Specimens of English Prose Style, From Malory to Macaulay, Selected and Annotated, With an Intro. Essay, by G. Saintsbury

You are holding a reproduction of an original work that is in the public domain in the United States of America, and possibly other countries. You may freely copy and distribute this work as no entity (individual or corporate) has a copyright on the body of the work. This book may contain prior copyright references, and library stamps (as most of these works were scanned from library copies). These have been scanned and retained as part of the historical artifact.

This book may have occasional imperfections such as missing or blurred pages, poor pictures, errant marks, etc. that were either part of the original artifact, or were introduced by the scanning process. We believe this work is culturally important, and despite the imperfections, have elected to bring it back into print as part of our continuing commitment to the preservation of printed works worldwide. We appreciate your understanding of the imperfections in the preservation process, and hope you enjoy this valuable book.

SPECIMENS OF
ENGLISH PROSE STYLE

SPECIMENS OF
ENGLISH PROSE STYLE

FROM MALORY TO MACAULAY

SELECTED AND ANNOTATED
WITH AN INTRODUCTORY ESSAY BY
GEORGE SAINTSBURY

The other harmony of prose

LONDON
KEGAN PAUL, TRENCH & CO.
MDCCCLXXXV

CONTENTS.

	PAGE
ENGLISH PROSE STYLE	xv
SIR THOMAS MALORY.	
THE DEATH OF LANCELOT	1
HUGH LATIMER. 14 —1555.	
THE DILIGENT BISHOP	5
SIR THOMAS ELYOT. 14 —1546.	
THE TRUE SIGNIFICATION OF TEMPERANCE A MORAL VIRTUE	8
ROGER ASCHAM. 1515—1568.	
THE WAY OF THE WIND	10
SIR WALTER RALEIGH. 1552—1618.	
THE END OF EMPIRES AND OF LIFE	13
EDMUND SPENSER. 1552?—1599.	
THE IRISH MANTLE	16
SIR PHILIP SIDNEY. 1554—1586.	
TO HIS SISTER	18
RICHARD HOOKER. 1554—1600.	
THE SANCTIONS OF HUMAN LAW	20
JOHN LYLY. 1554?—	
REMEDIA AMORIS	23

CONTENTS.

	PAGE
FRANCIS BACON, VISCOUNT ST. ALBANS. 1561—1626.	
OF MASQUES AND TRIUMPHS	26
OF STUDIES	27
BENJAMIN JONSON. 1574—1637.	
ON EDUCATION AND STYLE	30
ROBERT BURTON. 1576—1640.	
TERRESTRIAL DEVILS	34
THE CURE OF MELANCHOLY	38
EDWARD HERBERT, LORD HERBERT OF CHERBURY. 1581—1648.	
THE EVIDENCE OF ANOTHER LIFE	40
THOMAS HOBBES. 1588—1679.	
DREAMS AND APPARITIONS	42
IZAAC WALTON. 1593—1683.	
CHARACTER OF NOWEL	46
WILLIAM CHILLINGWORTH. 1602—1644.	
AGAINST THE PUNISHMENT OF DEATH	48
SIR THOMAS BROWNE. 1605—1682.	
BONES OF THE DEAD	51
CONSCIENCE	52
SELF OPINION	53
THOMAS FULLER. 1608—1661.	
ON SURGEONS	54
ON MUSIC	55
EDWARD HYDE, EARL OF CLARENDON. 1608—1674.	
THE CHARACTER OF LAUD	57
THE BATTLE OF LANSDOWN	59
JOHN MILTON. 1608—1674.	
THE SEARCH FOR DEAD TRUTH	63
THE TRAINING OF SCHOOLBOYS	66

CONTENTS.

	PAGE
JEREMY TAYLOR. 1613—1667.	
THE FRUITS OF SIN	69
THE WEAKNESS OF MAN	70
HENRY MORE. 1614—1687.	
THE WORKS OF THE DEVIL	73
ON DEATH	74
RICHARD BAXTER. 1615—1691.	
THE PEOPLE OF SOLDANIA	76
ABRAHAM COWLEY. 1618—1667.	
THE GARDEN	78
OLIVER CROMWELL	80
JOHN EVELYN. 1620—1706.	
THE LIFE OF TREES	82
ALGERNON SIDNEY. 1621—1683.	
HIS APOLOGY	84
JOHN BUNYAN. 1628—1688.	
THE HISTORY OF MR. FEARING	87
MANSOUL HELD BY THE DOUBTERS	91
THE SCIENCE OF BREAKING	92
SIR WILLIAM TEMPLE. 1628—1699.	
THE ENGLISH CLIMATE	95
THE USE OF POETRY AND MUSIC	97
GEORGE SAVILE, MARQUESS OF HALIFAX. 1630—1695.	
THE CHARACTER OF A TRIMMER	99
JOHN DRYDEN. 1631—1700.	
A LAYMAN'S FAITH	104
THE USE OF ARCHAIC WORDS	107
JOHN LOCKE. 1632—1704.	
PUBLIC SCHOOLS	110

CONTENTS.

ROBERT SOUTH. 1633—1716.
   THE EXECUTION OF CHARLES I. 113
   PLAINNESS OF APOSTOLIC SPEECH 115

APHRA BEHN. 1640?—1689.
   LOVE LETTERS 117

GILBERT BURNET. 1643—1715.
   ARCHBISHOP CRANMER 119

CHARLES LESLIE. 1650—1722.
   THE ARGUMENT FROM PROBABILITY 123

DANIEL DEFOE. 1661—1731.
   THE SHIPWRECK 125
   SIGNS AND WONDERS 127
   THE SKIRMISH AFTER MARSTON MOOR 129

RICHARD BENTLEY. 1662—1742.
   PHALARISM 133
   THE CHANGE OF LANGUAGE 135

JONATHAN SWIFT. 1667—1745.
   THE TRANSPORT OF GULLIVER TO THE CAPITAL . . 137
   THE KING'S OPINIONS ON GUNPOWDER 139
   CONCERNING MADNESS 141

SIR RICHARD STEELE. 1671?—1729.
   SARCASMS ON MARRIAGE 144

JOSEPH ADDISON. 1672—1719.
   ON ASKING ADVICE ON AFFAIRS OF LOVE 148
   LITERARY TASTE 151

HENRY ST. JOHN, VISCOUNT BOLINGBROKE.
   1678—1751.
   REMEDIES FOR AFFLICTION 153

CONYERS MIDDLETON. 1683—1750.
   CICERO CONSUL 156

CONTENTS.

	PAGE
GEORGE BERKELEY. 1684—1753.	
MATTER	159
LYSICLES ON AGNOSTICISM	161
ALEXANDER POPE. 1688—1744.	
A RECEIPT TO MAKE AN EPIC POEM	166
SAMUEL RICHARDSON. 1689—1761.	
THE DEATH OF LOVELACE	170
LADY MARY WORTLEY MONTAGU. 1690?—1762.	
LOUVERE	174
JOSEPH BUTLER. 1692—1752.	
THE DEATH OF THE RIGHTEOUS	177
PHILIP DORMER STANHOPE, EARL OF CHESTERFIELD. 1694—1773.	
THE CHARACTER OF RICHARD, EARL OF SCARBOROUGH	179
ROBERT PALTOCK.	
PETER'S COURTSHIP	183
HENRY FIELDING. 1707—1754.	
PARTRIDGE AT THE PLAY	185
SAMUEL JOHNSON. 1709—1784.	
ADDISON AS A PROSE WRITER	190
PUNCH AND CONVERSATION	193
DAVID HUME. 1711—1776.	
ON MIRACLES	196
HIS OWN CHARACTER	197
LAURENCE STERNE. 1713—1769.	
ON SLEEP	199
THE MONK	201
THOMAS GRAY. 1716—1771.	
A SUNRISE	204

CONTENTS.

HORACE WALPOLE. 1717—1797.
   THE JOYS OF LONDON 205

GILBERT WHITE. 1720—1793.
   THE HYBERNATION OF SWALLOWS 207
   NATURAL AFFECTION OF ANIMALS 208

TOBIAS SMOLLETT. 1721—1771.
   A BUDGET OF PARADOXES 211

ADAM SMITH. 1723—1790.
   PROFESSIONAL GAINS 216

SIR JOSHUA REYNOLDS. 1723—1792.
   THE CRITERION OF BEAUTY 219

OLIVER GOLDSMITH. 1728—1774.
   THE STROLLING PLAYER 223

EDMUND BURKE. 1730—1797.
   ON REFORM 226
   GROUNDS OF SYMPATHY WITH FRANCE . . . 228

EDWARD GIBBON. 1737—1794.
   THE HERESY OF APOLLINARIS 232
   HIS CONVERSION TO THE ROMAN CHURCH . . . 235

JAMES BOSWELL. 1740—1795.
   CHARACTER OF DR. JOHNSON 239

SIR PHILIP FRANCIS. 1740—1818.
   TO THE DUKE OF GRAFTON 242

WILLIAM PALEY. 1743—1805.
   OF THE SUCCESSION OF PLANTS AND ANIMALS . . . 244

THOMAS HOLCROFT. 1745—1805.
   THE LIFE OF A JOCKEY 248

HENRY MACKENZIE. 1745—1831.
   HARLEY'S COMPASSION 252

CONTENTS.

	PAGE
FRANCES BURNEY, MADAME D'ARBLAY. 1752—1840.	
A MIDDLE CLASS EXQUISITE	255
WILLIAM GODWIN. 1756—1836.	
OF JUSTICE	259
ST. LEON'S THOUGHTS ON GAINING THE ELIXIR OF LIFE	261
MARY WOLLSTONECRAFT. 1759—1797.	
WOMAN'S TRUE POSITION	264
WILLIAM COBBETT. 1762—1835.	
THE WICKED BOROUGH-MONGERS	265
ANNE RADCLIFFE. 1764—1823.	
EMILY'S MIDNIGHT ADVENTURE	267
ROBERT HALL. 1764—1831.	
REFLEXIONS ON WAR	272
SIR JAMES MACKINTOSH. 1765—1832.	
CHIVALRY	274
MARIA EDGEWORTH. 1766—1849.	
THE DUBLIN SHOEBLACK	276
SIR WALTER SCOTT. 1771—1832.	
AN ANTIQUARY'S STUDY	281
THE INSTALLATION OF THE ABBOT OF KENNAQUHAIR	283
SYDNEY SMITH. 1771—1845.	
THE PRODUCTIONS OF CEYLON	286
SAMUEL TAYLOR COLERIDGE. 1772—1834.	
COLERIDGE AS A LITERARY CANVASSER	288
THE BOOK OF NATURE	290
ROBERT SOUTHEY. 1774—1843.	
DANIEL DOVE'S BOOKS	294

CONTENTS.

JANE AUSTEN. 1775—1817.
    A STRAWBERRY PARTY 299

CHARLES LAMB. 1775—1834.
    THE CONVALESCENT 303

WALTER SAVAGE LANDOR. 1775—1864.
    THE DREAM OF BOCCACCIO 308
    CRITICS AS GENTLEMEN-USHERS 310

HENRY HALLAM. 1777—1859.
    THE SUPPRESSION OF CONVOCATION 312

WILLIAM HAZLITT. 1778—1830.
    THE ELGIN MARBLES 315
    COLERIDGE 317

THOMAS MOORE. 1779—1852.
    A FESTIVAL ON THE NILE 318

JOHN WILSON. 1785—1854.
    THE FAIRY'S FUNERAL 321

THOMAS DE QUINCEY. 1785—1859.
    THE POWER AND DANGER OF THE CÆSARS . . . 324
    OUR LADY OF DARKNESS 328

SIR WILLIAM FRANCIS PATRICK NAPIER. 1785—1860.
    THE BRITISH SOLDIER 329

MARY RUSSELL MITFORD. 1786—1855.
    THE COWSLIP BALL 331

THOMAS LOVE PEACOCK. 1788—1866.
    THE DRUNKENNESS OF SEITHENYN 335

HENRY HART MILMAN. 1791—1868.
    MONASTICISM 339

CONTENTS.

PERCY BYSSHE SHELLEY. 1792—1822.

THE LAKE OF COMO	342
POETRY	343

EDWARD IRVING. 1792—1834.

TRUE COURAGE	347

JOHN GIBSON LOCKHART. 1793—1854.

CHARACTER OF HOOK	350

THOMAS CARLYLE. 1795—1881.

OLD DRAGOON DROUET	354
COLERIDGE	357
ON STATUES	360

THOMAS BABINGTON, LORD MACAULAY. 1800—1859.

THE RELIEF OF LONDONDERRY	364
WARREN HASTINGS	366

ENGLISH PROSE STYLE.

"*The other harmony of prose.*"—*Dryden.*

A YEAR or more ago it was reported, perhaps falsely, that a great French writer, whose command of his own tongue was only equalled by his ignorance of the English language and literature, gave in some semi-public form his opinion of the difference between French and English prose and verse. A perfect language, he opined, should show a noteworthy difference between its style in prose and its style in verse: this difference existed in French and did not exist in English. I shall give no opinion as to the truth of this axiom in general, or as to its application to French. But it is not inappropriate to begin an essay on the subject of English prose style by observing that, whatever may be its merits and defects, it is entirely different—different by the extent of the whole heaven of language—from English verse style. We have had writers, including some of genius, who have striven to make prose like verse: and we have had other writers, including some of genius, who have striven to make verse like prose. Both in so doing have shown themselves to be radically mistaken. The actual vocabulary of the best English style of different periods is indeed almost entirely common to verse and to prose, and it is perhaps this fact which induced the distinguished person above referred to, and others not much less distinguished, to make a mistake of confusion. The times when the mere dictionary of poetic style has been distinct from the mere dictionary of prosaic style (for there have been such) have not been those in which English literature was at its highest point. But between the syntax, taking that word in its proper sense of the order of words, of prose and the syntax of verse; between the rhythm of prose and the rhythm of verse; between the sentence- and clause-architecture of prose and the sentence- and clause-architecture of verse, there has been since English literature took a durable form in the sixteenth century at least as strongly marked a difference in English as in other languages.

Good poets have usually been good writers of prose; but in English more than in any other tongue the prose style of these writers has differed from their verse style. The French prose and the French verse of Victor Hugo are remarkably similar in all but the most arbitrary differences, and the same may be said, to a less extent, of the prose and the verse style of Goethe. But Shelley's prose and Shelley's verse (to confine myself to examples taken from the present century) are radically different in all points of their style and verbal power; and so are Coleridge's prose and Coleridge's verse. The same is eminently true of Shakspere, and true to a very great extent of Milton. If it is less true of Dryden and of Pope (it is often true of Dryden to a great degree), that is exactly in virtue of the somewhat un-English influence which, though it benefited English prose not a little, worked upon both. In our own days prose style has become somewhat disarranged, but in the hands of those who have any pretence to style at all, its merits and its defects are in great part clearly traceable to discernment on the one hand, to confusion on the other, of the separate and distinct aims and methods of the prose-writer and the poet.

It should scarcely be necessary to say that no attempt is made in this essay to compile a manual of English prose-writing, or to lay down didactically the principles of the art. The most that can be done or that is aimed at is the discovery by a running critical and historical commentary on the illustrations which follow, and on the course of English prose generally, what have been the successive characteristics of its style, what the aims of its writers, and what the amount of success that they have attained. There is nothing presumptuous in the attitude of the student, whatever there may be in the attitude of the teacher. Nearly ten years ago, at the suggestion of Mr. John Morley, I attempted in the *Fortnightly Review* a study of the chief characteristics of contemporary prose. Since then I have reviewed many hundreds of new books, and have read again, or for the first time, many hundreds of old ones. I do not know that the two processes have altered my views much: they certainly have not lessened my estimate of the difficulty of writing good prose, or of the merit of good prose when written. During these ten years considerable attention has undoubtedly been given by English writers to style: I wish I could think that the result has been a distinct improvement in the quality of the product. If the present object were a study of contemporary prose, much would have to be said on the growth of what I may call the Aniline style and the style of Marivaudage, the first dealing in a gorgeous and glaring vocabulary, the second in unexpected turns and twists of thought or phrase, in long-winded description of incident, and in finical analysis of motive. Unexpectedness, indeed, seems to be the chief aim of the practitioners of both, and it lays them perhaps open to the damaging question of Mr. Milestone in *Headlong Hall*. When we hear that a bar of music has "veracity," that there is a finely-executed "passage" in a marble chimney-piece, that someone is "part of the conscience of a nation," that the "andante" of a sonnet is specially noteworthy, the quest after the unexpected has become sufficiently evident. But these things are not directly our subject, though we shall find other things remarkably like them in the history of the past. For there is nothing new in art except its beauties, and all the faults of French naturalism and English æstheticism were doubtless perfectly well known to critics and admired by the uncritical in the days of Hilpa and Shalum.

For reasons obvious enough, not the most or the least obvious being the necessity of beginning somewhere, we begin these specimens with the invention of printing; not of course denying the title of books written before Caxton set up his press to the title of English or of English prose, but simply fixing a term from which literary production has been voluminous and uninterrupted in its volume. In the earlier examples, however (up, it may be said, to Lyly), the character of the passages, though often interesting and noteworthy, is scarcely characteristic. All the writers of this period are, if not actually, yet in a manner, translators. The work of Malory, charming as it is, and worthy to occupy the place of honour here given to it, is notoriously an adaptation of French originals. Latimer and Ascham, especially the former, in parts highly vernacular, are conversational where they are not classical.

It was not till the reign of Elizabeth was some way advanced that a definite effort on the part of writers to make an English prose style can be perceived. It took for the most part one of two directions. The first was vernacular in the main, but very strongly tinged with a peculiar form of preciousness, the origin of which has been traced to various sources, but which appears clearly enough in the French *rhétoriqueurs* of the fifteenth century, from whom it spread to Italy, Spain, and England.

This style, in part almost vulgar, in part an *estilo culto* of the most quintessenced kind, is represented here only by Lyly. But it is in fact common to all the Elizabethan pamphleteers—Greene, Nash, Harvey, Dekker, Breton, and the rest. The vernacular in many of them descends even to vulgarity, and the cultivated in Lyly frequently ascends to the incomprehensible. Few things are more curious than this mixture of corduroy and *clinquant*, of slang and learning, of street repartees and elaborate coterie preciousnesses. On the other hand, the more sober writers were not less classical than their forerunners, though in the endeavour not merely to write Latin sentences rendered into English, or English sentences that would translate with little alteration into Latin, they fell into new difficulties. In all the Elizabethan, Jacobean, and Caroline writers, inelegancies and obscurities occur which may be traced directly to the attempt to imitate the forms of a language possessed of regular inflections and strict syntax in a language almost destitute of grammar. Especially fatal is the attempt to imitate the Latin relative and demonstrative pronouns, with their strict agreement of gender, number, and case, and to render them in usage and meaning by the English words of all work *who, which, he, they*, and to copy the *oratio obliqua* in a tongue where the verbs for the most are indistinguishable whether used in *obliqua* or in *recta*. These attempts lie at the root of the faults which are found even in the succinct style of Hooker and Jonson, which turn almost to attractions in the quaint paragraph-heaps of the *Anatomy of Melancholy*, which mar many of the finest passages of Milton and Taylor, and which in Clarendon perhaps reach their climax. The abuse of conjunctions—which is also noticeable in most of the writers of this period, and which leads them, apparently out of mere wantonness, to prefer a single sentence jointed and rejointed, parenthesised and postscripted, till it does the duty of a paragraph, to a succession of orderly sentences each containing the expression of a simple or moderately complex thought—is not chargeable quite so fairly on imitation of the classics. But it has something to do with this, or rather it has much to do with the absence of any model except the classics. Most of these writers had a great deal to say, and they were as much in want of models as of deterrent examples in regard to the manner of saying it. The feeling seems still to have prevailed, that if a man aimed at literary elegance and precision he should write in Latin, that English might be a convenient vehicle of matter, but was scarcely susceptible of form, that the audience was *ex hypothesi* incult, uncritical, exoteric, and neither required nor could understand refinements of phrase.

I have more than once seen this view of the matter treated with scorn or horror, or both, as if those who take it thought little of the beauty of seventeenth century prose before the Restoration. This treatment does not appear very intelligent. The business of the critic is to deal with and to explain the facts, and all the facts. It is the fact, no doubt, that detached phrases, sentences, even long passages of Milton, of Taylor, of Browne, equal if they do not excel in beauty anything that English prose has since produced. It is the fact that Clarendon is unmatched for moral portrait painting to this day; that phrase after phrase of Hobbes has the ring and the weight and the sharp outline of a bronze coin; that Bacon is often as glorious without as within. But it is, at the same time, and not less often, the fact that Clarendon gets himself into involutions through which no breath will last, and which cannot be solved by any kind effort of repunctuation; that Milton's sentences, beginning magnificently, often end in mere tameness, sometimes in mere discord; that all the authors of the period abound in what look like wilful and gratuitous obscurities, cacophonies, breaches of sense and grammar and rhythm. To anyone who considers the matter in any way critically, and not in the attitude of mind which shouts "Great is Diana of the Ephesians" by the space of as many hours as may be, it is perfectly evident that these great men, these great masters, were not thoroughly masters of their instrument; that their touch, for all its magic in its happier moments, was not certain; that they groped, and sometimes stumbled in their walk. When Browne begins the famous descant, "Now since these dead bones;" when Hobbes gathers up human vice and labels it unconcernedly as "either an effect of power or a cause of pleasure;" when Milton pours forth any one of the scores of masterpieces to be found here and there in his prose work, let us hold our tongues and simply admire. But it is a merely irrational admiration which refuses to recognize that Browne's antithesis is occasionally an anticlimax and his turn of words occasionally puerile; that Milton's sentences constantly descend from the *mulier formosa* to the *piscis;* and that Hobbes, after the very phrase above quoted, spoils its effect as style by a clumsy repetition of nearly but not quite the same form of words, after a fashion which few writers possessing a tithe of Hobbes's genius would have imitated in the eighteenth century. It is still more irrational to deny that most of this great group of writers occasionally make what are neither more nor less than "faults of English," grammatical blunders which actually vitiate their sense. Let us admire Alexander by all means, but let us not try to make out that Alexander's wry neck is worthy of an Apollo or an Antinous.

Among the chief reasons for this slowness on the part even of great writers in recognizing the more obvious requirements of English prose style, not the least perhaps may be found in the fact that English writers had no opportunity of comparison in modern tongues. German literature was not, and Spanish and Italian, which had been cultivated in England with some zeal, were too alien from English in all linguistic points to be of much service. The Restoration introduced the study and comparison of a language which, though still alien from English, was far less removed from it than the other Romance tongues, and which had already gone through its own reforming process with signal success. On the other hand, the period of original and copious thought ceased in England for a time, and men, having less to say, became more careful in saying it. The age of English prose which opens with Dryden and Tillotson (the former being really entitled to almost the sole credit of opening it, while Tillotson has enjoyed his reputation as a stylist and still more as an originator of style at a very easy rate) produced, with the exception of Swift and Dryden himself, no writer equal in genius to those of the age before it, but the talent of the writers that it did produce was infinitely better furnished with command of its weapons, and before the period itself had ceased English prose as an instrument may be said to have been perfected. Even in Dryden, though not very often, and in his followers Temple and Halifax occasionally, there appear examples of the old slovenlinesses; but in the writers of the Queen Anne school these entirely disappear. To the present day, though their vocabulary may have in places become slightly antiquated, and their phrase, especially in conversational passages, may include forms which have gone out of fashion, there is hardly anything in the structure of their clauses, their sentences, or their paragraphs, which is in any way obsolete.

The blemishes, indeed, which had to some extent disfigured earlier English prose, were merely of the kind that exists because no one has taken the trouble to clear it away. Given on the one side a certain conversational way of talking English, inaccurate or rather licentious as all conversational ways of speaking are, and on the other side a habit of writing exact and formal Latin, what had happened was what naturally would happen. Dryden himself, who during the whole of his life was a constant critical student of language and style, may be said, if not to have accomplished the change single-handed, at any rate to have given examples of it at all its stages. He in criticism chiefly, Temple in miscellaneous essay writing, and Halifax in the political pamphlet, left very little to be done, and the Queen Anne men found their tools ready for them when they began to write. It is moreover very observable that this literary change, unlike many if not most other literary changes, had hardly anything that was pedantic about it. So far was it from endeavouring to classicize English style, that most of its alterations were distinctly directed towards freeing English from the too great admixture of Latin grammar and style. The vernacular influence, of which almost in its purity the early part of the period affords such an admirable example in Bunyan, while the later part offers one not much less admirable in Defoe, is scarcely less perceptible in all the three writers just mentioned, Dryden, Temple, and Halifax, and in their three great successors, Swift, Addison, and Steele. Addison classicizes the most of the six, but Addison's style cannot be called exotic. The ordinary English of the streets and the houses helped these men to reform the long sentence, with its relatives and its conjunctions, clumsily borrowed from Latin, to reject inversions and involutions of phrase that had become bewildering in the absence of the clue of inflexional sounds, to avoid attempts at *oratio obliqua* for which the syntax of the language is ill fitted, to be plain, straightforward, unadorned. It is true that in rejecting what they thought, in many instances rightly, to be barbarisms, they to a great extent lost the secret of a splendour which had been by no means exclusively or often barbaric. They were unrivalled in vigour, not easily to be beaten in sober grace, abundantly capable of wit, but as a rule they lacked magnificence, and prose was with them emphatically a *sermo pedestris*. Except in survivors of the older school, it is difficult to find in post-Restoration prose an impassioned passage. When the men of the time wished to be impassioned they thought it proper to drop into poetry. South's satire on the "fringes of the North-star" and other Taylorisms expresses their attitude very happily. It is hardly an accident that Dryden's subjects, capable though the writer was of giving literary expression to every form of thought and feeling, never in prose lead him to the inditing of anything exalted ; that Temple gives a half sarcastic turn to the brief but exquisite passage on life which closes his essay on poetry; that Addison's renowned homilies on death and tombs and a future life have rather an unrivalled decency, a propriety that is quintessential, than solemnity in the higher sense of the term. The lack of ornament in the prose of this period is never perhaps more clearly shown than in the style of Locke, which, though not often absolutely incorrect, is to me, I frankly own, a disgusting style, bald, dull, plebeian, giving indeed the author's meaning, but giving it ungraced with any due apparatus or ministry. The defects, however, were for the most part negative. The writers of this time, at least the greater of them, spoilt nothing that they touched, and for the most part omitted to touch subjects for which their style was not suited. The order, lucidity, and proportion of Dryden's criticism, the ease and well-bred loquacity of Temple and the essayists, the mild or rough polemic of Halifax and Bentley, the incomparable ironic handling of Swift, the narrative and pictorial faculty, so sober and yet so vivid, of Bunyan and Defoe, are never likely to be surpassed in English literature. The generation which equals the least of them may be proud of its feat. This period, moreover, it must never be forgotten, was not merely a great period in itself as regarded production, but the schoolmaster of all periods to follow. It settled what the form, the technical form, of English prose was to be, and settled it once for all.

It is not usual to think or speak of the eighteenth century as reactionary, and yet, in regard to its prose style, it to some extent deserves this title. The peculiarities of this prose, the most famous names among whose practitioners are Johnson and Gibbon, exhibit a decided reaction against the plainness and vernacular energy which, as has been said, characterized writers from Dryden to Swift. Lord Chesterfield's well-known denunciation of proverbial phrases in speaking and writing, and the Latinisms of the extreme Johnsonian style, may seem to have but little to do with each other, but they express in different ways the revolt of the fine gentleman and the revolt of the scholar against the simplicity and homeliness of the style which had gone before. The men of 1660-1720 had not been afraid of Latinisms, but they had not sought them: the *ampullæ et sesquipedalia verba* of Johnson at his worst were by no means peculiar to himself, but may be found alike in the prose and the verse of writers over whom he exercised little or no influence. The altered style, however, in the hands of capable men became somewhat more suitable for the dignified branches of sustained prose-writing. We shall never have a greater historian in style as well as in matter than Gibbon; in style at least we have not beaten Hume, though there has been more than a century to do it in. Berkeley belongs mainly to the latest school of seventeenth century writers, to the Queen Anne men, but partly also to the eighteenth century proper; and he, again with Hume as a second, is as unlikely to be surpassed in mastery of philosophical style as Gibbon and Hume are unlikely to be surpassed in the style of history. Nor were there wanting tendencies and influences which counteracted to a great extent the striving at elaboration and dignity. The chief of these was the growth of the novel. This not only is in itself a kind unfriendly to the pompous style, but happened to attract to its practice the great genius of Fielding, which was from nothing so averse as from everything that had the semblance or the reality of pretension, pedantry, or conceit. Among the noteworthy writers of the time, not a few stand apart from its general tendencies, and others exhibit only part of those tendencies. The homely and yet graceful narrative of the author of *Peter Wilkins* derives evidently from Defoe; the *commérage* of the letters of Walpole, Gray, and others, is an attempt partly to imitate French models, partly to reproduce the actual talk of society; Sterne's deliberate eccentricity is an adaptation, as genius of course adapts, of Rabelais and Burton, while the curious and inimitable badness of the great Bishop Butler's form is evidently due, not like Locke's, to carelessness and contempt of good literary manners, but to some strange idiosyncrasy of defect. On the whole, however, the century not merely added immortal examples to English prose, but contributed not a little to the further perfecting of the general instrument. A novelist like Fielding, a historian like Gibbon, a philosopher like Hume, an orator and publicist like Burke, could not write without adding to the capacities of prose in the hands of others as well as to its performances in their own. They gave a further extension to the system of modulating sentences and clauses with a definite regard to harmony. Although there may be too much monotony in his method, it seems unlikely that Gibbon will soon be surpassed in the art of arranging the rhythm of a sentence of not inconsiderable length without ever neglecting co-ordination, and, at the same time, without ever committing the mistake of exchanging the rhythm proper to prose for the metre which is proper to poetry. Much the same may be said of Burke when he is at his best, while two earlier ornaments of the period, Bolingbroke and Conyers Middleton, though their prose is less rhythmical, are scarcely less remarkable for a deliberate and systematic arrangement of the sentence within itself and of the sentences in the paragraph. To enumerate separate particulars in which the eighteenth and late seventeenth centuries subjected English prose to laws would be rather appropriate to a manual of composition than to an essay like the present. For instance, such details as the reform of punctuation, and especially the more frequent use of the full stop, as the avoidance of the homoeoteleuton, and if possible of the same word, unless used emphatically, in the same sentence, can be only very summarily referred to. But undoubtedly the matter of principal importance was the practice, which as a regular practice began with Dryden and was perfected in Gibbon, of balancing and proportioning the sentence. Of course there are numerous or innumerable examples of exquisitely proportioned sentences in Milton and his contemporaries, but that is not to the point. What is to the point is such a sentence as the following from the *Areopagitica:*—"But if his rear and flanks be not impaled, if his back-door be not secured by the rigid licenser but that a bold book may now and then issue forth and give the assault to some of his old collections in their trenches, it will concern him then to keep waking, to stand in watch, to set good guards and sentinels about his received opinions, to walk the round and counter-round with his fellow-inspectors, fearing lest any of his flock be seduced, *who then also would be better instructed, better exercised and disciplined.*" Here the sentence begins excellently, winds up the height to "trenches," and descends again in an orderly and regular fashion to "seduced." There in sense, in sound, by all the laws of verbal architecture it should stop, but the author has an afterthought, and he tacks on the words italicised, thereby ruining the balance of his phrase, and adding an unnecessary and disturbing epexegesis to his thought. Had Milton lived a hundred years later he would no more have committed this merely careless and inerudite fault than Gibbon would.

Like all rules of general character, the balancing of the sentence has of course its difficulties and its dangers. Carried out on principles too uniform, or by means too obvious, it becomes monotonous and disgusting. It is a considerable encouragement to sonorous platitude, and (as satirists have sometimes amused themselves by showing) it can easily be used to disguise and carry off the simply unmeaning. When Mrs. St. Clair in *The Inheritance* uttered that famous sentence, "Happy the country whose nobles are thus gifted with the power of reflecting kindred excellence, and of perpetuating national virtue on the broad basis of private friendship," she owed everything to the fact that she was born after Dr. Johnson. Very large numbers of public speakers in and out of pulpits were, during the time that prose rhythm by means of balance was enforced or expected, in a similar case of indebtedness. But the amount of foolish speech and writing in the world has not appreciably lessened since every man became a law unto himself in the matter of composition, and for my part I own, though it may be immoral, that I prefer a platitude which seems as if it might have some meaning, and at any rate sounds well as sound, to a platitude which is nakedly and cacophonously platitudinous or senseless. The Latinizing of the language was a greater evil by far, but one of no lasting continuance. No permanent harm came to English literature from Johnson's noted second thought about vitality and putrefaction, or from Armstrong's singular fancy (it is true this was in verse) for calling a cold bath a gelid cistern. The fashion rose, lived, died, as fashions do. But beauty looks only a little less beautiful in the ugliest fashion, and so the genius and talent of the eighteenth century showed themselves only to a little less advantage because of their predilection for an exotic vocabulary. No harm was done, but much good, to the theory and practice of verbal architecture, and if inferior material was sometimes used, Time has long since dealt with each builder's work in his usual just and equal fashion.

With the eighteenth century speaking generally—with Burke and Gibbon speaking particularly—what may be called the consciously or unconsciously formative period of English prose came to an end. In the hundred years that have since passed we have had not a few prose writers of great genius, many of extreme talent. But they have all either deliberately innovated upon or obediently followed, or carefully neglected, the two great principles which were established between 1660 and 1760, the principle, that is to say, which limited the meaning of a sentence to a moderately complex thought in point of matter, and that which admitted the necessity of balance and coherent structure in point of form. One attempt at the addition of a special kind of prose, an attempt frequently made but foredoomed to failure, I shall have to notice, but only one.

The great period of poetical production which began with the French Revolution and lasted till about 1830, saw also much prose of merit. Coleridge, Southey, Shelley, are eminent examples in both prose and verse, while Wordsworth, Byron, Moore, and others, come but little behind. Scott, the most voluminous of all except perhaps Southey in prose composition, occupies a rather peculiar position. The astonishing rapidity of his production, and his defective education (good prose-writing is far more a matter of scholarship than good verse-writing), may have had a somewhat injurious influence on his style; but this style has on the whole been rated much too low, and at its best is admirable English. The splendour, however, of the poetical production of the later Georgian period in poetry no doubt eclipsed its production in prose, and as a general rule that prose was rather even and excellent in general characteristics than eminent or peculiar in special quality. The same good sense which banished an artificial vocabulary from poetry achieved the banishing of it from prose. But except that it is always a little less stiff, and sometimes a little more negligent, the best prose written by men of middle or advanced age when George the Third was dying does not differ very greatly from the best prose written by men of middle or advanced age when he came to the throne. The range of subjects, the tone of thought, might be altered, the style was very much the same; in fact, there can be very little doubt that while the poets deliberately rebelled against their predecessors, the prose writers, who were often the same persons in another function, deliberately followed, if they did not exactly imitate them.

It was not until the end of this period of brilliant poetry that certain persons more or less deliberately set themselves to revolutionize English prose, as the poets for a full generation had been revolutionizing English verse. I say more or less deliberately, for the revived fashion of "numerous" prose which one man of genius and one man of the greatest talent, Thomas de Quincey and John Wilson, proclaimed, which others seem to have adopted without much of set purpose, and which, owing especially to the great example of Mr. Ruskin, has enlisted so large a following, was in its origin partial and casual. The inducers of this style have hardly had due honour or due dishonour, for what they have done is not small, whatever may be thought of its character. Indeed, at the present day, among a very large proportion of general readers, and among a certain number of critics, "style" appears to be understood in the sense of ornate and semi-metrical style. A work which is "not remarkable for style" is a work which does not pile up the adjectives, which abstains from rhythm so pronounced and regular that it ceases to be rhythm merely and becomes metre, which avoids rather than seeks the drawing of attention to originality of thought by singularity of expression, and which worships no gods but proportion, clearness, closeness of expression to idea, and (within the limits incident to prose) rhythmical arrangement. To confess the truth, the public has so little prose of this latter quality put before it, and is so much accustomed to find that every writer whose style is a little above the school exercise, and his thought a little above platitude, aims at the distinction of prose-poet, that it has some excuse for its blunder. That it is a blunder I shall endeavour to show a little later. For the present, it is sufficient to indicate the period of George the Fourth's reign as the beginning of the flamboyant style in modern English prose. Besides the two persons just mentioned, whose writings were widely distributed in periodicals, three other great masters of prose, though not inclined to the same form of prose-poetry, did not a little to break down the tradition of English prose in which sobriety was the chief thing aimed at. These were Carlyle, with his Germanisms of phrase and his sacrifice (not at all German) of order to emphasis in arrangement; Macaulay with his spasmodic clause and his endless fire of snapping antitheses; and lastly, with not much influence on the general reader, but with much on the special writer, Landor, who together with much prose that is nearly perfect, gave the innovators the countenance of an occasional leaning to the florid and of a neo-classicism which was sometimes un-English. It is the nature of man to select the worst parts of his models for imitation.

Side by side with these great innovators there were no doubt many and very excellent practitioners of the older and simpler style. Southey survived and Lockhart flourished as accomplished examples of it in one great literary organ; the influence of Jeffrey was exerted rather vigorously than wisely to maintain it in another. Generally speaking, it was not admitted before 1850 that the best models for a young man in prose could be any other than the chief ornaments of English literature from Swift and Addison to Gibbon and Burke. The examples of the great writers above mentioned, however, could not fail to have a gradual effect; and, as time passed, more and more books came to be written in which one of two things was evident. The one was that the author had tried to write a prose-poem as far as style was concerned, the other that he was absolutely without principles of style. I can still find no better instance of this literary antinomianism than I found ten years ago in Grote's history, where there is simply no style at all. The chief political speeches and the most popular philosophical works of the day supply examples of this antinomian eminence in other departments, although, as their authors are living, it may be impertinent to name them. Take Grote and compare him with Hume, Gibbon, or even Thirlwall; take almost any chief speaker of either House and compare him with Burke or Canning or Lord Lyndhurst; take almost any living philosopher and compare him with Berkeley, with Hume, or even with Mill, and the difference is obvious at once. As history, as politics, as philosophy, the later examples may be excellent—no opinion on that point will be given here. But as examples of style they are not comparable with the earlier.

In the department of luxuriant ornament, the example of Mr. Ruskin may be said to have rendered all other examples comparatively superfluous. From the date of the first appearance of *Modern Painters*, the prose-poetry style has more and more engrossed attention and imitation. It has invaded history, permeated novel writing, affected criticism so largely that those who resist it in that department are but a scattered remnant. It is unnecessary to quote instances, for the fact is very little likely to be gainsaid, and if it is gainsaid at all, will certainly not be gainsaid by any person who has frequent and copious examples of English style coming before him for criticism.

At the same time the period of individualism has given rise, as a former period of something like individualism did in the seventeenth century, to some great and to many remarkable writers. Of these, so far as they have not been distinguished by an adherence to the ornate style, and so far as they have not, with the disciples of literary incuria, let style go to the winds altogether, Mr. Carlyle was during all his later days the chief, and in not a few cases the model. But he had seconds in the work, in many of whom literary genius to a great extent supplied the want of academic correctness. Thackeray, with some remarkable slovenlinesses (he is probably the last writer of the first eminence of whom the enemy "and which" has made a conquest), elaborated, rather it would seem by practice and natural genius, than in the carrying out of any theory, a style which for the lighter purposes of literature has no rival in urbanity, flexibility, and width of range since Addison, and which has found the widest acceptance among men of letters. Dickens again, despite very great faults of bad taste and mannerism, did not lack the qualities of a great writer. This is sufficiently shown in the excellent storm passage in *David*

Copperfield, as well as in not a few others scattered over his works. He seldom had occasion for a sustained effort of this kind, and the "tricks and manners" to which he was so unfortunately given lent themselves but too easily to imitation. Of the many writers of merit who stand beside and below these two space here forbids detailed mention. There are also many earlier authors who, either because they have been merely exceptional, or because they have been examples of tendencies which others have exhibited in a more characteristic manner, have not been noticed specially in the foregoing sketch. To take the last century only, Cobbett ranks with Bunyan and Defoe as the third of a trio of deliberately vernacular writers. The exquisite grace and charm of Lamb, springing in part no doubt from an imitation of the unreformed writers, especially Fuller, Browne, and Burton, had yet in it so much of idiosyncrasy that it has never been and is never likely to be successfully imitated. Peacock, an accomplished scholar and a master of irony, has a peculiarity which is rather one of thought than of style, of viewpoint towards the world at large than of expression of the views taken. The late Lord Beaconsfield, unrivalled at epigram and detached phrase, very frequently wrote and sometimes spoke below himself, and in particular committed the fault of substituting for a kind of English Voltairian style, which no one could have brought to greater perfection if he had given his mind to it, corrupt followings of the sensibility and philosophism of Diderot and the mere grandiloquence of Buffon.

In the same way, in the earlier and longer period, there are many names which, though claiming a place of right in the history of English prose, cannot claim a place in an essay on that history, while in some cases they have had to be excluded even from the list of selections. Many excellent theologians and sermon-writers have been shut out because the admission of one would require the admission of all. Philosophers of the second class are in the same case. The older novelists who are dead and the modern novelists who are dying cannot here be mummified, nor can anything but the faintest taste be given of the vast mass of periodical literature which has been produced in these latter days. Except in regard to peculiarities which are exclusively the peculiarities of recent writers, and which therefore fall out of the scheme, the main characteristics of English prose are, it is believed, here given in the work of their most distinguished representatives. *Vixere fortes*, many of them, outside the lists of this or any similar undertaking. But they must, in the words of Wharton's sarcasm to Harley's twelve peers, here applied with no sarcastic intent, "speak through their foreman," or the foremen of their several classes.

Thus then the course of English prose style presents, in little, the following picture. Beginning for the most part with translations from Latin or French, with prose versions of verse writings, and with theological treatises aiming more at edification, and at the edification of the vulgar, than at style, it was not till after the invention of printing that it attempted perfection of form. But in its early strivings it was much hindered, first by the persistent attempt to make an uninflected do the duty of an inflected language, and secondly, by the curious flood of conceits which accompanied, or helped, or were caused by the Spanish and Italian influences of the sixteenth and early seventeenth centuries. In the latter period we find men of the greatest genius producing singularly uneven and blemished work, owing to the want of an accepted theory and practice of style; each man writing as seemed good in his own eyes, and selecting not merely his vocabulary (as to that a great freedom, and rightly, has always prevailed in England), but his arrangement of clauses and sentences, and even to some extent his syntax. To this period of individualism an end was put by Dryden, whose example in codifying and reforming was followed for nearly a century. During this period the syntactical part of English grammar was settled very nearly as it has hitherto remained; the limitation of the sentence to a single moderately simple proposition, or at most to two or three propositions closely connected in thought, was effected; the arrangement of the single clause was prescribed as nearly as possible in the natural order of vocal speech, inversions being reserved as an exception and a license for the production of some special effect; the use of the parenthesis was (perhaps unduly) discouraged; and a general principle was established that the cadence as well as the sense of a sentence should rise gradually toward the middle, should if necessary continue there on a level for a brief period, and should then descend in a gradation corresponding to its ascent. These principles were observed during the whole of the eighteenth century, and with little variation during the first quarter of the nineteenth, a certain range of liberty being given by the increasing subdivision of the subjects of literature, and especially by the growth of fiction and periodical writing on more or less ephemeral matters. The continuance of this latter process, the increased study of foreign (especially German) literature, the disuse of Greek and Latin as the main instruments of education, and the example of eminent or popular writers, first in small and then in great numbers, have during the last fifty years induced a return of individualism. This has in most cases taken the form either of a neglect of regular and orderly style altogether, or of the preference of a highly ornamented diction and a poetical rather than prosaic rhythm. The great mass of writers belong to the first division, the smaller number who take some pains about the ordering of their sentences almost entirely to the second.

That this laboured and ornate manner will not last very long is highly probable, that it should last long would be out of keeping with experience. But it is not so certain that its disappearance will be followed by anything like a return to the simplicity of theory and practice in style which, while it left eighteenth-century and late seventeenth-century authors full room to display individual talents and peculiarities, still caused between them the same resemblance which exists in examples of an order of architecture or of a natural species.

So much has been said about the balancing of the sentence, and the rhythm appropriate to prose and distinct from metre, that the reader may fairly claim to be informed somewhat more minutely of the writer's views on the subject. They will have to be put to a certain extent scholastically, but the thing is really a scholastic question, and the impatience with "iambs and pentameters," which Mr. Lowell (a spokesman far too good for such a breed) condescended to express some forty years ago on behalf of the vulgar, is in reality the secret of much of the degradation of recent prose. In dealing with this subject I shall have to affront an old prejudice which has apparently become young again, the prejudice which deems terms of quantity inapplicable to the English and other modern languages. The truth is, that the metrical symbols and system of scansion which the genius of the Greeks invented, are applicable to all European languages, though (and this is where the thoroughgoing defenders of accent against quantity make their blunder) the quantity of particular syllables is much more variable. In other words, there are far more common syllables in English and other modern languages than in Latin, or even in the language of those

> Quibus est nihil negatum
> Et queis " ārēs ārēs " licet sonare.

A Greek would have laughed heartily enough at the notion that the alternative quantity of *Ares* made it impossible to scan Homer regularly, and so may an Englishman, even though a very large number of syllables (not by any means all) in his language are capable of being made long or short according to the pleasure of the writer and the exigencies of the verse. All good English verse, from the rudest ballad of past centuries to the most elaborate harmonies of Mr. Swinburne and Lord Tennyson, is capable of being exhibited in metrical form as strict in its final, if not in its initial laws, as that which governs the prosody of Horace or of Euripides. Most bad English verse is capable of having its badness shown by the application of the same tests. In using therefore longs and shorts, and the divisions of classical metre from Pyrrhic to dochmiac, in order to exhibit the characteristics of English prose rhythm and the differences which it exhibits from the metre which is verse rhythm, I am using disputed means deliberately and with the fullest intention and readiness to defend them if required.[1]

I take it that the characteristic of metre—that is to say, poetic rhythm—is not only the recurrence of the same feet in the same line, but also the recurrence of corresponding and similar arrangements of feet in different lines. The Greek chorus, and in a less degree the English pindaric, exhibit the first characteristic scantly, but they make up, in the one case by a rigid, and in the other by what ought to be a rigid, adherence to the second. In all other known forms of literary European verse, Greek, Latin, English, French, Italian, Spanish, German, both requirements are complied with in different measure or degree,

---

[1] It has been pointed out to me, since the following remarks were written, that I might have sheltered myself under a right reverend precedent in the shape of some criticism of Hurd's on the rhythmical peculiarities of Addison. I do so now all the more willingly, that no one who compares the two passages will suspect me of merely following the bishop.

from the cast-iron regularity of the Latin alcaic to the wide license of a Greek comic senarius or an English anapæstic tetrameter. In blank verse or in couplets every verse is (certain equivalent values being once recognized) exactly equal to every other verse. In stanzas from the quatrain to the Spenserian the parallelism, if more intricate, is equally exact.

Now the requirement of a perfect prose rhythm is that, while it admits of indication by quantity-marks, and even by divisions into feet, the simplicity and equivalence of feet within the clause answering to the line are absent, and the exact correspondence of clause for clause, that is to say, of line for line, is absent also, and still more necessarily absent. Let us take an example. I know no more perfect example of English prose rhythm than the famous verses of the last chapter of the Canticles in the Authorized Version; I am not certain that I know any so perfect. Here they are arranged for the purpose of exhibition in clause-lines, quantified and divided into feet.

Sĕt mĕ | ăs ă seăl | ŭpŏn thĭne heărt | ăs ă seăl | ŭpŏn thĭne ărm |
Fŏr lŏve | ĭs strŏng | ăs deăth | jeălŏusў | ĭs cruĕl | ăs thĕ grăve |
Thĕ coăls thĕreŏf | ăre coăls | ŏf fĭrĕ | whĭch hăth | ă mŏst vĕ | hĕmĕnt flăme |
Mănў wătĕrs | cănnŏt quĕnch lŏve | neĭthĕr | căn thĕ floŏds | drŏwn ĭt |
Ĭf ă măn | shoŭld gĭve | ăll thĕ sŭb | stănce | ŏf hĭs hoŭse | fŏr lŏve | ĭt shŏuld ŭt | tĕrlў bĕ cŭntĕmned. |

I by no means give the quantification of this, or the distribution into lines and feet as final or impeccable, though I think it is, on the whole—as a good elocutionist would read the passage—accurate enough. But the disposition will, I think, be sufficient to convince anyone who has an ear and a slight acquaintance with *res metrica*, that here is a system of rhythm irreducible to poetic form. The movement of the whole is perfectly harmonious, exquisitely modulated, finally complete. But it is the harmony of perfectly modulated speech, not of song; harmony, in short, but not melody, divisible into clauses, but not into bars or staves, having parts which continue each other, but do not correspond to each other. A similar example may be found in the almost equally beautiful Charity passage of the First Epistle to the Corinthians, and if the reader likes to see how the sense of rhythm flourishes in these days, he may compare that with the version which has been substituted for it by the persons called Revisers. But let us take an example of different kind and of less elaborate but still beautiful form, the already cited close of Sir William Temple's Essay on Poetry :—

"When all is done, human life is at the greatest and the best but like a froward child, that must be played with and humoured a little to keep it quiet till it falls asleep, and then the care is over."

Here the division is that which has been noted as the usual one in eighteenth century prose, an arsis (to alter the use of the word a little) as far as "child," a level space of progress till "asleep," and then a thesis, here unusually brief, but quite sufficient for the purpose. But here also the movement is quite different from that of poetry. Part of the centre clause, "but like a froward child that must be played with," may indeed be twisted into something like a heroic, but there is nothing corresponding to it earlier or later, and the twisting itself is violent and unnatural, for the clause or prose-line does not begin at "but," and does not end at "with."

Here is yet another and longer passage, this time from Mr. Ruskin, who, though he has by no means always observed the distinction we are discussing, and has taught many maladroit imitators to neglect it, is, when he is at his best, thoroughly sound. The sentence chosen shall be a long one, such as the writer loves :—

"He did not teach them how to build for glory and for

beauty, He did not give them the fearless, faithful, inherited energies that worked on and down from death to death, generation after generation, that we might give the work of their poured-out spirit to the axe and to the hammer: He has not cloven the earth with rivers that their wild white waves might turn wheels and push paddles, nor turned it up under, as it were fire, that it might heat wells and cure diseases: He brings not up His quails by the east wind only to let them fall in flesh about the camp of men: He has not heaped the rocks of the mountain only for the quarry, nor clothed the grass of the field only for the oven."

At first sight it may seem that this admirable passage (the brilliant effect of which is not in the least due to spilth of adjectives, or to selection of exotic words, or to eccentricity of word-order, for the vocabulary is very simple and plain, and the order is quite natural) incurs some of the blame due to the merely conglomerate sentence, in which the substitution of full-stops for colons or commas is sufficient to break up the whole into independent wholes. But it does not, and it is saved from this condemnation not merely by the close connection of its matter, but by the arrangement of its form. The separate members have a varying but compensating harmony, and the ascent and descent of the sentence never finally ends till the last word, which has been led up to by a most cunning and in no invidious sense prosaic concatenation of rhythm. Mr. Ruskin, it is true, is not always impeccable. In a fine passage of *The Harbours of England* (too long for quotation, but which may be conveniently found at p. 378 of the *Selections* from his works) I find the following complete heroics imbedded in the prose:—

> "Hot in the morning sun, rusty and seamed."
> "The grass of spring, the soft white cloud of foam."

> "Fading or flying high into the breeze."
> "Brave lives dashed
> Away about the rattling beach like weeds."
> "Still at the helm of every lonely boat,
> Through starless night and hopeless dawn, His hand."

Now this is wrong, though of course it is impossible always to avoid a complete heroic cadence. So is it, also, with a very elaborate, and in its somewhat illegitimate way, very beautiful passage of Charles Kingsley, which will be in all recollections, the Dream of Amyas at the Devil's Limekiln. This sins not by conscious or unconscious insertions of blank verse, but by the too definitely regular and lyrical sweep of the rhythm in the words, "I saw the grand old galleon," etc. This is the great difficulty of very ornate prose, that it is constantly tending to overstep the line between the two rhythms. When this fault is avoided, and the prose abides strictly by its own laws, and draws its ornament, not from aniline dyes of vocabulary, but from harmony of arrangement, nothing can be more beautiful and more satisfactory. But in fact such prose does not differ at all in kind from satisfactory specimens of the simpler style, and it was De Quincey's great critical fault that he not only overlooked but denied this identity in his scornful criticisms of the style of Swift and other severe writers. The same principles are applied with more or less elaboration as the case may be, the criterion of appropriateness in each case being the nature of the subject and the circumstances of the utterance.

It is because the rule of prose writing is in this way so entirely a μολύβδινος κανών, because between the limits of cacophony on the one hand and definitely metrical effect on the other, the practitioner must always choose and can never merely follow, that prose writing is so difficult, that the examples of great eminence in it are so rare, and that even these examples are for the most part so unequal. It is easy to produce long passages of English poetry which are absolutely flawless, which, each according to its own plan and requirements, could not be better. It is by no means easy to produce long passages of English prose, or of any prose, of which as much can be said. The artist lacks the help of obvious and striking error which he possesses in poetry. In poetry, as in the typewriter on which I write these words, a bell rings loudly to warn of certain simple dangers. The muse of prose is silent, however awkwardly her suitors make love to her. In arranging the passages which follow, not the least difficulty has been the occurrence of these sudden flaws and inequalities in specimens otherwise admirable. Omission, even indicated by asterisks, would have been fatal to the attainment of the object, which is to show the author's style in every case as the author wrote it, and not a *remaniement* by the editor. In some few cases passages exhibiting a glaring drop in style have been purposely chosen, but as a rule this naturally had to be avoided. In the simpler style there is of course less danger of flaws—Swift is often quite impeccable—but as the style rises the danger increases. I do not think that even in Landor or in Mr. Ruskin, the most accomplished, as the most opposed, English writers of the elaborate style during this century, it is possible to find an unbroken passage of very considerable length which is absolutely faultless.

This art of rhythmical arrangement, applicable in sentences so simple as that quoted from Temple, as much as in sentences so complex as that quoted from Mr. Ruskin, applicable indeed in sentences much simpler than the one and even more complicated (though such complication may be perhaps best avoided) than the other, is undoubtedly the principal thing in prose. Applied in its simplest forms, it is constantly missed by the vulgar, but is perhaps productive of not least pleasure to the critic. Of its subsidiary arts and arrangements of art space would fail me to speak at length, but the two most important articles, so important, indeed, that with the architectural process they may be said to form the three great secrets of prose success, are simplicity of language, and directness of expression in the shorter clause and phrase. It is against these two that the pseudo-stylists of our day sin most constantly. A gaudy vocabulary is thought a mark of style: a non-natural, twisted, allusive phrase is thought a mark of it. Now no reasonable person, certainly no competent critic, will advocate a *grisâtre* style; all that such a critic will contend for is a remembrance of the rule of the Good Clerk,—

"Red ink for ornament and black for use."

There are occasions for red ink in prose writing, no doubt; but they are not every man's occasions, nor are they for the men whose occasions they are on every day or on every subject. Not only the test passages taken above, but most of those which follow in the text, will show what extreme error, what bad art, what blind lack of observation, is implied in the peppering and salting of sentence after sentence with strange words or with familiar words used strangely. It is not wanted to produce the effect aimed at; it may safely be added that it produces the effect aimed at only in the case of persons who are not competent to judge whether the mark has been hit. Obscurity of phrase, on the other hand, is only a more venial crime than gaudiness of language because it takes a little more trouble on the part of the sinner. It is at least as bad in itself. It may safely be laid down that in almost any case where the phrase is not comprehended as soon as read by a person of decent intelligence and education—in almost any case where, without quite exceptional need for emphasis or for attracting his attention, a non-natural, involved, laboured diction is used—in almost any case where, as Addison has it of Durfey, "words are brought together that, without his good offices, would never have been acquainted with one another, so long as it had been a tongue"— there is bad style. Exceptions there are, no doubt, as in the other case; the fault, as always, is in making the exception the rule.

To conclude, the remarks which have been made in this Essay are no doubt in many cases disputable, probably in some cases mistaken. They are given, not as *dogma*, but as *doxa;* not as laws to guide practitioners whose practice is very likely better than the lawgiver's, but as the result of a good many years' reading of the English literature of all ages with a constantly critical intent. And of that critical intent one thing can be said with confidence, that the presence and the observation of it, so far from injuring the delight of reading, add to that delight in an extraordinary degree. It infuses toleration in the study of the worst writers— for there is at any rate the result of a discovery or an illustration of some secret of badness; it heightens the pleasure in the perusal of the best by transforming a confused into a rational appreciation. I do not think that keeping an eye on style ever interfered with attention to matter in any competent writer; I am quite sure that it never interfered with that attention in any competent reader. Less obvious, more contestable in detail, far more difficult of continuous observance than the technical excellences of verse, the technical excellences of prose demand, if a less rare, a not less alert and vigorous exercise of mental power to produce or to appreciate them. Nor will any time spent in acquiring pleasant and profitable learning be spent to much better advantage than the time necessary to master the principles and taste the expression of what has been called, by a master of both, "the *other* harmony of prose."

POSTSCRIPT.

The plan of the following Specimens will have been partly perceived from the foregoing Essay. A more direct and elaborate explanation of it would perhaps be out of place. Lectori benevolo supervacanea, nihil curat malevolus. *It is sufficient to say that the endeavour has been to provide, not a book of beauties, but a collection of characteristic examples of written style. This being so, examples of what may be called spoken style;—that is to say, letters, drama, and oratory, have been for the most part excluded, the first and last being in some rare cases admitted when it was difficult otherwise to exhibit the powers of some admitted master of prose. For a somewhat different reason, prose fiction has been but scantily drawn upon. For convenience' sake the* terminus a quo *has been fixed at the invention of printing: considerations of space, which with others from the first shut out living writers, have led to the inferior birth-limit being fixed at* 1800. *The head-notes aim only at the briefest outline of biographical information, and sometimes of general criticism, which will be found not unfrequently supplemented in the Essay. The foot-notes are intended to give such information on points both of matter and form as may be sufficient to prevent a reader of average intelligence and information from being molested in his reading by obvious difficulties. It should be added that in the selection of the passages I have received considerable assistance, though the final responsibility for their choice is in all cases mine. In the case of the Essay and the Notes this responsibility is both final and initial.*

G. S.

SIR THOMAS MALORY.

Nothing is known of the life of Sir Thomas Malory or Maleore. He is said to have been a Welshman and not Sir Knight but Sir Priest. He finished his work in the ninth year of King Edward the Fourth, and it was printed by Caxton in 1485. Compilation as it is, it has caught the whole spirit and beauty of the Arthurian legends, and is one of the first monuments of accomplished English prose.

THE DEATH OF LANCELOT.

OH ye mighty and pompous lords, winning in the glory transitory of this unstable life, as in reigning over great realms and mighty great countries, fortified with strong castles and towers, edified with many a rich city: Ye also, ye fierce and mighty knights, so valiant in adventurous deeds of arms, behold, behold, see how this mighty conqueror King Arthur, whom in his human life all the world doubted, yea also the noble Queen Guenever, which sometime sat in her chair adorned with gold, pearls, and precious stones, now lie full low in obscure foss or pit covered with clods of earth and clay. Behold also this mighty champion Sir Launcelot, peerless of all knighthood, see now how he lieth grovelling upon the cold mould, now being so feeble and faint, that sometime was so terrible, how and in what manner ought ye to be so desirous of worldly honour so dangerous. Therefore me thinketh this present book is right necessary often to be read, for in all ye find the most gracious, knightly and virtuous war of the most noble knights of the world, whereby they got praising continually. Also me seemeth by the oft reading thereof, ye shall greatly desire to accustom yourself in the following of those gracious knightly deeds, that is to say, to dread God and to love righteousness, faithfully and courageously to serve your sovereign Prince. And the more that God hath given you the triumphal honour, the meeker ye ought to be, ever fearing the unstableness of this deceitful world, and so I pass over and turn again unto my matter.

So within six weeks after Sir Launcelot fell sick, and lay in his bed; and then he sent for the bishop that there was hermit, and all his true fellows. Then Sir Launcelot said with dreary steven: "Sir Bishop, I pray you that ye will give me all my rights that belongeth unto a Christian man." "It shall not need you," said the hermit and all his fellows, "it is but a heaviness of the blood, ye shall be well amended by the grace of God tomorrow."

"My fair lords," said Sir Launcelot, "wit ye well, my careful body will into the earth, I have warning more than I will now say, therefore I pray you give me my rights." So when he was houseled and enealed and had all that a Christian man ought to have, he prayed the bishop that his fellows might bear his body unto Joyous Gard. Some men say Anwick, and some men's say is Bamborow.

"Howbeit," said Sir Launcelot, "me repenteth sore, but I made mine avow sometime, that in Joyous Gard I would be buried, and because of breaking of my vow I pray you all lead me thither." Then there was weeping and wringing of hands among all his fellows. So at the season of the night, they went all to their beds, for they all lay in one chamber; so after midnight against day, the bishop that was hermit, as he lay in his bed asleep he fell on a great laughter; and therewith the fellowship awoke, and came unto the bishop and asked him what he ailed. "Ah Jesus, mercy," said the bishop, "why did ye awake me, I was never in all my life so merry and so well at ease." "Why, wherefore?" said Sir Bors.

"Truly," said the bishop, "here was Sir Launcelot with me, with more angels than ever I saw men upon one day; and I saw the angels heave Sir Launcelot towards heaven, and the gates of heaven opened against him." "It is but dretching of swevens," said Sir Bors, "for I doubt not Sir Launcelot aileth nothing but good." "It may well be," said the bishop, "go ye to his bed, and then shall ye prove the sooth."

So when Sir Bors and his fellows came to his bed they found him stark dead, and he lay as he had smiled, and the sweetest savour about him that ever they smelled. Then was there weeping and wringing of hands, and the greatest dole they made that ever made men. And on the morrow the bishop sung his mass of *Requiem;* and after the bishop and all those nine knights put Sir Launcelot in the same horse bier that Queen Guenever was laid in before that she was buried.

And so the bishop and they altogether went with the corpse of Sir Launcelot daily, till they came unto Joyous Gard, and ever they had an hundred torches burning about him.

And so within fifteen days they came to Joyous Gard. And there they laid his corpse in the body of the choir, and sung and read many psalters and prayers over him and about him; and ever his visage was laid open and naked, that all folk might behold him; for such was the custom in those days that all men of worship should so lie with open visage till that they were buried. And right thus as they were at their service, there came Sir Ector de Maris that had sought seven years all England, Scotland and Wales, seeking his brother Sir Launcelot.

And when Sir Ector de Maris heard such noise and light in the choir of Joyous Gard, he alighted and put his horse away from him, and came into the choir, and there he saw men sing the service full lamentably. And all they knew Sir Ector, but he knew not them. Then went Sir Bors unto Sir Ector, and told him how there lay his brother Sir Launcelot dead.

And then Sir Ector threw his shield, his sword and his helm from him, and when he beheld Sir Launcelot's visage, he fell down in a swoon; and when he awaked it were hard for any tongue to tell the doleful complaints that he made for his brother. "Ah Sir Launcelot," said he, "thou were head of all christian knights." "And now I dare say," said Sir Bors, "that Sir Launcelot there thou liest, thou were never matched of none earthly knight's hands; and thou were the courteoust knight that ever bare shield; and thou were the truest friend to thy lover that ever bestrode horse, and thou were the truest lover of sinful man that ever loved woman; and thou were the kindest man that ever struck with sword; and thou were the goodliest person that ever came among press of knights; and thou were the meekest man and the gentlest, that ever eat in hall among ladies, and thou were the sternest knight to thy mortal foe that ever put spear in the rest."

La Morte d'Arthur.

P. 1, l. 1. Winning. *If this is the right reading, it must mean "succeeding," "having luck." Perhaps "wonning," i.e. "dwelling," is better.*

P. 1, l. 19. Yourself. *The confusion of singular and plural in this way is common in early modern English. In the present case there is some logical defence for it, the act being in each case individual.*

P. 2, l. 9. Steven, *"outcry," "utterance."*

P. 2, l. 18. Houseled and eneeled — *"received the Eucharist and extreme unction," as all readers of Shakespeare ought to know.*

P. 2, l. 20. Joyous Gard. *The curious gloss on this has been incorporated in most editions into the speech. It means only that in the attempt to localise the Arthurian myth different Northumbrian fortresses were chosen as the site of Sir Launcelot's famous hold.*

P. 2, l. 37. Dretching of swevens, *"troubling about dreams."*

P. 3, l. 36. Courteoust. *Others, "courtliest," and "wert" for "were" throughout.*

HUGH LATIMER.

Hugh Latimer, Bishop of Worcester, the honestest man among the English reformers, and one of the first writers of vigorous modern English, was born at an uncertain date in the last quarter of the fifteenth century, and was burnt at Oxford on the 16th October, 1555. His only literary work was his Sermons, from which the following extract is taken.

THE DILIGENT BISHOP.

AND now I would ask a strange question; who is the most diligentest bishop and prelate in all England, that passeth all the rest in doing his office? I can tell, for I know him who it is; I know him well. But now I think I see you listening and hearkening that I should name him. There is one that passeth all the other, and is the most diligent prelate and preacher in all England. And will ye know who it is? I will tell you: it is the devil. He is the most diligent preacher of all other; he is never out of his diocese; he is never from his cure; ye shall never find him unoccupied; he is ever in his parish; he keepeth residence at all times; ye shall never find him out of the way, call for him when you will he is ever at home; the diligentest preacher in all the realm; he is ever at his plough; no lording nor loitering can hinder him; he is ever applying his business, ye shall never find him idle I warrant you. And his office is to hinder religion, to maintain superstition, to set up idolatry, to teach all kind of popery. He is ready as can be wished for to set forth his plough; to devise as many ways as can be to deface and obscure God's glory. Where the devil is resident, and hath his plough going, there away with books and up with candles; away with bibles and up with beads; away with the light of the gospel, and up with the light of candles, yea, at noon days. Where the devil is resident, that he may prevail, up with all superstition and idolatry; censing, painting of images, candles, palms, ashes, holy water, and new service of men's inventing; as though man could invent a better way to honour God with, than God himself hath appointed. Down with Christ's cross, up with purgatory pickpurse, up with him, the popish purgatory, I mean. Away with clothing the naked, the poor and impotent, up with decking of images, and gay garnishing of stocks and stones: up with man's traditions and his laws, down with God's traditions and his most holy word. Down with the old honour due to God, and up with the new god's honour. Let all things be done in Latin: there must be nothing but Latin, not so much as *Memento homo quod cinis es, et in cinerem reverteris*. "Remember man that thou art ashes, and into ashes shalt thou return," which be the words that the minister speaketh unto the ignorant people, when he giveth them ashes upon Ash-Wednesday, but it must be spoken in Latin. God's word may in no wise be translated into English.

Oh that our prelates would be as diligent to sow the corn of good doctrine, as Satan is to sow cockle and darnel! And this is the devilish ploughing, the which worketh to have things in Latin, and letteth the fruitful edification. But here some man will say to me, What, Sir, are ye so privy of the devil's counsel that ye know all this to be true?—Truly I know him too well, and have obeyed him a little too much in condescending to some follies; and I know him as other men do, yea that he is ever occupied, and ever busy in following his plough. I know by Saint Peter, which saith of him, *Sicut leo rugiens circuit quærens quem devoret.* "He goeth about like a roaring lion, seeking whom he may devour." I would have this text well viewed and examined, every word of it: "*Circuit,*" he goeth about in every corner of his diocese; he goeth on visitation daily, he leaveth no place of his cure unvisited: he walketh round about from place to place, and ceaseth not. "*Sicut leo,*" as a lion, that is, strongly, boldly, and proudly, stately and fiercely with haughty looks, with his proud countenances, with his stately braggings. "*Rugiens,*" roaring; for he letteth not slip any occasion to speak or to roar out when he seeth his time. "*Quærens,*" he goeth about *seeking,* and not sleeping, as our bishops do; but he seeketh diligently, he searcheth diligently all corners, whereas he may have his prey. He roveth abroad in every place of his diocese; he standeth not still, he is never at rest, but ever in hand with his plough, that it may go forward. But there was never such a preacher in England as he is. Who is able to tell his diligent preaching, which every day, and every hour, laboureth to sow cockle and darnel, that he may bring out of form, and out of estimation and renown, the institution of the Lord's supper and Christ's cross? For there he lost his right; for Christ said, *Nunc judicium est mundi, princeps seculi hujus ejicietur foras. Et sicut exaltavit Moses serpentem in deserto, ita exaltavi oportet filium hominis. Et cum exaltatus fuero, a terra, omnia traham ad meipsum.* "Now is the judgment of this world, and the prince of this world shall be cast out. And as Moses did lift up the serpent in the wilderness, so must the son of man be lift up. And when I shall be lift up from the earth, I will draw all things unto myself." For the devil was disappointed of his purpose; for he thought all to be his own: and when he had once brought Christ to the cross, he thought all cocksure.

The Sermon of the Plough.

P. 5, l. 13. Lording nor loitering. *It must be remembered that alliteration, though English had grown out of it to some extent, still exercised considerable influence. It is therefore perhaps unnecessary to attempt to give any very precise sense to "lording," though "swaggering about" will give a good enough meaning.*

P. 5, l. 14. Applying his business, *i.q.* "*plying.*"

P. 6, l. 16. *Note that Latimer himself, despite his indignation at Latin, cites the Latin as well as the English of his texts, and cites it first. Whether this was due to mere habit, or was a precaution against the charge of garbling, or was, as Kingsley has it, because "a preacher was nothing thought of in those days who could not prove himself a good Latiner," may be left in doubt.*

P. 7, l. 23. Cocksure. *This word perhaps deserves a note because of the absurd derivation given in some dictionaries, as if from the superiority of firelocks to matchlocks. The idea probably came from the confident gait and voice of Chanticleer.*

SIR THOMAS ELYOT.

Sir Thomas Elyot was born towards the end of the fifteenth century, took his degree at Cambridge in 1507, was a protégé of Wolsey, but survived the Cardinal's fall, was more than once employed on embassies, and died at Carlton in Cambridgeshire in 1546. The Governour (a book conceived after the example of Plato and intended to sketch the character and duties of an active citizen) was published in 1531.

THE TRUE SIGNIFICATION OF TEMPERANCE A MORAL VIRTUE.

THIS blessed company of virtues in this wise assembled, followeth Temperance, as a sad and discreet matron and reverent governess, awaiting diligently that in any wise volupty or concupiscence have no preeminence in the soul of man. Aristotle defineth this virtue to be a mediocrity in the pleasures of the body, specially in taste and touching. Therefore he that is temperate fleeth pleasures voluptuous, and with the absence of them is not discontented, and from the presence of them he willingly abstaineth. But in mine opinion, Plotinus, the wonderful philosopher, maketh an excellent definition of temperance, saying, that the property or office thereof is to covet nothing which may be repented, also not to exceed the bounds of mediocrity, and to keep desire under the yoke of reason. He that practiseth this virtue is called a temperate man, and he that doeth contrary thereto is named intemperate. Between whom and a person incontinent Aristotle maketh this diversity; that he is intemperate which by his own election is led, supposing that the pleasure that is present, or, as I might say, in ure should alway be followed. But the person incontinent supposeth not so, and yet be notwithstanding doth follow it. The same author also maketh a diversity between him that is temperate and him that is continent; saying, that the continent man is such, one that nothing will do for bodily pleasure which shall stand against reason. The same is he which is temperate, saving that the other hath corrupt desires, which this man lacketh. Also the temperate man delighteth in nothing contrary to reason. But he that is continent delighteth, yet will he not be led against reason. Finally, to declare it in few words, we may well call him a temperate man that desireth the thing which he ought to desire, and as he ought to desire, and when he ought to desire. Notwithstanding there be divers other virtues which do seem to be as it were companions with temperance. Of whom, for the eschewing of tediousness, I will speak now only of two, moderation and soberness, which no man, I suppose, doubteth to be of such efficacy that without them no man may attain unto wisdom, and by them wisdom is soonest espied.

The Book named The Governour.

P. 8, l. 5. Mediocrity. *The reader will excuse a reminder that the bad sense of mediocrity is, as an exclusive sense, purely modern.*

ROGER ASCHAM.

Roger Ascham was born at Kirby Wiske in Yorkshire in 1515 and died at London in 1568. He was a member of St. John's College, Cambridge, an advocate of classical learning and education, tutor to Queen Elizabeth, and secretary to Edward VI., Mary, and Elizabeth herself. His English works are the Toxophilus, 1544, *and the* Schoolmaster, *published after his death.*

THE WAY OF THE WIND.

IN the whole year, Spring-time, Summer, Fall of the Leaf, and Winter: and in one day, Morning, Noontime, Afternoon, and Eventide, altereth the course of the weather, the pith of the bow, the strength of the man. And in every one of these times, the weather altereth, as sometime windy, sometime calm, sometime cloudy, sometime clear, sometime hot, sometime cold, the wind sometime moisty and thick, sometime dry and smooth. A little wind in a moisty day stoppeth a shaft more than a good whisking wind in a clear day. Yea, and I have seen when there hath been no wind at all, the air so misty and thick, that both the marks have been wonderful great. And once, when the plague was in Cambridge, the down wind twelve score mark for the space of three weeks was thirteen score and a half, and into the wind, being not very great, a great deal above fourteen score.

The wind is sometime plain up and down, which is commonly most certain, and requireth least knowledge, wherein a mean shooter with mean gear, if he can shoot home, may make best shift. A side wind trieth an archer and good gear very much. Sometime it bloweth aloft, sometime hard by the ground; sometime it bloweth by blasts, and sometime it continueth all in one; sometime full side wind, sometime quarter with him and more, and likewise against him, as a man with casting up light grass, or else if he take good heed, shall sensibly learn by experience. To see the wind, with a man his eyes, it is impossible, the nature of it is so fine and subtle, yet this experience of the wind had I once myself, and that was in the great snow that fell four years ago. I rode in the highway betwixt Topcliffe upon Swale, and Borough-bridge, the way being somewhat trodden before by wayfaring men. The fields on both sides were plain and lay almost yard deep with snow, the night before had been a little frost, so that the snow was hard and crusted above. That morning the sun shone bright and clear, the wind was whistling aloft, and sharp according to the time of year. The snow in the highway lay loose and trodden with horse feet : so as the wind blew, it took the loose snow with it, and made it so slide upon the snow in the field which was hard and crusted by reason of the frost over night, that thereby I might see very well the whole nature of the wind as it blew that day. And I had a great delight and pleasure to mark it, which maketh me now far better to remember it. Sometime the wind would be not past two yards broad, and so it would carry the snow as far as I could see. Another time the snow would blow over half the field at once. Sometime the snow would tumble softly, by and by it would fly wonderful fast. And this I perceived also, that the wind goeth by streams and not whole together. For I should see one stream within a score on me, then the space of two score no snow would stir, but after so much quantity of ground, another stream of snow at the same very time should be carried likewise, but not equally. For the one would stand still when the other flew apace, and so continue sometime swifter, sometime slower, sometime broader, sometime narrower, as far as I could see. Now it flew not straight, but sometime it crooked this way, sometime that way, and sometime it ran round about in a compass. And sometime the snow would be lift clean from the ground up into the air, and by and by it would be all clapped to the ground, as though there had been no wind at all, straightway it would rise and fly again.

And that which was the most marvel of all, at one time two drifts of snow flew, the one out of the west into the east, the other out of the north into the east: and I saw two winds by reason of the snow, the one cross over the other, as it had been two highways. And again, I should hear the wind blow in the air, when nothing was stirred at the ground. And when all was still where I rode, not very far from me the snow should be lifted wonderfully. This experience made me more marvel at the nature of the wind, than it made me cunning in the knowledge of the wind; but yet thereby I learned perfectly that it is no marvel at all though men in a wind loose their length in shooting, seeing so many ways the wind is so variable in blowing.

Toxophilus.

P. 11, l. 2. Quarter with him. *This use of the word quarter appears to coincide with the nautical sense of the term, where a wind blowing on the quarter is one midway between due astern and straight on the side or beam; in other words, a wind at an angle of 135 degrees to the course of the arrow.*

P. 11, l. 8. Topcliffe *and* Boroughbridge *are both on the Great North Road, the former a few miles N.E., the latter about the same distance S.E. of Ripon. Both, though now decayed, have been of some note in English history.*

P. 11, l. 27. A score, *x. yards.*

P. 12, l. 11. Length; *as we should now say, "range."*

SIR WALTER RALEIGH.

Sir Walter Raleigh, in his faults as in his merits a type and model of a great Englishman, was born at Hayes Barton in Devonshire in 1552, and was beheaded at London on Oct. 29th, 1618. His History of the World, composed during his long captivity in the Tower, is said to have received the collaboration of Jonson and other men of letters. Its finest passages are magnificent examples of sixteenth century style.

THE END OF EMPIRES AND OF LIFE.

NOW these great kings, and conquering nations have been the subject of those ancient histories, which have been preserved, and yet remain among us; and withal of so many tragical poets as in the persons of powerful princes, and other mighty men, have complained against infidelity, time, destiny; and most of all, against the variable success of worldly things, and instability of fortune. To these undertakings, these great lords of the world have been stirred up, rather by the desire of fame, which plougheth up the air, and soweth in the wind, than by the affection of bearing rule, which draweth after it so much vexation, and so many cares. And that this is true, the good advice of Cineas to Pyrrhus proves. And certainly, as fame hath often been dangerous to the living, so is it to the dead of no use at all; because separate from knowledge. Which were it otherwise, and the extreme ill bargain of buying this last discourse, understood by them which were dissolved; they themselves would then rather have wished, to have stolen out of the world without noise than to be put in mind, that they have purchased the report of their actions in the world, by rapine, oppression and cruelty, by giving in spoil the innocent and labouring soul to the idle and insolent, and by having emptied the cities of the world of their ancient inhabitants, and filled them again with so many and so variable sorts of sorrows.

Since the fall of the Roman empire, omitting that of the Germans, which had neither greatness nor continuance, there hath been no state fearful in the east, but that of the Turk; nor in the west any prince that hath spread his wings far over his nest, but the Spaniard; who since the time that Ferdinand expelled the Moors out of Granada, have made many attempts to make themselves masters of all Europe. And it is true, that by the treasures of both Indies, and by the many kingdoms which they possess in Europe, they are at this day the most powerful. But as the Turk is now counterpoised by the Persian, so instead of so many millions as have been spent by the English, French, and Netherlands in a defensive war, and in diversions against them, it is easy to demonstrate, that with the charge of two hundred thousand pounds, continued but for two years or three at the most, they may not only be persuaded to live in peace; but all their swelling and over-flowing streams may be brought back into their natural channels and old banks. These two nations, I say, are at this day the most eminent and to be regarded; the one seeking to root out the Christian religion altogether, the other the truth and sincere profession thereof; the one to join all Europe to Asia, the other the rest of all Europe to Spain.

For the rest, if we seek a reason of the succession and continuance of this boundless ambition in mortal men, we may add to that which hath been already said; That the kings and princes of the world have always laid before them, the actions, but not the ends, of those great ones which preceded them. They are always transported with the glory of the one; but they never mind the misery of the other, till they find the experience in themselves. They neglect the advice of God, while they enjoy life, or hope it; but they follow the counsel of death, upon his first approach. It is he that puts into man all the wisdom of the world, without speaking a word; which God with all the words of his law, promises or threats, doth not infuse. Death, which hateth and destroyeth man, is believed; God, which hath made him and loves him, is always deferred. "I have considered," saith Solomon, "all the works that are under the sun, and behold, all is vanity and vexation of spirit:" but who believes it, till death tells it us? It was death, which opening the conscience of Charles the fifth, made him enjoin his son Philip to restore Navarre; and king Francis the first of France, to command that justice should be done upon the murderers of the protestants in Merindol and Cabrières, which till then he neglected. It is therefore death alone, that can suddenly make man to know himself. He tells the proud and insolent, that they are but abjects, and humbles them at the instant; makes them cry, complain, and repent; yea, even to hate their fore-passed happiness. He takes the account of the rich, and proves him a beggar; a naked beggar, which hath interest in nothing, but in the gravel that fills his mouth. He holds a glass before the eyes of the most beautiful, and makes them see therein their deformity and rottenness; and they acknowledge it.

O eloquent, just and mighty death! whom none could advise, thou hast persuaded; what none hath dared, thou hast done; and whom all the world hath flattered, thou only hast cast out of the world and despised: thou hast drawn together all the far stretched greatness, all the pride, cruelty, and ambition of man, and covered it all over with these two narrow words, *Hic jacet*.

The History of the World.

P. 13, l. 15. Discourse. *This word at the date usually meant "argument," but here is taken in the least special and exact sense — "being talked about."*

P. 15, l. 9. Merindol and Cabrières. *Villages of the Vaudois, which were sacked and their inhabitants subjected to all possible outrages during the campaign of the President d'Oppède in 1545.*

EDMUND SPENSER.

Edmund Spenser was born about 1552, and died at Westminster in 1599. The View of the State of Ireland, *his only prose work of any magnitude, was posthumously published. It has interest not merely as his work and as a piece of prose of merit, but as one of the earliest political tractates of a finished and important kind in English.*

THE IRISH MANTLE.

IT is a fit house for an outlaw, a meet bed for a rebel, and an apt cloke for a thief. First the outlaw being for his many crimes and villanies banished from the towns and houses of honest men, and wandering in waste places, far from danger of law, maketh his mantle his house, and under it covereth himself from the wrath of heaven, from the offence of the earth, and from the sight of men. When it raineth it is his pent-house; when it bloweth it is his tent; when it freezeth it is his tabernacle. In summer he can wear it loose; at all times he can use it; never heavy, never cumbersome. Likewise for a rebel it is as serviceable. For in his war that he maketh, if at least it deserve the name of war, when he still flyeth from his foe, and lurketh in the thick woods and strait passages, waiting for advantages, it is his bed, yea and almost his household stuff. For the wood is his house against all weathers and his mantle is his couch to sleep in. Therein he wrappeth himself round, and coucheth himself strongly against the gnats, which in that country do more annoy the naked rebels, whilst they keep the wood, and do more sharply wound them than all their enemies swords, or spears, which can seldom come nigh them : yea and oftentimes their mantle serveth them, when they are near driven, being wrapped about their left arm, for it is hard to cut through with a sword. Besides it is light to bear, light to throw away, and, being, as they commonly are, naked, it is to them all in all. Lastly for a thief it is so handsome, as it may seem it was first invented for him, for under it he may cleanly convey any fit pillage that cometh handsomely in his way, and when he goeth abroad in the night in freebooting, it is his best and surest friend ; for lying, as they often do, two or three nights together abroad to watch for their booty, with that they can prettily shroud themselves under a bush or a bank side, till they may conveniently do their errand : and, when all is over, he can in his mantle pass through any town or company, being close hooded over his head as he useth, from knowledge of any to whom he is endangered. Besides this, he, or any man else that is disposed to mischief or villany, may under his mantle go privily armed without suspicion of any, carry his head-piece, his skean, or pistol if he please to be always in readiness.

A View of the State of Ireland.

P. 17, l. 6. Handsome, *it must be remembered, is here used in its original sense, implying "handy."*
P. 17, l. 18. Skean, *knife.*

SIR PHILIP SIDNEY.

Sir Philip Sidney was born at Penshurst in 1554, and died of his wounds at the battle of Zutphen in 1586. All his work was posthumously published, but all is of a very high order as literature, the Arcadia *being the chief example of its peculiar style in English, and the* Defence of Poetry *the earliest noteworthy piece of English criticism.*

TO HIS SISTER.

TO my dear Lady and Sister the Countess of Pembroke.

Here have you now, most dear, and most worthy to be most dear lady! this idle work of mine; which I fear, like the spider's web, will be thought fitter to be swept away, than worn to any other purpose. For my part, in very truth, as the cruel fathers among the Greeks were wont to do to the babes they would not foster, I could well find in my heart to cast out, in some desert of forgetfulness, this child, which I am loth to father. But you desired me to do it, and your desire, to my heart is an absolute commandment. Now, it is done only for you, only to you: if you keep it to yourself, or commend it to such friends, who will weigh errors in the balance of good will, I hope, for the father's sake, it will be pardoned, perchance made much of, though in itself it have deformities. For indeed, for severer eyes it is not, being but a trifle, and that triflingly handled. Your dear self can best witness the manner, being done in loose sheets of paper, most of it in your presence; the rest by sheets sent unto you as fast as they were done. In sum, a young head, not so well stayed as I would it were, and shall be when God will, having many fancies begotten in it, if it had not been in some way delivered, would have grown a monster and more sorry might I be that they came in, than that they gat out. But his chief safety shall be the not walking abroad; and his chief protection, the bearing the livery of your name, which, if much good will do not deceive me, is worthy to be a sanctuary for a greater offender. This say I, because I know thy virtue so, and this say I, because it may be for ever so, or to say better, because it will be ever so.

Read it then at your idle times, and the follies your good judgment will find in it, blame not, but laugh at. And so, looking for no better stuff than as in a haberdasher's shop, glasses or feathers, you will continue to love the writer, who doth exceedingly love you, and most heartily prays you may long live, to be a principal ornament to the family of the Sidneys.

Dedication to the Arcadia.

P. 19, ll. 8, 9. *And this say I—ever so. This phrase, which is one of the rather indefensible jingles in which Elizabethan writers delighted, comes to little more than "and because I have no doubt of its continuance."*

RICHARD HOOKER.

Richard Hooker was born near Exeter in 1554. He was scholar and fellow of Corpus Christi College, Oxford, took orders, and was appointed to the cure of Drayton Beauchamp. Made Master of the Temple by Whitgift, he engaged in active controversy. He died at his living of Bishopsbourne in Kent in 1600. The first part of the Ecclesiastical Polity *appeared in* 1594.

THE SANCTIONS OF HUMAN LAW.

IN laws, that which is natural bindeth universally, that which is positive not so. To let go those kind of positive laws which men impose upon themselves, as by vow unto God, contract with men, or such like; somewhat it will make unto our purpose, a little more fully to consider what things are incident unto the making of the positive laws for the government of them that live united in public society. Laws do not only teach what is good, but they enjoin it, they have in them a certain constraining force. And to constrain men unto any thing inconvenient doth seem unreasonable. Most requisite therefore it is that to devise laws which all men shall be forced to obey none but wise men be admitted. Laws are matters of principal consequence; men of common capacity and but ordinary judgment are not able,—for how should they?—to discern what things are fittest for each kind and state of regiment. We cannot be ignorant how much our obedience unto laws dependeth upon this point. Let a man though never so justly oppose himself unto them that are disordered in their ways, and what one amongst them commonly doth not stomach at such contradiction, storm at reproof, and hate such as would reform them? Notwithstanding even they which brook it worst that men should tell them of their duties, when they are told the same by a law, think very well and reasonably of it. For why? They presume that the law doth speak with all indifferency; that the law hath no side-respect to their persons; that the law is as it were an oracle proceeded from wisdom and understanding.

Howbeit laws do not take their constraining force from the quality of such as devise them, but from that power which doth give them the strength of laws. That which we spake before concerning the power of government must here be applied unto the power of making laws whereby to govern; which power God hath over all: and by the natural law, whereunto he hath made all subject, the lawful power of making laws to command whole politic societies of men belongeth so properly unto the same entire societies, that for any prince or potentate of what kind soever upon earth to exercise the same of himself, and not either by express commission immediately and personally received from God, or else by authority derived at the first from their consent upon whose persons they impose laws, it is no better than mere tyranny.

Laws they are not therefore which public approbation hath not made so. But approbation not only they give who personally declare their assent by voice, sign or act, but also when others do it in their names by right originally at the least derived from them. As in parliaments, councils, and the like assemblies, although we be not personally ourselves present, notwithstanding our assent is by reason of others, agents there in our behalf. And what we do by others, no reason but that it should stand as our deed, no less effectually to bind us than if ourselves had done it in person. In many things assent is given, they that give it not imagining they do so, because the manner of their assenting is not apparent. As for example, when an absolute monarch commandeth his subjects that which seemeth good in his own discretion, hath not his edict the force of a law whether they approve or dislike it? Again, that which hath been received long sithence and is by custom now established, we keep as a law which we may not transgress; yet what consent was ever thereunto sought or required at our hands?

Of this point therefore we are to note, that sith men naturally have no full and perfect power to command whole politic multitudes of men, therefore utterly without our consent we could in such sort be at no man's commandment living. And to be commanded we do consent, when that society whereof we are part hath at any time before consented, without revoking the same after by the like universal agreement. Wherefore as any man's deed past is good as long as himself continueth; so the act of a public society of men done five hundred years sithence standeth as theirs who presently are of the same societies, because corporations are immortal; we were then alive in our predecessors, and they in their successors do live still. Laws therefore human, of what kind soever, are available by consent.

Of the Laws of Ecclesiastical Polity.

P. 20, l. 15. Regiment = *"government," as in the famous instance of Knox's "monstrous regiment of women."*

JOHN LYLY.

John Lyly was born in Kent about 1554: the exact date of his death is uncertain. He was educated at Oxford, and for a time held a place at Court. Euphues (the first part) was published in 1579; the plays by which the author is also known, later.

REMEDIA AMORIS.

DO you not know the nature of women which is grounded only upon extremities? Do they think any man to delight in them, unless he dote on them? Any to be zealous except they be jealous? Any to be fervent in case he be not furious? If he be cleanly, then term they him proud, if mean in apparel a sloven, if tall a lungis, if short a dwarf, if bold, blunt: if shamefaced, a coward: insomuch as they have neither mean in their frumps, nor measure in their folly. But at the first the ox wieldeth not the yoke, nor the colt the snaffle, nor the lover good counsel, yet time causeth the one to bend his neck, the other to open his mouth, and should enforce the third to yield his right to reason. Lay before thine eyes the slights and deceits of thy lady, her snatching in jest and keeping in earnest, her perjury, her impiety, the countenance she showeth to thee of course, the love she beareth to others of zeal, her open malice, her dissembled mischief.

O I would in repeating their vices thou couldst be as eloquent as in remembering them thou oughtest to be penitent: be she never so comely call her counterfeit, be she never so straight think her crooked. And wrest all parts of her body to the worst, be she never so worthy. If she be well set, then call her a boss ; if slender, a hazel twig ; if nutbrown, as black as a coal ; if well coloured, a painted wall ; if she be pleasant, then is she a wanton ; if sullen, a clown ; if honest, then is she coy ; if impudent, a harlot.

Search every vein and sinew of their disposition ; if she have no sight in descant, desire her to chant it ; if no cunning to dance, request her to trip it ; if no skill in music, proffer her the lute ; if an ill gait, then walk with her ; if rude in speech, talk with her ; if she be gag-toothed, tell her some merry jest to make her laugh ; if pink-eyed, some doleful history to cause her weep ; in the one her grinning will show her deformed, in the other her whining like a pig half roasted.

It is a world to see how commonly we are blinded with the collusions of women, and more enticed by their ornaments being artificial, than their proportion being natural. I loathe almost to think on their ointments and apothecary drugs, the sleeking of their faces, and all their slibber sauces, which bring queesiness to the stomach, and disquiet to the mind.

Take from them their periwigs, their paintings, their jewels, their rolls, their bolsterings, and thou shalt soon perceive that a woman is the least part of herself. When they be once robbed of their robes, then will they appear so odious, so ugly, so monstrous, that thou wilt rather think them serpents than saints, and so like hags that thou wilt fear rather to be enchanted than enamoured. Look in their closets, and there shalt thou find an apothecary's shop of sweet confections, a surgeon's box of sundry salves, a pedlar's pack of new fangles. Besides all this their shadows, their spots, their lawns, their leefikyes, their ruffs, their rings, shew them rather cardinal's courtesans, than modest matrons, and more carnally affected, than moved in conscience. If every one of these things severally be not of force to move thee, yet all of them jointly should mortify thee.

Moreover, to make thee the more stronger to strive against these sirens, and more subtle to deceive these tame serpents, my counsel is that thou have more strings to thy bow than one, it is safe riding at two anchors, a fire divided in twain burneth slower, a fountain running into many rivers is of less force, the mind enamoured on two women is less affected with desire, and less infected with despair, one love expelleth another, and the remembrance of the latter quencheth the concupiscence of the first.

Euphues.

P. 23, l. 1. *Most of this passage is taken directly, and many of its phrases are literally translated from Ovid's* Remedia Amoris, *especially from lines* 315-355. *This is characteristic of Lyly and his school.*
P. 23, l. 6. Lungis, *a lounging, slouching fellow.*
P. 23, l. 7. Frumps, *"tempers," "cross speeches."*
P. 23, l. 8. Wieldeth, *in the sense of "abide," "brook;" so not common.*
P. 23, ll. 14, 15. "Of course," "of zeal," *contrasted as we should now contrast "as a matter of course" and "by predilection."*
P. 24, l. 2. Boss, *a hump, a lump.*
P. 24, l. 7. Sight in. *Compare the phrase "to be well seen in."*
P. 24, l. 10. Gag-toothed, *with projecting teeth.*
P. 24, l. 18. Slibber, *slippery.*
P. 24, l. 29. Leefikyes, *apparently from "lief," "playthings," "toys." Chosen, no doubt, for its alliteration with "lawns."*

FRANCIS BACON, VISCOUNT ST. ALBANS.

Francis Bacon was born in London in 1561. Leaving Cambridge young, he went to Paris in the suite of Sir Amyas Paulet, there studied law, became M.P. for Middlesex in 1595, Attorney-General in 1613, Lord Keeper in 1617, in 1619 Lord Chancellor and Baron Verulam, in 1620 Viscount St. Albans. He died in 1626. His fall is notorious, his character disputed, his genius incontestable.

OF MASQUES AND TRIUMPHS.

THESE things are but toys, to come amongst such serious observations. But yet, since princes will have such things, it is better they should be graced with elegancy, than daubed with cost. Dancing to song, is a thing of great state and pleasure. I understand it, that the song be in quire, placed aloft, and accompanied with some broken music; and the ditty fitted to the device. Acting in song, especially in dialogues, hath an extreme good grace; I say acting, not dancing, for that is a mean and vulgar thing; and the voices of the dialogue would be strong and manly, a bass and a tenor; no treble; and the ditty high and tragical; not nice or dainty. Several quires, placed one over against another, and taking the voice by catches, anthem-wise, give great pleasure. Turning dances into figure is a childish curiosity. And generally let it be noted, that those things which I here set down are such, as do naturally take the sense, and not respect petty wonderments. It is true, the alterations of scenes, so it be quietly and without noise, are things of great beauty and pleasure; for they feed and relieve the eye, before it be full of the same object. Let the scenes abound with light, specially coloured and varied; and let the masquers, or any other, that are to come down from the scene, have some motions upon the scene itself before their coming down; for it draws the eye strangely, and makes it with great pleasure to desire to see that it cannot perfectly discern. Let the songs be loud and cheerful, and not chirpings or pulings. Let the music likewise be sharp and loud, and well placed. The colours that shew best by candle-light, are white, carnation, and a kind of sea-water-green; and oes or spangs, as they are of no great cost, so they are of most glory. As for rich embroidery, it is lost and not discerned. Let the suits of the masquers be graceful, and such as become the person when the vizards are off; not after examples of known attires; Turks, soldiers, mariners, and the like. Let anti-masques not be long; they have been commonly of fools, satyrs, baboons, wild-men, antics, beasts, sprites, witches, Ethiops, pigmies, turquets, nymphs, rustics, cupids, statuas moving, and the like. As for angels, it is not comical enough to put them in anti-masques; and anything that is hideous, as devils, giants, is on the other side as unfit. But chiefly, let the music of them be recreative, and with some strange changes. Some sweet odours suddenly coming forth, without any drops falling, are, in such a company as there is steam and heat, things of great pleasure and refreshment. Double masques, one of men, another of ladies, addeth state and variety. But all is nothing except the room be kept clear and neat.

For jousts, and tourneys, and barriers, the glories of them are chiefly in the chariots, wherein the challengers make their entry; especially if they be drawn with strange beasts, as lions, bears, camels, and the like; or in the devices of their entrance; or in the bravery of their liveries; or in the goodly furniture of their horses and armour. But enough of these toys.

Essays.

OF STUDIES.

STUDIES serve for delight, for ornament, and for ability. Their chief use for delight, is in privateness and retiring; for ornament, is in discourse; and for ability, is in the judgment and disposition of business. For expert men can execute, and perhaps judge of particulars, one by one; but the general counsels, and the plots and marshalling of affairs, come best from those that are learned. To spend too much time in studies is sloth; to use them too much for ornament, is affectation; to make judgment wholly by their rules, is the humour of a scholar. They perfect Nature, and are perfected by experience: for natural abilities are like natural plants, that need pruning by study; and studies themselves do give forth directions too much at large, except they be bounded in by experience. Crafty men contemn studies, simple men admire them, and wise men use them; for they teach not their own use; but that is a wisdom without them, and above them, won by observation. Read not to contradict and confute; nor to believe and take for granted; nor to find talk and discourse; but to weigh and consider. Some books are to be tasted, others to be swallowed, and some few to be chewed and digested; that is, some books are to be read only in parts; others to be read, but not curiously; and some few to be read wholly, and with diligence and attention. Some books also may be read by deputy, and extracts made of them by others; but that would be only in the less important arguments, and the meaner sort of books; else distilled books are like common distilled waters, flashy things. Reading maketh a full man; conference a ready man; and writing an exact man. And therefore, if a man write little, he had need have a great memory; if he confer little, he had need have a present wit; and if he read little, he had need have much cunning, to seem to know that he doth not. Histories make men wise; poets witty; the mathematics subtle; natural philosophy deep; moral grave; logic and rhetoric able to contend. *Abeunt studia in mores.* Nay there is no stond or impediment in the wit, but may be wrought out by fit studies: like as diseases of the body may have appropriate exercises. Bowling is good for the stone and reins; shooting for the lungs and breast; gentle walking for the stomach; riding for the head; and the like. So if a man's wit be wandering, let him study the mathematics; for in demonstrations, if his wit be called away never so little, he must begin again. If his wit be not apt to distinguish or find differences, let him study the schoolmen; for they are *cymini sectores*. If he be not apt to beat over matters, and to call up one thing to prove and illustrate another, let him study the lawyers' cases. So every defect of the mind may have a special receipt.

Essays.

P. 26, l. 11. Quires *seems here to have the double sense, referring both to the place of singing and to the choristers.*
P. 27, l. 2. Motions, *acting in dumb show.*
P. 27, ll. 8, 9. Oes or spangs, *metallic spots and spangles.*
P. 27, l. 15. Turquets, *a kind of pug-dog.*
P. 28, l. 1. Expert men, *practical men, or, as we say more usually now, specialists: this barbarism, however, has not come into legal use where expert holds its ground.*
P. 28, l. 31. Stond, "*stoppage.*"

BENJAMIN JONSON.

Ben Jonson, who was born at Westminster in 1574, and died there in 1637, is not often thought of as a prose writer. His Discoveries, *however, a collection of critical and miscellaneous essays, which form his principal work in prose, are of very great merit, showing a conception of English style which for order and symmetry is hardly equalled before Dryden.*

ON EDUCATION AND STYLE.

IT pleased your Lordship of late, to ask my opinion, touching the education of your sons, and especially to the advancement of their studies. To which, though I returned somewhat for the present; which rather manifested a will in me, than gave any just resolution to the thing propounded: I have upon better cogitation called those aids about me, both of mind and memory, which shall venture my thoughts clearer, if not fuller, to your Lordship's demand. I confess, my Lord, they will seem but petty, and minute things I shall offer to you, being writ for children, and of them. But studies have their infancy as well as creatures—we see in men, even the strongest compositions had their beginnings from milk, and the cradle; and the wisest tarried some times about apting their mouths to letters and syllables. In their education therefore, the care must be the greater had of their beginnings, to know, examine, and weigh their natures; which though they be proner in some children to some disciplines; yet are they naturally prompt to taste all by degrees, and with change. For change is a kind of refreshing in studies, and infuseth knowledge by way of recreation. Thence the school itself is called a play, or game ; and all letters are so best taught to scholars. They should not be affrighted, or deterred in their entry, but drawn on with exercise and emulation. A youth should not be made to hate study, before he know the causes to love it ; or taste the bitterness before the sweet ; but called on, and allured, entreated, and praised : yea, when he deserves it not. For which cause I wish them sent to the best school, and a public ; which I think the best. Your Lordship I fear hardly hears of that, as willing to breed them in your eye, and at home ; and doubting their manners may be corrupted abroad. They are in more danger in your own family, among ill servants, allowing they be safe in their schoolmaster, than amongst a thousand boys, however immodest : would we did not spoil our own children, and overthrow their manners ourselves by too much indulgence ! To breed them at home is to breed them in a shade, where in a school they have the light and heat of the sun. They are used and accustomed to things and men. When they come forth into the common wealth, they find nothing new, or to seek. They have made their friendships and aids, some to last till their age. They hear what is commanded to others, as well as themselves ; much approved, much corrected ; all which they bring to their own store and use ; and learn as much as they hear. Eloquence would be but a poor thing, if we should only converse with singulars ; speak but man and man together. Therefore I like no private breeding. I would send them where their industry should be daily increased by praise, and that kindled by emulation. It is a good thing to inflame the mind. And though ambition itself be a vice, it is often the cause of great virtue. Give me that wit, whom praise excites, glory puts on, or disgrace grieves : he is to be nourished with ambition, pricked forward with honour, checked with reprehension, and never to be suspected of sloth. Though he be given to play, it is a sign of spirit and liveliness ; so there be a mean had of their sports and relaxations. And from the rod or ferule I would have them free, as from the menace of them ; for it is both deformed and servile.

For a man to write well, there are required three necessaries. To read the best authors, observe the best speakers : and much exercise of his own style. In style to consider, what ought to be written; and after what manner. He must first think and excogitate his matter; then choose his words, and examine the weight of either. Then take care in placing, and ranking both matter, and words, that the composition be comely; and to do this with diligence, and often. No matter how slow the style be at first, so it be laboured, and accurate; seek the best, and be not glad of the forward conceits, or first words that offer themselves to us, but judge of what we invent, and order what we approve. Repeat often what we have formerly written; which beside that it helps the consequence, and makes the juncture better, it quickens the heat of imagination, that often cools in the time of setting down, and gives it new strength, as if it grew lustier by the going back. As we see in the contention of leaping, they jump farthest that fetch their race largest: or, as in throwing a dart or javelin, we force back our arms to make our loose the stronger. Yet, if we have a fair gale of wind, I forbid not the steering out of our sail, so the favour of the gale deceive us not. For all that we invent doth please us in the conception or birth; else we would never set it down. But the safest is to return to our judgment, and handle over again those things, the easiness of which might make them justly suspected. So did the best writers in their beginnings; they imposed upon themselves care, and industry. They did nothing rashly. They obtained first to write well, and then custom made it easy and a habit. By little and little, their matter showed itself to them more plentifully; their words answered, their composition followed; and all, as in a well ordered family, presented itself in the place. So that the sum of all is: ready writing makes not good writing; but good writing brings on ready writing. Yet when we think we have got the faculty, it is even then good to resist it; as to give a horse a check sometimes with bit, which doth not so much stop his course, as stir his mettle. Again, whether a man's genius is best able to reach thither, it should more and more contend, lift and dilate itself, as men of low stature raise themselves on their toes, and so oft times get even, if not eminent. Besides, as it is fit for grown and able writers to stand of themselves, and work with their own strength, to trust and endeavour by their own faculties; so it is fit for the beginner, and learner, to study others, and the best. For the mind and memory are more sharply exercised in comprehending another man's things than our own; and such as accustom themselves, and are familiar with the best authors, shall ever and anon find somewhat of them in themselves, and in the expression of their minds, even when they feel it not, be able to utter something like theirs, which hath an authority above their own. Nay, sometimes it is the reward of a man's study, the praise of quoting another man fitly: and though a man be more prone and able for one kind of writing than another, yet he must exercise all. For as in an instrument, so in style, there must be a harmony and consent of parts.

Timber, or Discoveries, made upon Men and Matter.

P. 30, l. 2. To—"*as to*," *to be construed with* "*opinion*," *not* "*touching*."
P. 30, l. 5. Resolution, *explanation or answer, a sense neglected in modern English, though* "*resolve*" *retains it as a verb.*
P. 30, l. 11. Compositions—"*constitutions*."
P. 31, l. 9. "Hardly hears of." *To translate this sense of* audio *we now chiefly use* "listen to," *though oddly enough* "hear of" *maintains its use with the auxiliary* "will not" *and* "would not."
P. 32, l. 4. To do. *Notice the way in which Jonson varies between imperative and infinitive, according to his classical models.*
P. 32, l. 10. Consequence. "*Sequence*" *is now more exact to the sense.*
P. 32, l. 17. Steering out of our sails, *shaking the reefs out, setting full sail.*

ROBERT BURTON.

Robert Burton was born at Lindley in Leicestershire in 1576, and died at Oxford in 1640. The Anatomy of Melancholy by Democritus Junior appeared in 1621. It has been constantly pillaged, sometimes imitated, never equalled. Burton held preferment in the Church, and lived all his days at Oxford. That his melancholy or his conceit as an astrologer induced him to shorten his life is a mere legend

TERRESTRIAL DEVILS.

TERRESTRIAL devils are those Lares, Genii, Fauns, Satyrs, Wood nymphs, Foliots, Fairies, Robin Goodfellows, Trulli, etc. which as they are most conversant with men, so they do them most harm. Some think it was they alone that kept the heathen people in awe of old, and had so many idols and temples erected to them. Of this range was Dagon amongst the Philistines, Bel amongst the Babylonians, Astarte amongst the Sidonians, Baal amongst the Samaritans, Isis and Osiris amongst the Egyptians, etc. Some put our fairies into this rank, which have been in former times adored with much superstition, with sweeping their houses, and setting of a pail of clean water, good victuals, and the like, and then they should not be pinched, but find money in their shoes, and be fortunate in their enterprizes. These are they that dance on heaths and greens, as Lavater thinks with Tritemius, and as Olaus Magnus adds, leave that green circle, which we commonly find in plain fields, which others hold to proceed from a meteor falling, or some accidental rankness of the ground, so Nature sports herself; they are sometimes seen by old women and children. Hierom. Pauli. in his description of the city of Bercino in Spain, relates how they have been familiarly seen near that town, about fountains and hills; *Nonnunquam,* saith Tritemius, *in sua latibula montium simpliciores homines ducant, stupenda mirantibus ostentes miracula, nolarum sonitus, spectacula,* etc. Giraldus Cambrensis, gives instance in a monk of Wales that was so deluded. Paracelsus reckons up many places in Germany, where they do usually walk in little coats some two foot long. A bigger kind there is of them, called with us Hobgoblins, and Robin Goodfellows, that would in those superstitious times grind corn for a mess of milk, cut wood, or do any manner of drudgery work. They would mend old irons in those Æolian Isles of Lipara, in former ages, and have been often seen and heard. Tholosanus calls them Trullos and Getulos, and saith, that in his days they were common in many places of France. Dithmarus Bleshenius in his description of Iceland, reports for a certainty, that almost in every family they have yet some such familiar spirits; and Felix Malleolus in his book *De Crudel. Dæmon.* affirms as much, that these Trolli, or Telchines, are very common in Norway, "and seen to do drudgery work;" to draw water, saith Wierus lib. 1. cap. 22., dress meat, or any such thing. Another sort of these there are, which frequent forlorn houses, which the Italians call Foliots, most part innoxious, Cardan holds; "They will make strange noises in the night, howl sometimes pitifully, and then laugh again, cause great flame and sudden lights, fling stones, rattle chains, shave men, open doors, and shut them, fling down platters, stools, chests, sometime appear in the likeness of hares, crows, black dogs, etc." of which read Pet. Thyræus the Jesuit in his Tract, *de locis infestis,* part 1 *et* cap. 4. who will have them to be devils, or the souls of damned men that seek revenge, or else souls out of Purgatory that seek ease; for such examples peruse Sigismundus Scheretzius lib. de spectris, part 1. c. 1. which he saith he took out of Luther most part; there be many instances. Plinius Secundus remembers such a house at Athens, which Athenodorus the Philosopher hired, which no man durst inhabit for fear of devils. Austin *de Civ. Dei.* lib. 22. cap. 1. relates as much of Hesperius the Tribune's house at Zubeda near their city of Hippo, vexed with evil spirits to his great hindrance, *Cum afflictione animalium et servorum suorum.* Many such instances are to be read in Niderius Formicar. lib. 5. cap. 12. 3. *etc.* Whether I may call these Zim and Ophim, which Isaiah cap. 13. 21. speaks of, I make a doubt. See more of these in the said Scheretz. lib. 1. *de spect.* cap. 4. he is full of examples. These kind of devils many times appear to men, and affright them out of their wits, sometimes walking at noon day, sometimes at nights, counterfeiting dead men's ghosts, as that of Caligula, which, saith Suetonius, was seen to walk in Lavinia's garden, where his body was buried, spirits haunted, and the house where he died, *Nulla nox sine terrore transacta, donec incendio consumpta;* every night this happened, there was no quietness, till the house was burned. About Hecla in Iceland ghosts commonly walk, *animas mortuorum simulantes,* saith Joh. Anan. lib. 3. *de nat dæm. Olaus.* lib. 2. cap. 2. *Natal. Tallopid. lib. de apparit. spir. Kornmannus de mirac. mort.* part 1. cap. 44 : such sights are frequently seen *circa Sepulchra et Monasteria,* saith Lavat. lib. 1. cap. 19, in Monasteries and about Churchyards, *loca paludinosa, ampla ædificia, solitaria, et cæde hominum notata, etc.* Thyreus adds, *ubi gravius peccatum est commissum, impii, pauperum oppressores et nequiter insignes habitant.* These spirits often foretell men's deaths, by several signs, as knocking, groanings, etc. though Rich. Argentine c. 18. *de præstigiis dæmonum,* will ascribe these predictions to good angels, out of the authority of Ficinus and others ; *prodigia in obitu principum sæpius contingunt, etc.* as in the Lateran Church in Rome, the Popes' deaths are foretold by Sylvester's tomb. Near Rupes Nova in Finland, in the Kingdom of Sweden, there is a lake, in which, before the Governor of the Castle dies, a spectrum, in the habit of Arion with his harp appears, and makes excellent music, like those blocks in Cheshire, which, they say, presage death to the master of the family ; or that oak in Lanthadran Park in Cornwall, which foreshows as much. Many families in Europe are so put in mind of their last, by such predictions, and many men are forewarned, if we may believe Paracelsus, by familiar spirits in divers shapes, as cocks, crows, owls, which often hover about sick men's chambers, *vel quia morientium fæditatem sentiunt,* as

Barcellus conjectures, *et ideo super tectum infermorum crocitant*, because they smell a corse;—or for that, as Bernardinus de Bustis thinketh, God permits the devil to appear in the form of crows, and such like creatures, to scare such as live wickedly here on earth. A little before Tully's death, saith Plutarch, the crows made a mighty noise about him, *tumultuose perstrepentes*, they pulled the pillow from under his head. Rob. Gaguinus hist. Franc. lib. 8. telleth such another wonderful story at the death of Johannes de Monteforti, a French lord, Anno 1345. *tanta Corvorum multitudo ædibus morientis insedit, quantam esse in Gallia nemo judicasset.* Such prodigies are very frequent in authors. See more of these in the said Lavater, *Thyreus de locis infestis*, part 3. cap. 58. Pictorius, Delrio, Cicogna, lib. 3. cap. 9. Necromancers take upon them to raise and lay them at their pleasures: And so likewise those which Mizaldus calls Ambulones, that walk about midnight on great heaths and desert places, which, saith Lavater, "draw men out of the way, and lead them all night a by-way, or quite bar them of their way;" these have several names in several places; we commonly call them Pucks. In the deserts of Lop in Asia, such illusions of walking spirits are often perceived, as you may read in M. Paulus the Venetian his travels; If one lose his company by chance, these devils will call him by his name, and counterfeit voices of his companions to seduce him. Hieronym Pauli in his book of the hills of Spain, relates of a great mount in Cantabria, where such spectrums are to be seen; Lavater and Cicogna have variety of examples of spirits and walking devils in this kind. Sometimes they sit by the highway side, to give men falls, and make their horses stumble and start as they ride, if you will believe the relation of that holy man Ketellus in Nubrigensis, that had an especial grace to see devils, *Gratiam divinitus collatam*, and talk with them, *Et impavidus cum spiritibus sermonem miscere*, without offence, and if a man curse or spur his horse for stumbling, they do heartily rejoice at it; with many such pretty feats.

The Anatomy of Melancholy.

THE CURE OF MELANCHOLY.

IF princes would do justice, judges be upright, clergymen truly devout, and so live as they teach, if great men would not be so insolent, if soldiers would quietly defend us, the poor would be patient, rich men would be liberal and humble, citizens honest, magistrates meek, superiors would give good example, subjects peaceable, young men would stand in awe : if parents would be kind to their children, and they again obedient to their parents, brethren agree amongst themselves, enemies be reconciled, servants trusty to their masters, virgins chaste, wives modest, husbands would be loving and less jealous : If we could imitate Christ and his Apostles, live after God's laws, these mischiefs would not so frequently happen amongst us ; but being most part so irreconcileable as we are, perverse, proud, insolent, factious and malicious, prone to contention, anger and revenge, of such fiery spirits, so captious, impious, irreligious, so opposite to virtue, void of grace, how should it otherwise be ? Many men are very testy by nature, apt to mistake, apt to quarrel, apt to provoke and misinterpret to the worst, everything that is said or done, and thereupon heap unto their selves a great deal of trouble, and disquietness to others, smatterers in other men's matters, tale-bearers, whisperers, liars, they cannot speak in season, or hold their tongues when they should, *Et suam partem itidem tacere, cum aliena est oratio :* they will speak more than comes to their shares, in all companies, and by those bad courses accumulate much evil to their own souls, *qui contendit, sibi convicium facit*, their life is a perpetual brawl, they snarl like so many dogs, with their wives, children, servants, neighbours, and all the rest of their friends, they can agree with nobody. But to such as are judicious, meek, submiss, and quiet, these matters are easily remedied : they will forbear upon all such occasions, neglect, contemn, or take no notice of them, dissemble, or wisely turn it off. If it be a natural impediment, as a red nose, squint eyes, crooked legs, or any such imperfection, infirmity, disgrace, reproach, the best way is to speak of it first thyself, and so thou shalt surely take away all occasions from others to jest at, or contemn, that they may perceive thee to be careless of it. Vatinius was wont to scoff at his own deformed feet, to prevent his enemies' obloquies and sarcasms in that kind ; or else by prevention, as Cotys king of Thrace, that brake a company of fine glasses presented to him, with his own hands, lest he should be overmuch moved when they were broken by chance. And sometimes again, so that it be discreetly and moderately done, it shall not be amiss to make resistance, to take down such a saucy companion, no better means to vindicate himself to purchase final peace : for he that suffers himself to be ridden, or through pusillanimity or sottishness will let every man baffle him, shall be a common laughing stock to flout at. As a cur that goes through a village, if he clap his tail between his legs, and run away, every cur will insult over him : but if he bristle up himself, and stand to it, give but a counter-snarl, there's not a dog dares meddle with him : much is in a man's courage and discreet carriage of himself.

The Anatomy of Melancholy.

P. 34, l. 2. Foliots, *stated below to be Italian, but connected apparently with Fr. follets, pucks, will-o'-the wisps : Trulli, the Scandinavian trolls.*

P. 35, l. 19. Telchines, *of Rhodes and other places, a tribe or family of half divine or superhuman attributes, to whom Greek mythology assigns attributes not unlike those of trolls and brownies.*

P. 37, l. 20. Lop, *i.e. Lob Nor, north of Thibet.*

P. 37, l. 22. M. Paulus, *better recognised, perhaps, as Marco Polo.*

P. 38, l. 3. The poor would be. *This must not be mistaken for a consequence. It and the other clauses in the same case are part of the hypothesis, "if" being alternately dropped and inserted at the writer's pleasure.*

P. 39, l. 3. Vatinius. *Both the later or Neronian Vatinius and Cæsar's friend, of whom it was said,* per consulatum pejerat, *were ill favoured in person. I am not certain to which this story refers. Cotys again was the name of at least four kings of Thrace.*

EDWARD HERBERT, LORD HERBERT OF CHERBURY.

Edward Herbert, elder brother of the poet George, was born at Montgomery Castle in 1581. He was educated at Oxford, travelled much abroad with some romantic adventures, and was raised to the peerage for diplomatic services. He died at London in 1648. His theological writings have caused him to be rather loosely styled the first English deist: his autobiography is curious and characteristic of the time.

THE EVIDENCE OF ANOTHER LIFE.

AND certainly since in my mother's womb this Plastica or Formatrix which formed my eyes, ears, and other senses, did not intend them for that dark and noisome place, but as being conscious of a better life, made them as fitting organs to apprehend and perceive those things which should occur in this world: so I believe since my coming into this world my soul hath formed or produced certain faculties which are almost as useless for this life, as the above-named senses were for the mother's womb; and these faculties are Hope, Faith, Love, and Joy, since they never rest or fix upon any transitory or perishing object in this world, as extending themselves to something further than can be here given, and indeed acquiesce only in the perfect, eternal, and infinite. I confess they are of some use here, yet I appeal to every body whether any worldly felicity did so satisfy their hope here, that they did not wish and hope for something more excellent, or whether they had ever that faith in their own wisdom, or in the help of man, that they were not constrained to have recourse to some diviner and superior power, than they could find on earth, to relieve them in their danger or necessity; whether ever they could place their love on any earthly beauty, that it did not fade and wither, if not frustrate or deceive them, or whether ever their joy was so consummate in any thing they delighted in, that they did not want much more than it, or indeed this world can afford to make them happy. The proper objects of these faculties therefore though framed, or at least appearing in this world, is God only, upon whom Faith, Hope, and Love were never placed in vain, or remain long unrequited.

Life of Lord Herbert.

P. 40, l. 1. Plastica or Formatrix, sc. *Natura.*

THOMAS HOBBES.

Thomas Hobbes was born at Malmesbury in 1588. After leaving Oxford he became tutor in the Cavendish family, with whom he long resided. He abode also much in France, especially during the Civil War. At the Restoration he was pensioned. His work is voluminous: the Leviathan, *his most famous book, was published in 1651. He died in 1679.*

DREAMS AND APPARITIONS.

THE imaginations of them that sleep are those we call *dreams*. And these also, as all other imaginations, have been before, either totally or by parcels, in the sense. And because in sense, the brain and nerves, which are the necessary organs of sense, are so benumbed in sleep, as not easily to be moved by the action of external objects, there can happen in sleep no imagination, and therefore no dream, but what proceeds from the agitation of the inward parts of man's body; which inward parts, for the connexion they have with the brain, and other organs, when they be distempered, do keep the sense in motion; whereby the imaginations there formerly made, appear as if a man were waking; saving that the organs of sense being now benumbed, so as there is no new object, which can master and obscure them with a more vigorous impression, a dream must needs be more clear, in this silence of sense, than our waking thoughts. And hence it cometh to pass, that it is a hard matter, and by many thought impossible, to distinguish exactly between sense and dreaming. For my part, when I consider that in dreams I do not often nor constantly think of the same persons, places, objects, and actions, that I do waking; nor remember so long a train of coherent thoughts, dreaming, as at other times; and because waking I often observe the absurdity of dreams, but never dream of the absurdities of my waking thoughts; I am well satisfied, that being awake, I know I dream not, though when I dream I think myself awake.

And seeing dreams are caused by the distemper of some of the inward parts of the body, divers distempers must needs cause different dreams. And hence it is that lying cold breedeth dreams of fear, and raiseth the thought and image of some fearful object, the motion from the brain to the inner parts and from the inner parts to the brain being reciprocal; and that as anger causeth heat in some parts of the body when we are awake, so when we sleep the overheating of the same parts causeth anger, and raiseth up in the brain the imagination of an enemy. In the same manner, as natural kindness, when we are awake, causeth desire, and desire makes heat in certain other parts of the body; so also too much heat in those parts, while we sleep, raiseth in the brain an imagination of some kindness shown. In sum, our dreams are the reverse of our waking imaginations; the motion when we are awake beginning at one end, and when we dream at another.

The most difficult discerning of a man's dream, from his waking thoughts, is then, when by some accident we observe not that we have slept: which is easy to happen to a man full of fearful thoughts, and whose conscience is much troubled; and that sleepeth, without the circumstances of going to bed or putting off his clothes, as one that noddeth in a chair. For he that taketh pains, and industriously lays himself to sleep, in case any uncouth and exorbitant fancy come unto him, cannot easily think it other than a dream. We read that Marcus Brutus, one that had his life given him by Julius Cæsar, and was also his favourite, and notwithstanding murdered him, how at Philippi, the night before he gave battle to Augustus Cæsar, he saw a fearful apparition, which is commonly related by historians as a vision; but considering the circumstances, one may easily judge to have been but a short dream. For sitting in his tent, pensive and troubled with the horror of his rash act, it was not hard for him, slumbering in the cold, to dream of that which most affrighted him; which fear, as by degrees it made him wake, so also it must needs make the apparition by degrees to vanish; and having no assurance that he slept, he could have no cause to think it a dream, or any thing but a vision. And this is no very rare accident; for even they that be perfectly awake, if they be timorous and superstitious, possessed with fearful tales, and alone in the dark, are subject to the like fancies, and believe they see spirits and dead men's ghosts walking in churchyards; whereas it is either their fancy only, or else the knavery of such persons as make use of such superstitious fear, to pass disguised in the night, to places they would not be known to haunt.

From this ignorance of how to distinguish dreams, and other strong fancies, from vision and sense, did arise the greatest part of the religion of the Gentiles in time past, that worshipped satyrs, fauns, nymphs, and the like; and now-a-days the opinion that rude people have of fairies, ghosts, and goblins, and of the power of witches. For as for witches, I think not that their witchcraft is any real power; but yet that they are justly punished, for the false belief they have that they can do such mischief, joined with their purpose to do it, if they can; their trade being nearer to a new religion than to a craft or science. And for fairies, and walking ghosts, the opinion of them has, I think, been on purpose either taught or not confuted, to keep in credit the use of exorcism, of crosses, of holy water, and other such inventions of ghostly men. Nevertheless, there is no doubt, but God can make unnatural apparitions; but that he does it so often, as men need to fear such things, more than they fear the stay or change of the course of nature, which he also can stay, and change, is no point of Christian faith. But evil men under pretext that God can do any thing, are so bold as to say any thing when it serves their turn, though they think it untrue; it is the part of a wise man, to believe them no farther, than right reason makes that which they say, appear credible. If this superstitious fear of spirits were taken away, and with it, prognostics from dreams, false prophecies, and many other things depending thereon, by which crafty ambitious persons abuse the simple people, men would be much more fitted than they are for civil obedience.

And this ought to be the work of the Schools: but they rather nourish such doctrine. For, not knowing what imagination or the senses are, what they receive, they teach: some saying, that imaginations rise of themselves, and have no cause: others that they rise most commonly from the will; and that good thoughts are blown, inspired, into a man, by God; and evil thoughts by the Devil: or that good thoughts are poured, infused, into a man, by God, and evil ones by the Devil. Some say the senses receive the species of things, and deliver them to the common-sense; and the common-sense delivers them over to the fancy, and the fancy to the memory, and the memory to the judgment, like handing of things from one to another, with many words making nothing understood.

Leviathan.

P. 43, l. 36. That ... how ... but. *Observe the confusion of these constructions, even in so clear a writer as Hobbes. He has forgotten "that" when he comes to "how;" he has forgotten "which" when he comes to "but."*

P. 44, l. 19. *This sentence is very noticeable in matter, because of Hobbes's agreement, from a quite different point of view, with the opinions of Hale and Browne on the punishment of witchcraft, and because of the astonishing foresight of the last clause.*

IZAAC WALTON.

Izaak Walton was born at Stafford in 1593, and died at Winchester in 1683. Most of his life, however, was passed in London, where he was for a time in trade. The Complete Angler *appeared in 1653; the not less charming* Lives *at different periods earlier and later. All his work has the same quiet grace which seems to have distinguished his character.*

CHARACTER OF NOWEL.

THE first is Doctor Nowel, sometimes Dean of the Cathedral Church of St. Paul's in London, where his monument stands yet undefaced: a man that in the Reformation of Queen Elizabeth, not that of Henry VIII., was so noted for his meek spirit, deep learning, prudence and piety, that the then Parliament and Convocation both, chose, enjoined, and trusted him to be the man to make a Catechism for public use, such a one as should stand as a rule for faith and manners to their posterity. And the good old man, though he was very learned, yet knowing that God leads us not to heaven by many nor by hard questions, like an honest angler, made that good, plain, unperplexed catechism which is printed with our good old Service-Book. I say, this good man was a dear lover, and constant practiser of angling, as any age can produce; and his custom was to spend besides his fixed hour of prayer, those hours which by command of the Church were enjoined the Clergy and voluntarily dedicated to devotion by many primitive Christians: I say, besides those hours, this good man was observed to spend a tenth part of his time in angling; and also, for I have conversed with those which have conversed with him, to bestow a tenth part of his revenue, and usually all his fish, amongst the poor that inhabited near to those rivers in which it was caught: saying often, "That charity gave life to religion:" and at his return to his house, would praise God he had spent that day free from worldly trouble; both harmlessly, and in a recreation that became a churchman. And this good man was well content, if not desirous, that posterity should know he was an angler, as may appear by his picture, now to be seen, and carefully kept in Brazen-nose College, to which he was a liberal benefactor; in which picture he is drawn leaning on a desk with his Bible before him, and on one hand of him his lines, hooks, and other tackling lying in a round; and on his other hand are his angle-rods of several sorts: and by them this is written, "That he died 13 Feb. 1601, being aged 95 years, 44 of which he had been Dean of St. Paul's Church; and that his age had neither impaired his hearing, nor dimmed his eyes, nor weakened his memory, nor made any of the faculties of his mind weak or useless." It is said that angling and temperance were great causes of these blessings; and I wish the like to all that imitate him, and love the memory of so good a man.

Complete Angler.

P. 47, l. 19. Temperance. *But Nowel was not a total abstainer, and according to a story told by Fuller, and quoted by Southey in the* Doctor, *he accidentally invented bottled beer.*

WILLIAM CHILLINGWORTH.

William Chillingworth was born at Oxford in 1602, and was the godson of Laud. While a member of Trinity College he was converted to Roman Catholicism, but reverted to the Anglican Church in 1631. His Religion of Protestants *appeared in 1635. He took orders and received preferment. He died in 1644, having distinguished himself as a partisan of the Royal cause.*

AGAINST THE PUNISHMENT OF DEATH.

MY fourth notion is, that they who by the rigour of the laws are to suffer death, and especially thieves, may by the clemency of this present parliament be saved from death, and made public slaves. My reasons are, first, because the chief end of punishment being, that others may fear to offend, the punishment of public slavery, as it may be ordered, being a long and lasting punishment, is like to work more effectually to this end, than putting to death, which is despatched in a moment. Lasting pain and public shame, though in true account not so great a punishment as death, especially if we remember the danger that follows after, yet certainly to the generality of men is much more terrible than speedy death; especially to Englishmen. For the best observers of their natures and disposition have out of their experience assured us, that they are generally not so much afraid of death, as of pain and shame. So that we have reason to expect, that this punishment will be more available for achieving the end of all punishment, which is by fear to keep others from transgressing; and therefore, in policy, we should rather make use of it than the other.

Secondly, it seems better in order to justice; because this kind of punishment, besides the benefit of a more lasting and a more public example, leaves the criminal a possibility and power to make some kind of satisfaction for the injury done by him to his neighbour, by restitution, and to the commonwealth, by doing some service to the public; both which by capital punishments are quite taken away. Our commonwealth for want of public slaves wants many great advantages; as the use of galleys, the making or repairing of public ways, the opening the passages of all our great rivers, and making an intercourse between them; which, and many other noble works of great benefit to the public, by the labour of public slaves might be obtained, and that without any prejudice or danger, if they be wisely ordered.

Thirdly, it is more agreeable to charity. For it is, I conceive, most evidently demonstrable out of the principles of charity, as a certain conclusion, that destructive punishments ought not to be used against any delinquents whatsoever, if in reason we may expect, that such as are medicinal and not destructive, will be as exemplary and as beneficial to the commonwealth, or rather much more. For certainly nothing can be more agreeable to charity, than all possible and lawful parsimony of the blood of Christians, nay even of the blood of men; nor anything more apparently repugnant to Christian charity, and the bowels of compassion, and even to humanity itself, than to hurt, much more to destroy any person, unless this severity be necessary, or may at least be useful for the public good: for that were to shed the blood of a man and of a Christian to no purpose.

Fourthly, capital punishments as they are now ordered, are ordinarily, if not necessarily, as we may well fear, joined with the eternal destruction of the delinquents' souls; who are commonly turned out of the world without other preparation for their last account, than only some sad short recollections, and constrained sorrow for their sins and their calamities, with some stupifying comfort grounded thereupon, which is commonly, but grossly, mistaken to be true repentance. But repentance is not so ordinary a thing, nor of so easy dispatch, as most mistake it, who conceive it to be nothing more, but true sorrow for sin past, with true intention to forsake it. Whereas it is a true and an habitual change of the soul and the whole man, an effectual forsaking of sin, and an effectual and constant practice of Christian holiness, and an universal obedience to the law of Christ. The scripture assures us expressly, that without the knowledge of God's will revealed to us by Jesus Christ, without effectual forsaking and mortifying our sins, and without the effectual practice of Christian virtues, such as may truly denominate us new creatures and holy men, without true mortification and sanctification, briefly, "without holiness, no man shall see God." This being so, it is easy to judge, that it is morally impossible for our miserable delinquents ordinarily to be so qualified with true repentance, as to be in the state of salvation, experience showing, that few of them are truly mortified and sanctified men. And indeed the course now taken, as it gives them not means, so it allows them not time between their imprisonment and execution necessary for the effecting of this great work in themselves, which yet God is willing to grant them; and therefore it cannot be excused from a most bloody and horrible uncharitableness, and a base esteem of men's souls, if we allow them not all possible means to effect this great work in themselves, and all that time and space, even to a minute, which God in his mercy is pleased to allow them. Whereas we take from them that time, and inflict on them a punishment, the consequents whereof, though we intend it not, are infinitely more grievous than the punishments which we inflict, too frequently destroying the delinquents, both body and soul.

Sermons.

P. 50, l. 2. Habitual change. *That is to say, a change of the habit—the ἕξις—of the soul. Usage has somewhat obscured this.*

SIR THOMAS BROWNE.

Sir Thomas Browne was born in London in 1605, and died at Norwich, where he practised as a physician, in 1682. In his Vulgar Errors he is chiefly learned and quaint, tempering strong sense with humour. But in passages there, and in most part of his Christian Morals, Urn Burial, and Religio Medici, he is Jeremy Taylor's rival, and sometimes his superior in the use of ornate and cadenced prose.

BONES OF THE DEAD.

NOW since these dead bones have already outlasted the living ones of Methuselah, and in a yard underground, and thin walls of clay, out-worn all the strong and spacious buildings above it, and quietly rested under the drums and tramplings of three conquests, what prince can promise such diuturnity unto his relics, or might not gladly say

Sic ego componi versus in ossa velim?

Time, which antiquates antiquities, and hath an art to make dust of all things, hath yet spared these minor monuments. In vain we hope to be known by open and visible conservatories, when to be unknown was the means of their continuation, and obscurity their protection. If they died by violent hands, and were thrust into their urns, these bones become considerable, and some old philosophers would honour them, whose souls they conceived most pure, which were thus snatched from their bodies, and to retain a stronger propension unto them : whereas they weariedly left a languishing corpse, and with faint desires of reunion. If they fell by long and aged decay, yet wrapt up in the bundle of time, they fall into indistinction, and make but one blot with infants. If we begin to die when we live, and long life be but a prolongation of death, our life is a sad composition; we live with death, and die not in a moment. How many pulses made up the life of Methuselah, were work for Archimedes: common counters sum up the life of Moses's man. Our days become considerable like petty sums by minute accumulations; where numerous fractions make up but small round numbers; and our days of a span long make not one little finger.

If the nearness of our last necessity, brought a nearer conformity unto it, there were a happiness in hoary hairs, and no calamity in half senses. But the long habit of living indisposeth us for dying; when avarice makes us the sport of death, when even David grew politically cruel, and Solomon could hardly be said to be the wisest of men. But many are too early old, and before the date of age. Adversity stretcheth our days, misery makes Alcmena's nights, and time hath no wings unto it. But the most tedious being is that which can unwish itself, content to be nothing, or never to have been, which was beyond the malcontent of Job, who cursed not the day of his life, but his nativity. Content to have so far been, as to have a title to future being; although he had lived here but in an hidden state of life, and, as it were, an abortion.

Hydriotaphia or Urn Burial.

CONSCIENCE.

PAINT not the sepulchre of thyself, and strive not to beautify thy corruption. Be not an advocate for thy vices, nor call for many hour-glasses to justify thy imperfections. Think not that always good which thou thinkest thou canst always make good, nor that concealed which the sun doth not behold: that which the sun doth not now see, will be visible when the sun is out, and the stars are fallen from heaven. Meanwhile there is no darkness unto conscience; which can see without light, and in the deepest obscurity give a clear draught of things, which the cloud of dissimulation hath concealed from all eyes. There is a natural standing court within us, examining, acquitting, and condemning at the tribunal of ourselves ; wherein iniquities have their natural thetas and no nocent is absolved by the verdict of himself. And therefore although our transgressions shall be tried at the last bar, the process need not be long : for the judge of all knoweth all, and every man will nakedly know himself; and when so few are like to plead not guilty, the assize must soon have an end.

Christian Morals.

SELF OPINION.

COMPLY with some humours, bear with others, but serve none. Civil complacency consists with decent honesty : Flattery is a juggler, and no kin unto sincerity. But while thou maintainest the plain path, and scornest to flatter others, fall not into self-adulation, and become not thine own parasite. Be deaf unto thyself, and be not betrayed at home. Self-credulity, pride, and levity, lead unto self-idolatry. There is no Damocles like unto self-opinion, nor any siren to our own fawning conceptions. To magnify our minor things, or hug ourselves in our apparitions ; to afford a credulous ear unto the clawing suggestions of fancy ; to pass our days in painted mistakes of ourselves ; and though we behold our own blood, to think ourselves the sons of Jupiter ; are blandishments of self-love, worse than outward delusion. By this imposture wise men sometimes are mistaken in their elevation, and look above themselves. And fools, which are antipodes unto the wise, conceive themselves to be but their Periœci, and in the same parallel with them.

Christian Morals.

P. 51, l. 1. These dead bones. *Some funeral urns had been discovered in Norfolk. They formed the subject of* Hydriotaphia or Urn Burial.
P. 51, l. 10. Conservatories, *literally, i.e. places of conservation.*
P. 52, l. 15. To retain, *construed with "they conceived."*
P. 52, l. 9. One little finger, *which, in the language of signs, denotes a hundred.*
P. 52, l. 17. Alcmena's nights, *as long as three.*
P. 53, l. 16. Any siren to, *i.e. "equal to."*

THOMAS FULLER.

Thomas Fuller was born in 1608 at Aldwinkle, was educated at Cambridge, held various benefices, and, though a Royalist, was not wholly deprived under the Commonwealth. He died in 1661. His Worthies did not appear till after his death. He had written much else, while he was also celebrated as a preacher. For quaintness which is not buffoonery Fuller has no rival in English.

ON SURGEONS.

NECESSARY and ancient their profession, ever since man's body was subject to enmity and casualty. For that promise, "A bone of him shall not be broken," is peculiar to Christ. As for the other, "To keep them in all their ways, that they dash not their foot against a stone," though it be extended to all Christians, yet it admitteth, as other temporal promises, of many exceptions, according to God's will and pleasure.

It seemeth by the parable of the good Samaritan, who "bound up" the passenger's "wounds, pouring in oil and wine," that, in that age, ordinary persons had a general insight in chirurgery, for their own and others' use. And it is reported, to the just praise of the Scotch nobility, that anciently they all were very dexterous thereat; particularly it is written of James, the fourth king of Scotland, *quod vulnera scientissime tractaret*, "he was most skilful at the handling of wounds." But we speak of chirurgery, as it is a particular mystery, professed by such as make a vocation thereof. Of whom we have inserted some (eminent for their writings or otherwise), amongst physicians, and that, as we hope, without any offence, seeing the healing of diseases and wounds were anciently one calling, as still great the sympathy betwixt them; many diseases causing wounds, as ulcers; as wounds occasioning diseases, as fevers; till in process of time they were separated, and chirurgeons only consigned to the manual operation. Thus, wishing unto them the three requisites for their practice, an eagle's eye, a lady's hand, and a lion's heart, I leave them, and proceed.

The Worthies of England.

ON MUSIC.

RIGHT glad I am, that when music was lately shut out of our churches, on what default of hers I dare not to inquire, it hath since been harboured and welcomed in the halls, parlours, and chambers, of the primest persons of this nation. Sure I am, it could not enter into my head, to surmise that music would have been so much discouraged by such who turned our kingdom into a Commonwealth, seeing they prided themselves in the arms thereof, an impaled harp being moiety of the same. When it was asked, "what made a good musician?" one answered, a good voice; another, that it was skill. But he said the truth, who said, it was encouragement. It was therefore my constant wish, that seeing most of our musicians were men of maturity, and arrived at their full age and skill, before these distracted times began, and seeing what the historian wrote in another sense is true here in our acceptation and application thereof, "Res est unius seculi populus virorum;" I say, I did constantly wish, that there might have been some seminary of youth set up, to be bred in the faculty of music, to supply succession, when this set of masters in that science had served their generation.

Yet although I missed of what I did then desire; yet, thanks be to God, I have lived to see music come into request, since our nation came into right tune, and begin to flourish in our churches and elsewhere; so that now no fear but we shall have a new generation skilful in that science, to succeed such whose age shall call upon them to pay their debt to nature.

If any who dislike music in churches object it as useless, if not hurtful, in Divine service, let them hear what both a learned and able divine allegeth in defence thereof; "So that although we lay altogether aside the consideration of ditty or matter, the very harmony of sounds being framed in due sort, and carried from the ear through the spiritual faculties to the soul, it is by a native puissance and efficacy greatly available to bring to a perfect temper, whatsoever is there tumbled; apt, as well to quicken the spirits, as to allay that which is too eager; sovereign against melancholy and despair, forcible to draw forth tears of devotion, if the mind be such as can yield them, able both to move and moderate all affections."

In recounting up of musicians, I have only insisted on such who made it their profession; and either have written books of that faculty, or have attained to such an eminence therein as is generally acknowledged. Otherwise the work would be endless, to recount all up who took it as a quality of accomplishment; amongst whom king Henry the Eighth must be accounted; who, as Erasmus testifies to his knowledge, did not only sing his part sure, but also compose services for his chapel, of four, five, and six parts, though as good a professor as he was, he was a great destroyer of music in this land; surely not intentionally, but accidentally, when he suppressed so many choirs at the Dissolution.

The Worthies of England.

P. 54, ll. 12, 13. *Fuller is quite capable of having made the obvious insinuation that the dexterity of the Scotch nobility arose from the abundance of their practice.*

P. 55, ll. 1-3. *Observe the confusion and repetition of "as" in different senses. Half a century later no writer of anything like Fuller's scholarship and talent would have failed to avoid such obscurity of sense and inelegance of sound.*

P. 56, l. 3. Ditty. *In the proper sense of "words."*

EDWARD HYDE, EARL OF CLARENDON.

Edward Hyde, Earl of Clarendon, was born at Dinton, Wiltshire, in 1608, and died at Rouen in 1674, but was buried in Westminster Abbey. His political career, and the singular fortune which made him the grandfather of two reigning queens of England, concern us not here. But his History of the Rebellion *is one of the epoch-making books of English prose.*

THE CHARACTER OF LAUD.

HE was a man of great parts, and very exemplar virtues, allayed and discredited by some unpopular natural infirmities; the greatest of which was, besides a hasty, sharp way of expressing himself, that he believed innocence of heart, and integrity of manners, was a guard strong enough to secure any man in his voyage through this world, in what company soever he travelled, and through what ways soever he was to pass: and sure never any man was better supplied with that provision. He was born of honest parents, who were well able to provide for his education in the schools of learning, from whence they sent him to Saint John's College in Oxford, the worst endowed at that time of any in that famous university. From a scholar he became a fellow, and then the president of that college, after he had received all the graces and degrees, the proctorship and the doctorship, could be obtained there. He was always maligned and persecuted by those who were of the Calvinian faction, which was then very powerful, and who, according to their useful maxim and practice, call every man they do not love, papist; and under this senseless appellation they created him many troubles and vexations ; and so far suppressed him, that though he was the king's chaplain, and taken notice of for an excellent preacher, and a scholar of the most sublime parts, he had not any preferment to invite him to leave his poor college, which only gave him bread, till the vigour of his age was past : and when he was promoted by king James, it was but to a poor bishopric in Wales, which was not so good a support for a bishop, as his college was for a private scholar, though a doctor.

Parliaments in that time were frequent, and grew very busy ; and the party under which he had suffered a continual persecution, appeared very powerful, and full of design, and they who had the courage to oppose them, began to be taken notice of with approbation and countenance : and under this style he came to be first cherished by the duke of Buckingham, after he had made some experiments of the temper and spirit of the other people, nothing to his satisfaction. From this time he prospered at the rate of his own wishes, and being transplanted out of his cold barren diocese of Saint David's, into a warmer climate, he was left, as was said before, by that omnipotent favourite in that great trust with the king, who was sufficiently indisposed towards the persons or the principles of Mr. Calvin's disciples.

When he came into great authority, it may be, he retained too keen a memory of those who had so unjustly and uncharitably persecuted him before; and, I doubt, was so far transported with the same passions he had reason to complain of in his adversaries, that, as they accused him of popery, because he had some doctrinal opinions which they liked not, though they were nothing allied to popery; so he entertained too much prejudice to some persons, as if they were enemies to the discipline of the church, because they concurred with Calvin in some doctrinal points ; when they abhorred his discipline, and reverenced the government of the church, and prayed for the peace of it with as much zeal and fervency as any in the kingdom; as they made manifest in their lives, and in their sufferings with it and for it. He had, from his first entrance into the world, without any disguise or dissimulation, declared his own opinion of that classis of men ; and, as soon as it was in his power, he did all he could to hinder the growth and increase of that faction, and to restrain those who were inclined to it, from doing the mischief they desired to do. But his power at court could not enough qualify him to go through with that difficult reformation, whilst he had a superior in the church, who, having the reins in his hand, could slacken them according to his own humour and indiscretion; and was thought to be the more remiss, to irritate his choleric disposition. But when he had now the primacy in his own hand, the king being inspired with the same zeal, he thought he should be to blame, and have much to answer, if he did not make haste to apply remedies to those diseases, which he saw would grow apace.

The History of the Rebellion, Book I.

THE BATTLE OF LANSDOWN.

SIR WILLIAM WALLER had the advantage in his ground, having a good city, well furnished with provisions, to quarter his army together in; and so in his choice not to fight but upon extraordinary advantage. Whereas the king's forces must either disperse themselves, and so give the enemy advantage upon their quarters, or, keeping near together, lodge in the field, and endure great distress of provision; the county being so disaffected that only force could bring in any supply or relief. Hereupon, after several attempts to engage the enemy to a battle upon equal terms, which, having the advantage, he wisely avoided, the marquis and prince Maurice advanced with their whole body to Marsfield, five miles beyond Bath towards Oxford; presuming, that by this means they should draw the enemy from the place of advantage, their chief business being to hinder them from joining with the king. And if they had been able to preserve that temper, and neglected the enemy till they had quitted their advantages, it is probable they might have fought upon as good terms as they desired. But the unreasonable contempt they had of the enemy, and confidence they should prevail in any ground, with the straits they endured for want of provisions, and their waste of ammunition, which was spent as much in the daily hedge-skirmishes, and upon their guards, being so near, as could have been in battle, would not admit that patience; for Sir William Waller, who was not to suffer that body to join with the king, no sooner drew out his whole army to Lansdown, which looked towards Marsfield, but they suffered themselves to be engaged upon great disadvantage.

It was upon the fifth of July when Sir William Waller, as soon as it was light, possessed himself of that hill; and after he had, upon the brow of the hill over the high way, raised breast-works with fagots and earth, and planted cannon there, he sent a strong party of horse towards Marshfield, which quickly alarumed the other army, and was shortly driven back to their body. As great a mind as the king's forces had to cope with the enemy, when they had drawn into battalia, and found the enemy fixed on the top of the hill, they resolved not to attack them upon so great disadvantage; and so retired again towards their old quarters: which Sir William Waller perceiving, sent his whole body of horse and dragoons down the hill, to charge the rear and flank of the king's forces; which they did throughly, the regiment of cuirassiers so amazing the horse they charged, that they totally routed them; and standing firm and unshaken themselves, gave so great terror to the king's horse, who had never before turned from an enemy, that no example of their officers, who did their parts with invincible courage, could make them charge with the same confidence and in the same manner they had usually done. However, in the end, after Sir Nicholas Slanning, with three hundred musketeers, had fallen upon and beaten their reserve of dragooners, prince Maurice and the earl of Carnarvon, rallying their horse, and winging them with the Cornish musketeers, charged the enemy's horse again, and totally routed them; and in the same manner received two bodies more, and routed and chased them to the hill; where they stood in a place almost inaccessible. On the brow of the hill there were breast-works, on which were pretty bodies of small shot, and some cannon; on either flank grew a pretty thick wood towards the declining of the hill, in which strong parties of musketeers were placed; at the rear was a very fair plain, where the reserves of horse and foot stood ranged; yet the Cornish foot were so far from being appalled at this disadvantage, that they desired to fall on, and cried out, "that they might have leave to fetch off those cannon." In the end, order was given to attempt the hill with horse and foot. Two strong parties of musketeers were sent into the woods, which flanked the enemy. And the horse and musketeers up the road way, which were charged by the enemy's horse and routed; then Sir Bevil Greenvil advanced, with a party of horse on his right hand, that ground being best for them, and his musketeers on the left, himself leading up his pikes in the middle; and in the face of their cannon, and small shot from their breast-works, gained the brow of the hill, having sustained two full charges of the enemy's horse; but in their third charge, his horse failing, and giving ground, he received, after other wounds, a blow on the head with a poleaxe, with which he fell, and many of his officers about him; yet the musketeers fired so fast upon the horse, that they quit their ground, and the two wings, who were sent to clear the woods, having done their work, and gained those parts of the hill, at the same time they beat off their foot, and became possessed of their breast-works; and so made way for their whole body of horse, foot, and cannon to ascend the hill; which they quickly did, and planted themselves on the ground which they had won; the enemy retiring about demi-culverin shot behind a stone wall upon the same level, and standing in reasonable good order.

Either party was sufficiently tired and battered to be contented to stand still. The king's horse were so shaken, that of two thousand which were upon the field in the morning, there were not above six hundred on the top of the hill. The enemy was exceedingly scattered too, and had no mind to venture on plain ground with those who had beaten them from the hill; so that, exchanging only some shot from their ordnance, they looked one at another till the night interposed. About twelve of the clock, it being very dark, the enemy made a show of moving towards the ground they had lost; but giving a smart volley of small shot, and finding themselves answered with the like, they made no more noise: which the prince observing, he sent a common soldier to hearken as near the place where they were as he could; who brought word, that the enemy had left lighted matches in the wall behind which they had lain, and were drawn off the field; which was true; so that as soon as it was day the king's army found themselves possessed entirely of the field, and the dead, and all other ensigns of victory; Sir William Waller being marched to Bath, in so much disorder and apprehension, that he left a great store of arms and ten barrels of powder behind him; which was a very seasonable supply to the other side, who had spent in that day's service no less than fourscore barrels, and had not a safe proportion left.

In this battle, on the king's part, there were more officers and gentlemen of quality slain than common men, and more hurt than slain. That which would have clouded any victory, and made the loss of others the less spoken of, was the death of Sir Bevil Greenvil; who was indeed an excellent person, whose activity, interest, and reputation was the foundation of what had been done in Cornwall; and his temper and affections so public, that no accidents which happened could make any impression in him; and his example kept others from taking any thing ill, or at least seeming to do so. In a word a brighter courage and a gentler disposition were never married together to make the most cheerful and innocent conversation.

The History of the Rebellion, Book VII.

P. 57, l. 2. Allayed *and* alloyed *are constantly used as identical words in seventeenth century English.*

P. 57, l. 5. Manners *in the sense of* mores — "*morals.*"

P. 57, ll. 14, 15. Proctorship and doctorship *would seem meant, not literally, but* — "*experience in business and teaching.*"

P. 59, l. 5. Superior. *Abbot, who favoured the Puritans and shot a keeper.*

P. 60, l. 14. Battalia, *not the plural of battalion, but* "*battle array*" *generally.*

JOHN MILTON.

John Milton was born in London in 1608, and died there in 1674. His prose, less valuable absolutely, is not less relatively important than his verse. With his contemporary Clarendon he shows more strongly than any other writer the general organic defects of the prose of his day, and its excellence in particular passages.

THE SEARCH FOR DEAD TRUTH.

TRUTH indeed came once into the world with her divine Master, and was a perfect shape most glorious to look on: but when he ascended, and his Apostles after him were laid asleep, then straight arose a wicked race of deceivers, who as that story goes of the Egyptian Typhon with his conspirators, how they dealt with the good Osiris, took the virgin Truth, hewed her lovely form into a thousand pieces, and scattered them to the four winds. From that time ever since, the sad friends of Truth, such as durst appear, imitating the careful search that Isis made for the mangled body of Osiris, went up and down gathering up limb by limb still as they could find them. We have not yet found them all, Lords and Commons, nor ever shall do, till her Master's second coming; he shall bring together every joint and member, and shall mould them into an immortal feature of loveliness and perfection. Suffer not these licensing prohibitions to stand at every place of opportunity forbidding and disturbing them that continue seeking, that continue to do our obsequies to the torn body of our martyred Saint. We boast our light; but if we look not wisely on the sun itself, it smites us into darkness. Who can discern those planets that are oft combust, and those stars of brightest magnitude that rise and set with the sun, until the opposite motion of their orbs bring them to such a place in the firmament, where they may be seen evening or morning. The light which we have gained, was given us not to be ever staring on, but by it to discover onward things more remote from our knowledge. It is not the unfrocking of a priest, the unmitring of a bishop, and the removing him from off the Presbyterian shoulders that will make us a happy nation, no, if other things as great in the Church, and in the rule of life both economical and political be not looked into and reformed, we have looked so long upon the blaze that Zuinglius and Calvin hath beaconed up to us, that we are stark blind. There be who perpetually complain of schisms and sects, and make it such a calamity that any man dissents from their maxims. 'Tis their own pride and ignorance which causes the disturbing, who neither will hear with meekness, nor can convince, yet all must be suppressed which is not found in their Syntagma. They are the troublers, they are the dividers of unity, who neglect and permit not others to unite those dissevered pieces which are yet wanting to the body of Truth. To be still searching what we know not, by what we know, still closing up truth to truth as we find it, for all her body is homogeneal and proportional, this is the golden rule in Theology as well as in Arithmetic, and makes up the best harmony in a Church; not the forced and outward union of cold, and neutral, and inwardly divided minds.

Lords and Commons of England, consider what Nation it is whereof ye are, and whereof ye are the governors: a Nation not slow and dull, but of a quick, ingenious, and piercing spirit, acute to invent, subtle and sinewy to discourse, not beneath the reach of any point the highest that human capacity can soar to. Therefore the studies of learning in her deepest sciences have been so ancient, and so eminent among us, that writers of good antiquity, and ablest judgment have been persuaded that even the school of Pythagoras, and the Persian wisdom took beginning from the old philosophy of this island. And that wise and civil Roman, Julius Agricola, who governed once here for Cæsar, preferred the natural wits of Britain, before the laboured studies of the French. Nor is it for nothing that the grave and frugal Transylvanian sends out yearly from as far as the mountainous borders of Russia, and beyond the Hercynian wilderness, not their youth, but their staid men, to learn our language, and our theologic arts. Yet that which is above all this, the favour and the love of heaven we have great argument to think in a peculiar manner propitious and propending towards us. Why else was this Nation chosen before any other, that out of her as out of Sion should be proclaimed and sounded forth the first tidings and trumpet of Reformation to all Europe. And had it not been the obstinate perverseness of our prelates against the divine and admirable spirit of Wiclif, to suppress him as a schismatic and innovator, perhaps neither the Bohemian Huss and Jerome, no nor the name of Luther, or of Calvin had been ever known: the glory of reforming all our neighbours had been completely ours. But now, as our obdurate clergy have with violence demeaned the matter, we are become hitherto the latest and the backwardest scholars, of whom God offered to have made us the teachers. Now once again by all concurrence of signs, and by the general instinct of holy and devout men, as they daily and solemnly express their thoughts, God is decreeing to begin some new and great period in his church, even to the reforming of Reformation itself: what does he then but reveal himself to his servants, and as his manner is, first to his Englishmen; I say as his manner is, first to us, though we mark not the method of his counsels, and are unworthy. Behold now this vast city; a city of refuge, the mansion house of liberty, encompassed and surrounded with his protection; the shop of war hath not there more anvils and hammers working, to fashion out the plates and instruments of armed Justice in defence of beleaguered Truth, than there be pens and heads there, sitting by their studious lamps, musing, searching, revolving new notions and ideas wherewith to present, as with their homage and their fealty the approaching Reformation: others as fast reading, trying all things, assenting to the force of reason and convincement. What could a man require more from a Nation so pliant and so prone to seek after knowledge? What wants there to such a towardly and pregnant soil, but wise and faithful labourers, to make a knowing people, a nation of prophets, of sages, and of worthies? We reckon more than five months yet to harvest; there need not be five weeks, had we but eyes to lift up, the fields are white already. Where there is much desire to learn, there of necessity will be much arguing, much writing, many opinions; for opinion in good men is but knowledge in the making. Under these fantastic terrors of sect and schism, we wrong the earnest and zealous thirst after knowledge and understanding which God hath stirred up in this city. What some lament of, we rather should rejoice at, should rather praise this pious forwardness among men, to reassume the ill deputed care of their religion into their own hands again. A little generous prudence, a little forbearance of one another, and some grain of charity might win all these diligencies to join and unite into one general and brotherly search after Truth; could we but forego this prelatical tradition of crowding free consciences and Christian liberties into canons and precepts of men. I doubt not, if some great and worthy stranger should come among us, wise to discern the mould and temper of a people, and how to govern it, observing the high hopes and aims, the diligent alacrity of our extended thoughts and reasonings in the pursuance of truth and freedom, but that he would cry out as Pyrrhus did, admiring the Roman docility and courage: If such were my Epirots, I would not despair the greatest design that could be attempted to make a church or kingdom happy.

Areopagitica.

THE TRAINING OF SCHOOLBOYS.

ABOUT an hour and a half ere they eat at noon should be allowed them for exercise, and due rest afterwards : but the time for this may be enlarged at pleasure, according as their rising in the morning shall be early. The exercise which I commend first is the exact use of their weapon; to guard and to strike safely with edge, or point; this will keep them healthy, nimble, strong and well in breath, is also the likeliest means to make them grow large, and tall, and to inspire them with a gallant and fearless courage, which being tempered with seasonable lectures and precepts to make them of true fortitude, and patience, will turn into a native and heroic valour, and make them hate the cowardice of doing wrong. They must be also practised in all the locks and gripes of wrestling, wherein Englishmen were wont to excel, as need may often be in fight to tug, to grapple and to close. And this perhaps will be enough, wherein to prove and heat their single strength. The interim of unsweating themselves regularly, and convenient rest before meat may both with profit and delight be taken up in recreating and composing their travailed spirits with the solemn and divine harmonies of music heard, or learnt; either while the skilful organist plies his grave and fancied descant, in lofty fugues, or the whole symphony with artful and unimaginable touches adorn and grace the well studied chords of some choice composer; some times the lute, or soft organ stop waiting on elegant voices either to religious, martial, or civil ditties; which if wise men and prophets be not extremely out, have a great power over dispositions and manners, to smooth and make them gentle from rustic harshness and distempered passions. The like also would not be unexpedient after meat to assist and cherish nature in her first concoction, and send their minds back to study in good tune and satisfaction. Where having followed it close under vigilant eyes till about two hours before supper, they are by a sudden alarum or watch word, to be called out to their military motions, under sky or covert, according to the season, as was the Roman wont; first on foot, then as their age permits, on horse back, to all the art of cavalry; That having in sport, but with much exactness, and daily muster, served out the rudiments of their soldiership in all the skill of embattailing, marching, encamping, fortifying, beseiging and battering, with all the helps of ancient and modern stratagems, tactics and warlike maxims, they may as it were out of a long war come forth renowned and perfect commanders in the service of their country. They would not then, if they were trusted with fair and hopeful armies, suffer them for want of just and wise discipline to shed away from about them like sick feathers, though they be never so oft supplied; they would not suffer their empty and unrecruitible colonels of twenty men in a company to quaff out, or convey into secret hoards, the wages of a delusive list, and a miserable remnant: yet in the mean while to be overmastered with a score or two of drunkards, the only soldiery left about them, or else to comply with all rapines and violences. No certainly, if they knew aught of that knowledge that belongs to good men or good governors, they would not suffer these things.

Of Education : To Master Samuel Hartlib.

P. 65, l. 8. Propending — *inclining*. *Of the once numerous group of words to which this belongs, only "propensity" survives in common use.*

P. 65, l. 18. Demeaned the matter. *Milton has ample warrant for this rare use in the O. F. employment of* demener. *In modern French, as in modern English, the verb is reflexive only.*

P. 65, l. 19. Of whom. *We could not now dispense with the double genitive, "of those, of whom," and it may be doubted whether the compression was ever good English, though it was common.*

P. 67, ll. 35, 36. They would not then. *The drop in style ("unrecruitible," for instance, is little better than a* vox nihili) *as well as in tone here is very noteworthy, and very characteristic of Milton. He passes in both from the poet to the pamphleteer.*

JEREMY TAYLOR.

Jeremy Taylor, Bishop of Down and Connor, was born at Cambridge in 1613, and died at Lisburn in 1667. The greatest of all sacred orators in English, and perhaps the greatest ancient master of the florid and ornate style of English prose, he was a voluminous writer, but he is nowhere read to such literary advantage as in his sermons.

THE FRUITS OF SIN.

THE fruits of its present possession, the pleasures of its taste, are no less pleasant, because no sober person, no man that can discourse, does like it long.

——— Breve sit quod turpiter audes. Juv. 8. 165.

But he approves it in the height of passion, and in the disguises of a temptation; but at all other times he finds it ugly and unreasonable; and the very remembrance of it must at all times abate its pleasures, and sour its delicacies. In the most parts of a man's life he wonders at his own folly, and prodigious madness, that it should ever be possible for him to be deluded by such trifles; and he sighs next morning, and knows it over night; and is it not therefore certain that he leans upon a thorn which he knows will smart, and he dreads the event of to-morrow? But so have I known a bold trooper fight in the confusion of a battle, and being warm with heat and rage, received, from the swords of his enemy, wounds open like a grave; but he felt them not, and when, by the streams of blood, he found himself marked for pain, he refused to consider then what he was to feel to-morrow; but when his rage had cooled into the temper of a man, and clammy moisture had checked the fiery emission of spirits, he wonders at his own boldness, and blames his fate, and needs a mighty patience to bear his great calamity. So is the bold and merry sinner, when he is warm with wine and lust, wounded and bleeding with the strokes of hell, he twists with the fatal arm that strikes him and cares not; but yet it must abate his gaiety, because he remembers that when his wounds are cold and considered, he must roar or perish, repent, or do worse, that is be miserable or undone.

Apples of Sodom.

THE WEAKNESS OF MAN.

WE are as water, weak, and of no consistence, always descending, abiding in no certain place, unless we are detained with violence; and every little breath of wind makes us rough and tempestuous, and troubles our faces; every trifling accident discomposes us; and as the face of the waters wafting in a storm so wrinkles itself that it makes upon its forehead furrows deep and hollow like a grave; so do our great and little cares and trifles first make the wrinkles of old age and then they dig a grave for us: and there is in nature nothing so contemptible, but it may meet with us in such circumstances, that it may be too hard for us in our weaknesses; and the sting of a bee is a weapon sharp enough to pierce the finger of a child or the lip of a man; and those creatures which nature hath left without weapons, yet they are armed sufficiently to vex those parts of man which are left defenceless and obnoxious to a sunbeam, to the roughness of a sour grape, to the unevenness of a gravel stone, to the dust of a wheel, or the unwholesome breath of a star looking awry upon a sinner.

But besides the weaknesses and natural decayings of our bodies, if chances and contingencies be innumerable, then no man can reckon our dangers, and the preternatural causes of our deaths: so that he is a vain person, whose hopes of life are too confidently increased by reason of his health: and he is too

unreasonably timorous, who thinks his hopes at an end when
he dwells in sickness. For men die without rule, and with and
without occasions, and no man suspecting or foreseeing any of
death's addresses; and no man in his whole condition is weaker
than another. A man in a long consumption is fallen under
one of the solemnities and preparations to death; but at the
same instant the most healthful person is as near death, upon a
more fatal and a more sudden but a less discerned cause. There
are but few persons upon whose foreheads every man can read
the sentence of death, written in the lines of a lingering sickness,
but they sometimes hear the passing bell ring for stronger men,
even long before their own knell calls at the house of their
mother to open her womb and make a bed for them. No man
is surer of to-morrow than the weakest of his brethren: and
when Lepidus and Aufidius stumbled at the threshold of the
senate, and fell down and died, the blow came from heaven in a
cloud; but it struck more suddenly than upon the poor slave
that made sport upon the theatre with a premeditated and fore-
described death: "Quod quisque vitet, nunquam homini satis
Cautum est in horas." There are sicknesses that walk in darkness; and there are exterminating angels, that fly wrapt up in
the curtains of immateriality and an uncommunicating nature;
whom we cannot see, but we feel their force, and sink under
their sword; and from heaven the veil descends that wraps our
heads in the fatal sentence. There is no age of man but it hath
proper to itself some posterns and outlets for death, besides
those infinite and open ports out of which myriads of men and
women every day pass into the dark, and the land of forgetfulness. Infancy hath life but in effigy, or like a spark dwelling
in a pile of wood: the candle is so newly lighted, that every
little shaking of the taper, and every ruder breath of air puts it
out, and it dies. Childhood is so tender, and yet so unwary;
so soft to all the impressions of chance, and yet so forward to
run into them, that God knew there could be no security without
the care and vigilance of an angel keeper: and the eyes of
parents and the arms of nurses, the provisions of art, and all
the effects of human love and providence are not sufficient to
keep one child from horrid mischiefs, from strange and early

calamities and deaths, unless a messenger be sent from heaven to stand sentinel, and watch the very playings and sleepings, the eatings and drinkings of the children; and it is a long time before nature maketh them capable of help: for there are many deaths, and very many diseases to which poor babes are exposed; but they have but very few capacities of physic; to shew that infancy is as liable to death as old age, and equally exposed to danger, and equally incapable of a remedy; with this only difference, that old age hath diseases incurable by nature, and the diseases of childhood are incurable by art; and both the states are the next heirs of death.

Funeral Sermon on the Countess of Carbery.

P. 69, l. 3. Discourse. *That is to say, "reason."*
P. 69, l. 5. One suspects *"he but approves it."*
P. 69, l. 15. Received. *A noteworthy instance of the disorderly syntax of the day. "Receive" or "he received" are of course required. Similarly in the end of the sentence the tenses are in complete confusion.*
P. 71, l. 6. Solemnities, *in the strict sense of "usual formalities," "customary accompaniments."*
P. 71, l. 11. They, *referring to the "few persons."*

HENRY MORE.

Henry More, one of the chiefs of the group called the Cambridge Platonists, was born in 1614 at Grantham, and died in 1687. Almost the whole of his life was passed at Christ's College, Cambridge, of which he was fellow. His elaborate philosophical poetry is little more than a curiosity, but in prose he is a writer of importance both in matter and manner, being, as far as style goes, the superior of Cudworth.

THE WORKS OF THE DEVIL.

WE might abound in instances of this kind, I mean supernatural effects unattended with miraculous apparitions, if I would bring in all that I have myself been informed of by either eye-witnesses themselves, or by such as have had the narrations immediately from them. As for example, bricks being carried round about a room without any visible hand; multitudes of stones flung down at a certain time of the day from the roof of an house for many months together, to the amazement of the whole country; pots carried off from the fire, and set on again, no body meddling with them; the violent flapping of a chest-cover, no hand touching it; the carrying up linens that have been a-bleaching, so high into the air, that tablecloths and sheets looked but like napkins, and this when there was no wind, but all calm and clear; glass windows struck with that violence as if all had been broken to shivers, the glass jingling all over the floor, and this for some quarter of an hour together, when yet all has been found whole in the morning; boxes carefully locked, unlocking themselves, and flinging the flax out of them; bread tumbling off from a form of its own

accord; women's pattens rising up from the floor, and whirling against people; the breaking of a comb in two pieces of itself in the window, the pieces also flying in men's faces; the rising up of a knife also from the same place, being carried with its haft forwards; stones likewise flung about the house, but not hurting any man's person; with several things, which would be too voluminous to repeat with their due circumstances; and the less needful, there being already published to our hands such narrations as will store us with examples enough of this kind.
An Antidote against Atheism.

ON DEATH.

I CANNOT but confess that the tragic pomp and preparation to dying, that lays waste the operations of the mind, putting her into fits of dotage or fury, making the very visage look ghastly and distracted, and at the best sadly pale and consumed, as if life and soul were even almost quite extinct, cannot but imprint strange impressions even upon the stoutest mind, and raise suspicions that all is lost in so great a change. But the knowing and benign spirit, though he may flow in tears at so dismal a spectacle, yet it does not at all suppress his hope and confidence of the soul's safe passage into the other world; and is no otherwise moved than the more passionate spectators of some cunningly-contrived tragedy, where persons, whose either virtues or misfortunes, or both, have won the affection of the beholders, are at last seen wallowing in their blood, and after some horrid groans and gasps, lie stretched stark dead upon the stage : but being once drawn off, find themselves well and alive, and are ready to taste a cup of wine with their friends in the attiring room, to solace themselves really, after their fictitious pangs of death, and leave the easy-natured multitude to indulge to their soft passions for an evil that never befel them.

The fear and abhorrency therefore we have of death, and the sorrow that accompanies it, is no argument but that we may live after it, and are but due affections for those that are to be spectators of the great tragic-comedy of the world; the whole plot whereof being contrived by infinite wisdom and goodness, we cannot but surmise, that the most sad representations are but a shew, but the delight real to such as are not wicked and impious; and that what the ignorant call evil in this universe, is but as a shadowy stroke in a fair picture, or the mournful notes in music, by which the beauty of the one is more lively and express, and the melody of the other more pleasing and melting.

An Antidote against Atheism.

P. 74, l. 19. Is *instead of "he is"*; l. 28, indulge to *instead of "indulge"*; ll. 31, 32, is, are. *All these are instances of constructions foreign to the genius of English, and defensible only on classical rules.*

RICHARD BAXTER.

Richard Baxter was born at Rowton in 1615. He was irregularly educated, but took orders, and received the living of Kidderminster. He was chaplain in the Parliament army, but of moderate views, and was prominent at the Savoy Conference. The Act of Uniformity deprived him, and in 1685 he was fined and imprisoned. He died in 1691. His Saint's Rest *has been immensely popular.*

THE PEOPLE OF SOLDANIA.

THIS is the case of the miserable world ; but they have not hearts to pity themselves, nor can we make them willing to be delivered, because we cannot make them know their case. If a man fall into a pit, we need not spend all the day to persuade him that he is there, and to be willing to be helped out of it. But with these fleshly, miserable souls, the time that should be spent by themselves and us for their recovery, must be spent to make them believe that they are lost ; and when all is done we leave them lost, and have lost our labour, because we cannot prevail with them to believe it. Drown they will, and perish everlastingly, because the time that should be spent in saving them, must be spent in making them know that they are sinking, and after all they will not believe it; and therefore will not lay hold on the hand that is stretched forth to pull them out. The narrative of the savage people of Soldania doth notably represent their state. Those people lived naked, and fed upon the carrion-like carcases of beasts, and hang the stinking guts about their necks for ornaments, and wear hats made of the dung, and carve their skins, and will not change these loathsome customs.

Some of them being drawn into our ships, were carried away for England. When they came to London and saw our stately buildings, and clothing, and provisions, they were observed to sigh much, which was thought to have been in compassion of their miserable country, which so much differed from ours. When they had stayed long among us, and got so much acquaintance with our civility and order, and all that belongs to the life of man, as that they were thought fit to communicate it to their countrymen, the next voyage they were brought back, and set on shore in their own country, to draw some of the rest to come into the ships, and see and enjoy what they had done, who had purposely been used as might most content them. But as soon as they were landed, they leaped for joy, and cried, "Soldania," and cast away their clothes, and came again in the sight of our ships, with dung on their heads and guts hanging about their necks, triumphing in their sordid nakedness. Just so do worldly, sensual men, in the matters of salvation. If against their wills they are carried into cleaner ways and company, and the beauty of holiness, and the joys of heaven are opened to them, they are weary of it all the while; and when we expect they should delight themselves in the felicity that is opened to them, and draw their old acquaintance to it, and be utterly ashamed of their former base and sinful state, they are gone when the next temptation comes, and return with the dog unto their vomit, and with the washed swine to wallow in the mire, and glory in their filth and shame, and only mind their earthly things.

A Saint or a Brute.

P. 76, l. 15. Soldania *is apparently Saldanha Bay, and the peculiar necklaces described are eminently Hottentot.*

ABRAHAM COWLEY.

Abraham Cowley was born in London in 1618, and died at Chertsey in 1667. His prose is small in quantity, but wonderfully good and advanced in form. The two following extracts show both its sides, the second that in which it approximates to Milton, and the first that in which it anticipates Dryden and Temple.

THE GARDEN.

I NEVER had any other desire so strong and so like to covetousness, as that one which I have had always, that I might be master at last of a small house and large garden, with very moderate conveniences joined to them, and there dedicate the remainder of my life only to the culture of them, and study of nature;

> And there, with no design beyond my wall, whole and intire to lie,
> In no unactive ease, and no unglorious poverty.

Or, as Virgil has said, shorter and better for me, that I might there

> "Studiis florere ignobilis oti:"

(though I could wish that he had rather said, "nobilis oti," when he spoke of his own). But several accidents of my ill-fortune have disappointed me hitherto, and do still, of that felicity; for though I have made the first and hardest step to it, by abandoning all ambitions and hopes in this world, and by retiring from the noise of all business, and almost company, yet I stick still in the inn of a hired house and garden, among weeds and rubbish; and without that pleasantest work of human industry, the improvement of something which we call (not very properly, but yet we call) our own. I am gone out from Sodom, but I am not yet arrived at my little Zoar. "O let me escape thither (is it not a little one?) and my soul shall live." I do not look back yet; but I have been forced to stop, and make too many halts. You may wonder, Sir (for this seems a little too extravagant and pindarical for prose), what I mean by all this preface: it is to let you know, that though I have missed, like a chemist, my great end, yet I account my affections and endeavours well rewarded by something that I have met with by the bye; which is, that they have procured to me some part in your kindness and esteem; and thereby the honour of having my name so advantageously recommended to posterity, by the epistle you are pleased to prefix to the most useful book that has been written in that kind, and which is to last as long as months and years.

Among many other arts and excellencies which you enjoy, I am glad to find this favourite of mine the most predominant; that you choose this for your wife, though you have hundreds of other arts for your concubines; though you know them, and beget sons upon them all (to which you are rich enough to allow great legacies), yet the issue of this seems to be designed by you to the main of the estate; you have taken most pleasure in it, and bestowed most charges upon its education: and I doubt not to see that book, which you are pleased to promise to the world, and of which you have given us a large earnest in your calendar, as accomplished, as anything can be expected from an extraordinary wit, and no ordinary expenses, and a long experience. I know nobody that possesses more private happiness than you do in your garden; and yet no man, who makes his happiness more public, by a free communication of the art and knowledge of it to others. All that I myself am able yet to do, is only to recommend to mankind the search of that felicity, which you instruct them how to find and to enjoy.

Essay on The Garden to J. Evelyn, Esq.

OLIVER CROMWELL.

WHAT can be more extraordinary, than that a person of mean birth, no fortune, no eminent qualities of body, which have sometimes, or of mind, which have often, raised men to the highest dignities, should have the courage to attempt, and the happiness to succeed in, so improbable a design, as the destruction of one of the most ancient and most solidly-founded monarchies upon the earth? that he should have the power or boldness to put his prince and master to an open and infamous death; to banish that numerous and strongly-allied family; to do all this under the name and wages of a parliament; to trample upon them too as he pleased, and spurn them out of doors when he grew weary of them; to raise up a new and unheard of monster out of their ashes; to stifle that in the very infancy, and set up himself above all things that ever were called sovereign in England; to oppress all his enemies by arms, and all his friends afterwards by artifice; to serve all parties patiently for a while, and to command them victoriously at last; to overrun each corner of the three nations, and overcome with equal facility both the riches of the south and the poverty of the north; to be feared and courted by all foreign princes and adopted a brother to the gods of the earth; to call together parliaments with a word of his pen, and scatter them again with the breath of his mouth; to be humbly and daily petitioned that he would please to be hired, at the rate of two millions a year, to be the master of those who had hired him before to be their servant; to have the estates and lives of three kingdoms as much at his disposal, as was the little inheritance of his father, and to be as noble and liberal in the spending of them; and lastly, for there is no end of all the particulars of his glory, to bequeath all this with one word to his posterity; to die with peace at home, and triumph abroad; to be buried among kings, and with more than regal solemnity; and to leave a name behind him, not to be extinguished, but with the whole world; which, as it is now too little for his praises, so might have been

too for his conquests, if the short line of his human life could have been stretched out to the extent of his immortal designs?
Essay on the Government of Oliver Cromwell.

P. 80, l. 5. Happiness *has, of course, nothing of its modern connotation of approval on the part of the writer. It simply* = "*luck.*"
P. 80, l. 15. Oppress = "*put down.*"

JOHN EVELYN.

John Evelyn was born at Wotton in 1620, was educated at Oxford, entered the Temple, and during the Civil War spent his time mostly abroad. Under the Commonwealth he lived quietly in England, but after the Restoration he took much part in public, and some in political, affairs. He died in 1706. His Silva *is most remarkable for style, his* Diary *for matter.*

THE LIFE OF TREES.

FOR their preservation, nature has invested the whole tribe and nation (as we may say) of vegetables, with garments suitable to their naked and exposed bodies, temper, and climate: Thus some are clad with a coarser, and resist all extremes of weather; others with more tender and delicate skins and scarfs, as it were, and thinner raiment. *Quid foliorum describam diversitates?* What shall we say of the mysterious forms, variety, and variegation of the leaves and flowers, contrived with such art, yet without art; some round, others long, oval, multangular, indented, crisped, rough, smooth, and polished, soft and flexible at every tremulous blast, as if it would drop in a moment, and yet so obstinately adhering, as to be able to contest against the fiercest winds that prostrate mighty structures!—There it abides till God bids it fall: for so the wise Disposer of things has placed it, not only for ornament, but use and protection both of body and fruit; from the excessive heat of summer, and colds of the sharpest winters, and their immediate impressions; as we find it in all such places and trees, as, like the blessed and good man, have always fruit upon them, ripe, or preparing to mature; such as the Pine, Fir, Arbutus, Orange, and most of those which the Indies and more southern tracts plentifully abound in, where Nature provides this continual shelter, and clothes them with perennial garments.

Let us examine with what care the seeds, (in which the whole and complete tree, though invisible to our dull sense, is yet perfectly and entirely wrapped up,) exposed, as they seem to be, to all those accidents of weather, storms, and rapacious birds, are yet preserved from avólation, diminution, and detriment, within their spiny, armed, and compacted receptacles; where they sleep as in their causes, till their prisons let them gently fall into the embraces of the earth, now made pregnant with the season, and ready for another burden: for at the time of year she fails not to bring them forth. With what delight have I beheld this tender and innumerable offspring repullulating at the feet of an aged tree! from whence the suckers are drawn, transplanted and educated by human industry, and, forgetting the ferity of their nature, become civilized to all his employments.

Can we look on the prodigious quantity of liquor, which one poor wounded birch will produce in a few hours, and not be astonished? Is it not wonderful that some trees should, in a short space of time, weep more than they weigh? And that so dry, so feeble, and wretched a branch, as that which bears the grape, should yield a juice that cheers the heart of man? That the Pine, Fir, Larch, and other resinous trees, planted in such rude and uncultivated places, amongst rocks and dry pumices, should transude into turpentine, and pearl out into gums and precious balms?

Silva, or a Discourse of Forest Trees.

P. 82, l. 11. It, *i.e.*, *the individual leaf or flower, though there is no antecedent except in the plural. A good instance of the negligence of the older style.*

P. 83, l. 9. Avolation, *flying, or being blown away.*

P. 83, l. 11. Causes. *According to the Realist idea of things being essentially contained, and, so to speak, wrapped up in their causes.*

P. 83, l. 18. Ferity, *wildness.*

ALGERNON SIDNEY.

Algernon Sidney, born at Penshurst in 1621, was in his time the chief literary exponent of theoretical Republicanism. He fought for the Parliament, was one of the king's judges, though he did not sign the warrant, and was opposed to Cromwell. Exiled at the Restoration, he was pardoned in 1677, but being implicated in the Rye House Plot, was executed on Dec. 7, 1683.

HIS APOLOGY.

WHEN I heard the judgment, to the best of my remembrance I said these words.

Why then, oh Lord! sanctify, I beseech thee, these my sufferings unto me; sanctify me through my sufferings; sanctify me through thy truth; thy word is truth; impute not my blood unto this nation; impute it not unto the great city through which I shall be led to the place of death; let not my soul cry, though it lie under the altar; make no inquisition for it; or, if innocent blood must be expiated, let thy vengeance fall only upon the head of those, who knowingly and maliciously persecute me for righteousness sake.

The Chief Justice then speaking, as if I had been a distempered man, I held out my arm, and desired any that were present to feel my pulse, and whether any man could be more free from emotion; and I do profess, that so far as I do know, and did then feel myself, I was never in a more quiet temper; glory and thanks be unto God for ever, who had filled me with comforts, and so upheld me, that having, as I hope, through Christ, vanquished sin, he doth preserve me from the fears of death.

The Chief Justice, having performed this exploit, is said to have bragged unto the king, that no man in his place had ever rendered unto any king of England such services as he had done, in making it to pass for law, that any man might be now tried by a jury not consisting of freeholders; and that one witness, with any concurrent circumstance (as that of the buying the knife) was sufficient to convict him. In this he seems to have spoken very modestly; for he might truly have said, that he had overruled eight or ten very important points of law, and decided them without hearing; whereby the law itself was made a snare, which no man could avoid, nor have any security for his life or fortune, if one wild wretch could be found to swear against him, such circumstances as he required: nevertheless we all know, that the like had been done in former times: in the days of Richard II. the nation was brought into such a condition, through the perversion of the law, that no man knew what to say or do, for fear of treason, as is expressed in the stat. 1 Hen. IV. and were thereby driven upon the most violent remedies: God only knows what will be the issue of the like practice in these our days: perhaps he will in mercy speedily visit his afflicted people. I die in the faith that he will do it, though I know not the time or ways; and am so much the more confident he will do it, that his cause, and his people, is more concerned now than it was in former time: the lust of one man and his favourites was then only to be set up in the exercise of an arbitrary power over persons and states; but now the tyranny over consciences is principally affected, and the civil powers are stretched unto this exorbitant height, for the establishment of popery. I believe that the people of God in England have, in these late years, generally grown faint; some, through fear, have deflected from the integrity of their principles; some have been too deeply plunged themselves in worldly cares, and, so as they might enjoy their trades and wealth, have less regarded the treasure that is laid up in heaven: but I think there are very many who have kept their garments unspotted; and hope that God will deliver them, and the nation for their sakes. God will not suffer this land, where the gospel hath of late flourished more than any part of the world, to become a slave of the world; he will not suffer it to be made a land of graven images: he will stir up witnesses of the truth, and, in his own time, spirit his people to stand up for his cause, and deliver them. I lived in this belief, and am now about to die in it: I know my Redeemer lives; and, as he hath in a great measure upheld me in the day of my calamity, hope that he will still uphold me by his spirit in this last moment, and, giving me grace to glorify him in my death, receive me into the glory prepared for those that fear him, when my body shall be dissolved. Amen.

Discourses concerning Government.

P. 84, l. 12. The Chief Justice. *Jeffries.*
P. 85, l. 6. The buying the knife. *This refers to a dictum of Jeffries, that "if one man swore that he would with his knife kill the king, and another that he had of him bought that knife, it was sufficient evidence." The parallel was to Sidney's written justification of rebellion, and Howard's testimony that rebellion was intended.*

JOHN BUNYAN.

John Bunyan was born at Elstow in 1628. He served in the (probably Royalist) army, but at a comparatively early time of life was convinced of sin, and became a Baptist preacher. After the Restoration he was convicted of holding conventicles, and spent twelve years in Bedford Gaol. He died at London in 1688. The Pilgrim's Progress, the masterpiece of all vernacular literature, appeared in 1678.

THE HISTORY OF MR. FEARING.

GREAT-HEART. Why, he was always afraid that he should come short of whither he had a desire to go. Every thing frightened him that he heard any body speak of, that had but the least appearance of opposition in it. I hear that he lay roaring at the Slough of Despond for about a month together; nor durst he, for all he saw several go over before him, venture, though they, many of them, offered to lend him their hand. He would not go back again neither. The Celestial City, he said, he should die if he came not to it; and yet was dejected at every difficulty, and stumbled at every straw that any body cast in his way. Well, after he had lain at the Slough of Despond a great while, as I have told you, one sunshine morning, I do not know how, he ventured, and so got over; but when he was over, he would scarce believe it. He had, I think, a Slough of Despond in his mind; a slough that he carried everywhere with him, or else he could never have been as he was. So he came up to the gate, you know what I mean, that stands at the head of this way; and there also he stood a good while, before he would adventure to knock. When the gate was opened, he would give back, and give place to others, and say that he was not worthy. For, for all he got before some to the gate, yet many of them went in before him. There the poor man would stand, shaking and shrinking. I dare say, it would have pitied one's heart to have seen him; nor would he go back again. At last, he took the hammer that hanged on the gate in his hand, and gave a small rap or two; then one opened to him, but he shrank back as before. He that opened stepped out after him, and said, Thou trembling one, what wantest thou? With that he fell down to the ground. He that spoke to him wondered to see him so faint. So he said to him, Peace be to thee; up, for I have set open the door to thee. Come in, for thou art blessed. With that he got up, and went in trembling; and when he was in, he was ashamed to show his face. Well, after he had been entertained there a while, as you know how the manner is, he was bid go on his way, and also told the way he should take. So he came till he came to our house. But as he behaved himself at the gate, so he did at my master the Interpreter's door. He lay thereabout in the cold a good while, before he would adventure to call; yet he would not go back, and the nights were long and cold then. Nay, he had a note of necessity in his bosom to my master, to receive him and grant him the comfort of his house, and also to allow him a stout and valiant conductor, because he was himself so chicken-hearted a man; and yet, for all that, he was afraid to call at the door. So he lay up and down thereabouts, till, poor man! he was almost starved. Yea, so great was his dejection, that though he saw several others, for knocking, get in, yet he was afraid to venture. At last, I think, I looked out of the window, and perceiving a man to be up and down about the door, I went out to him, and asked what he was; but, poor man! the water stood in his eyes; so I perceived what he wanted. I went, therefore, in and told it in the house, and we showed the thing to our Lord. So he sent me out again, to entreat him to come in; but, I dare say, I had hard work to do it. At last he came in; and I will say that for my Lord, he carried it wonderfully lovingly to him. There were but a few good bits at the table, but some of it was laid upon his trencher. Then he presented the note, and my Lord looked thereon, and said his desire should be granted. So, when he had been there a good while, he seemed to get some heart, and to be a little more comfortable; for my master, you must know, is one of very tender bowels, especially to them that are afraid; wherefore he carried it so towards him, as might tend most to his encouragement. Well, when he had had a sight of the things of the place, and was ready to take his journey to go to the city, my Lord, as he did to Christian before, gave him a bottle of spirits, and some comfortable things to eat. Thus we set forward, and I went before him; but the man was but of few words, only he would sigh aloud.

When we were come to where the three fellows were hanged, he said that he doubted that that would be his end also. Only he seemed glad when he saw the Cross and the Sepulchre. There, I confess, he desired to stay a little to look, and he seemed, for a while after, to be a little cheery. When we came at the Hill Difficulty, he made no stick at that, nor did he much fear the lions; for you must know that his trouble was not about such things as those; his fear was about his acceptance at last.

I got him in at the House Beautiful, I think, before he was willing. Also when he was in, I brought him acquainted with the damsels that were of the place; but he was ashamed to make himself much for company. He desired much to be alone, yet he always loved good talk, and often would get behind the screen to hear it. He also loved much to see ancient things, and to be pondering them in his mind. He told me afterwards that he loved to be in those two houses from which he came last, to wit, at the gate, and that of the Interpreter, but that he durst not be so bold to ask.

When we went also from the House Beautiful, down the hill, into the Valley of Humiliation, he went down as well as ever I saw man in my life; for he cared not how mean he was, so he might be happy at last. Yea, I think, there was a kind of a sympathy betwixt that valley and him; for I never saw him better in all his pilgrimage than when he was in that valley.

Here he would lie down, embrace the ground, and kiss the very flowers that grew in this valley. He would now be up every morning by break of day, tracing and walking to and fro in this valley.

But when he was come to the entrance of the Valley of the Shadow of Death, I thought I should have lost my man; not for that he had any inclination to go back; that he always abhorred; but he was ready to die for fear. Oh! the hobgoblins will have me! the hobgoblins will have me! cried he; and I could not beat him out on it. He made such a noise, and such an outcry here, that, had they but heard him, it was enough to encourage them to come and fall upon us.

But this I took very great notice of, that this valley was as quiet while he went through it, as ever I knew it before or since. I suppose these enemies here had now a special check from our Lord, and a command not to meddle until Mr. Fearing was passed over it.

It would be too tedious to tell you of all. We will, therefore, only mention a passage or two more. When he was come at Vanity Fair, I thought he would have fought with all the men at the fair. I feared there we should both have been knocked on the head, so hot was he against their fooleries. Upon the Enchanted Ground, he was also very wakeful. But when he was come at the river, where was no bridge, there again he was in a heavy case. Now, now, he said, he should be drowned for ever, and so never see that face with comfort that he had come so many miles to behold.

And here, also, I took notice of what was very remarkable; the water of that river was lower at this time than ever I saw it in all my life. So he went over at last, not much above wet-shod. When he was going up to the gate, Mr. Great-heart began to take his leave of him, and to wish him a good reception above. So he said, I shall, I shall. Then parted we asunder, and I saw him no more.

The Pilgrim's Progress.

MANSOUL HELD BY THE DOUBTERS.

Now a man might have walked for days together in Mansoul, and scarce have seen one in the town that looked like a religious man. O the fearful state of Mansoul now! Now every corner swarmed with outlandish Doubters; red-coats and black-coats walked the town by clusters, and filled up all the houses with hideous noises, vain songs, lying stories, and blasphemous language against Shaddai and his Son. Now, also, those Diabolonians that lurked in the walls and dens and holes that were in the town of Mansoul, came forth and showed themselves, yea, walked with open face in company with the Doubters that were in Mansoul. Yea, they had more boldness now to walk the streets, to haunt the houses, and to show themselves abroad, than had any of the honest inhabitants of the now woful town of Mansoul.

But Diabolus and his outlandish men were not at peace in Mansoul, for they were not there entertained as were the captains and forces of Emmanuel; the townsmen did browbeat them what they could; nor did they partake or make stroy of any of the necessaries of Mansoul, but that which they seized on against the townsmen's will; what they could they hid from them, and what they could not they had with an ill-will. They, poor hearts, had rather have had their room than their company, but they were at present their captives, and their captives for the present they were forced to be. But, I say, they discountenanced them as much as they were able, and showed them all the dislike that they could.

The captains also from the castle did hold them in continual play with their slings, to the chasing and fretting of the minds of the enemies. True, Diabolus made a great many attempts to have broken open the gates of the castle, but Mr. Godly-fear was made the keeper of that; and he was a man of that courage, conduct and valour, that it was in vain, as long as life lasted within him, to think to do that work though mostly desired, wherefore all the attempts that Diabolus made against him were fruitless. I have wished sometimes that that man had had the whole rule of the town of Mansoul.

Well, this was the condition of the town of Mansoul for about two years and an half; the body of the town was the seat of war; the people of the town were driven into holes, and the glory of Mansoul was laid in the dust; what rest then could be to the inhabitants, what peace could Mansoul have, and what sun could shine upon it? had the enemy lain so long without in the plain against the town, it had been enough to have famished them; but now when they shall be within, when the town shall be their tent, their trench, and fort against the castle that was in the town, when the town shall be against the town, and shall serve to be a defence to the enemies of her strength and life: I say, when they shall make use of the forts, and town-holds, to secure themselves in, even till they shall take, spoil, and demolish the castle, this was terrible; and yet this was now the state of the town of Mansoul.

The Holy War.

THE SCIENCE OF BREAKING.

Wise. I will tell you; it was this, he had an art to break, and get hatfuls of money by breaking.

Atten. But what do you mean by Mr. Badman's breaking? You speak mystically, do you not?

Wise. No, no, I speak plainly. Or, if you will have it in plainer language, it is this;—when Mr. Badman had swaggered and whored away most of his wife's portion, he began to feel that he could not much longer stand upon his legs in this course of life and keep up his trade and repute—such as he had—in the world, but by the new engine of breaking. Wherefore upon a time he gives a great and sudden rush into several men's debts, to the value of about four or five thousand pounds, driving at the same time a very great trade, by selling many things for less than they cost him, to get him custom, therewith to blind his creditor's eyes. His creditors therefore seeing that he had a great employ, and dreaming that it must needs at

length turn to a very good account to them, trusted him freely
without mistrust, and so did others too, to the value of what was
mentioned before. Well, when Mr. Badman had well feathered
his nest with other men's goods and money, after a little time
he breaks, and by and by it was noised abroad that Mr. Badman
had shut up shop, was gone, and could trade no longer. Now
by that time his breaking was come to his creditors' ears, he had
by craft and knavery made so sure of what he had, that his
creditors could not touch a penny. Well, when he had done,
he sends his mournful sugared letters to his creditors, to let
them understand what had happened unto him, and desired
them not to be severe with him, for he bore towards all men an
honest mind, and would pay so far as he was able. Now he
sends his letters by a man confederate with him, who could
make both the worst and best of Mr. Badman's case; the best
for Mr. Badman and the worst for his creditors. So when he
comes to them he both bemoans them and condoles Mr. Badman's condition, telling of them that, without a speedy bringing
of things to a conclusion, Mr. Badman would be able to make
them no satisfaction, but at present he both could and would,
and that to the utmost of his power, and to that end he desired
that they would come over to him. Well, his creditors appoint
him a time and come over, and he, meanwhile, authorizes
another to treat with them, but will not be seen himself, unless
it was on a Sunday, lest they should snap him with a writ. So
his deputed friend treats with them about their concern with
Mr. Badman, first telling them of the great care that Mr. Badman took to satisfy them and all men for whatsoever he owed,
as far as in him lay, and how little he thought a while since to
be in this low condition. He pleaded also the greatness of his
charge, the greatness of taxes, the badness of the times, and the
great losses that he had by many of his customers; some of
which died in his debt, others were run away, and for many that
were alive he never expected a farthing from them. Yet nevertheless he would show himself an honest man, and would pay
as far as he was able; and if they were willing to come to terms,
he would make a composition with them, for he was not able to
pay them all. The creditors asked what he would give? It was

replied, Half-a-crown in the pound. At this they began to huff, and he to renew his complaint and entreaty, but the creditors would not hear, and so for that time their meeting without success broke up. But after his creditors were in cool blood, and admitting of second thoughts, and fearing lest delays should make them lose all, they admit of a second debate, come together again, and, by many words and great ado, they obtained five shillings in the pound. So the money was produced, releases and discharges drawn, signed, and sealed, books crossed, and all things confirmed; and then Mr. Badman can put his head out a-doors again, and be a better man than when he shut up shop, by several thousands of pounds.

The Life and Death of Mr. Badman.

P. 88, l. 28. Starved. *Probably in the sense of "perished with cold," not with hunger. See l. 22.*

P. 90, l. 2. Tracing — *"quartering the ground backwards, forwards, and sideways." So frequently in Malory when he describes fights.*

P. 91, l. 4. Red-coats and black-coats. *It is worth noting, though of course not conclusive, on the question of the side Bunyan took in the Civil War, that red was chiefly a Parliamentary uniform colour.*

P. 91, l. 18. Stroy — *"destroy," though it does not seem to be used elsewhere as a noun. Timid editors changed it early into "destruction."*

P. 91, l. 33. Mostly — *"most."*

P. 94, l. 9. Books crossed, *i.e., accounts crossed off, cancelled.*

SIR WILLIAM TEMPLE.

Sir William Temple was born in London in 1628, and died at Moor Park, Surrey, in 1699. The epithet of "genteel" which has stuck to his style is unfortunate, because the adjective has perpetually sunk in value, till it has become, at least in educated mouths and pens, definitely satirical. In its proper sense of refinement combined with urbanity, and dignity associated with grace, it is applicable enough.

THE ENGLISH CLIMATE.

MY orange-trees are as large as any I saw, when I was young, in France, except those of Fontainebleau, or what I have seen since in the Low Countries, except some very old ones of the prince of Orange's; as laden with flowers as any can well be, as full of fruit as I suffer or desire them, and as well tasted as are commonly brought over, except the best sorts of Seville and Portugal. And thus much I could not but say in defence of our climate, which is so much and so generally decried abroad by those who never saw it; or, if they have been here, have yet perhaps seen no more of it than what belongs to inns, or to taverns and ordinaries; who accuse our country for their own defaults, and speak ill, not only of our gardens and houses, but of our humours, our breeding, our customs and manners of life, by what they have observed of the meaner and baser sort of mankind; and of company among us, because they wanted themselves, perhaps, either fortune or birth, either quality or merit, to introduce them among the good.

I must needs add one thing more in favour of our climate, which I heard the king say, and I thought new and right, and truly like a king of England, that loved and esteemed his own country; it was in reply to some of the company that were reviling our climate, and extolling those of Italy and Spain, or at least of France: he said, he thought that was the best climate, where he could be abroad in the air with pleasure, or at least without trouble or inconvenience, the most days of the year, and the most hours of the day; and this he thought he could be in England, more than in any country he knew of in Europe. And I believe it is true, not only of the hot and the cold, but even among our neighbours in France, and the Low Countries themselves, where the heats or the colds, and changes of seasons, are less treatable than they are with us.

The truth is, our climate wants no heat to produce excellent fruits; and the default of it is only the short season of our heats or summers, by which many of the latter are left behind and imperfect with us. But all such as are ripe before the end of August, are, for aught I know, as good with us as any where else. This makes me esteem the true region of gardens in England to be the compass of ten miles about London, where the accidental warmth of air, from the fires and steams of so vast a town, makes fruits, as well as corn, a great deal forwarder than in Hampshire or Wiltshire, though more southward by a full degree.

There are, besides the temper of our climate, two things particular to us, that contribute much to the beauty and elegance of our gardens, which are the gravel of our walks, and the fineness and almost perpetual greenness of our turf. The first is not known anywhere else, which leaves all their dry walks in other countries, very unpleasant and uneasy. The other cannot be found in France or in Holland as we have it, the soil not admitting that fineness of blade in Holland, nor the sun that greenness in France, during most of the summer; nor indeed is it to be found but in the finest of our soils.

Essay on Gardening.

THE USE OF POETRY AND MUSIC.

WHETHER it be that the fierceness of the Gothic humours, or noise of their perpetual wars, frighted it away, or that the unequal mixture of the modern languages would not bear it; certain it is, that the great heights and excellency both of poetry and music fell with the Roman learning and empire, and have never since recovered the admiration and applauses that before attended them; yet, such as they are among us, they must be confessed to be the softest and sweetest, the most general and most innocent amusements of common time and life. They still find room in the courts of princes and the cottages of shepherds: they serve to revive and animate the dead calm of poor or idle lives, and to allay or divert the violent passions and perturbations of the greatest and the busiest men. And both these effects are of equal use to human life: for the mind of man is like the sea, which is neither agreeable to the beholder nor the voyager in a calm or in a storm, but is so to both when a little agitated by gentle gales; and so the mind, when moved by soft and easy passions and affections. I know very well that many, who pretend to be wise by the forms of being grave, are apt to despise both poetry and music as toys and trifles too light for the use or entertainment of serious men: but whoever find themselves wholly insensible to these charms, would, I think, do well to keep their own counsel, for fear of reproaching their own temper, and bringing the goodness of their natures, if not of their understandings, into question: it may be thought at least an ill sign, if not an ill constitution, since some of the fathers went so far, as to esteem the love of music a sign of predestination, as a thing divine, and reserved for the felicities of heaven itself. While this world lasts, I doubt not but the pleasure and requests of these two entertainments will do so too: and happy those that content themselves with these, or any other so easy and so innocent and do not trouble the world, or other men, because they cannot be quiet themselves though no body hurts them!

When all is done, human life is, at the greatest and the best, but like a froward child, that must be played with and humoured a little to keep it quiet till it falls asleep, and then the care is over.

Essay on Poetry.

P. 95, l. 10. **It.** *Here Sir William falls into the obscurity of the elder style, for what follows concerns not "climate" but "country." In itself, however, the censure is just, and has not lost its force to-day.*

P. 95, l. 19. **The king.** *Charles II.*

P. 96, l. 15. **The latter** *is not a slip of Temple's; it is opposed, not to "former," but to "early." But the distinct use of the two forms "later" and "latter" in modern English is certainly a gain in clearness, as this instance, among many, shows.*

P. 97, l. 1. *The assertion in the first sentence of this passage cannot of course be admitted, but the singular beauty of the passage itself far more than redeems it.*

GEORGE SAVILE, MARQUESS OF HALIFAX.

George Savile, Marquess of Halifax, was born in 1630, of an old Yorkshire family. He first came into great political prominence in the struggles of the Exclusion Bill, and was recognised chief of the "Trimmers." His pamphlets were mostly anonymous, but their style is unmistakable, and they are among the origins of pointed political writing in England. He died in 1695.

THE CHARACTER OF A TRIMMER.

TO conclude; our Trimmer is so fully satisfied of the truth of these principles by which he is directed, in reference to the public, that he will neither be hectored and threatened, laughed nor drunk out of them; and instead of being converted by the arguments of his adversaries to their opinions, he is very much confirmed in his own by them. He professes solemnly, that were it in his power to choose, he would rather have his ambition bounded by the commands of a great and wise master, than let it range with a popular license, though crowned with success; yet he cannot commit such a sin against the glorious thing called Liberty, nor let his soul stoop so much below itself, as to be content without repining to have his reason wholly subdued, or the privilege of acting like a sensible creature torn from him by the imperious dictates of unlimited authority, in what hand soever it happens to be placed. What is there in this that is so criminal, as to deserve the penalty of that most singular apophthegm, "A Trimmer is worse than a rebel!" What do angry men ail, to rail so against moderation? Does it not look as if they were going to some very scurvy extreme, that is too strong to be digested by the more considering part of mankind? These arbitrary methods, besides the injustice of them, are, God be thanked, very unskilful too; for they fright the birds, by talking so loud, from coming into the nets that are laid for them; and when men agree to rifle a house, they seldom give warning, or blow a trumpet; but there are some small statesmen, who are so full charged with their own expectations, that they cannot contain.

And kind Heaven, by sending such a seasonable curse upon their undertakings, has made their ignorance an antidote against their malice. Some of these cannot treat peaceably; yielding will not satisfy them, they will have men by storm. There are others that must have plots to make their service more necessary, and have an interest to keep them alive, since they are to live upon them; and persuade the king to retrench his own greatness, so as to shrink into the head of a party, which is the betraying him into such an unprincely mistake, and to such a wilful diminution of himself, that they are the last enemies he ought to allow himself to forgive. Such men, if they could, would prevail with the sun to shine only upon them and their friends, and to leave all the rest of the world in the dark. This is a very unusual monopoly, and may come within the equity of the law, which makes it treason to imprison the king: When such unfitting bounds are put to his favour, and he confined to the narrow limits of a particular set of men, that would inclose him; these honest and loyal gentlemen, if they may be allowed to bear witness for themselves, make a king their engine, and degrade him into a property, at the very time that their flattery would make him believe they paid divine worship to him. Besides these, there is a flying squadron on both sides, they are afraid the world should agree; small dabblers in conjuring, that raise angry apparitions to keep men from being reconciled, like wasps that fly up and down, buz and sting men to keep them unquiet; but these insects are commonly short-lived creatures, and no doubt in a little time mankind will be rid of them. They were giants at least who fought once against heaven, but for such pigmies as these to contend against it, is such a provoking folly, that the insolent bunglers ought to be laughed and hissed out of the world for it. They should consider, there is a soul in that great body the people, which may for a time be drowsy and unactive, but when the leviathan is roused, it moves like an angry creature, and will neither be convinced nor resisted. The people can never agree to show their united powers, till they are extremely tempted and provoked to it; so that to apply cupping-glasses to a great beast naturally disposed to sleep, and to force the tame thing, whether it will or no, to be valiant, must be learnt out of some other book than Machiavil, who would never have prescribed such a preposterous method. It is to be remembered, that if princes have law and authority on their sides, the people on theirs may have Nature, which is a formidable adversary. Duty, Justice, Religion, nay, even human prudence too, bids the people suffer anything rather than resist; but uncorrected Nature, where'er it feels the smart, will run to the nearest remedy. Men's passions, in this case, are to be considered as well as their duty, let it be never so strongly enforced; for if their passions are provoked, they being as much a part of us as our limbs, they lead men into a short way of arguing, that admits no distinction; and from the foundation of self-defence, they will draw inferences that will have miserable effects upon the quiet of a government.

Our Trimmer therefore dreads a general discontent, because he thinks it differs from a rebellion, only as a spotted fever does from the plague, the same species under a lower degree of malignity; it works several ways, sometimes like a slow poison that has its effects at a great distance from the time it was given; sometimes like dry flag prepared to catch at the first fire, or like seed in the ground ready to sprout up on the first shower: In every shape 'tis fatal, and our Trimmer thinks no pains or precaution can be so great as to prevent it.

In short, he thinks himself in the right, grounding his opinion upon that truth, which equally hates to be under the oppressions of wrangling sophistry on the one hand, or the short dictates of mistaken authority on the other.

Our Trimmer adores the goddess Truth, though in all ages she has been scurvily used, as well as those that worshipped her: 'Tis of late become such a ruining virtue, that Mankind seems to be agreed to commend and avoid it; yet the want of practice, which repeals the other laws, has no influence upon the law of truth, because it has root in Heaven, and an intrinsic value in itself, that can never be impaired: She shows her greatness in this, that her enemies, even when they are successful, are ashamed to own it. Nothing but power full of truth has the prerogative of triumphing, not only after victories, but in spite of them, and to put conquest herself out of countenance. She may be kept under and suppressed, but her dignity still remains with her, even when she is in chains. Falsehood with all her impudence, has not enough to speak ill of her before her face: such majesty she carries about her, that her most prosperous enemies are fain to whisper their treason; all the power upon the earth can never extinguish her: she has lived in all ages; and let the mistaken zeal of prevailing authority christen any opposition to it with what name they please, she makes it not only an ugly and unmannerly, but a dangerous thing to persist: She has lived very retired indeed, nay, sometimes so buried, that only some few of the discerning part of Mankind could have a glimpse of her; with all that, she has eternity in her, she knows not how to die, and from the darkest clouds that shade and cover her, she breaks from time to time with triumph for her friends, and terror to her enemies.

Our Trimmer therefore, inspired by this divine virtue, thinks fit to conclude with these assertions, that our climate is a Trimmer, between that part of the world where men are roasted, and the other where they are frozen: That our church is a Trimmer, between the frenzy of platonic visions, and the lethargic ignorance of popish dreams: That our laws are Trimmers, between the excess of unbounded power, and the extravagance of liberty not enough restrained: That true virtue hath ever been thought a Trimmer, and to have its dwelling in the middle between the two extremes: That even God Almighty himself is divided between his two great attributes, his Mercy and his Justice.

In such company, our Trimmer is not ashamed of his name, and willingly leaves to the bold champions of either extreme, the honour of contending with no less adversaries than

Nature, Religion, Liberty, Prudence, Humanity, and Common Sense.

Miscellanies.

P. 100, l. 22. Equity, *i.e. reasonable construction, range.*
P. 100, l. 30. They. *Demonstrative for relative. So not very uncommon.*
P. 101, l. 31. So great as to prevent it. *Not that it is impossible to prevent it by pains and precaution, but that no exertion or precaution is of such importance as the prevention of it.*

JOHN DRYDEN.

John Dryden was born at Aldwinkle in 1631, and died in London in 1700. What has been said of Milton may be said with more emphasis of him. His prose is less good than his verse, but it is fully as important historically, and its influence, unlike that of his verse, was almost unmixedly good.

A LAYMAN'S FAITH.

A POEM, with so bold a title, and a name prefixed from which the handling of so serious a subject would not be expected, may reasonably oblige the author to say somewhat in defence, both of himself and of his undertaking. In the first place, if it be objected to me, that, being a layman, I ought not to have concerned myself with speculations, which belong to the profession of divinity; I could answer, that perhaps laymen, with equal advantages of parts and knowledge, are not the most incompetent judges of sacred things; but, in the due sense of my own weakness, and want of learning, I plead not this, I pretend not to make myself a judge of faith in others, but only to make a confession of my own. I lay no unhallowed hand upon the ark, but wait on it, with the reverence that becomes me, at a distance. In the next place, I will ingenuously confess, that the helps I have used in this small treatise, were many of them taken from the works of our own reverend divines of the church of England; so that the weapons with which I combat irreligion, are already consecrated; though I suppose they may be taken down as lawfully as the sword of Goliah was by David, when they are to be employed for the common cause against the enemies of piety. I intend not by this to entitle them to any of my errors, which yet I hope are only those of charity to mankind; and such as my own charity has caused me to commit, that of others may more easily excuse. Being naturally inclined to scepticism in philosophy, I have no reason to impose my opinions in a subject which is above it; but whatever they are, I submit them with all reverence to my mother church, accounting them no further mine, than as they are authorized, or at least uncondemned, by her. And, indeed, to secure myself on this side, I have used the necessary precaution of shewing this paper before it was published to a judicious and learned friend; a man indefatigably zealous in the service of the church and state, and whose writings have highly deserved of both. He was pleased to approve the body of the discourse, and I hope he is more my friend than to do it out of complaisance: It is true, he had too good a taste to like it all; and, amongst some other faults, recommended to my second view, what I have written, perhaps too boldly, on St. Athanasius, which he advised me wholly to omit. I am sensible enough, that I had done more prudently to have followed his opinion; but then I could not have satisfied myself, that I had done honestly not to have written what was my own. It has always been my thought, that heathens, who never did, nor without miracle could, hear of the name of Christ, were yet in a possibility of salvation. Neither will it enter easily into my belief, that before the coming of our Saviour, the whole world, excepting only the Jewish nation, should lie under the inevitable necessity of everlasting punishment, for want of that revelation, which was confined to so small a spot of ground as that of Palestine. Among the sons of Noah, we read of one only who was accursed; and, if a blessing, in the ripeness of time, was reserved for Japhet, of whose progeny we are, it seems unaccountable to me, why so many generations of the same offspring, as preceded our Saviour in the flesh, should be all involved in one common condemnation, and yet that their posterity should be entitled to the hopes of salvation; as if a bill of exclusion had passed only on the fathers, which debarred not the sons from their succession: or, that so

many ages had been delivered over to hell, and so many reserved
for heaven, and that the devil had the first choice, and God the
next. Truly I am apt to think, that the revealed religion, which
was taught by Noah to all his sons, might continue for some
ages in the whole posterity. That afterwards it was included
wholly in the family of Shem, is manifest; but when the pro-
genies of Cham and Japhet swarmed into colonies, and those
colonies were subdivided into many others, in process of time
their descendants lost, by little and little, the primitive and purer
rites of divine worship, retaining only the notion of one deity;
to which succeeding generations added others; for men took
their degrees in those ages from conquerors to gods. Revelation
being thus eclipsed to almost all mankind, the light of nature,
as the next in dignity, was substituted; and that is it which
St. Paul concludes to be the rule of the heathens, and by which
they are hereafter to be judged. If my supposition be true, then
the consequence, which I have assumed in my poem, may be
also true; namely, that Deism, or the principles of natural
worship, are only faint remnants, or dying flames, of revealed
religion, in the posterity of Noah; and that our modern philosophers, nay, and some of our philosophizing divines, have too
much exalted the faculties of our souls, when they have maintained, that, by their force, mankind has been able to find out,
that there is one supreme agent, or intellectual being, which
we call God; that praise and prayer are his due worship; and
the rest of those deducements, which I am confident are the
remote effects of revelation, and unattainable by our discourse,
I mean as simply considered, and without the benefit of divine
illumination. So that we have not lifted up ourselves to God,
by the weak pinions of our reason, but he has been pleased to
descend to us, and what Socrates said of him, what Plato writ,
and the rest of the heathen philosophers of several nations, is
all no more than the twilight of revelation, after the sun of it
was set in the race of Noah. That there is something above us,
some principle of motion, our reason can apprehend, though it
cannot discover what it is by its own virtue: and, indeed, it is
very improbable that we, who, by the strength of our faculties,
cannot enter into the knowledge of any being, not so much as

of our own, should be able to find out, by them, that supreme nature, which we cannot otherwise define, than by saying it is infinite; as if infinite were definable, or infinity a subject for our narrow understanding. They, who would prove religion by reason, do but weaken the cause which they endeavour to support: it is to take away the pillars from our faith, and to prop it only with a twig; it is to design a tower, like that of Babel, which, if it were possible, as it is not, to reach heaven, would come to nothing by the confusion of the workmen. For every man is building a several way; impotently conceited of his own model and his own materials, reason is always striving, and always at a loss; and of necessity it must so come to pass, while it is exercised about that which is not its proper object. Let us be content at last, to know God by his own methods; at least, so much of him as he is pleased to reveal to us in the sacred Scriptures. To apprehend them to be the word of God is all our reason has to do; for all beyond it is the work of faith, which is the seal of heaven impressed upon our human understanding.

Preface to Religio Laici.

THE USE OF ARCHAIC WORDS.

BUT there are other judges, who think I ought not to have translated Chaucer into English, out of quite a contrary notion: they suppose there is a certain veneration due to his old language; and that it is little less than profanation and sacrilege to alter it. They are farther of opinion, that somewhat of his good sense will suffer in this transfusion, and much of the beauty of his thoughts will infallibly be lost, which appear with more grace in their old habit. Of this opinion was that excellent person, whom I mentioned, the late Earl of Leicester, who valued Chaucer as much as Mr. Cowley despised him. My lord dissuaded me from this attempt, (for I was thinking of it some years before his death) and his authority prevailed so far with me, as to defer my undertaking while he lived, in deference to him: yet my reason was not convinced with what he urged against it. If the first end of a writer be to be understood, then, as his language grows obsolete, his thoughts must grow obscure:

> "Multa renascentur, quæ jam cecidere; cadentque
> Quæ nunc sunt in honore vocabula, si volet usus,
> Quem penes arbitrium est et jus et norma loquendi."

When an ancient word, for its sound and significancy, deserves to be revived, I have that reasonable veneration for antiquity to restore it. All beyond this is superstition. Words are not like landmarks, so sacred as never to be removed; customs are changed, and even statutes are silently repealed, when the reason ceases for which they were enacted. As for the other part of the argument,—that his thoughts will lose of their original beauty by the innovation of words,—in the first place, not only their beauty, but their being is lost, where they are no longer understood, which is the present case. I grant that something must be lost in all transfusion, that is, in all translations; but the sense will remain, which would otherwise be lost, or at least be maimed, when it is scarce intelligible, and that but to a few. How few are there, who can read Chaucer, so as to understand him perfectly? And if imperfectly, then with less profit, and no pleasure. It is not for the use of some old Saxon friends, that I have taken these pains with him: let them neglect my version, because they have no need of it. I made it for their sakes, who understand sense and poetry as well as they, when that poetry and sense is put into words which they understand. I will go farther, and dare to add, that what beauties I lose in some places, I give to others which had them not originally: but in this I may be partial to myself; let the reader judge, and I submit to his decision. Yet I think I have just occasion to complain of them, who, because they understand Chaucer, would deprive the greater part of their countrymen of the same advantage, and hoard him up, as misers do their grandam gold, only to look on it themselves, and hinder others from making use of it. In sum, I seriously protest, that no man ever had, or can have, a greater veneration for Chaucer than myself. I have translated some part of his works, only that I might perpetuate his memory, or at least refresh it, amongst my countrymen. If I have altered him anywhere for the better, I must at the same time acknowledge, that I could have done nothing without him. "*Facile est inventis addere*" is no great commendation; and I am not so vain to think I have deserved a greater.

Preface to the Fables.

P. 105, l. 2. Entitle them to, *i.e.* "*father my errors upon them*," *put as it were their names on the title-page. A common use in Dryden.*

P. 105, l. 6. Scepticism *is here used in its proper sense as opposed to "dogmatism," not to "faith."*

P. 106, ll. 11, 12. Took their degrees, *i.e. became gods after being conquerors, as a man proceeds from one academical degree to another.*

P. 106. l. 27. Discourse, *as often, — reason.*

P. 107, l. 28. The late Earl of Leicester. *Algernon Sidney's elder brother.*

P. 108, l. 34. Grandam gold. *This phrase is very characteristic of Dryden, being easily intelligible, though not strictly to be interpreted.*

JOHN LOCKE.

John Locke was born at Wrington in 1632, and died at Oates, a now destroyed house of the Mashams in Essex, in 1704. His style is slovenly but clear: that is to say, there is no possibility of mistaking his meaning. The meaning in his case being the result of important and forcible thought, his directness of expression has gained him credit as a writer which is not strictly deserved.

PUBLIC SCHOOLS.

TILL you can find a school, wherein it is possible for the master to look after the manners of his scholars, and can show as great effects of his care of forming their minds to virtue, and their carriage to good breeding, as of forming their tongues to the learned languages; you must confess, that you have a strange value for words, when, preferring the languages of the ancient Greeks and Romans to that which made them such brave men, you think it worth while to hazard your son's innocence and virtue, for a little Greek and Latin. For, as for that boldness and spirit, which lads get amongst their playfellows at school, it has ordinarily such a mixture of rudeness, and an ill-turned confidence, that those misbecoming and disingenuous ways of shifting in the world must be unlearned, and all the tincture washed out again, to make way for better principles, and such manners as make a truly worthy man. He that considers how diametrically opposite the skill of living well, and managing, as a man should do, his affairs in the world, is to that malapertness, tricking, or violence, learnt among schoolboys, will think the faults of a privater education infinitely to be preferred to such improvements; and will take care to preserve his child's innocence and modesty at home, as being nearer of kin, and more in the way of those qualities, which make an useful and able man. Nor does any one find, or so much as suspect, that the retirement and bashfulness, which their daughters are brought up in, makes them less knowing or less able women. Conversation, when they come into the world, soon gives them a becoming assurance; and whatsoever, beyond that, there is of rough and boisterous, may in men be very well spared too: for courage and steadiness, as I take it, lie not in roughness and ill-breeding.

Virtue is harder to be got, than a knowledge of the world; and, if lost in a young man, is seldom recovered. Sheepishness and ignorance of the world, the faults imputed to a private education, are neither the necessary consequences of being bred at home; nor, if they were, are they incurable evils. Vice is the more stubborn, as well as the more dangerous evil of the two; and therefore, in the first place, to be fenced against. If that sheepish softness, which often enervates those, who are bred like fondlings at home, be carefully to be avoided, it is principally so for virtue's sake; for fear lest such a yielding temper should be too susceptible of vicious impressions, and expose the novice too easily to be corrupted. A young man, before he leaves the shelter of his father's house, and the guard of a tutor, should be fortified with resolution, and made acquainted with men, to secure his virtue; lest he should be led into some ruinous course, or fatal precipice, before he is sufficiently acquainted with the dangers of conversation, and has steadiness enough not to yield to every temptation. Were it not for this, a young man's bashfulness, and ignorance of the world, would not so much need an early care. Conversation would cure it in a great measure; or, if that will not do it early enough, it is only a stronger reason for a good tutor at home. For, if pains be to be taken to give him a manly air and assurance betimes, it is chiefly as a fence to his virtue, when he goes into the world under his own conduct.

It is preposterous, therefore, to sacrifice his innocency to the attaining of confidence, and some little skill of bustling for himself among others, by his conversation with ill-bred and vicious boys; when the chief use of that sturdiness, and standing upon his own legs, is only for the preservation of his virtue. For if confidence or cunning come once to mix with vice, and support his miscarriages, he is only the surer lost, and you must undo again, and strip him of that he has got from his companions, or give him up to ruin. Boys will unavoidably be taught assurance by conversation with men when they are brought into it; and that is time enough. Modesty and submission, till then, better fits them for instruction: and therefore there needs not any great care to stock them with confidence beforehand. That which requires most time, pains, and assiduity, is to work into them the principles and practice of virtue and good breeding. This is the seasoning they should be prepared with, so as not easily to be got out again: this they had need to be well provided with. For conversation, when they come into the world, will add to their knowledge and assurance, but be too apt to take from their virtue; which therefore they ought to be plentifully stored with, and have that tincture sunk deep into them.

Some Thoughts concerning Education.

P. 111, l. 7. Conversation, *it is perhaps not superfluous to remind the reader, does not mean "talking," but "intercourse." The comparison of the matter of this passage with that of Ben Jonson supra is so interesting as also to excuse the suggestion of it.*

ROBERT SOUTH.

Robert South was born at Hackney in 1633, was educated at Westminster and Christ Church, and became Public Orator at Oxford. Clarendon made him his chaplain, and introduced him to a series of preferments, which is said to have stopped short of the Bench by his own desire merely. He died in 1716, leaving a very high reputation for soundness in Toryism, Churchmanship, morals, and style.

THE EXECUTION OF CHARLES I.

"AND it shall come to pass, when your children shall say unto you, What mean you by this service? that you shall say, It is the Lord's Passover; who passed over the houses of the children of Israel in Egypt, when he smote the Egyptians and delivered our fathers," etc. So say I to all true English parents. When your children shall ask you, Why do we keep the thirtieth of January as a fast? and the twenty-ninth of May as a festival? What mean you by this service? Then is the time to rip up and lay before them the tragical history of the late rebellion, and unnatural civil war. A war commenced without the least shadow or pretence of right; as being notoriously against all law. A war begun without any provocation, as being against the justest, the mildest, and most pious prince, that had ever reigned. A war raised upon clamours of grievances; while the subject swam in greater plenty and riches than had ever been known in these islands before; and no grievances to be found in the three kingdoms, besides the persons who cried out of them. Next to this let them tell their children over and over of the villainous imprisonments, and contumelious trial, and the barbarous murder of that blessed and royal martyr, by a company of cobblers, tailors, draymen, drunkards, whoremongers, and broken tradesmen; though since, I confess, dignified with the title of *the sober part of the nation.* These, I say, were the illustrious judges of that great monarch. Whereas the whole people of England, nobles, and commons together, neither in Parliament, nor out of Parliament, as that great judge in the trial of the regicides affirmed, had power by law to touch one hair of his head, or judicially to call him to account for any of his actions. And then in the last place, they are to tell their children also of the base and brutish cruelties practised by those bloodhounds in the plunders, sequestrations, decimations, and murders of their poor fellow subjects: likewise of their horrid oaths, covenants, and perjuries; and of their shameless, insatiable, and sacrilegious avarice, in destroying the purest church in the world, and seizing its revenues, and all this under the highest pretences of zeal for religion, and with the most solemn appeals to the great God, while they were actually spitting in his face.

These things, I say, and a thousand more, they are to be perpetually inculcating into the minds of their children, according to that strict injunction of God himself to the Israelites, Deut. vi. 6, 7, 8. "These words shall be in thine heart, and thou shalt diligently teach them thy children, and shalt talk of them, when thou sittest in thy house, and when thou walkest by the way, and when thou liest down, and when thou risest up." Such discourses should open their eyes in the morning, and close them in the evening. And I dare undertake, that if this one thing had been faithfully and constantly practised, even but since the late Restoration, which came upon these poor kingdoms like life from the dead, the fanatics had never been so considerable, as to cause those terrible convulsions in Church and State, and those misunderstandings between the king and his people, which we have seen and trembled at, and must expect to see, as long as the same spirit, which governed in forty-one, continues still so powerful, as it does, amongst us. For, I am sure, no king and that, can ever reign quietly together.

Sermons.

PLAINNESS OF APOSTOLIC SPEECH.

A SECOND property of the ability of speech, conferred by Christ upon his apostles, was its unaffected plainness and simplicity: it was to be easy, obvious and familiar; with nothing in it strained, or far fetched: no affected scheme, or airy fancies, above the reach or relish of an ordinary apprehension; no, nothing of all this; but their grand subject was truth, and consequently above all these petit arts, and poor additions; as not being capable of any greater lustre or advantage, than to appear just as it is. For there is a certain majesty in plainness; as the proclamation of a prince never frisks it in tropes, or fine conceits, in numerous and well-turned periods, but commands in sober, natural expressions. A substantial beauty, as it comes out of the hands of nature, needs neither paint nor patch: things never made to adorn, but to cover something that would be hid. It is with expression, and the clothing of a man's conceptions, as with the clothing of a man's body. All dress and ornament supposes imperfection, as designed only to supply the body with something from without, which it wanted, but had not of its own. Gaudery is a pitiful and a mean thing, not extending farther than the surface of the body; nor is the highest gallantry considerable to any, but to those, who would hardly be considered without it: for in that case indeed there may be great need of an outside, when there is little or nothing within.

And thus also it is with the most necessary and important truths; to adorn and clothe them is to cover them, and that to obscure them. The eternal salvation and damnation of souls, are not things to be treated of with jests and witticisms. And he, who thinks to furnish himself out of plays and romances with language for the pulpit, shews himself much fitter to act a part in the revels, than for a cure of souls.

I speak the words of soberness, said St. Paul, Acts xxvi. 25. And I preach the Gospel not with the enticing words of man's wisdom, 1 Cor. ii. 4. This was the way of the apostles discoursing of things sacred. Nothing here of the fringes of the

North-star; nothing of Nature's becoming unnatural; nothing of the down of angels' wings, or the beautiful locks of cherubims: no starched similitudes, introduced with a thus have I seen a cloud rolling in its airy mansion, and the like. No, these were sublimities above the rise of the Apostolic Spirit. For the apostles, poor mortals, were content to take lower steps, and to tell the world in plain terms, that he who believed should be saved, and that he who believed not should be damned. And this was the dialect, which pierced the conscience, and made the hearers cry out, Men and brethren, what shall we do? It tickled not the ear, but sunk into the heart: and when men came from such sermons, they never commended the preacher for his taking voice or gesture; for the fineness of such a simile, or the quaintness of such a sentence; but they spoke like men conquered with the overpowering force and evidence of the most concerning truths; much in the words of the two disciples going to Emmaus; Did not our hearts burn within us, while he opened to us the Scriptures?

In a word, the apostles' preaching was therefore mighty, and successful, because plain, natural, and familiar, and by no means above the capacity of their hearers: nothing being more preposterous, than for those, who were professedly aiming at men's hearts, to miss the mark, by shooting over their heads.

Sermon on Ascension Day.

P. 113, l. 18. Cried out of them. *There is a slight difference of sense between this and the more usual "cried out on them."*

P. 115, l. 1. *The whole of this passage indirectly, and the sentence from "Nothing" to "the like" directly, is levelled at Jeremy Taylor. I do not know whether this attack on a brother preacher is apostolic, but it is very amusing.*

P. 115, l. 7. *The original form* petit *is now confined to legal use, and even there is sometimes changed to* petty. *But it was common in South's time.*

P. 115, ll. 19, 20. Gaudery *and* gallantry, *both in the sense of "finery," are both old-fashioned and the former is rare; but both are good.*

APHRA BEHN.

Aphra Behn was born at Canterbury about 1640. She visited the West Indies, married a Dutch merchant, and held some dubious diplomatic appointments. Her plays have in relation to those of her contemporaries a rather unfair reputation for license, but are of small literary worth. Her prose has much merit, and she ranks early and high in the list of English novelists. She died in 1689.

LOVE LETTERS.

IT is an art too ingenious to have been found out by man, and too necessary to lovers, not to have been invented by the God of Love himself. But, Damon, I do not pretend to exact from you those letters of gallantry, which, I have told you, are filled with nothing but fine thoughts, and writ with all the arts of wit and subtilty: I would have yours still all tender unaffected love, words unchosen, thoughts unstudied, and love unfeigned. I had rather find more softness than wit in your passion; more of nature than of art; more of the lover than the poet.

Nor would I have you write any of those little short letters, that are read over in a minute; in love, long letters bring a long pleasure; Do not trouble yourself to make them fine, or write a great deal of wit and sense in a few lines; that is the notion of a witty billet, in any affair but that of love. And have a care rather to avoid these graces to a mistress; and assure yourself, dear Damon, that what pleases the soul pleases the eye, and the largeness or bulk of your letter shall never offend me; and that I only am displeased when I find them small. A letter is ever the best and most powerful agent to a mistress, it almost always persuades, 'tis always renewing little impressions, that possibly otherways absence would deface. Make use then, Damon, of your time while it is given you, and thank me that I permit you to write to me : Perhaps I shall not always continue in the humour of suffering you to do so ; and it may so happen, by some turn of chance and fortune, that you may be deprived, at the same time, both of my presence, and of the means of sending to me. I will believe that such an accident would be a great misfortune to you, for I have often heard you say that, " To make the most happy lover suffer martyrdom, one need only forbid him seeing, speaking and writing to the object he loves." Take all the advantages then you can, you cannot give me too often marks too powerful of your passion : Write therefore during this hour, every day. I give you leave to believe, that while you do so, you are serving me the most obligingly and agreeably you can, while absent ; and that you are giving me a remedy against all grief, uneasiness, melancholy, and despair ; nay, if you exceed your hour, you need not be ashamed. The time you employ in this kind devoir, is the time that I shall be grateful for, and no doubt will recompense it. You ought not however to neglect heaven for me ; I will give you time for your devotion, for my Watch tells you 'tis time to go to the temple.

The Lover's Watch.

P. 118, l. 23. The Lover's Watch *is a time-table in verse and prose of imaginary employments for the lover and his mistress during the twenty-four hours. In justice to "the divine Astrea," it should be said that the treatment is almost entirely unobjectionable.*

GILBERT BURNET.

Gilbert Burnet was born in Edinburgh in 1643. Educated chiefly at Aberdeen and Amsterdam, he took orders, and in 1674 came to London. He belonged to the Whig party, lived abroad during the reign of James II., and was appointed to the see of Salisbury by William of Orange. He died in 1715. Burnet had talent and merit, but was hot-headed, pragmatical, and injudicious.

ARCHBISHOP CRANMER.

WHEN he came to the stake, he first prayed, and then undressed himself; and, being tied to it, as the fire was kindling, he stretched forth his right hand towards the flame; never moving it, save that once he wiped his face with it, till it was burnt away, which was consumed before the fire reached his body. He expressed no disorder for the pain he was in; sometimes saying, "That unworthy hand!" and oft crying out, "Lord Jesus, receive my spirit!" He was soon after quite burnt.

But it was no small matter of astonishment to find his heart entire, and not consumed among the ashes: which, though the reformed would not carry so far as to make a miracle of it, and a clear proof that his heart had continued true, though his hand had erred; yet they objected it to the papists, that it was certainly such a thing, that, if it had fallen out in any of their church, they had made it a miracle.

Thus did Thomas Cranmer end his days, in the sixty-seventh year of his age. He was a man raised of God for great services, and well fitted for them. He was naturally of a mild and gentle

temper, not soon heated, nor apt to give his opinion rashly of
things or persons : and yet his gentleness, though it oft exposed
him to his enemies, who took advantages from it to use him ill,
knowing he would readily forgive them, did not lead him into
such a weakness of spirit, as to consent to everything that was
uppermost : for as he stood firmly against the Six Articles in
king Henry's time, notwithstanding all his heat for them, so he
also opposed the duke of Somerset in the matter of the sale and
alienation of the chantry lands, and the duke of Northumberland
during his whole government, and now resisted unto blood : so
that his meekness was really a virtue in him, and not a pusillanimity in his temper. He was a man of great candour : he
never dissembled his opinion, nor disowned his friend; two rare
qualities in that age, in which there was a continued course of
dissimulation, almost in the whole English clergy and nation,
they going backward and forward, as the court turned. But
this had got him that esteem with king Henry, that it always
preserved him in his days. He knew, what complaints soever
were brought against him, he would freely tell him the truth :
so, instead of asking it from other hands, he began at himself.
He neither disowned his esteem of queen Anne, nor his friendship to Cromwell and the duke of Somerset in their misfortunes ;
but owned he had the same thoughts of them in their lowest
condition, that he had in their greatest state.

He being thus prepared by a candid and good nature for the
searches into truth, added to these a most wonderful diligence ;
for he drew out of all the authors that he read every thing that
was remarkable, digesting these quotations into common-places.
This begat in king Henry an admiration of him : for he had
often tried it, to bid him bring the opinions of the fathers and
doctors upon several questions ; which he commonly did in two
or three days' time : this flowed from the copiousness of his
common-place books. He had a good judgment, but no great
quickness of apprehension, nor closeness of style, which was
diffused and unconnected ; therefore when anything was to be
penned that required more nerves, he made use of Ridley. He
laid out all his wealth on the poor, and pious uses : he had
hospitals and surgeons in his house for the king's seamen : he

gave pensions to many of those that fled out of Germany into England; and kept up that which is hospitality indeed at his table, where great numbers of the honest and poor neighbours were always invited, instead of the luxury and extravagance of great entertainments, which the vanity and excess of the age we live in has honoured with the name of hospitality, to which too many are led by the authority of custom to comply too far. He was so humble and affable, that he carried himself in all conditions at the same rate. His last fall was the only blemish of his life; but he-expiated it with a sincere repentance, and a patient martyrdom. He had been the chief advancer of the reformation in his life; and God so ordered it, that his death should bear a proportion to the former parts of his life, which was no small confirmation to all that received his doctrine, when they heard how constantly he had at last sealed it with his blood. And though it is not to be fancied that king Henry was a prophet, yet he discovered such things in Cranmer's temper as made him conclude he was to die a martyr for his religion; and therefore he ordered him to change his coat of arms, and to give *pelicans* instead of *cranes*, which were formerly the arms of his family; intimating withal, that as it is reported of the *pelican*, that she gives her blood to feed her young ones; so he was to give his blood for the good of the church. That king's kindness to him subjected him too much to him; for great obligations do often prove the greatest snares to generous and noble minds. And he was so much overborne by his respects to him, and was so affected with king Henry's death, that he never after that shaved his beard, but let it grow to a great length: which I the rather mention, because the pictures that were afterwards made for him, being taken according to what he was at his death, differ much from that which I have put in my former volume. Those who compared modern and ancient times, found in him so many and excellent qualities, that they did not doubt to compare him to the greatest of the primitive bishops; not only to the Chrysostoms, Ambroses, and Austins; but to the fathers of the first rate that immediately followed the apostles, to the Ignatiuses, Polycarps, and Cyprians. And it seemed necessary that the reformation of this church, which was indeed nothing else but restoring of the primitive and apostolical doctrine, should have been chiefly carried on by a man so eminent in all primitive and apostolical virtues. And to those who upbraided the reformed with his fall, it was answered, that Liberius, whom they so much magnify, had fallen as foully upon a much slighter temptation, only out of a desire to re-enter to his see, from which he had been banished; and that he persisted much longer in it.

History of Reformation.

P. 119, l. 15. In any of their church, *i.e.*, *in any one*.

P. 120, l. 7. Heat *seems here to have the sense which we now colloquially assign to "hot water." "Notwithstanding the troubles into which he got as regarded them." It cannot mean "his zeal for them."*

P. 121, l. 36. Rate, *in its proper sense of "rank" or "order," with no allusion to merit.*

P. 122, l. 5. Liberius, *who, in* A.D. 355, *refused to concur in the condemnation of Athanasius, despite the commands of the Emperor Constantius. Banishment broke his resolution and he submitted, but afterwards repented of his complaisance.*

CHARLES LESLIE.

Charles Leslie was born at Dublin in 1650; his father was Bishop of the Isles, Raphoe, and Clogher. He first studied law, but was ordained in 1680, and for a short time held the Chancellorship of Connor. The Revolution made him a nonjuror and a Jacobite. In the Rehearsal newspaper and in his polemic against deists and dissenters he showed controversial powers of the highest kind. He died in 1722.

THE ARGUMENT FROM PROBABILITY.

THERE are several other topics from whence the truth of the Christian religion is evinced to all who will judge by reason, and give themselves leave to consider :—as the improbability that ten or twelve poor illiterate fishermen should form a design of converting the whole world to believe their delusions, and the impossibility of their effecting it, without force of arms, learning, oratory, or any one visible thing that could recommend them! And to impose a doctrine quite opposite to the lusts and pleasures of men, and all worldly advantages or enjoyments! And this in an age of so great learning and sagacity as that wherein the Gospel was first preached! That these Apostles should not only undergo all the scorn and contempt, but the severest persecutions and most cruel deaths that could be inflicted, in attestation to what themselves knew to be a mere deceit and forgery of their own contriving! Some have suffered for errors which they thought to be truth, but never any for what themselves knew to be lies. And the Apostles must know what they taught to be lies, if it was so, because they spoke of those things which, they said, they had both seen and heard, had looked upon and handled with their hands, etc.

Neither can it be said, that they, perhaps, might have proposed some temporal advantages to themselves, but missed of them, and met with sufferings instead of them: for, if it had been so, it is more than probable that, when they saw their disappointment, they would have discovered their conspiracy; especially when they might have not only saved their lives, but got great rewards for doing of it. That not one of them should ever have been brought to do this!

But this is not all: for they tell us that their Master bid them expect nothing but sufferings in this world. This is the tenure of all that Gospel which they taught; and they told the same to all whom they converted. So that here was no disappointment.

For all that were converted by them, were converted upon the certain expectation of suffering, and bidden prepare for it. Christ commanded His disciples to take up their cross daily, and follow Him; and told them that in the world they should have tribulation; that whoever did not forsake father, mother, wife, children, lands, and their very lives, could not be His disciples: that he who sought to save his life in this world, should lose it in the next.

Now, that this despised doctrine of the cross should prevail so universally against the allurements of flesh and blood, and all the blandishments of this world, against the rage and persecution of all the kings and powers of the earth, must show its original to be Divine, and its Protector Almighty. What is it else could conquer without arms, persuade without rhetoric; overcome enemies; disarm tyrants; and subdue empires without opposition?

A Short and Easy Method with the Deists.

P. 124, l. 9. That. *This, like the preceding "thats," depends on "the improbability" at p. 123, l. 3. The construction is rhetorical, and better suited to spoken than to written style; but it is effective enough.*

DANIEL DEFOE.

Daniel Defoe was born in London in 1661, and died there in 1731. He conducted the first daily review in English; he was the first English novelist properly so called; he has never been equalled for realism without tediousness of detail; his variety is extraordinary, and with Bunyan he stands at the head of all writers who have employed vernacular English as a written language.

THE SHIPWRECK.

AND now our case was very dismal indeed; for we all saw plainly, that the sea went so high, that the boat could not live, and that we should be inevitably drowned. As to making sail, we had none, nor, if we had, could we have done anything with it; so we worked at the oar towards the land, though with heavy hearts, like men going to execution; for we all knew, that when the boat came nearer the shore, she would be dashed in a thousand pieces by the breach of the sea. However, we committed our souls to God in the most earnest manner; and the wind driving us towards the shore, we hastened our destruction with our own hands, pulling as well as we could towards land.

What the shore was, whether rock or sand, whether steep or shoal, we knew not; the only hope that could rationally give us the least shadow of expectation, was, if we might happen into some bay or gulf, or the mouth of some river, where, by great chance, we might have run our boat in, or got under the lee of the land, and perhaps made smooth water. But there was nothing of this appeared; but, as we made nearer and nearer the shore, the land looked more frightful than the sea.

After we had rowed, or rather driven, about a league and a half, as we reckoned it, a raging wave, mountain-like, came rolling astern of us, and plainly bade us expect the *coup de grace*. In a word, it took us with such a fury, that it overset the boat at once; and, separating us as well from the boat, as from one another, gave us not time hardly to say O God! for we were all swallowed up in a moment.

Nothing can describe the confusion of thought which I felt when I sunk into the water; for though I swam very well, yet I could not deliver myself from the waves so as to draw breath, till that wave having driven me, or rather carried me, a vast way on towards the shore, and, having spent itself, went back, and left me upon the land almost dry, but half dead with the water I took in. I had so much presence of mind, as well as breath left, that, seeing myself nearer the main land than I expected, I got upon my feet, and endeavoured to make on towards the land as fast as I could, before another wave should return, and take me up again. But I soon found it was impossible to avoid it; for I saw the sea come after me as high as a great hill, and as furious as an enemy, which I had no means or strength to contend with; my business was to hold my breath, and raise myself upon the water, if I could; and so, by swimming, to preserve my breathing, and pilot myself towards the shore, if possible; my greatest concern now being, that the sea, as it would carry me a great way towards the shore when it came on, might not carry me back again with it when it gave back towards the sea.

The wave that came upon me again, buried me at once twenty or thirty foot deep in its own body; and I could feel myself carried with a mighty force and swiftness towards the shore a very great way; but I held my breath, and assisted myself to swim still forward with all my might. I was ready to burst with holding my breath, when, as I felt myself rising up, so, to my immediate relief, I found my head and hands shoot out above the surface of the water; and though it was not two seconds of time that I could keep myself so, yet it relieved me greatly, gave me breath, and new courage. I was covered again with water a good while, but not so long but I held it out; and finding the water had spent itself, and began to return, I struck forward against the return of the waves, and felt ground again with my feet. I stood still a few moments to recover my breath, and till the water went from me, and then took to my heels, and ran with what strength I had farther towards the shore. But neither would this deliver me from the fury of the sea, which came pouring in after me again ; and twice more I was lifted up by the waves, and carried forward as before, the shore being very flat.

The last time of these two had well near been fatal to me ; for the sea having hurried me along as before, landed me, or rather dashed me against a piece of rock, and that with such force, as it left me senseless, and indeed helpless, as to my own deliverance ; for the blow taking my side and breast, beat the breath as it were quite out of my body; and had it returned again immediately, I must have been strangled in the water ; but I recovered a little before the return of the waves, and seeing that I should be covered again with the water, I resolved to hold fast by a piece of the rock, and so to hold my breath, if possible, till the wave went back. Now, as the waves were not so high as at first, being near land, I held my hold till the wave abated, and then fetched another run, which brought me so near the shore, that the next wave, though it went over me, yet did not so swallow me up as to carry me away ; and the next run I took I got to the main land, where, to my great comfort, I clambered up the cliffs of the shore, and sat me down upon the grass, free from danger, and quite out of the reach of the water.

The Life and Adventures of Robinson Crusoe.

SIGNS AND WONDERS.

NEXT to these public things, were the dreams of old women ; or, I should say, the interpretation of old women upon other people's dreams ; and these put abundance of people even out of their wits. Some heard voices warning them to be gone, for that there would be such a plague in London, so that the living would not be able to bury the dead ; others saw apparitions in the air, and I must be allowed to say of both, I hope without breach of charity, that they heard voices that never spake, and saw sights that never appeared; but the imagination of the people was really turned wayward and possessed; and no wonder if they who were poring continually at the clouds, saw shapes and figures, representations and appearances, which had nothing in them but air and vapour. Here they told us they saw a flaming sword held in a hand, coming out of a cloud, with a point hanging directly over the city. There they saw hearses and coffins in the air carrying to be buried. And there again, heaps of dead bodies lying unburied and the like; just as the imagination of the poor terrified people furnished them with matter to work upon.

> So hypochondriac fancies represent
> Ships, armies, battles, in the firmament;
> Till steady eyes the exhalations solve,
> And all to its first matter, cloud, resolve.

I could fill this account with the strange relations such people give every day of what they have seen; and every one was so positive of their having seen what they pretended to see, that there was no contradicting them, without breach of friendship, or being accounted rude and unmannerly on the one hand, and profane and impenetrable on the other. One time before the plague was begun, otherwise than as I have said in St. Giles's, I think it was in March, seeing a crowd of people in the street, I joined with them to satisfy my curiosity, and found them all staring up into the air to see what a woman told them appeared plain to her, which was an angel clothed in white, with a fiery sword in his hand, waving it or brandishing it over his head. She described every part of the figure to the life, showed them the motion and the form, and the poor people came into it so eagerly and with so much readiness: Yes! I see it all plainly, says one, there's the sword as plain as can be; another saw the angel; one saw his very face, and cried out, What a glorious creature he was! One saw one thing, and one another. I looked as earnestly as the rest, but, perhaps, not with so much willingness to be imposed upon; and I said indeed, that I could see nothing but a white cloud, bright on one side, by the shining of the sun upon the other part. The woman endeavoured to show it me, but could not make me confess that I saw it, which, indeed, if I had, I must have lied: but the woman turning to me looked me in the face and fancied I laughed, in which her imagination deceived her too, for I really did not laugh, but was seriously reflecting how the poor people were terrified by the force of their own imagination. However, she turned to me, called me profane fellow, and a scoffer, told me that it was a time of God's anger, and dreadful judgments were approaching, and that despisers, such as I, should wander and perish.

The people about her seemed disgusted as well as she, and I found there was no persuading them that I did not laugh at them, and that I should be rather mobbed by them than be able to undeceive them. So I left them, and this appearance passed for as real as the blazing star itself.

The History of the Plague in London.

THE SKIRMISH AFTER MARSTON MOOR.

THESE few of us that were left together, with whom I was, being now pretty clear of pursuit, halted, and began to inquire who and what we were, and what we should do; and on a short debate, I proposed we should make to the first garrison of the king's that we could recover, and that we should keep together, lest the country people should insult us upon the roads. With this resolution we pushed on westward for Lancashire; but our misfortunes were not yet at an end: we travelled very hard, and got to a village upon the river Wharfe, near Wetherby. At Wetherby there was a bridge, but we understood that a party from Leeds had secured the town and the post, in order to stop the flying cavaliers, and that it would be very hard to get through there, though, as we understood afterwards, there were no soldiers there but a guard of the townsmen. In this pickle we consulted what course to take; to stay where we were till morning we all concluded would not be safe; some advised to take the stream with our horses, but the river, which is deep, and the current strong, seemed to bid us have a care what we did of that kind, especially in the night. We resolved therefore to refresh ourselves and our horses, which indeed is more than we did, and go on till we might come to a ford or bridge, where we might get over. Some guides we had, but they either were foolish or false, for after we had rid eight or nine miles, they plunged us into a river at a place they called a ford, but it was a very ill one, for most of our horses swam, and seven or eight were lost, but we saved the men; however, we got all over.

We made bold with our first convenience to trespass upon the country for a few horses, where we could find them, to remount our men whose horses were drowned, and continued our march; but being obliged to refresh ourselves at a small village on the edge of Bramham-Moor, we found the country alarmed by our taking some horses, and we were no sooner got on horseback in the morning, and entering on the moor, but we understood we were pursued by some troops of horse. There was no remedy but we must pass this moor; and though our horses were exceedingly tired, yet we pressed on upon a round trot, and recovered an enclosed country on the other side, where we halted. And here, necessity putting us upon it, we were obliged to look out for more horses, for several of our men were dismounted, and others' horses disabled by carrying double, those who lost their horses getting up behind them; but we were supplied by our enemies against their will.

The enemy followed us over the moor, and we having a woody enclosed country about us, where we were, I observed by their moving, they had lost sight of us; upon which I proposed concealing ourselves till we might judge of their numbers. We did so, and lying close in a wood, they past hastily by us, without skirting or searching the wood, which was what on another occasion they would not have done. I found they were not above a hundred and fifty horse, and considering that to let them go before us, would be to alarm the country, and stop our design; I thought, since we might be able to deal with them, we should not meet with a better place for it, and told the rest of our officers my mind, which all our party presently (for we had not time for a long debate) agreed to. Immediately upon this I caused two men to fire their pistols in the wood, at two different places, as far asunder as I could. This I did to give them an alarm, and amuse them; for being in the lane, they would otherwise have got through before we had been ready, and I resolved to engage them there, as soon as it was possible. After this alarm, we rushed out of the wood, with about a hundred horse, and charged them on the flank in a broad lane, the wood being on their right. Our passage into the lane being narrow, gave us some difficulty in our getting out; but the surprise of the charge did our work; for the enemy thinking we had been a mile or two before, had not the least thoughts of this onset, till they heard us in the wood, and then they who were before could not come back. We broke into the lane just in the middle of them, and by that means divided them; and facing to the left, charged the rear. First our dismounted men, which were near fifty, lined the edge of the wood, and fired with their carabines upon those which were before, so warmly, that they put them into a great disorder. Meanwhile, fifty more of our horse from the further part of the wood showed themselves in the lane upon their front; this put them of the foremost party into a great perplexity, and they began to face about, to fall upon us who were engaged in the rear: but their facing about in a lane where there was no room to wheel, and one who understands the manner of wheeling a troop of horse must imagine, put them into a great disorder. Our party in the head of the lane taking the advantage of this mistake of the enemy, charged in upon them, and routed them entirely. Some found means to break into the enclosures on the other side of the lane, and get away. About thirty were killed, and about twenty-five made prisoners, and forty very good horses were taken; all this while not a man of ours was lost, and not above seven or eight wounded. Those in the rear behaved themselves better; for they stood our charge with a great deal of resolution, and all we could do could not break them; but at last our men, who had fired on foot through the hedges at the other party, coming to do the like here, there was no standing it any longer. The rear of them faced about, and retreated out of the lane, and drew up in the open field to receive and rally their fellows. We killed about seventeen of them, and followed them to the end of the lane, but had no mind to have any more fighting than needs must; our condition at that time not making it proper, the towns round us being all in the enemy's hands, and the country but indifferently pleased with us; however, we stood facing them till they thought fit to march away. Thus we were supplied with horses enough to remount our men, and pursued our first design of getting into Lancashire. As for our prisoners, we let them off on foot.

Memoirs of a Cavalier.

P. 125, l. 8. Breach. *In the changed use of English, "breaking" would now be more usual in this sense. The phrase "making a clean breach," however, survives.*

P. 129, l. 17. *This (third) passage is perhaps the most marvellous example of Defoe's power of realist description. I have heard or read somewhere of a military man of distinction who declared that no one—certainly no civilian—could have written such an account unless he had seen the action.*

P. 131, l. 23. And *seems to be a mistake for "as."*

RICHARD BENTLEY.

Richard Bentley, greatest of English scholars, was born at Oulton in 1662, and died Master of Trinity at Cambridge in 1742. Throughout his life he displayed immense learning, the utmost vigour and acuteness of mind, combined with an intolerant and intolerable temper. No example of polemic in English excels the Phalaris dissertation in the union of knowledge, argument, and wit.

PHALARISM.

THERE is a certain temper of mind, that Cicero calls Phalarism, "a spirit like Phalaris's;" and one would be apt to imagine that a portion of it had descended upon some of his translators. The gentleman has given a broad hint more than once in his book, that, if I proceed further against Phalaris, I may draw perhaps a duel or a stab upon myself; which is a generous threat, especially to a divine, who neither carries arms nor principles fit for that sort of controversy. It is the same kind of generosity, though in a lower degree, when he forbids me "to meddle with banter and ridicule, which, even when luckily hit on, are not very suitable to my character." And yet the sharpest, nay almost the only arguments that he himself uses, are banter and ridicule; so that "we two," as he says, "must end this dispute;" but he takes care to allow me none of the offensive arms that himself fights with. These are the extraordinary instances both of his candour and his courage. However, I have endeavoured to take his advice, and avoid all ridicule where it was possible to avoid it; and if ever "that odd work of his" has irresistibly moved me to a little jest and laughter, I am content that what is the greatest virtue of *his* book should be counted the greatest fault of *mine*.

The facetious Examiner seems resolved to vie with Phalaris himself in the science of Phalarism; for his revenge is not satisfied with one single death of his adversary, but he will kill me over and over again. He has slain me twice by two several deaths; one in the first page of his book, and another in the last. In the title-page I die the death of Milo the Crotonian :—

"—— Remember Milo's end !
"Wedg'd in that timber which he strove to rend."

The application of which must be this : That as Milo, after his victories at six several Olympiads, was at last conquered and destroyed in wrestling with a tree, so I, after I had attained to some small reputation in letters, am to be quite baffled and run down by wooden antagonists :—but, in the end of his book, he has got me into Phalaris's bull ; and he has the pleasure of fancying that he hears me " begin to bellow." Well, since it is certain then that I am in the bull, I have performed the part of a sufferer ; for as the cries of the tormented in old Phalaris's bull, being conveyed through pipes lodged in the machine, were turned into music for the entertainment of the tyrant, so the complaints which my torments express for me, being conveyed to Mr. B—— by this Answer, are all dedicated to his pleasure and diversion ; but yet, methinks, when he was setting up to be Phalaris junior, the very omen of it might have deterred him ; for, as the old tyrant himself at last bellowed in his own bull, so his imitators ought to consider, that at long run their own actions may chance to overtake them.

But it is not enough for him that I die a bodily death, unless my reputation too die with me. He accuses me of one of the meanest and basest of actions: " That when Sir Edward Sherburn put a MS. into my hands to get it published by Mr. Grævius, desiring me to let him know from whom he had it, that he might make an honourable mention of him, I concealed the kindness of Sir Edward, and took the honour of it to myself; so that the book was dedicated to *me*, and not one word said of *him*." This is both a very black and a very false accusation; and yet I own I am neither sorry nor surprised to see it in print. Not sorry, because I can so fully confute it, that with all ingenuous readers it will turn to my applause;—not surprised, because I expected such usage from the spirit of Phalarism. I am morally sure that the very persons that printed this story knew how to give a good answer to it; for I heard of it by some common friends some time before it was printed, who, I question not, gave them an account how I justified myself; but, however, it seems they would not lay aside this calumny; for, as in war sometimes it is an useful stratagem to spread a false report, though it certainly must be dispersed in two or three days; so here it was thought a serviceable falsehood, if it could be credited for a few months. Besides that, it is the old rule to accuse strenuously, and something will stick; and it is almost the same thing with men's reputations as with their lives: he that is prodigal of his own, is master of another man's.

Dissertation upon the Epistles of Phalaris.

THE CHANGE OF LANGUAGE.

BUT, since tyrants will not be confined by laws, let us suppose, if you will, that our Phalaris might make use of the Attic, for no reason at all but his own arbitrary humour and pleasure; yet we have still another indictment against the credit of the Epistles; for even the Attic of the true Phalaris's age is not there represented; but a more recent idiom and style, that by the whole thread and colour of it betrays itself to be many centuries younger than he. Every living language, like the perspiring bodies of living creatures, is in perpetual motion and alteration; some words go off, and become obsolete; others are taken in, and by degrees grow into common use; or the same word is inverted to a new sense and notion, which in tract of time makes as observable a change in the air and features of a language, as age makes in the lines and mien of a face. All are sensible of this in their own native tongue, where continual use makes every man a critic; for what Englishman does not think himself able, from the very turn and fashion of the style, to distinguish a fresh English composition from another a hundred years old? Now there are as real and sensible differences in the several ages of Greek, were there as many that could discern them; but very few are so versed and practised in that language as ever to arrive at that subtilty of taste. And yet as few will be content to relish or dislike a thing, not by their own sense, but by another man's palate;—so that, should I affirm that I know the novity of these Epistles from the whole body and form of the work, none, perhaps, would be convinced by it, but those that, without my indication, could discover it by themselves.

Dissertation upon the Epistles of Phalaris.

P. 134, l. 23. Mr. B——, *Boyle.*
P. 135, ll. 29, 30. Tract of time, "*space or process of time.*" So still in "*protract,*" *but not in the simple noun.*
P. 136, l. 9. Novity. *It is rather a pity that this opposite to "antiquity" has been allowed to become obsolete; for it is a useful subdivision of "newness."*

JONATHAN SWIFT.

Jonathan Swift, an Englishman of Englishmen, was born at Dublin in 1667, and was educated at Trinity College. After being dependent on Temple, he obtained some small livings in Ireland, drifted into connection with the English Tories, was made Dean of St. Patrick's, and died in 1745. In most qualifications of the prose writer Swift has few equals and no superiors in English.

THE TRANSPORT OF GULLIVER TO THE CAPITAL.

THESE people are most excellent mathematicians, and arrived to a great perfection in mechanics, by the countenance and encouragement of the emperor, who is a renowned patron of learning. This prince has several machines fixed on wheels, for the carriage of trees and other great weights. He often builds his largest men-of-war, whereof some are nine feet long, in the woods where the timber grows, and has them carried on these engines three or four hundred yards to the sea. Five hundred carpenters and engineers were immediately set at work to prepare the greatest engine they had. It was a frame of wood raised three inches from the ground, about seven feet long, and four wide, moving upon twenty-two wheels. The shout I heard was upon the arrival of this engine, which, it seems, set out in four hours after my landing. It was brought parallel to me as I lay. But the principal difficulty was to raise and place me in this vehicle. Eighty poles, each of one foot high, were erected for this purpose, and very strong cords, of the bigness of pack-thread, were fastened by hooks to many bandages, which the workmen had girt round my neck, my hands, my body, and my legs. Nine hundred of the strongest men were employed to draw up these cords, by many pulleys fastened on the poles; and thus, in less than three hours, I was raised and slung into the engine, and there tied fast. All this I was told; for, while the whole operation was performing, I lay in a profound sleep, by the force of that soporiferous medicine infused into my liquor. Fifteen hundred of the emperor's largest horses, each about four inches and a half high, were employed to draw me towards the metropolis, which, as I said, was half a mile distant.

'About four hours after we began our journey, I awaked by a very ridiculous accident; for the carriage being stopped awhile, to adjust something that was out of order, two or three of the young natives had the curiosity to see how I looked when I was asleep; they climbed up into the engine, and advancing very softly to my face, one of them, an officer in the guards, put the sharp end of his half-pike a good way up into my left nostril, which tickled my nose like a straw, and made me sneeze violently; whereupon they stole off unperceived, and it was three weeks before I knew the cause of my waking so suddenly. We made a long march the remaining part of the day, and rested at night with five hundred guards on each side of me, half with torches, and half with bows and arrows, ready to shoot me if I should offer to stir. The next morning at sunrise we continued our march, and arrived within two hundred yards of the city gates about noon. The emperor, and all his court, came out to meet us, but his great officers would by no means suffer his majesty to endanger his person, by mounting on my body.

At the place where the carriage stopped there stood an ancient temple, esteemed to be the largest in the whole kingdom; which, having been polluted some years before by an unnatural murder, was, according to the zeal of those people, looked upon as profane, and therefore had been applied to common use, and all the ornaments and furniture carried away. In this edifice it was determined I should lodge. The great gate fronting to the north, was about four feet high, and almost two feet wide, through which I could easily creep. On each side of the gate was a small window, not above six inches from the ground: into that on the left side, the king's smith conveyed fourscore and eleven chains, like those that hang to a lady's watch in Europe, and almost as large, which were locked to my left leg with six-and-thirty padlocks. Over against this temple, on the other side of the great highway, at twenty feet distance, there was a turret at least five feet high. Here the emperor ascended, with many principal lords of his court, to have an opportunity of viewing me, as I was told, for I could not see them. It was reckoned that above a hundred thousand inhabitants came out of the town upon the same errand; and, in spite of my guards, I believe there could not be fewer than ten thousand at several times, who mounted my body by the help of ladders. But a proclamation was soon issued, to forbid it upon pain of death. When the workmen found it was impossible for me to break loose, they cut all the strings that bound me; whereupon I rose up, with as melancholy a disposition as ever I had in my life. But the noise and astonishment of the people, at seeing me rise and walk, are not to be expressed. The chains that held my left leg were about two yards long, and gave me not only liberty of walking backwards and forwards in a semicircle, but being fixed within four inches of the gate, allowed me to creep in, and lie at my full length in the temple.

A Voyage to Lilliput.

THE KING'S OPINIONS ON GUNPOWDER.

IN hopes to ingratiate myself farther into his majesty's favour, I told him of "an invention, discovered between three and four hundred years ago, to make a certain powder, into a heap of which, the smallest spark of fire falling, would kindle the whole in a moment, although it were as big as a mountain, and make it all fly up in the air together, with a noise and agitation greater than thunder. That a proper quantity of this powder, rammed into a hollow tube of brass or iron, according to its bigness, would drive a ball of iron or lead with such violence and speed, as nothing was able to sustain its force. That the largest balls, thus discharged, would not only destroy whole ranks of an army at once, but batter the strongest walls to the ground, sink down ships, with a thousand men in each, to the bottom of the sea; and when linked together by a chain, would cut through masts and rigging, divide hundreds of bodies in the middle, and lay all waste before them. That we often put this powder into large, hollow balls of iron, and discharged them by an engine into some city we were besieging, which would rip up the pavements, tear the houses to pieces, burst, and throw splinters on every side, dashing out the brains of all who came near. That I knew the ingredients very well, which were cheap and common; I understood the manner of compounding them, and could direct his workmen how to make those tubes, of a size proportionable to all other things in his majesty's kingdom, and the largest need not be above a hundred feet long; twenty or thirty of which tubes, charged with the proper quantity of powder and balls, would batter down the walls of the strongest town in his dominions in a few hours, or destroy the whole metropolis, if ever it should pretend to dispute his absolute commands. This I humbly offered to his majesty, as a small tribute of acknowledgment, in return of so many marks that I had received of his royal favour and protection."

The king was struck with horror at the description I had given of these terrible engines, and the proposal I had made. "He was amazed, how so impotent and grovelling an insect as I," (these were his expressions,) "could entertain such inhuman ideas, and in so familiar a manner, as to appear wholly unmoved at all the scenes of blood and desolation which I had painted, as the common effects of those destructive machines; whereof," he said, "some evil genius, enemy to mankind, must have been the first contriver." As for himself, he protested, that although few things delighted him so much as new discoveries in art or in nature, yet he would rather lose half his kingdom than be privy to such a secret; which he commanded me, as I valued my life, never to mention any more.

A strange effect of narrow principles and views! that a prince, possessed of every quality which procures veneration, love, and esteem; of strong parts, great wisdom, and profound learning, endued with admirable talents, and almost adored by his subjects, should, from a nice, unnecessary scruple, whereof in Europe we can have no conception, let slip an opportunity put into his hands, that would have made him absolute master of the lives, liberties, and the fortunes of his people! Neither do I say this with the least intention to detract from the many virtues of that excellent king, whose character, I am sensible, will, on this account, be very much lessened in the opinion of an English reader; but, I take this defect among them to have risen from their ignorance, by not having hitherto reduced politics into a science, as the more acute wits of Europe have done. For, I remember very well, in a discourse one day with the king, when I happened to say, "there were several thousand books among us written upon the art of government," it gave him (directly contrary to my intention) a very mean opinion of our understandings. He professed both to abominate and despise all mystery, refinement, and intrigue, either in a prince or in a minister. He could not tell what I meant by secrets of state, where an enemy, or some rival nation, were not in the case. He confined the knowledge of governing within very narrow bounds, to common sense and reason, to justice and lenity, to the speedy determination of civil and criminal causes; with some other obvious topics, which are not worth considering. And he gave it for his opinion "That whoever could make two ears of corn, or two blades of grass, to grow upon a spot of ground where only one grew before, would deserve better of mankind, and do more essential service to his country, than the whole race of politicians put together."

A Voyage to Brobdingnag.

CONCERNING MADNESS.

LET us next examine the great introducers of new schemes in philosophy, and search till we can find from what faculty of the soul the disposition arises in mortal man, of taking it into his head to advance new systems, with such an eager zeal, in things agreed on all hands impossible to be known: from what seeds this disposition springs, and to what quality of human nature

these grand innovators have been indebted for their number of
disciples. Because it is plain, that several of the chief among
them, both ancient and modern, were usually mistaken by their
adversaries, and indeed by all, except their own followers, to
have been persons crazed, or out of their wits; having generally
proceeded, in the common course of their words and actions,
by a method very different from the vulgar dictates of unrefined
reason; agreeing for the most part in their several models, with
their present undoubted successors in the academy of modern
Bedlam; whose merits and principles I shall farther examine in
due place. Of this kind were Epicurus, Diogenes, Apollonius,
Lucretius, Paracelsus, Des Cartes, and others; who, if they were
now in the world, tied fast, and separate from their followers,
would, in this our undistinguishing age, incur manifest danger
of phlebotomy, and whips, and chains, and dark chambers,
and straw. For what man, in the natural state or course of
thinking, did ever conceive it in his power to reduce the notions
of all mankind exactly to the same length, and breadth, and
height of his own? yet this is the first humble and civil design
of all innovators in the empire of reason. Epicurus modestly
hoped, that, one time or other, a certain fortuitous concourse of
all men's opinions, after perpetual justlings, the sharp with the
smooth, the light and the heavy, the round and the square,
would, by certain clinamina, unite in the notions of atoms and
void, as these did in the originals of all things. Cartesius
reckoned to see, before he died, the sentiments of all philosophers,
like so many lesser stars in his romantic system, wrapped and
drawn within his own vortex. Now, I would gladly be informed,
how it is possible to account for such imaginations as these in
particular men, without recourse to my phenomenon of vapours,
ascending from the lower faculties to overshadow the brain, and
there distilling into conceptions, for which the narrowness of
our mother-tongue has not yet assigned any other name beside
that of madness or phrensy. Let us therefore now conjecture
how it comes to pass, that none of these great prescribers
do ever fail providing themselves and their notions with a
number of implicit disciples. And, I think, the reason is easy
to be assigned: for there is a peculiar string in the harmony of

human understanding, which, in several individuals, is exactly of the same tuning. This, if you can dexterously screw up to its right key, and then strike gently upon it, whenever you have the good fortune to light among those of the same pitch, they will, by a secret necessary sympathy, strike exactly at the same time. And in this one circumstance lies all the skill or luck of the matter; for, if you chance to jar the string among those who are either above or below your own height, instead of subscribing to your doctrine, they will tie you fast, call you mad, and feed you with bread and water. It is therefore a point of the nicest conduct, to distinguish and adapt this noble talent, with respect to the differences of persons and times. Cicero understood this very well, when writing to a friend in England, with a caution, among other matters, to beware of being cheated by our hackney-coachmen, (who it seems, in those days were as arrant rascals as they are now,) has these remarkable words: *Est quod gaudeas te in ista loca venisse, ubi aliquid sapere viderere.* For, to speak a bold truth, it is a fatal miscarriage so ill to order affairs, as to pass for a fool in one company, when, in another, you might be treated as a philosopher. Which I desire some certain gentlemen of my acquaintance to lay up in their hearts, as a very seasonable *innuendo.*

A Tale of a Tub.

P. 137, l. 2. Arrived. *Participle, not verb. "Is arrived" is now thought a Gallicism, perhaps not justly.*

P. 141, l. 8. Them, *the Brobdingnagians, though nobody but the king has been the subject of discourse.*

P. 142, l. 24. Clinamina. *The Epicurean postulate of a slight declension from the perpendicular in the rain of atoms through space, which brings them together.*

P. 142, l. 36. Fail providing. *This, like "agreed impossible," is characteristic of Swift's elliptic shortenings of phrase.*

P. 143, l. 12. Cicero. *The actual quotation is from Ep. ad Fam.* vii. 10. *The reader will hardly need to be told that there is nothing about hackney coachmen in the original. The series of letters to Trebatius is, however, full of "chaff," and in a previous epistle* (7) *Cicero suggests that if his friend finds that there is nothing to be made in Britain, he shall take an* essedum (*the war chariots which Cæsar's expedition had made famous*) *and come back.*

SIR RICHARD STEELE.

Richard Steele was born at Dublin in 1671 (?) He entered Merton College, Oxford, but went into the army. In 1709 he founded with the Tatler an unrivalled series of periodicals. Despite many gifts of fortune, he was always in difficulties till his death, near Carmarthen, in 1729. He ranks first among English humourists for geniality without boisterousness, and sentiment without gush.

SARCASMS ON MARRIAGE.

WHEN I consider the false impressions which are received by the generality of the world, I am troubled at none more than a certain levity of thought, which many young women of quality have entertained, to the hazard of their characters, and the certain misfortune of their lives. The first of the following letters may best represent the faults I would now point at, and the answer to it, the temper of mind in a contrary character.

"My dear Harriot,

"If thou art she, but oh! how fallen, how changed, what an apostate! how lost to all that is gay and agreeable! To be married I find is to be buried alive; I cannot conceive it more dismal to be shut up in a vault to converse with the shades of my ancestors, than to be carried down to an old manor-house in the country, and confined to the conversation of a sober husband, and an awkward chambermaid. For variety I suppose you may entertain yourself with madam in her grogram gown, the spouse of your parish vicar, who has by this time, I am sure, well furnished you with receipts for making salves and possets, distilling cordial waters, making syrups, and applying poultices.

"Blest solitude! I wish thee joy, my dear, of thy loved retirement, which indeed you would persuade me is very agreeable, and different enough from what I have here described: but, child, I am afraid thy brains are a little disordered with romances and novels. After six months' marriage to hear thee talk of love, and paint the country scenes so softly, is a little extravagant; one would think you lived the lives of sylvan deities, or roved among the walks of Paradise, like the first happy pair. But pray thee leave these whimsies, and come to town in order to live, and talk like other mortals. However, as I am extremely interested in your reputation, I would willingly give you a little good advice at your first appearance under the character of a married woman. It is a little insolent in me, perhaps, to advise a matron; but I am so afraid you will make so silly a figure as a fond wife, that I cannot help warning you not to appear in any public places with your husband, and never to saunter about St. James's Park together: if you presume to enter the ring at Hyde Park together, you are ruined for ever; nor must you take the least notice of one another at the playhouse, or opera, unless you would be laughed at for a very loving couple, most happily paired in the yoke of wedlock. I would recommend the example of an acquaintance of ours to your imitation; she is the most negligent and fashionable wife in the world; she is hardly ever seen in the same place with her husband, and if they happen to meet, you would think them perfect strangers; she never was heard to name him in his absence, and takes care he shall never be the subject of any discourse that she has a share in. I hope you will propose this lady as a pattern, though I am very much afraid you will be so silly to think Portia, etc., Sabine and Roman wives, much brighter examples. I wish it may never come into your head to imitate these antiquated creatures so far as to come into public in the habit, as well as air, of a Roman matron. You make already the entertainment at Mrs. Modish's tea-table: she says, she always thought you a discreet person, and qualified to manage a family with admirable prudence; she dies to see what demure and serious airs wedlock has given you; but she says, she shall never forgive your choice of so gallant a man as Bellamour to transform him into a mere sober husband; it was unpardonable. You see, my dear, we all envy your happiness, and no person more than

"Your humble servant,
"LYDIA."

"Be not in pain, good madam, for my appearance in town; I shall frequent no public places, or make any visits where the character of a modest wife is ridiculous. As for your wild raillery on matrimony, it is all hypocrisy; you, and all the handsome young women of your acquaintance, show yourselves to no other purpose, than to gain a conquest over some man of worth, in order to bestow your charms and fortune on him. There is no indecency in the confession, the design is modest and honourable, and all your affectation can't disguise it.

"I am married, and have no other concern but to please the man I love; he is the end of every care I have; if I dress, it is for him; if I read a poem, or a play, it is to qualify myself for a conversation agreeable to his taste: he is almost the end of my devotions; half my prayers are for his happiness. I love to talk of him, and never hear him named but with pleasure and emotion. I am your friend, and wish you happiness, but am sorry to see, by the air of your letter, that there are a set of women who are got into the common-place raillery of everything that is sober, decent, and proper: matrimony and the clergy are the topics of people of little wit, and no understanding. I own to you, I have learned of the vicar's wife all you tax me with. She is a discreet, ingenious, pleasant, pious, woman; I wish she had the handling of you and Mrs. Modish; you would find, if you were too free with her, she would soon make you as charming as ever you were; she would make you blush as much as if you never had been fine ladies. The vicar, madam, is so kind as to visit my husband, and his agreeable conversation has brought him to enjoy many sober happy hours when even I am shut out, and my dear master is entertained only with his own thoughts. These things, dear madam, will be lasting satisfactions, when the fine ladies, and the coxcombs, by whom they form themselves, are irreparably ridiculous, ridiculous in old age.

"I am, madam,
"Your most humble servant,
"MARY HOME."

"Dear Mr. Spectator,
"You have no goodness in the world, and are not in earnest in anything you say that is serious, if you do not send me a plain answer to this. I happened some days past to be at the play, where, during the time of performance, I could not keep my eyes off from a beautiful young creature who sat just before me, and who, I have been since informed, has no fortune. It would utterly ruin my reputation for discretion to marry such a one, and by what I can learn she has a character of great modesty, so that there is nothing to be thought on any other way. My mind has ever since been so wholly bent on her, that I am much in danger of doing something very extravagant, without your speedy advice to,
"Sir,
"Your most humble servant."

I am sorry I cannot answer this impatient gentleman, but by another question.

"Dear Correspondent,
"Would you marry to please other people, or yourself?"
Spectator.

P. 144, l. 9. Harriot. *This form, now rarely used, is not only the oldest but perhaps the most correct.*

P. 145, ll. 3, 4. Thee .... you. *This ugly variation, which all careful writers denounce, and which Johnson (I think) somewhere calls "disgusting," is but too common. Below (l. 9) the you is of course justified as applying to both husband and wife.*

JOSEPH ADDISON.

Joseph Addison was born near Amesbury in 1672, obtained much reputation at Oxford, was pensioned in 1699, travelled abroad, and after the Battle of Blenheim was patronized by the Whigs. He was Secretary of State in 1717, and died at Holland House in 1719. Destitute of the strength of Swift and the softness of Steele, Addison outwent both these his friends in even finish of style.

ON ASKING ADVICE ON AFFAIRS OF LOVE.

IT is an old observation, which has been made of politicians who would rather ingratiate themselves with their sovereign, than promote his real service, that they accommodate their counsels to his inclinations, and advise him to such actions only as his heart is naturally set upon. The privy councillor of one in love must observe the same conduct, unless he would forfeit the friendship of the person who desires his advice. I have known several odd cases of this nature. Hipparchus was going to marry a common woman, but being resolved to do nothing without the advice of his friend Philander, he consulted him upon the occasion. Philander told him his mind freely, and represented his mistress to him in such strong colours, that the next morning he received a challenge for his pains, and before twelve o'clock was run through the body by the man who had asked his advice. Celia was more prudent on the like occasion. She desired Leonilla to give her opinion freely upon the young fellow who made his addresses to her. Leonilla, to oblige her, told her with great frankness, that she looked upon him as one of the most worthless—— Celia, foreseeing what a character she was to expect, begged her not to go on, for that she had been privately married to him above a fortnight. The truth of it is, a woman seldom asks advice before she has bought her wedding clothes. When she has made her own choice, for form's sake, she sends a *congé d'élire* to her friends.

If we look into the secret springs and motives that set people at work on these occasions, and put them upon asking advice which they never intend to take; I look upon it to be none of the least, that they are incapable of keeping a secret which is so very pleasing to them. A girl longs to tell her confidante, that she hopes to be married in a little time: and, in order to talk of the pretty fellow that dwells so much in her thoughts, asks her very gravely, what she would advise her to in a case of so much difficulty. Why else should Melissa, who had not a thousand pounds in the world, go into every quarter of the town to ask her acquaintance, whether they would advise her to take Tom Townly, that made his addresses to her with an estate of five thousand a year? It is very pleasant, on this occasion, to hear the lady propose her doubts; and to see the pains she is at to get over them.

I must not here omit a practice that is in use among the vainer part of our own sex, who will often ask a friend's advice in relation to a fortune whom they are never like to come at. Will Honeycomb, who is now on the verge of threescore, took me aside not long since, and asked me, in his most serious look, whether I would advise him to marry my lady Betty Single, who, by the way, is one of the greatest fortunes about town. I stared him full in the face, upon so strange a question; upon which he immediately gave me an inventory of her jewels and estate, adding that he was resolved to do nothing in a matter of such consequence without my approbation. Finding he would have an answer, I told him if he could get the lady's consent, he had mine. This is about the tenth match which, to my knowledge, Will has consulted his friends upon, without ever opening his mind to the party herself.

I have been engaged in this subject by the following letter, which comes to me from some notable young female scribe, who, by the contents of it, seems to have carried matters so far, that she is ripe for asking advice; but as I would not lose her good will, nor forfeit the reputation which I have with her for wisdom, I shall only communicate the letter to the public, without returning any answer to it.

"Mr. Spectator,

"Now, sir, the thing is this; Mr. Shapely is the prettiest gentleman about town. He is very tall, but not too tall neither. He dances like an angel. His mouth is made I do not know how, but it is the prettiest that I ever saw in my life. He is always laughing, for he has an infinite deal of wit. If you did but see how he rolls his stockings! He has a thousand pretty fancies, and I am sure, if you saw him, you would like him. He is a very good scholar, and can talk Latin as fast as English. I wish you could but see him dance. Now you must understand poor Mr. Shapely has no estate; but how can he help that, you know? and yet my friends are so unreasonable as to be always teasing me about him, because he has no estate; but I am sure he has that that is better than an estate; for he is a good-natured, ingenious, modest, civil, tall, well-bred, handsome, man; and I am obliged to him for his civilities ever since I saw him. I forgot to tell you that he has black eyes, and looks upon me now and then as if he had tears in them. And yet my friends are so unreasonable, that they would have me be uncivil to him. I have a good portion which they cannot hinder me of, and I shall be fourteen on the 29th day of August next, and am therefore willing to settle in the world as soon as I can, and so is Mr. Shapely. But everybody I advise with here is poor Mr. Shapely's enemy. I desire, therefore, you will give me your advice, for I know you are a wise man; and if you advise me well, I am resolved to follow it. I heartily wish you could see him dance; and am,

"Sir,
"Your most humble servant,
"B. D.

"He loves your Spectators mightily."

Spectator.

LITERARY TASTE.

AFTER having thus far explained what is generally meant by a fine taste in writing, and shown the propriety of the metaphor which is used on this occasion, I think I may define it to be "that faculty of the soul, which discerns the beauties of an author with pleasure, and the imperfections with dislike." If a man would know whether he is possessed of this faculty, I would have him read over the celebrated works of antiquity, which have stood the test of so many different ages and countries, or those works among the moderns which have the sanction of the politer part of our contemporaries. If, upon the perusal of such writings he does not find himself delighted in an extraordinary manner, or if, upon reading the admired passages in such authors, he finds a coldness and indifference in his thoughts, he ought to conclude, not, as is too usual amongst tasteless readers, that the author wants those perfections which have been admired in him, but that he himself wants the faculty of discovering them.

He should, in the second place, be very careful to observe, whether he tastes the distinguishing perfections, or, if I may be allowed to call them so, the specific qualities of the author whom he peruses; whether he is particularly pleased with Livy for his manner of telling a story, with Sallust for his entering into those internal principles of action which arise from the characters and manners of the persons he describes, or with Tacitus for his displaying those outward motives of safety and interest which give birth to the whole series of transactions which he relates.

He may likewise consider, how differently he is affected by the same thought which presents itself in a great writer, from what he is when he finds it delivered by a person of an ordinary genius; for there is as much difference in apprehending a thought clothed in Cicero's language, and that of a common author, as in seeing an object by the light of a taper, or by the light of the sun.

It is very difficult to lay down rules for the acquirement of such a taste as that I am here speaking of. The faculty must in some degree be born with us; and it very often happens, that those who have other qualities in perfection are wholly void of this. One of the most eminent mathematicians of the age has assured me, that the greatest pleasure he took in reading Virgil was in examining Æneas his voyage by the map; as I question not but many a modern compiler of history would be delighted with little more in that divine author than the bare matters of fact.

But, notwithstanding this faculty must in some measure be born with us, there are several methods for cultivating and improving it, and without which it will be very uncertain, and of little use to the person that possesses it. The most natural method for this purpose is to be conversant among the writings of the most polite authors. A man who has any relish for fine writing, either discovers new beauties, or receives stronger impressions, from the masterly strokes of a great author every time he peruses him; besides that he naturally wears himself into the same manner of speaking and thinking.

Spectator.

P. 150, l. 6. *This letter is one of the most perfect examples of Addisonian humour, polished, demure, and a little cruel.*

HENRY ST. JOHN, VISCOUNT BOLINGBROKE.

Henry St. John, Viscount Bolingbroke, was born at Battersea in 1678. He rose early to eminence, and for a few days at the end of Queen Anne's reign held, but failed to use, supreme power. He fled the country, was attainted, but returned in 1724. As an orator Bolingbroke was ranked very high, but his speeches are lost. His written style is exemplary. He died in 1751.

REMEDIES FOR AFFLICTION.

DISSIPATION of mind, and length of time, are the remedies to which the greatest part of mankind trust in their afflictions. But the first of these works a temporary, the second a slow, effect: and both are unworthy of a wise man. Are we to fly from ourselves that we may fly from our misfortunes, and fondly to imagine that the disease is cured because we find means to get some moments of respite from pain? Or shall we expect from time, the physician of brutes, a lingering and uncertain deliverance? shall we wait to be happy till we can forget that we are miserable, and owe to the weakness of our faculties a tranquillity which ought to be the effect of their strength? Far otherwise. Let us set all our past and present afflictions at once before our eyes. Let us resolve to overcome them, instead of flying from them, or wearing out the sense of them by long and ignominious patience. Instead of palliating remedies, let us use the incision-knife and the caustic, search the wound to the bottom, and work an immediate and radical cure. The recalling of former misfortunes serves to fortify the mind against later. He must blush to sink under the anguish of one wound, who surveys a body seamed over with the scars of many, and who has come victorious out of all the conflicts wherein he received them. Let sighs, and tears, and fainting under the lightest strokes of adverse fortune, be the portion of those unhappy people whose tender minds a long course of felicity has enervated : while such, as have passed through years of calamity, bear up, with a noble and immoveable constancy, against the heaviest. Uninterrupted misery has this good effect, as it continually torments, it finally hardens.

Such is the language of philosophy: and happy is the man who acquires the right of holding it. But this right is not to be acquired by pathetic discourse. Our conduct can alone give it us: and therefore, instead of presuming on our strength, the surest method is to confess our weakness, and, without loss of time, to apply ourselves to the study of wisdom. This was the advice which the oracle gave to Zeno, and there is no other way of securing our tranquillity amidst all the accidents to which human life is exposed. Philosophy has, I know, her Thrasos, as well as War : and among her sons many there have been, who, while they aimed at being more than men, became something less. The means of preventing this danger are easy and sure. It is a good rule, to examine well before we addict ourselves to any sect: but I think it is a better rule, to addict ourselves to none. Let us hear them all, with a perfect indifferency on which side the truth lies : and, when we come to determine, let nothing appear so venerable to us as our own understandings. Let us gratefully accept the help of everyone who has endeavoured to correct the vices, and strengthen the minds of men ; but let us choose for ourselves, and yield universal assent to none. Thus, that I may instance the sect already mentioned, when we have laid aside the wonderful and surprising sentences, and all the paradoxes of the Portique, we shall find in that school such doctrines as our unprejudiced reason submits to with pleasure, as nature dictates, and as experience confirms. Without this precaution, we run the risk of becoming imaginary kings, and real slaves. With it, we may learn to assert our native freedom, and live independent on fortune.

In order to which great end, it is necessary that we stand watchful, as sentinels, to discover the secret wiles and open attacks of this capricious goddess, before they reach us. Where she falls upon us unexpected it is hard to resist: but those who wait for her, will repel her with ease. The sudden invasion of an enemy overthrows such as are not on their guard; but they who foresee the war, and prepare themselves for it before it breaks out, stand, without difficulty, the first and the fiercest onset. I learned this important lesson long ago, and never trusted to fortune even while she seemed to be at peace with me. The riches, the honours, the reputation, and all the advantages which her treacherous indulgence poured upon me, I placed so, that she might snatch them away without giving me any disturbance. I kept a great interval between me and them. She took them, but she could not tear them from me. No man suffers by bad fortune, but he who has been deceived by good. If we grow fond of her gifts, fancy that they belong to us, and are perpetually to remain with us, if we lean upon them, and expect to be considered for them; we shall sink into all the bitterness of grief, as soon as these false and transitory benefits pass away, as soon as our vain and childish minds, unfraught with solid pleasures, become destitute even of those which are imaginary. But, if we do not suffer ourselves to be transported by prosperity, neither shall we be reduced by adversity. Our souls will be of proof against the dangers of both these states: and having explored our strength, we shall be sure of it; for in the midst of felicity, we shall have tried how we can bear misfortune.

Reflections upon Exile.

P. 154, L 24. Indifferency. *Here used in the sense of "impartiality" or "freedom from bias," not "lack of interest."*

CONYERS MIDDLETON.

Conyers Middleton, a Rationalist theologian, a biographer of Cicero, and one of the chief opponents of Bentley at Trinity College, was born at Richmond (Yorkshire) in 1683, and died in 1750 at Hildersham. His honesty has been perhaps justly attacked; the general merit and accomplishment of his style is, despite De Quincey's attempt to depreciate it, undeniable.

CICERO CONSUL.

CICERO was now arrived through the usual gradation of honours, at the highest which the people could regularly give, or an honest citizen desire. The offices which he had already borne had but a partial jurisdiction, confined to particular branches of the government; but the consuls held the reins, and directed the whole machine with an authority as extensive as the empire itself. The subordinate magistracies, therefore, being the steps only to this sovereign dignity, were not valued so much for their own sake, as for bringing the candidates still nearer to the principal objects of their hopes, who, through this course of their ambition, were forced to practise all the arts of popularity: to court the little as well as the great, to espouse the principles and politics in vogue, and to apply their talents to conciliate friends, rather than to serve the public. But the consulship put an end to this subjection, and with the command of the state gave them the command of themselves: so that the only care left was, how to execute this high office with credit and dignity, and employ the power entrusted to them for the benefit and service of their country.

We are now therefore to look upon Cicero in a different light, in order to form a just idea of his character: to consider him, not as an ambitious courtier, applying all his thoughts and pains to his own advancement; but as a great magistrate and statesman, administering the affairs and directing the councils of a mighty empire. And, according to the accounts of all the ancient writers, Rome never stood in greater need of the skill and vigilance of an able consul than in this very year. For besides the traitorous cabals and conspiracies of those who were attempting to subvert the whole Republic, the new tribunes were also labouring to disturb the present quiet of it: some of them were publishing laws to abolish everything that remained of Sylla's establishment, and to restore the sons of the proscribed to their estates and honours; others to reverse the punishment of P. Sylla and Autronius, condemned for bribery, and replace them in the senate: some were for expunging all debts, and others for dividing the lands of the public to the poorer citizens: so that, as Cicero declared, both to the senate and the people, the Republic was delivered into his hands full of terrors and alarms; distracted by pestilent laws and seditious haranguers; endangered, not by foreign wars, but intestine evils, and the traitorous designs of profligate citizens; and that there was no mischief incident to a state which the honest had not cause to apprehend, the wicked to expect.

What gave the greater spirit to the authors of these attempts, was Antonius's advancement to the consulship: they knew him to be of the same principles, and embarked in the same designs with themselves, which, by his authority, they now hoped to carry into effect. Cicero was aware of this; and foresaw the mischief of a colleague equal to him in power, yet opposite in views, and prepared to frustrate all his endeavours for the public service; so that his first care, after their election, was to gain the confidence of Antonius, and to draw him from his old engagements to the interests of the Republic; being convinced that all the success of his administration depended upon it. He began therefore to tempt him by a kind of argument, which seldom fails of its effect with men of his character, the offer of power to his ambition, and of money to his pleasures: with these baits he caught him; and a bargain was presently agreed upon between them, that Antonius should have the choice of the best province, which was to be assigned to them at the expiration of their year. It was the custom for the senate to appoint what particular provinces were to be distributed every year to the several magistrates, who used afterward to cast lots for them among themselves; the prætors for the prætorian, the consuls for the consular provinces. In this partition, therefore, when Macedonia, one of the most desirable governments of the empire, both for command and wealth, fell to Cicero's lot, he exchanged it immediately with his colleague for Cisalpine Gaul, which he resigned also soon after in favour of Q. Metellus'; being resolved, as he declared in his inauguration speech, to administer the consulship in such a manner, as to put it out of any man's power either to tempt or terrify him from his duty; since he neither sought, nor would accept, any province, honour, or benefit from it whatsoever: "The only way," says he, "by which a man can discharge it with gravity and freedom, so as to chastise those tribunes who wish ill to the Republic, or despise those who wish ill to himself:" a noble declaration, and worthy to be transmitted to posterity, for an example to all magistrates in a free state. By this address he entirely drew Antonius into his measures, and had him ever after obsequious to his will; or, as he himself expresses it, by his patience and complaisance he softened and calmed him, eagerly desirous of a province, and projecting many things against the state. The establishment of this concord between them, was thought to be of such importance to the public quiet, that, in his first speech to the people, he declared it to them from the rostra, as an event the most likely to curb the insolence of the factious, and raise the spirits of the honest, and prevent the dangers with which the city was then threatened.

The Life of Cicero.

P. 157, l. 28. Which *is a blemish; for in strict English "with themselves" exhausts the antecedent "the same," and does not allow "which" to refer to it.*

GEORGE BERKELEY.

George Berkeley, the greatest master of English philosophical style and perhaps the greatest of English metaphysicians, was born "in the county of Kilkenny" in 1684. Educated at Trinity College, Dublin, he became chaplain to Peterborough, sojourned in America as a missionary and teacher, was made Bishop of Cloyne, and died at Oxford in 1753.

MATTER.

BUT let us examine a little the received opinion.—It is said extension is a mode or accident of Matter, and that Matter is the *substratum* that supports it. Now I desire that you would explain to me what is meant by Matter's *supporting* extension. Say you, I have no idea of Matter and therefore cannot explain it. I answer, though you have no positive, yet, if you have any meaning at all, you must at least have a relative idea of Matter; though you know not what it is, yet you must be supposed to know what relation it bears to accidents, and what is meant by its supporting them. It is evident "support" cannot here be taken in its usual or literal sense—as when we say that pillars support a building; in what sense therefore must it be taken?

If we inquire into what the most accurate philosophers declare themselves to mean by *material substance*, we shall find them acknowledge they have no other meaning annexed to those sounds but the idea of Being in general, together with the relative notion of its supporting accidents. The general idea of Being appeareth to me the most abstract and incomprehensible of all other; and as for its supporting accidents, this, as we have just now observed, cannot be understood in the common sense of those words; it must therefore be taken in some other sense, but what that is they do not explain. So that when I consider the two parts or branches which make the signification of the words *material substance*, I am convinced there is no distinct meaning annexed to them. But why should we trouble ourselves any farther, in discussing this material *substratum* or support of figure and motion, and other sensible qualities? Does it not suppose they have an existence without the mind? and is not this a direct repugnancy, and altogether inconceivable?

But, though it were possible that solid, figured, moveable substances may exist without the mind, corresponding to the ideas we have of bodies, yet how is it possible for us to know this? Either we must know it by sense or by reason. As for our senses, by them we have the knowledge only of our sensations, ideas, or those things that are immediately perceived by senses call them what you will: but they do not inform us that things exist without the mind, or unperceived, like to those which are perceived. This the materialists themselves acknowledge.—It remains therefore that if we have any knowledge at all of external things, it must be by reason, inferring their existence from what is immediately perceived by sense. But what reason can induce us to believe the existence of bodies without the mind, from what we perceive, since the very patrons of Matter themselves do not pretend there is any necessary connexion betwixt them and our ideas? I say it is granted on all hands, and what happens in dreams, frensies, and the like, puts it beyond dispute, that it is possible we might be affected with all the ideas we have now, though there were no bodies existing without resembling them. Hence, it is evident the supposition of external bodies is not necessary for the producing our ideas; since it is granted they are produced sometimes, and might possibly be produced always in the same order we see them in at present, without their concurrence.

But, though we might possibly have all our sensations without them, yet perhaps it may be thought easier to conceive and explain the manner of their production, by supposing external bodies in their likeness rather than otherwise; and so it might be at least probable there are such things as bodies that excite their ideas in our minds. But neither can this be said; for, though we give the materialists their external bodies, they by their own confession are never the nearer knowing how our ideas are produced; since they own themselves unable to comprehend in what manner body can act upon spirit, or how it is possible it should imprint any idea in the mind. Hence it is evident the production of ideas or sensations in our minds, can be no reason why we should suppose Matter or corporeal substances, since that is acknowledged to remain equally inexplicable with or without this supposition. If therefore it were possible for bodies to exist without the mind, yet to hold they do so, must needs be a very precarious opinion; since it is to suppose, without any reason at all, that God has created innumerable beings that are entirely useless, and serve to no manner of purpose.

In short, if there were external bodies, it is impossible we should ever come to know it; and if there were not, we might have the very same reasons to think these were that we have now. Suppose—what no one can deny possible—an intelligence without the help of external bodies, to be affected with the same train of sensations or ideas that you are, imprinted in the same order and with like vividness in his mind. I ask whether that intelligence hath not all the reason to believe the existence of corporeal substances, represented by his ideas, and exciting them in his mind, that you can possibly have for believing the same thing? Of this there can be no question—which one consideration were enough to make any reasonable person suspect the strength of whatever arguments he may think himself to have, for the existence of bodies without the mind.

Of the Principles of Human Knowledge.

LYSICLES ON AGNOSTICISM.

Lys. You must know then that at bottom the being of a God is a point in itself of small consequence, and a man may make this concession without yielding much. The great point is what sense the word *God* is to be taken in. The very Epicureans allowed the being of gods; but then they were indolent gods, unconcerned with human affairs. Hobbes allowed a corporeal God: and Spinosa held the universe to be God. And yet nobody doubts they were staunch free-thinkers. I could wish indeed the word God were quite omitted; because in most minds it is coupled with a sort of superstitious awe, the very root of all religion. I shall not, nevertheless, be much disturbed, though the name be retained, and the being of a God allowed in any sense but in that of a Mind—which knows all things, and beholds human actions, like some judge or magistrate, with infinite observation and intelligence. The belief of a God in this sense fills a man's mind with scruples, lays him under constraints, and embitters his very being: but in another sense it may be attended with no great ill consequence. This I know was the opinion of our great Diagoras, who told me he would never have been at the pains to find out a demonstration that there was no God, if the received notion of God had been the same with that of some Fathers and Schoolmen.

Euph. Pray what was that?

Lys. You must know, Diagoras, a man of much reading and inquiry, had discovered that once upon a time the most profound and speculative divines, finding it impossible to reconcile the attributes of God, taken in the common sense, or in any known sense, with human reason, and the appearances of things, taught that the words *knowledge, wisdom, goodness,* and such like, when spoken of the Deity, must be understood in a quite different sense from what they signify in the vulgar acceptation, or from anything that we can form a notion of or conceive. Hence, whatever objections might be made against the attributes of God they easily solved—by denying those attributes belonged to God, in this, or that, or any known particular sense or notion; which was the same thing as to deny they belonged to him at all. And thus denying the attributes of God, they in effect denied his being, though perhaps they were not aware of it.

Suppose, for instance, a man should object that future contingencies were inconsistent with the Foreknowledge of God, because it is repugnant that certain knowledge should be of an uncertain thing: it was a ready and an easy answer to say that this may be true with respect to knowledge taken in the common sense, or in any sense that we can possibly form any notion of; but that there would not appear the same inconsistency between the contingent nature of things and Divine Foreknowledge, taken to signify somewhat that we know nothing of, which in God supplies the place of what we understand by knowledge, from which it differs not in quantity or degree of perfection, but altogether, and in kind, as light doth from sound;—and even more, since these agree in that they are both sensations; whereas knowledge in God hath no sort of resemblance or agreement with any notion that man can frame of knowledge. The like may be said of all the other attributes, which indeed may by this means be equally reconciled with everything or with nothing. But all men who think must needs see this is cutting knots and not untying them. For, how are things reconciled with the Divine attributes when these attributes themselves are in every intelligible sense denied; and, consequently, the very notion of God taken away, and nothing left but the name, without any meaning annexed to it? In short, the belief that there is an unknown subject of attributes absolutely unknown is a very innocent doctrine; which the acute Diagoras well saw, and was therefore wonderfully delighted with this system.

For, said he, if this could once make its way and obtain in the world, there would be an end of all natural or rational religion, which is the basis both of the Jewish and the Christian: for he who comes to God, or enters himself in the church of God, must first believe that there is a God in some intelligible sense; and not only that there is *something in general*, without any proper notion, though never so inadequate, of any of its qualities or attributes: for this may be fate, or chaos, or plastic nature, or anything else as well as God. Nor will it avail to say—There is something in this unknown being *analogous* to knowledge and goodness; that is to say, which produceth those effects which we could not conceive to be produced by men, in any degree, without knowledge and goodness. For, this is in fact to give up the point in dispute between theists and atheists —the question having always been, not whether there was a

Principle, which point was allowed by all philosophers, as well before as since Anaxagoras, but whether this Principle was a νοῦς, a thinking intelligent being; that is to say, whether that order, and beauty, and use, visible in natural effects, could be produced by anything but a Mind or Intelligence, in the proper sense of the word? And whether there must not be true, real, and proper knowledge, in the First Cause? We will, therefore, acknowledge that all those natural effects which are vulgarly ascribed to knowledge and wisdom proceed from a being in which there is, properly speaking, no knowledge or wisdom at all, but only something else, which in reality is the cause of those things which men, for want of knowing better, ascribe to what they call knowledge and wisdom and understanding. You wonder perhaps to hear a man of pleasure, who diverts himself as I do, philosophize at this rate. But you should consider that much is to be got by conversing with ingenious men, which is a short way to knowledge, that saves a man the drudgery of reading and thinking.

And, now we have granted to you that there is a God in this indefinite sense, I would fain see what use you can make of this concession. You cannot argue from unknown attributes, or, which is the same thing, from attributes in an unknown sense. You cannot prove that God is to be loved for his goodness, or feared for his justice, or respected for his knowledge: all which consequences, we own, would follow from those attributes admitted in an intelligible sense. But we deny that those or any other consequences can be drawn from attributes admitted in no particular sense, or in a sense which none of us understand. Since, therefore, nothing can be inferred from such an account of God, about conscience, or worship, or religion, you may even make the best of it. And, not to be singular, we will use the name too, and so at once there is an end of atheism.

Euph. This account of a Deity is new to me. I do not like it, and therefore shall leave it to be maintained by those who do.

Cri. It is not new to me. I remember not long since to have heard a minute philosopher triumph upon this very point; which put me on inquiring what foundation there was for it in the Fathers or Schoolmen. And, for aught that I can find, it owes its original to those writings which have been published under the name of Dionysius the Areopagite. The author of which, it must be owned, hath written upon the Divine attributes in a very singular style.

Alciphron, or the Minute Philosopher.

P. 160, l. 20. Repugnancy, *contradiction.*
P. 161, l. 13. Precarious. *"Arbitrary" would now be more commonly used in this sense.*
P. 162, l. 16. *It has sometimes been thought that Diagoras (the name of a well-known Greek atheist) is used by Berkeley to denote some special contemporary free-thinker. This, however, is improbable and unnecessary. The opinion which he "discovered" appears earliest in the* Pseudo-Dionysius *(prob. fifth century). It is there urged on the orthodox side. The two most notable followers in the same line (though in each case with important and independent modifications) have been William of Occam and the late Dean Mansel.*

ALEXANDER POPE.

Alexander Pope was born in London in 1688, and died at Twickenham in 1744. His life was, except from the point of view of literary production and literary quarrels, wholly uneventful; his character, literary and moral, has never ceased to be the subject of debate; his style in prose, as in poetry, is a triumph of elegant artifice.

A RECEIPT TO MAKE AN EPIC POEM.

FOR THE FABLE.

"TAKE out of any old poem, history books, romance, or legend, for instance Geoffrey of Monmouth, or Don Belianis of Greece, those parts of story which afford most scope for long descriptions. Put these pieces together, and throw all the adventures you fancy into one tale. Then take a hero whom you may choose for the sound of his name, and put him into the midst of these adventures. There let him work, for twelve books; at the end of which you may take him out ready prepared to conquer, or to marry; it being necessary that the conclusion of an epic poem be fortunate."

To make an episode.—"Take any remaining adventure of your former collection, in which you could no way involve your hero; or any unfortunate accident that was too good to be thrown away; and it will be of use, applied to any other person, who may be lost and evaporate in the course of the work, without the least damage to the composition."

For the moral and allegory.—"These you may extract out of the fable afterwards at your leisure. Be sure you strain them sufficiently."

FOR THE MANNERS.

"For those of the hero, take all the best qualities you can find in all the celebrated heroes of antiquity; if they will not be reduced to a consistency, lay them all on a heap upon him. But be sure they are qualities which your patron would be thought to have; and to prevent any mistake which the world may be subject to, select from the alphabet those capital letters that compose his name, and set them at the head of a dedication before your poem. However, do not absolutely observe the exact quantity of these virtues, it not being determined, whether or no it be necessary for the hero of a poem, to be an honest man.—For the under-characters, gather them from Homer and Virgil, and change the names as occasion serves."

FOR THE MACHINES.

"Take of deities, male and female, as many as you can use. Separate them into two equal parts, and keep Jupiter in the middle. Let Juno put him in a ferment, and Venus mollify him. Remember on all occasions to make use of volatile Mercury. If you have need of devils, draw them out of Milton's Paradise, and extract your spirits from Tasso. The use of these machines is evident; for since no epic poem can possibly subsist without them, the wisest way is to reserve them for your greatest necessities. When you cannot extricate your hero by any human means, or yourself by your own wit, seek relief from heaven, and the gods will do your business very readily. This is according to the direct prescription of Horace in his Art of Poetry:

> Nec Deus intersit, nisi dignus vindice nodus
> Inciderit.—
>
> Never presume to make a God appear
> But for a business worthy of a God.
> *Roscommon.*

That is to say, a poet should never call upon the gods for their assistance, but when he is in great perplexity."

FOR THE DESCRIPTIONS.

For a tempest.—"Take Eurus, Zephyr, Auster and Boreas, and cast them together in one verse. Add to these of rain, lightning, and of thunder, the loudest you can, *quantum sufficit*. Mix your clouds and billows well together, till they foam, and thicken your description here and there with a quicksand. Brew your tempest well in your head, before you set it a blowing."

For a battle.—"Pick a large quantity of images and descriptions from Homer's Iliad, with a spice or two of Virgil, and if there remain any overplus you may lay them by for a skirmish. Season it well with similes, and it will make an excellent battle."

For a burning town.—"If such a description be necessary, because it is certain there is one in Virgil, Old Troy is ready burnt to your hands. But if you fear that would be thought borrowed, a chapter or two of the Theory of the Conflagration, well circumstanced, and done into verse, will be a good succedaneum."

"As for similes and metaphors, they may be found all over the creation; the most ignorant may gather them, but the danger is in applying them. For this, advise with your bookseller."

FOR THE LANGUAGE.

I mean the diction. "Here it will do well to be an imitator of Milton, for you will find it easier to imitate him in this than anything else. Hebraisms and Grecisms are to be found in him, without the trouble of learning the languages. I knew a painter who, like our poet, had no genius, made his daubings be thought originals by setting them in the smoke. You may in the same manner give the venerable air of antiquity to your piece, by darkening it up and down with old English. With this you may be easily furnished upon any occasion, by the dictionary commonly printed at the end of Chaucer."

I must not conclude without cautioning all writers without genius in one material point, which is never to be afraid of having too much fire in their works. I should advise rather to

take their warmest thoughts, and spread them abroad upon paper; for they are observed to cool before they are read.
Guardian.

P. 168, l. 16. Conflagration. *This is a reference (frequent in the wits of the time) to Thomas Burnet, an unequal but remarkable writer, who has been somewhat reluctantly excluded from this volume.*

P. 168, l. 28. Made. *Pope has here dropped "who" or "but."*

SAMUEL RICHARDSON.

Samuel Richardson, printer and novelist, was born Derbyshire in 1689, and died in London in 1761. The vast length of Richardson's works, his jealousy of Fielding, his court of lady-admirers, his immense popularity at home and abroad, are known to all. Not so, perhaps, his books, the style of which is certainly not their weakest part.

THE DEATH OF LOVELACE.

SIR,

I HAVE melancholy news to inform you of, by order of the Chevalier Lovelace. He shewed me his letter to you before he sealed it; signifying, that he was to meet the Chevalier Morden on the 15th. Wherefore, as the occasion of the meeting is so well known to you, I shall say nothing of it here.

I had taken care to have ready, within a little distance, a surgeon and his assistant, to whom, under an oath of secrecy, I had revealed the matter, though I did not own it to the two gentlemen; so that they were prepared with bandages, and all things proper. For well was I acquainted with the bravery and skill of my chevalier; and had heard the character of the other; and knew the animosity of both. A post-chaise was ready, with each of their footmen, at a little distance.

The two chevaliers came exactly at their time: They were attended by Monsieur Margate, the Colonel's gentleman, and myself. They had given orders overnight, and now repeated them in each other's presence, that we should observe a strict impartiality between them; And that, if one fell, each of us should look upon himself, as to any needful help or retreat, as the servant of the survivor, and take his commands accordingly.

After a few compliments, both the gentlemen, with the greatest presence of mind that I ever beheld in men, stript to their shirts, and drew.

They parried with equal judgment several passes. My chevalier drew the first blood, making a desperate push, which, by a sudden turn of his antagonist, missed going clear through him, and wounded him on the fleshy part of the ribs of his right side; which part the sword tore out, being on the extremity of the body; but, before my chevalier could recover himself, his adversary, in return, pushed him into the inside of the left arm, near the shoulder; and the sword, raking his breast as it passed, being followed by a great effusion of blood, the Colonel said, Sir, I believe you have enough.

My chevalier swore by G—d he was not hurt; 'twas a pin's point; and so made another pass at his antagonist; which he, with a surprising dexterity, received under his arm, and run my dear chevalier into the body; who immediately fell; saying, The luck is your's, Sir,—O my beloved Clarissa!—Now art thou—Inwardly he spoke three or four words more. His sword dropt from his hand. Mr. Morden threw his down, and ran to him; saying in French,—Ah, Monsieur! you are a dead man!—Call to God for mercy.

We gave the signal agreed upon to the footmen; and they to the surgeons; who instantly came up.

Colonel Morden, I found, was too well used to the bloody work; for he was as cool as if nothing extraordinary had happened, assisting the surgeons, though his own wound bled much. But my dear chevalier fainted away two or three times running, and vomited blood besides.

However, they stopped the bleeding for the present; and we helped him into the voiture; and then the Colonel suffered his own wound to be dressed; and appeared concerned that my chevalier was between whiles, when he could speak and struggle, extremely outrageous.—Poor gentleman! he had made quite sure of victory!

The Colonel, against the surgeon's advice, would mount on

horseback to pass into the Venetian territories; and generously gave me a purse of gold to pay the surgeons; desiring me to make a present to the footman; and to accept of the remainder, as a mark of his satisfaction in my conduct, and in my care and tenderness of my master.

The surgeons told him that my chevalier could not live over the day.

When the Colonel took leave of him, Mr. Lovelace said, You have well revenged the dear creature.

I have, sir, said Mr. Morden; and perhaps shall be sorry that you called upon me to this work, while I was balancing whether to obey, or disobey, the dear angel.

There is a fate in it! replied my chevalier—a cursed fate!—or this could not have been!—But be ye all witnesses, that I have provoked my destiny, and acknowledge that I fall by a man of honour.

Sir, said the Colonel, with the piety of a confessor, wringing Mr. Lovelace's hand, snatch these few fleeting moments, and commend yourself to God.

And so he rode off.

The voiture proceeded slowly with my chevalier; yet the motion set both his wounds bleeding afresh; and it was with difficulty they again stopped the blood.

We brought him alive to the nearest cottage; and he gave orders to me to dispatch to you the packet I herewith send sealed up; and bid me write to you the particulars of this most unhappy affair; and to give you thanks, in his name, for all your favours and friendship to him.

Contrary to all expectation, he lived over the night; but *suffered much*, as well from his *impatience* and *disappointment*, as from his *wounds;* for he seemed *very unwilling to die.*

He was delirious at times, in the two last hours; and then several times cried out, as if he had seen some frightful spectre, Take her away! Take her away! but named nobody. And sometimes praised some lady, that Clarissa, I suppose, whom he had invoked when he received his death's wound, calling her Sweet Excellence! Divine Creature! Fair Sufferer!—And once he said, Look down, Blessed Spirit, look down!—And there stopt;—his lips, however, moving.

At nine in the morning, he was seized with convulsions, and fainted away; and it was a quarter of an hour before he came out of them.

His few last words I must not omit, as they shew an ultimate composure; which may administer some consolation to his honourable friends.

Blessed—said he, addressing himself no doubt to Heaven; for his dying eyes were lifted up—a strong convulsion prevented him for a few moments saying more—but recovering, he again, with great fervour, lifting up his eyes and his spread hands, pronounced the word *blessed!* Then, in a seeming ejaculation, he spoke inwardly, so as not to be understood; at last, he distinctly pronounced these three words,—

LET THIS EXPIATE!

And then, his head sinking on his pillow, he expired, at about half an hour after ten.

Clarissa Harlowe.

P. 170, l. 12. *The writer is Lovelace's valet. Colonel Morden, Clarissa's cousin, challenges Lovelace, to revenge her seduction and death.*

LADY MARY WORTLEY MONTAGU.

Lady Mary Pierrepont, eldest daughter of the first Duke of Kingston, was born about 1690, married Edward Wortley Montagu in 1712, accompanied her husband when he went as ambassador to Constantinople, lived much in literary society at home and abroad, and died in 1762. Her rank as the best letter-writer of her sex in English is undisputed.

LOUVERE.

I HAVE already described to you this extraordinary spot of land, which is almost unknown to the rest of the world, and indeed does not seem to be destined by nature to be inhabited by human creatures, and I believe would never have been so, without the cruel civil war between the Guelps and Gibellines. Before that time here were only the huts of a few fishermen, who came at certain seasons on account of the fine fish with which this lake abounds, particularly trouts, as large and red as salmon. The lake itself is different from any other I ever saw or read of, being the colour of the sea, rather deeper tinged with green, which convinced me that the surrounding mountains are full of minerals, and it may be rich in mines yet undiscovered, as well as quarries of marble, from whence the churches and houses are ornamented, and even the streets paved, which, if polished and laid with art, would look like the finest mosaic work, being a variety of beautiful colours. I ought to retract the honourable title of street, none of them being broader than an alley, and impassable for any wheel carriage except a wheelbarrow. This town, which is the largest of twenty-five that are built on the banks of the lake of Iseo, is near two miles long, and the figure of a semi-circle, and situated at the northern extremity. If it was a regular range of building, it would appear magnificent; but being founded accidentally by those who sought a refuge from the violences of those times, it is a mixture of shops and palaces, gardens and houses, which ascend a mile high, in a confusion which is not disagreeable. After this salutary water was found, and the purity of the air experienced, many people of quality chose it for their summer residence, and embellished it with several fine edifices. It was populous and flourishing, till that fatal plague, which over-ran all Europe in the year 1626. It made a terrible ravage in this place: the poor were almost destroyed, and the rich deserted it. Since that time it has never recovered its former splendour; few of the nobility returned; it is now only frequented during the water-drinking season. Several of the ancient palaces are degraded into lodging-houses, and others stand empty in a ruinous condition: one of these I have bought. I see you lift up your eyes in wonder at my indiscretion. I beg you to hear my reasons before you condemn me. In my infirm state of health the unavoidable noise of a public lodging is very disagreeable; and here is no private one: secondly, and chiefly, the whole purchase is but one hundred pounds, with a very pretty garden in terraces down to the water, and a court behind the house. It is founded on a rock, and the walls so thick, they will probably remain as long as the earth. It is true the apartments are in most tattered circumstances, without doors or windows. The beauty of the great saloon gained my affection; it is forty-two feet in length by twenty-five, proportionably high, opening into a balcony of the same length, with a marble ballustre: the ceiling and flooring are in good repair, but I have been forced to the expense of covering the wall with new stucco; and the carpenter is at this minute taking measure of the windows in order to make frames for sashes. The great stairs are in such a declining way, it would be a very hazardous exploit to mount them: I never intend to attempt it. The state bed-chamber shall also remain for the sole use of the spiders that have taken possession of it, along with the grand cabinet, and some other pieces of magnificence, quite useless to me, and which would cost a great deal to make habitable. I have fitted up six rooms with lodging for five servants, which are all I ever will have in this place; and I am persuaded that I could make a profit if I would part with my purchase, having been very much favoured in the sale, which was by auction, the owner having died without children, and I believe he had never seen this mansion in his life, it having stood empty from the death of his grandfather. The governor bid for me, and nobody would bid against him. Thus I am become a citizen of Louvere, to the great joy of the inhabitants, not, as they would pretend, from their respect for my person, but I perceive they fancy I shall attract all the travelling English; and, to say truth, the singularity of the place is well worth their curiosity; but, as I have no correspondents, I may be buried here thirty years, and nobody know anything of the matter.

Letters, during her last residence abroad.

P. 174, l. 1. Spot. *Louvere, or rather Lovere, at the head of the Lago d'Iseo and the mouth of the Val Camonica.*

P. 175, l. 38. Pieces. *It is uncertain whether Lady Mary uses this in the French sense (= "rooms") or not.*

JOSEPH BUTLER.

Joseph Butler was born in 1692 at Wantage of a Nonconformist family, but joined the Church and became Rolls Preacher, Bishop of Bristol, and Bishop of Durham. His two books, the Analogy and the Sermons, are not bulky, and exhibit a strange incapacity for clothing thought in fit language. But the thought is always noble, and sometimes it forces the rebellious style into harmony. He died in 1752.

THE DEATH OF THE RIGHTEOUS.

HOW much soever men differ in the course of life they prefer, and in their ways of palliating and excusing their vices to themselves; yet all agree in the one thing, desiring to "die the death of the righteous." This is surely remarkable. The observation may be extended further, and put thus: Even without determining what that is which we call guilt or innocence, there is no man but would choose, after having had the pleasure or advantage of a vicious action, to be free of the guilt of it, to be in the state of an innocent man. This shows at least the disturbance, and implicit dissatisfaction in vice. If we inquire into the grounds of it, we shall find it proceeds partly from an immediate sense of having done evil; and partly from an apprehension that this inward sense shall, one time or another, be seconded by an higher judgment, upon which our whole being depends. Now, to suspend and drown this sense, and these apprehensions, be it by the hurry of business or of pleasure, or by superstition, or moral equivocations, this is in a manner one and the same, and makes no alteration at all in the nature of our case. Things and actions are what they are, and the consequences of them will be what they will be: Why then should we desire to be deceived? As we are reasonable creatures, and have any regard to ourselves, we ought to lay these things plainly and honestly before our mind, and upon this, act as you please, as you think most fit; make that choice, and prefer that course of life, which you can justify to yourselves, and which sits most easy upon your own mind. It will immediately appear, that vice cannot be the happiness, but must, upon the whole, be the misery of such a creature as man; a moral, and accountable agent. Superstitious observances, self-deceit, though of a more refined sort, will not, in reality, at all amend matters with us. And the result of the whole can be nothing else, but that with simplicity and fairness we "keep innocency, and take heed unto the thing that is right; for this alone shall bring a man peace at the last."

Sermon on Balaam.

P. 177, l. 10. Implicit. *Implied or underlying—the proper sense, which in modern usage is constantly obscured by a misunderstanding of the phrase "implicit obedience."*

P. 178, ll. 2-7. We .... you. *A confusion which in the preceding century would have been nothing wonderful, but which shows Butler's awkwardness at writing clearly enough.*

PHILIP DORMER STANHOPE, EARL OF CHESTERFIELD.

Philip Dormer Stanhope, Earl of Chesterfield, was born in 1694. He was a great gambler, a statesman of no small ability, an admirable writer. The letters to his natural son put the most questionable side of eighteenth century manners somewhat prominently forward; his miscellaneous writings have equal or greater literary elegance, and better if not always more amusing subjects. He died in 1773.

THE CHARACTER OF RICHARD, EARL OF SCARBOROUGH.

IN drawing the character of Lord Scarborough, I will be strictly upon my guard against the partiality of that intimate and unreserved friendship, in which we lived for more than twenty years; to which friendship, as well as to the public notoriety of it, I owe much more than my pride will let my gratitude own. If this may be suspected to have biassed my judgment, it must, at the same time, be allowed to have informed it; for the most secret movements of his soul were, without disguise, communicated to me only. However, I will rather lower than heighten the colouring; I will mark the shades, and draw a credible rather than an exact likeness.

He had a very good person, rather above the middle size; a handsome face, and when he was cheerful, the most engaging countenance imaginable; and when grave, which he was oftenest, the most respectable one. He had in the highest degree the air, manners and address of a man of quality, politeness with ease, and dignity without pride.

Bred in camps and courts, it cannot be supposed that he was untainted with the fashionable vices of these warm climates;

but, if I may be allowed the expression, he dignified them, instead of their degrading him into any mean or indecent action. He had a good degree of classical, and a great one of modern, knowledge; with a just, and, at the same time, a delicate taste.

In his common expenses he was liberal within bounds; but in his charities and bounties he had none. I have known them put him to some present inconveniencies.

He was a strong, but not an eloquent or florid speaker in parliament. He spoke so unaffectedly the honest dictates of his heart, that truth and virtue, which never want, and seldom wear, ornaments, seemed only to borrow his voice. This gave such an astonishing weight to all he said, that he more than once carried an unwilling majority after him. Such is the authority of unsuspected virtue, that it will sometimes shame vice into decency at least.

He was not only offered, but pressed to accept, the post of Secretary of State; but he constantly refused it. I once tried to persuade him to accept it; but he told me, that both the natural warmth and melancholy of his temper made him unfit for it; and that moreover he knew very well that, in those ministerial employments, the course of business made it necessary to do many hard things, and some unjust ones, which could only be authorised by the jesuitical casuistry of the direction of the intention; a doctrine which he said he could not possibly adopt. Whether he was the first that ever made that objection, I cannot affirm; but I suspect that he will be the last.

He was a true constitutional, and yet practicable patriot; a sincere lover and a zealous asserter of the natural, the civil, and the religious rights of his country. But he would not quarrel with the crown, for some slight stretches of the prerogative; nor with the people, for some unwary ebullitions of liberty; nor with any one, for a difference of opinion in speculative points. He considered the constitution in the aggregate, and only watched that no one part of it should preponderate too much.

His moral character was so pure, that if one may say of that imperfect creature man, what a celebrated historian says of Scipio, *nihil non laudandum aut dixit, aut fecit, aut sensit,* I sincerely think, I had almost said I know, one might say it with great truth of him, one single instance excepted, which shall be mentioned.

He joined to the noblest and strictest principles of honour and generosity the tenderest sentiments of benevolence and compassion; and as he was naturally warm, he could not even hear of an injustice or a baseness, without a sudden indignation, nor of the misfortunes or miseries of a fellow-creature, without melting into softness, and endeavouring to relieve them. This part of his character was so universally known, that our best and most satirical English poet says;

> When I confess, there is one who feels for fame,
> And melts to goodness, Scarb'rough need I name?

He had not the least pride of birth and rank, that common narrow notion of little minds, that wretched mistaken succedaneum of merit; but he was jealous to anxiety of his character, as all men are who deserve a good one. And such was his diffidence upon that subject, that he never could be persuaded that mankind really thought of him as they did. For surely never man had a higher reputation, and never man enjoyed a more universal esteem. Even knaves respected him; and fools thought they loved him. If he had any enemies, for I protest I never knew one, they could only be such as were weary of always hearing of Aristides the Just.

He was too subject to sudden gusts of passion, but they never hurried him into any illiberal or indecent expression or action; so invincibly habitual to him were good nature and good manners. But, if ever any word happened to fall from him in warmth, which upon subsequent reflection he himself thought too strong, he was never easy till he had made more than a sufficient atonement for it.

He had a most unfortunate, I will call it a most fatal kind of melancholy in his nature, which often made him both absent and silent in company, but never morose or sour. At other times he was a cheerful and agreeable companion; but, conscious that he was not always so, he avoided company too much, and was too often alone, giving way to a train of gloomy reflections.

His constitution, which was never robust, broke rapidly at the latter end of his life. He had two severe strokes of apoplexy or palsy, which considerably affected his body and his mind.

I desire that this may not be looked upon as a full and finished character, writ for the sake of writing it; but as my solemn deposit of the truth to the best of my knowledge. I owed this small tribute of justice, such as it is, to the memory of the best man I ever knew, and of the dearest friend I ever had.

Miscellanies.

P. 179, l. 1. Lord Scarborough. *The seventh earl, who committed suicide in 1740.*
P. 180, l. 23. Of the direction of the intention, *i.e. that the end justifies the means.*
P. 180, l. 27. Practicable. *We should now use "practical" in this sense.*
P. 181, l. 10. Poet. *Of course Pope. See* Epilogue to Satires, l. 64.
P. 182, l. 6. Deposit, *in the sense of deposition.*

ROBERT PALTOCK.

Robert Paltock is little more than a nominis umbra, but someone of the name who lived in Clement's Inn was connected with the authorship of Peter Wilkins. Whoever wrote it, wrote what has almost all the vividness and nature of Defoe with a treble portion of tenderness and grace.

PETER'S COURTSHIP.

AS we talked and walked by the lake, she made a little run before me and sprung into it. Perceiving this, I cried out; whereupon she merrily called on me to follow her. The light was then so dim, as prevented my having more than a confused sight of her when she jumped in; and looking earnestly after her, I could discern nothing more than a small boat on the water, which skimmed along at so great a rate that I almost lost sight of it presently; but running along the shore for fear of losing her, I met her gravely walking to meet me; and then had entirely lost sight of the boat upon the lake.—"This," accosting me with a smile, "is my way of sailing, which I perceive by the fright you were in, you are altogether unacquainted with: and as you tell me, you came from so many thousand miles off, it is possible you may be made differently from me: but surely we are the part of the creation which has had most care bestowed upon it; and I suspect from all your discourse to which I have been very attentive, it is possible you may no more be able to fly than to sail as I do."—"No, charming creature, that I cannot, I'll assure you." She then stepping to the edge of the lake, for the advantage of a descent before her, sprung up into the air, and away she went, farther than my eyes could follow her.

I was quite astonished. "So," said I, "then all is over! all a delusion which I have so long been in! a mere phantom! Better had it been for me never to have seen her than thus to lose her again! But what could I expect had she staid? For it is plain she is no human composition.—But, she felt like flesh too, when I lifted her out at the door!" I had but very little time for reflection; for in about ten minutes after she had left me in this mixture of grief and amazement, she alighted just by me on her feet.

Her return as she plainly saw filled me with a transport not to be concealed; and which as she afterwards told me was very agreeable to her. Indeed I was some moments in such an agitation of mind from these unparalleled incidents, that I was like one thunderstruck; but coming presently to myself, and clasping her in my arms with as much love and passion as I was capable of expressing, and for the first time with any desire, "Are you returned again, kind angel," said I, "to bless a wretch who can only be happy in adoring you! Can it be, that you, who have so many advantages over me, should quit all the pleasures that nature has formed you for, and all your friends and relations to take an asylum in my arms! But I here make you a tender of all I am able to bestow—my love and constancy."—"Come, come," replied she, "no more raptures; I find you are a worthier man than I thought I had reason to take you for, and I beg your pardon for my distrust, whilst I was ignorant of your imperfections; but now I verily believe all you have said is true; and I promise you as you have seemed so much to delight in me, I will never quit you till death, or other fatal accident shall part us. But we will now if you choose go home; for I know you have been some time uneasy in this gloom, though agreeable to me: for giving my eyes the pleasure of looking eagerly on you it conceals my blushes from your sight."

Life and Adventures of Peter Wilkins.

P. 183, l. 1. She. *Youwarkee, the gawry or flying girl whom accident has brought to Peter.*

HENRY FIELDING.

Henry Fielding was born at Sharpham in Somersetshire in 1707, and died at Lisbon in 1754. He divided his life between hard spending as a man of pleasure, and hard earning as a man of letters and a police magistrate. His four great novels put him, if not at the head of all English novelists, at least in a position shared only by Scott and Thackeray.

PARTRIDGE AT THE PLAY.

IN the first row, then, of the first gallery, did Mr. Jones, Mrs. Miller, her youngest daughter, and Partridge, take their places. Partridge immediately declared, it was the finest place he had ever been in. When the music was played, he said, "It was a wonder how so many fiddlers could play at one time, without putting one another out." While the fellow was lighting the upper candles, he cried out to Mrs. Miller, "Look, look, madam, the very picture of the man in the end of the Common-prayer-book, before the gunpowder-treason service." Nor could he help observing, with a sigh, when all the candles were lighted, "That here were candles enough burnt in one night, to keep an honest poor family for a twelvemonth."

As soon as the play, which was Hamlet Prince of Denmark, began, Partridge was all attention, nor did he break silence till the entrance of the ghost; upon which he asked Jones, what man that was in the strange dress? "Something," said he, "like what I have seen in a picture. Sure it is not armour, is it?" Jones answered, "That is the ghost." To which Partridge replied with a smile, "Persuade me to that, sir, if you can.

Though I can't say I ever actually saw a ghost in my life, yet I am certain I should know one, if I saw him, better than that comes to. No, no, sir, ghosts don't appear in such dresses as that, neither." In this mistake, which caused much laughter in the neighbourhood of Partridge, he was suffered to continue, till the scene between the ghost and Hamlet, when Partridge gave that credit to Mr. Garrick which he had denied to Jones, and fell into so violent a trembling, that his knees knocked against each other. Jones asked him what was the matter, and whether he was afraid of the warrior upon the stage? "O la! sir," said he, "I perceive now it is what you told me. I am not afraid of anything; for I know it is but a play. And if it was really a ghost, it could do no one no harm at such a distance, and in so much company; and yet, if I was frightened, I am not the only person."—"Why, who," cries Jones, "dost thou take to be such a coward here besides thyself?"—"Nay, you may call me coward if you will; but if that little man there upon the stage is not frightened, I never saw any man frightened in my life. Ay, ay; go along with you! ay, to be sure! who's fool then? Will you? Lud have mercy upon such fool-hardiness! Whatever happens, it is good enough for you.—Follow you? I'd follow the devil as soon. Nay, perhaps, it is the devil—for they say he can put on what likeness he pleases.—Oh! here he is again. —No farther! No, you have gone far enough already; farther than I'd have gone for all the king's dominions." Jones offered to speak, but Partridge cried, "Hush, hush, dear sir, don't you hear him!" And during the whole speech of the ghost, he sat with his eyes fixed partly on the ghost, and partly on Hamlet, and with his mouth open; the same passions which succeeded each other in Hamlet, succeeding likewise in him.

When the scene was over, Jones said, "Why, Partridge, you exceed my expectations. You enjoy the play more than I conceived possible."—"Nay, sir," answered Partridge, "if you are not afraid of the devil, I can't help it; but, to be sure, it is natural to be surprised at such things, though I know there is nothing in them: not that it was the ghost that surprised me neither; for I should have known that to have been only a man in a strange dress: but when I saw the little man so frightened himself, it was that which took hold of me."—"And dost thou imagine, then, Partridge," cried Jones, "that he was really frightened?"—"Nay, sir," said Partridge, "did not you yourself observe afterwards, when he found it was his own father's spirit, and how he was murdered in the garden, how his fear forsook him by degrees, and he was struck dumb with sorrow, as it were, just as I should have been, had it been my own case.—But hush! O la! what noise is that? There he is again!—Well, to be certain, though I know there is nothing at all in it, I am glad I am not down yonder, where those men are." Then turning his eyes again upon Hamlet, "Ay, you may draw your sword; what signifies a sword against the power of the devil?"

During the second act, Partridge made very few remarks. He greatly admired the fineness of the dresses; nor could he help observing upon the king's countenance. "Well," said he, "how people may be deceived by faces! *Nulla fides fronti*, is, I find, a true saying. Who would think, by looking in the king's face, he had ever committed a murder?" He then enquired after the ghost; but Jones, who intended that he should be surprised, gave him no other satisfaction, than that he might possibly see him again soon, and in a flash of fire.

Partridge sat in fearful expectation of this; and now, when the ghost made his next appearance, Partridge cried out, "There, sir, now; what say you now? is he frightened now or no? As much frightened as you think me, and, to be sure, nobody can help some fears. I would not be in so bad a condition as, what's his name, Squire Hamlet, is there, for all the world.—Bless me! what's become of the spirit? As I am a living soul, I thought I saw him sink into the earth."—"Indeed you saw right," answered Jones.—"Well, well," cries Partridge, "I know it is only a play; and, besides, if there was anything in all this, Madame Miller would not laugh so: for as to you, sir, you would not be afraid, I believe, if the devil was here in person.—There, there—Ay, no wonder you are in such a passion; shake the vile wicked wretch to pieces. If she was my own mother, I should serve her so. To be sure, all duty to a mother is forfeited by such wicked doings. —Ay, go about your business; I hate the sight of you."

Our critic was now pretty silent till the play which Hamlet introduces before the king. This he did not at first understand, till Jones explained it to him; but he no sooner entered into the spirit of it, than he began to bless himself that he had never committed murder. Then, turning to Mrs. Miller, he asked her, if she did not imagine the king looked as if he was touched? "Though he is," said he, "a good actor, and doth all he can to hide it. Well, I would not have so much to answer for, as that wicked man there hath, to sit upon a much higher chair than he sits upon.—No wonder he runs away; for your sake I'll never trust an innocent face again."

The grave-digging scene next engaged the attention of Partridge, who expressed much surprise at the number of skulls thrown upon the stage. To which Jones answered, that it was one of the most famous burial-places about town. "No wonder, then," cries Partridge, "that the place is haunted. But I never saw in my life a worse grave-digger. I had a sexton, when I was clerk, that should have dug three graves while he is digging one. The fellow handles a spade as if it was the first time he had ever had one in his hand.—Ay, ay, you may sing. You had rather sing than work, I believe." Upon Hamlet's taking up the skull, he cried out, "Well, it is strange to see how fearless some men are: I never could bring myself to touch anything belonging to a dead man on any account. He seemed frightened enough too, at the ghost, I thought. *Nemo omnibus horis sapit.*"

Little more worth remembering occurred during the play; at the end of which Jones asked him, which of the players he had liked best? To this he answered, with some appearance of indignation at the question, "The king, without doubt."—"Indeed, Mr. Partridge," says Mrs. Miller, "you are not of the same opinion with the town; for they are all agreed, the Hamlet is acted by the best player who was ever on the stage."—"He the best player!" cries Partridge, with a contemptuous sneer; "Why, I could act as well as he myself. I am sure if I had seen a ghost, I should have looked in the very same manner, and done just as he did. And then, to be sure, in that scene, as you called it, between him and his mother, where you told me he acted so fine, why, Lord help me! any man, that is, any good man, that had such a mother, would have done exactly the same. I know you are only joking with me; but indeed, madam, though I was never at a play in London, yet I have seen acting before in the country; and the king for my money. He speaks all his words distinctly, half as loud again as the other. Any body may see he is an actor."

While Mrs. Miller was thus engaged in conversation with Partridge, a lady came up to Mr. Jones, whom he immediately knew to be Mrs. Fitzpatrick. She said she had seen him from the other part of the gallery, and had taken that opportunity of speaking to him, as she had something to say which might be of great service to himself. She then acquainted him with her lodgings, and made him an appointment the next day in the morning; which, upon recollection, she presently changed to the afternoon; at which time Jones promised to attend her.

Thus ended the adventure at the playhouse; where Partridge had afforded great mirth, not only to Jones and Mrs. Miller, but to all who sat within hearing, who were more attentive to what he said, than to anything that passed on the stage.

He durst not go to bed all that night for fear of the ghost; and for many nights after sweated for two or three hours before he went to sleep with the same apprehensions, and waked several times in great horrors, crying out, "Lord have mercy upon us! there it is."

Tom Jones..

SAMUEL JOHNSON.

Samuel Johnson was born at Lichfield in 1709; he died in London in 1784. His life was one of hard literary struggle till he was fifty years old; he was then pensioned and at ease. His own work has been eclipsed by Boswell's Life of him, yet those who best know his own books are not those who like them least. The sesquipedalian style with which he is reproached is only occasional.

ADDISON AS A PROSE WRITER.

ADDISON is now to be considered as a critic; a name which the present generation is scarcely willing to allow him. His criticism is condemned as tentative or experimental, rather than scientific; and he is considered as deciding by taste rather than by principles.

It is not uncommon, for those who have grown wise by the labour of others, to add a little of their own, and overlook their masters. Addison is now despised by some who, perhaps, would never have seen his defects, but by the lights which he afforded them. That he always wrote as he would think it necessary to write now, cannot be affirmed; his instructions were such as the character of his readers made proper. That general knowledge which now circulates in common talk, was in his time rarely to be found. Men not professing learning were not ashamed of ignorance; and, in the female world, any acquaintance with books was distinguished only to be censured. His purpose was to infuse literary curiosity, by gentle and unsuspected conveyance, into the gay, the idle, and the wealthy; he therefore presented knowledge in the most alluring form, not lofty and austere, but accessible and familiar. When he showed them their defects, he showed them, likewise, that they might be easily supplied. His attempt succeeded; inquiry was awakened, and comprehension expanded. An emulation of intellectual elegance was excited, and, from his time to our own, life has been gradually exalted, and conversation purified and enlarged.

Dryden had, not many years before, scattered criticism over his prefaces with very little parsimony; but, though he sometimes condescended to be familiar, his manner was in general too scholastic for those who had yet their rudiments to learn, and found it not easy to understand their master. His observations were framed rather for those that were learning to write than for those that read only to talk.

An instructor like Addison was now wanting, whose remarks being superficial, might be easily understood, and being just, might prepare the mind for more attainments. Had he presented Paradise Lost to the public with all the pomp of system and severity of science, the criticism would, perhaps, have been admired, and the poem still have been neglected; but, by the blandishments of gentleness and facility, he has made Milton an universal favourite, with whom readers of every class think it necessary to be pleased.

He descended, now and then, to lower disquisitions; and, by a serious display of the beauties of Chevy-Chase, exposed himself to the ridicule of Wagstaffe, who bestowed a like pompous character on Tom Thumb, and to the contempt of Dennis, who, considering the fundamental position of his criticism, that Chevy-Chase pleases, and ought to please, because it is natural, observes, "that there is a way of deviating from nature, by bombast or tumour, which soars above nature, and enlarges images beyond their real bulk; by affectation, which forsakes nature in quest of something unsuitable; and by imbecility, which degrades nature by faintness and diminution, by obscuring its appearances, and weakening its effects." In Chevy-Chase there is not much of either bombast or affectation; but there is chill and lifeless imbecility. The story cannot possibly be told in a manner that shall make less impression on the mind.

Before the profound observers of the present race repose too securely on the consciousness of their superiority to Addison, let them consider his Remarks on Ovid, in which may be found specimens of criticism sufficiently subtle and refined; let them peruse, likewise, his essays on Wit, and on the Pleasures of Imagination, in which he founds art on the base of nature, and draws the principles of invention from dispositions inherent in the mind of man with skill and elegance, such as his contemners will not easily attain.

As a describer of life and manners, he must be allowed to stand, perhaps, the first of the first rank. His humour which, as Steele observes, is peculiar to himself, is so happily diffused as to give the grace of novelty to domestic scenes and daily occurrences. He never "outsteps the modesty of nature," nor raises merriment or wonder by the violation of truth. His figures neither divert by distortion, nor amaze by aggravation. He copies life with so much fidelity, that he can be hardly said to invent; yet his exhibitions have an air so much original, that it is difficult to suppose them not merely the product of imagination.

As a teacher of wisdom, he may be confidently followed. His religion has nothing in it enthusiastic or superstitious: he appears neither weakly credulous, nor wantonly sceptical; his morality is neither dangerously lax, nor impracticably rigid. All the enchantment of fancy, and all the cogency of argument, are employed to recommend to the reader his real interest, the care of pleasing the Author of his being. Truth is shown sometimes as the phantom of a vision; sometimes appears half-veiled in an allegory; sometimes attracts regard in the robes of fancy, and sometimes steps forth in the confidence of reason. She wears a thousand dresses, and in all is pleasing.

"Mille habet ornatus, mille decenter habet."

His prose is the model of the middle style; on grave subjects not formal, on light occasions not grovelling, pure without scrupulosity, and exact without apparent elaboration; always equable, and always easy, without glowing words or pointed sentences. Addison never deviates from his track to snatch a grace; he seeks no ambitious ornaments, and tries no hazardous innovations. His page is always luminous, but never blazes in unexpected splendour.

It was, apparently, his principal endeavour to avoid all harshness and severity of diction; he is, therefore, sometimes verbose in his transitions and connexions, and sometimes descends too much to the language of conversation; yet if his language had been less idiomatical, it might have lost somewhat of its genuine Anglicism. What he attempted, he performed; he is never feeble, and he did not wish to be energetic; he is never rapid, and he never stagnates. His sentences have neither studied amplitude, nor affected brevity: his periods, though not diligently rounded, are voluble and easy. Whoever wishes to attain an English style, familiar but not coarse, and elegant but not ostentatious, must give his days and nights to the volumes of Addison.

Life of Addison.

PUNCH AND CONVERSATION.

OF the parallels which have been drawn by wit and curiosity, some are literal and real, as between poetry and painting, two arts which pursue the same end, by the operation of the same mental faculties, and which differ only as the one represents things by marks permanent and natural, the other by signs accidental and arbitrary. The one, therefore, is more easily and generally understood, since similitude of form is immediately perceived; the other is capable of conveying more ideas, for men have thought and spoken of many things which they do not see.

Other parallels are fortuitous and fanciful, yet these have sometimes been extended to many particulars of resemblance by a lucky concurrence of diligence and chance. The animal body is composed of many members, united under the direction of one mind: any number of individuals, connected for some common purpose, is therefore called a body. From this participation of the same appellation arose the comparison of the body natural and body politic, of which, how far soever it has been deduced, no end has hitherto been found.

In these imaginary similitudes, the same word is used at once in its primitive and metaphorical sense. Thus health, ascribed to the body natural, is opposed to sickness; but attributed to the body politic stands as contrary to adversity. These parallels therefore have more of genius, but less of truth; they often please, but they never convince.

Of this kind is a curious speculation frequently indulged by a philosopher of my acquaintance, who had discovered, that the qualities requisite to conversation are very exactly represented by a bowl of punch.

Punch, says this profound investigator, is a liquor compounded of spirit and acid juices, sugar and water. The spirit, volatile and fiery, is the proper emblem of vivacity and wit; the acidity of the lemon will very aptly figure pungency of raillery, and acrimony of censure; sugar is the natural representative of luscious adulation and gentle complaisance; and water is the proper hieroglyphic of easy prattle, innocent and tasteless.

Spirit alone is too powerful for use. It will produce madness rather than merriment; and instead of quenching thirst will inflame the blood. Thus wit, too copiously poured out, agitates the hearer with emotions rather violent than pleasing; every one shrinks from the force of its oppression, the company sits entranced and overpowered; all are astonished, but nobody is pleased.

The acid juices give this genial liquor all its power of stimulating the palate. Conversation would become dull and vapid, if negligence were not sometimes roused, and sluggishness quickened, by due severity of reprehension. But acids unmixed will distort the face and torture the palate; and he that has no other qualities than penetration and asperity, he whose constant employment is detection and censure, who looks only to find faults, and speaks only to punish them, will soon be dreaded, hated and avoided.

The taste of sugar is generally pleasing, but it cannot long be eaten by itself. Thus meekness and courtesy will always recommend the first address, but soon pall and nauseate, unless they are associated with more sprightly qualities. The chief use of sugar is to temper the taste of other substances; and softness of behaviour, in the same manner, mitigates the roughness of contradiction, and allays the bitterness of unwelcome truth.

Water is the universal vehicle by which are conveyed the particles necessary to sustenance and growth, by which thirst is quenched, and all the wants of life and nature are supplied. Thus all the business of the world is transacted by artless and easy talk, neither sublimed by fancy, nor discoloured by affectation, without either the harshness of satire, or the lusciousness of flattery. By this limpid vein of language, curiosity is gratified, and all the knowledge is conveyed which one man is required to impart for the safety or convenience of another. Water is the only ingredient in punch which can be used alone, and with which man is content till fancy has framed an artificial want. Thus while we only desire to have our ignorance informed, we are most delighted with the plainest diction; and it is only in the moments of idleness or pride, that we call for the gratifications of wit or flattery.

He only will please long, who, by tempering the acidity of satire with the sugar of civility, and allaying the heat of wit with the frigidity of humble chat, can make the true punch of conversation; and, as that punch can be drunk in the greatest quantity which has the largest proportion of water, so that companion will be oftenest welcome, whose talk flows out with inoffensive copiousness, and unenvied insipidity.

The Idler.

P. 191, l. 11. *The scholastic character of Dryden's criticism is not very apparent. But it is true that he generally gives reasons for his views, which Addison does not often and sometimes could not do.*

P. 191, l. 25. *These remarks on* Chevy Chase *are among the texts which should be written at the bed-head of every critic to teach him not to presume.*

P. 194, l. 13. Punch. *By etymology and custom, punch consists of five ingredients, though different recipes differ greatly as to the fifth. But it would not be at all difficult to find a fifth conversational equivalent.*

P. 194, l. 19. Hieroglyphic. *Not improperly used, hieroglyphics being symbols in the shape of natural objects.*

P. 194, l. 28. Become dull and vapid. *The writer at least could not be charged with allowing this.*

DAVID HUME.

David Hume was born at Edinburgh in 1711 and died there in 1776. His character was amiable and upright; his literary achievements in two different branches extraordinary. He remains to this day the only historian of the whole, not a part, of English history, whose literary merit is very high, and the clearness, pregnancy, and elegance of his philosophical style have never been surpassed.

ON MIRACLES.

A MIRACLE is a violation of the laws of nature; and as a firm and unalterable experience has established these laws, the proof against a miracle, from the very nature of the fact, is as entire as any argument from experience can possibly be imagined. Why is it more than probable, that all men must die; that lead cannot, of itself, remain suspended in the air; that fire consumes wood, and is extinguished by water; unless it be, that these events are found agreeable to the laws of nature, and there is required a violation of these laws, or in other words, a miracle to prevent them? Nothing is esteemed a miracle, if it ever happen in the common course of nature. It is no miracle that a man, seemingly in good health, should die on a sudden: because such a kind of death, though more unusual than any other, has yet been frequently observed to happen. But it is a miracle, that a dead man should come to life; because that has never been observed, in any age or country. There must, therefore, be an uniform experience against every miraculous event, otherwise the event would not merit that appellation. And as an uniform experience amounts to a proof, there is here a direct and full *proof*, from the nature of the fact, against the existence of any miracle; nor can such a proof be destroyed, or the miracle rendered credible, but by an opposite proof, which is superior.

The plain consequence is—and it is a general maxim worthy of our attention,—' That no testimony is sufficient to establish a miracle, unless the testimony be of such a kind, that its falsehood would be more miraculous, than the fact, which it endeavours to establish; and even in that case there is a mutual destruction of arguments, and the superior only gives us an assurance suitable to that degree of force, which remains, after deducting the inferior.' When anyone tells me, that he saw a dead man restored to life, I immediately consider with myself, whether it be more probable, that this person should either deceive or be deceived, or that the fact, which he relates, should really have happened. I weigh the one miracle against the other; and according to the superiority, which I discover, I pronounce my decision, and always reject the greater miracle. If the falsehood of his testimony would be more miraculous, than the event which he relates; then, and not till then, can he pretend to command my belief or opinion.

An Enquiry concerning Human Understanding.

HIS OWN CHARACTER.

IN spring 1775, I was struck with a disorder in my bowels, which at first gave me no alarm, but has since, as I apprehend it, become mortal and incurable. I now reckon upon a speedy dissolution. I have suffered very little pain from my disorder; and what is more strange, have, notwithstanding the great decline of my person, never suffered a moment's abatement of my spirits; insomuch, that were I to name the period of my life, which I should most choose to pass over again, I might be tempted to point to this latter period. I possess the same ardour as ever in study, and the same gaiety in company. I consider, besides, that a man of sixty-five, by dying, cuts off only a few years of infirmities; and though I see many symptoms of my literary reputation's breaking out at last with additional lustre, I know that I could have but few years to enjoy it. It is difficult to be more detached from life than I am at present.

To conclude historically with my own character. I am, or rather was,—for that is the style I must now use in speaking of myself, which emboldens me the more to speak my sentiments; —I was, I say, a man of mild dispositions, of command of temper, of an open, social, and cheerful humour, capable of attachment, but little susceptible of enmity, and of great moderation in all my passions. Even my love of literary fame, my ruling passion, never soured my temper, notwithstanding my frequent disappointments. My company was not unacceptable to the young and careless, as well as to the studious and literary; and as I took a particular pleasure in the company of modest women, I had no reason to be displeased with the reception I met with from them. In a word, though most men anywise eminent, have found reason to complain of calumny, I never was touched, or even attacked by her baleful tooth: and though I wantonly exposed myself to the rage of both civil and religious factions, they seemed to be disarmed in my behalf of their wonted fury. My friends never had occasion to vindicate any one circumstance of my character and conduct: not but that the zealots, we may well suppose, would have been glad to invent and propagate any story to my disadvantage, but they could never find any which they thought would wear the face of probability. I cannot say there is no vanity in making this funeral oration of myself, but I hope it is not a misplaced one; and this is a matter of fact which is easily cleared and ascertained.

My Own Life.

P. 196, l. 19. Uniform experience amounts to a proof. *Formal logic, it must be remembered, had been almost entirely neglected in Hume's time. It would have saved one of the acutest of reasoners from making an obvious blunder. Uniform experience of course amounts to no proof except with the aid of a postulate or assumption as to the "uniformity of nature," which is in fact a circular argument.*

LAURENCE STERNE.

Laurence Sterne, a rather sorry man but a great writer, was born at Clonmel in 1713. He took orders and held preferment in Yorkshire, travelled abroad, and died in London in 1769. Sterne was a plagiarist, a sentimentalist to the gushing point, a deliberate dabbler in indecency for the sake of attracting readers, but he was one of the first of English humorists, and a perfect literary artist.

ON SLEEP.

I WISH I could write a chapter upon sleep.

A fitter occasion could never have presented itself, than what this moment offers, when all the curtains of the family are drawn—the candles put out—and no creature's eyes are open but a single one, for the other has been shut these twenty years, of my mother's nurse. It is a fine subject!

And yet, as fine as it is, I would undertake to write a dozen chapters upon button-holes, both quicker and with more fame than a single chapter upon this. Button-holes!—there is something lively in the very idea of 'em—and trust me, when I get among 'em—You gentry with great beards—look as grave as you will—I'll make merry work with my button-holes—I shall have 'em all to myself . . . . 'tis a maiden subject . . . . I shall run foul of no man's wisdom or fine sayings in it.

But for sleep——I know I shall make nothing of it before I begin—I am no dab at your fine sayings in the first place—and in the next, I cannot for my soul set a grave face upon a bad matter, and tell the world——'tis the refuge of the unfortunate——the enfranchisement of the prisoner——the downy lap of the hopeless, the weary, and the broken-hearted; nor could I set out with a lie in my mouth by affirming that of all the soft and delicious functions of our nature, by which the great author of it, in his bounty, has been pleased to recompense the sufferings wherewith his justice and his good pleasure has wearied us—that this is the chiefest (I know pleasures worth ten of it) or what a happiness it is to man, when the anxieties and passions of the day are over, and he lays down upon his back, that his soul shall be so seated within him, that whichever way she turns her eyes, the heavens shall look calm and sweet above her—no desire—or fear—or doubt that troubles the air, nor any difficulty past, present or to come, that the imagination may not pass over without offence, in that sweet secession.

.... " God's blessing," said Sancho Pancha, " be upon the man who first invented this selfsame thing called sleep—it covers a man all over like a cloak." Now there is more to me in this, and it speaks warmer to my heart and affections, than all the dissertations squeezed out of the heads of the learned together upon the subject.

—Not that I altogether disapprove of what Montaigne advances upon it—'tis admirable in its way.—(I quote by memory.)

The world enjoys other pleasures, says he, as they do that of sleep without tasting or feeling it as it slips and passes by— We should study and ruminate upon it, in order to render proper thanks to him who grants it to us—for this end I cause myself to be disturbed in my sleep, that I may the better and more sensibly relish it—And yet I see few, says he again, who live with less sleep when need requires; my body is capable of a firm, but not of a violent and sudden agitation—I evade of late all violent exercises—I am never weary with walking— but from my youth, I never like to ride upon pavements. I love to lie hard and alone, and even without my wife—This last word may stagger the faith of the world—but remember, " La Vraisemblance" (as Baylet says in the affair of Liceti) " n'est pas toujours du Côté de la Verité." And so much for sleep.

The Life and Opinions of Tristram Shandy, Gentleman.

THE MONK.

—Now, was I a King of France, cried I—what a moment for an orphan to have begged his father's portmanteau of me!

I had scarce uttered the words, when a poor monk of the order of St. Francis came into the room to beg something for his convent. No man cares to have his virtues the sport of contingencies—or one man may be generous, as another man is puissant—*sed non, quoad hanc*—or be it as it may—for there is no regular reasoning upon the ebbs and flows of our humours; they may depend upon the same causes, for aught I know, which influence the tides themselves—'twould oft be no discredit to us to suppose it was so: I'm sure at least for myself, that in many a case I should be more highly satisfied, to have it said by the world, "I had had an affair with the moon, in which there was neither sin or shame," than have it pass altogether as my own act and deed, wherein there was so much of both.

—But be this as it may. The moment I cast my eyes upon him, I was predetermined not to give him a single sous, and accordingly I put my purse into my pocket—buttoned it up—set myself a little more upon my centre, and advanced up gravely to him: there was something, I fear, forbidding in my look: I have his figure this moment before my eyes, and think there was that in it which deserved better.

The monk, as I judged from the break in his tonsure, a few scattered white hairs upon his temples, being all that remained of it, might be about seventy—but from his eyes, and that sort of fire which was in them, which seemed more tempered by courtesy than years, could be no more than sixty—Truth might lie between—he was certainly sixty-five; and the general air of his countenance, notwithstanding something seemed to have been planting wrinkles in it before their time, agreed to the account.

It was one of those heads, which Guido has often painted—mild, pale—penetrating, free from all common-place ideas of fat contented ignorance looking downwards upon the earth—it looked forwards; but looked, as if it looked at something beyond this world. How one of his order came by it, heaven above, who let it fall upon a monk's shoulders, best knows; but it would have suited a Bramin, and had I met it upon the plains of Indostan, I had reverenced it.

The rest of his outline may be given in a few strokes; one might put it into the hands of anyone to design, for 'twas neither elegant or otherwise, but as character and expression made it so: it was a thin, spare form, something above the common size, if it lost not the distinction by a bend forwards in the figure —but it was the attitude of Intreaty; and as it now stands present to my imagination, it gained more than it lost by it.

When he had entered the room three paces, he stood still; and laying his left hand upon his breast, a slender white staff with which he journeyed being in his right—when I had got close up to him, he introduced himself with the little story of the wants of his convent, and the poverty of his order—and did it with so simple a grace—and such an air of deprecation was there in the whole cast of his look and figure—I was bewitched not to have been struck with it—

—A better reason was, I had predetermined not to give him a single sous.

—'Tis very true, said I, replying to a cast upwards with his eyes, with which he had concluded his address—'tis very true— and heaven be their resource who have no other but the charity of the world, the stock of which, I fear, is no way sufficient for the many *great claims* which are hourly made upon it.

As I pronounced the words *great claims*, he gave a slight glance with his eye downwards upon the sleeve of his tunic—I felt the full force of the appeal—I acknowledge it, said I,—a coarse habit, and that but once in three years with meagre diet are—no great matters: and the true point of pity is, as they can be earned in the world with so little industry, that your order should wish to procure them by pressing upon a fund which is the property of the lame, the blind, the aged, and the infirm—; the captive who lies down counting over and over again the days of his afflictions, languishes also for his share of it; and had you been of the *order of mercy*, instead of the order of St. Francis, poor as I am, continued I, pointing at my portmanteau, full cheerfully should it have been opened to you, for the ransom of the unfortunate.—The monk made me a bow—but of all others, resumed I, the unfortunate of our own country, surely, have the first rights; and I have left thousands in distress upon our own shore—The monk gave a cordial wave with his head—as much as to say, No doubt, there is misery enough in every corner of the world, as well as within our convent—But we distinguish, said I, laying my hand upon the sleeve of his tunic, in return for his appeal—we distinguish, my good father! betwixt those who wish only to eat the bread of their own labour—and those who eat the bread of other people's, and have no other plan in life, but to get through it in sloth and ignorance, *for the love of God*.

The poor Franciscan made no reply: a hectic of a moment passed across his cheek, but could not tarry—Nature seemed to have had done with her resentments in him; he shewed none—but letting his staff fall within his arm, he pressed both his hands with resignation upon his breast, and retired.

A Sentimental Journey.

P. 200, l. 8. Lays down. "*There let him lay," for it can only be admitted that, despite the certainty and obvious use of the distinction between "lie" and "lay," it has been often neglected by great writers.*

P. 200, l. 21. Montaigne. *The passage is in Book III. Chapter xiii. of the Essays. It is quoted desultorily and without regard to context, but not unfaithfully.*

THOMAS GRAY.

Thomas Gray was born in London in 1716, was brought up at Eton and Cambridge, travelled with Horace Walpole, and then returned to Cambridge, which was the headquarters of his life of studious ease till his death in 1771. His prose has not the elaborate perfection of his poetry, but exhibits much of the same scholarly character. In appreciating nature he has few predecessors in English.

A SUNRISE.

I MUST not close my letter without giving you one principal event of my history; which was that, in the course of my late tour, I set out one morning before five o'clock, the moon shining through a dark and misty autumnal air, and got to the sea coast time enough to be at the sun's levee. I saw the clouds and dark vapours open gradually to right and left, rolling over one another in great smoky wreaths, and the tide, as it flowed gently in upon the sands, first whitening, then slightly tinged with gold and blue; and all at once a little line of insufferable brightness that, before I can write these five words, was grown to half an orb, and now to a whole one, too glorious to be distinctly seen. It is very odd it makes no figure on paper; yet I shall remember it as long as the sun, or at least as I endure. I wonder whether any body ever saw it before; I hardly believe it.

Letter to Bonstetten.

This brief passage gives what hardly exists before in prose English, an attempt to describe landscape from nature and not conventionally. It is probably this very difference from conventional writing which made the author complain that it "made no figure upon paper." We do not think so now.

HORACE WALPOLE.

Horace Walpole, younger son of Sir Robert, was born in London in 1717 and died there in 1797, by which time he had succeeded to the earldom of Orford. A dilettante, a coxcomb, and cold-hearted towards all but a narrow circle of personal friends, Walpole was a man of very considerable sense and culture, the best of all English letter-writers, and capable of much better work, of other kinds, than he chose to do.

THE JOYS OF LONDON.

I AM writing to you in an inn on the road to London. What a paradise should I have thought this when I was in the Italian inns! in a wide barn with four ample windows, which had nothing more like glass than shutters and iron bars! no tester to the bed, and the saddles and portmanteaus heaped on me to keep off the cold. What a paradise did I think the inn at Dover when I came back! and what magnificence were twopenny prints, salt-cellars, and boxes to hold the knives; but the *summum bonum* was small-beer and the newspaper.

"I bless'd my stars, and called it luxury!"

Who was the Neapolitan ambassadress that could not live at Paris, because there was no maccaroni? Now am I relapsed into all the dissatisfied refinement of a true English grumbling voluptuary. I could find in my heart to write a Craftsman against the Government, because I am not quite so much at my ease as on my own sofa. I could persuade myself that it is my Lord Carteret's fault that I am only sitting in a common armchair, when I would be lolling in a *péché-mortel*. How dismal, how solitary, how scrub does this town look; and yet it has actually a street of houses better than Parma or Modena. Nay, the houses of the people of fashion, who come hither for the races, are palaces to what houses in London itself were fifteen years ago. People do begin to live again now, and I suppose in a term we shall revert to York Houses, Clarendon Houses, etc. But from that grandeur all the nobility had contracted themselves to live in coops of a dining-room, a dark back-room, with one eye in a corner, and a closet. Think what London would be, if the chief houses were in it, as in the cities in other countries, and not dispersed like great rarity-plums in a vast pudding of country. Well, it is a tolerable place as it is! Were I a physician, I would prescribe nothing but Recipe, CCCLXV drachm. Londin. Would you know why I like London so much? Why, if the world must consist of so many fools as it does, I choose to take them in the gross, and not made into separate pills, as they are prepared in the country. Besides, there is no being alone but in a metropolis: the worst place in the world to find solitude is the country: questions grow there, and that unpleasant Christian commodity, neighbours. Oh! they are all good Samaritans, and do so pour balms and nostrums upon one, if one has but the toothache, or a journey to take, that they break one's head. A journey to take —ay! they talk over the miles to you, and tell you, you will be late in. My Lord Lovel says, *John* always goes two hours in the dark in the morning, to avoid being one hour in the dark in the evening. I was pressed to set out to-day before seven! I did before nine; and here am I arrived at a quarter past five, for the rest of the night.

Letters.

P. 205, l. 14. Craftsman. *The famous Opposition newspaper in which for ten years (1726-1736) Pulteney, Bolingbroke, and many minor writers carried on war against Walpole.*

P. 205, l. 18. Péché-mortel. *The eighteenth century was fond of these fantastic names for pieces of furniture.* Cf. *bonheur-du-jour*, etc.

GILBERT WHITE.

Gilbert White was born in 1720, and derives his whole celebrity from the elaborate observations of natural objects which he carried on in his parish of Selborne, and the simple but admirable English in which he set down their results. He has had no small influence on the descriptive school in England. He died in 1793.

THE HYBERNATION OF SWALLOWS.

AS to swallows being found in a torpid state during the winter in the Isle of Wight, or any part of this country, I never heard any such account worth attending to. But a clergyman of an inquisitive turn, assures me, that, when he was a great boy, some workmen, in pulling down the battlements of a church tower early in the spring, found two or three swifts among the rubbish, which seemed, at their first appearance, dead; but on being carried toward the fire, revived. He told me that, out of his care to preserve them, he put them in a paper bag, and hung them by the kitchen fire, where they were suffocated.

Another intelligent person has informed me that, while he was a schoolboy at Brighthelmstone, in Sussex, a great fragment of the chalk cliff fell down one stormy winter on the beach; and that many people found swallows among the rubbish: but, on my questioning him whether he saw any of those birds himself, to my no small disappointment he answered me in the negative; but that others assured him they did. Young broods of swallows began to appear this year on July the eleventh, and young martins were then fledged in their nests. Both species will

142

these g
disciple
them, b
adversa
have bee
proceede
by a met
reason ; ;
their pre:
Bedlam ;
due place
Lucretius,
now in th
would, in 1
of phlebot
and straw.
thinking, d
of all mar
height of
of all inno
hoped, that
all men's c
smooth, th
would, by c
void, as th
reckoned to
like so ma:
drawn with
how it is p
particular m
ascending fr
there distill
our mother-
that of mad
how it com
do ever fail
number of in
to be assigne

WHEN I
by the
more than a ce
of quality her
and the certain
ing letters ma
and the answe
racter.

"My des
"If thou art
apostate! how
married I find i
dismal to be sh
my ancestors, th
in the country,
husband, and an
you may enterta
the spouse of yo

breed again once: for I see by my *fauna* of last year, that young broods came forth as late as September the eighteenth. Are not these late hatchings more in favour of hiding than migration? Nay, some young martins remained in their nests last year so late as September the twenty-ninth; and yet they totally disappeared with us by the fifth of October. How strange it is that the swift which seems to live exactly the same life with the swallow and house martin should leave us before the middle of August invariably! while the latter stay often till the middle of October; once I even saw numbers of house martins on the seventh of November. The martins, red-wings and fieldfares were flying in sight together; an uncommon assemblage of summer and winter birds!

The Natural History of Selborne.

NATURAL AFFECTION OF ANIMALS.

THE more I reflect on the στοργή of animals, the more I am astonished at its effects. Nor is the violence of this affection more wonderful than the shortness of its duration. Thus every hen is in her turn the virago of the yard in proportion to the helplessness of her brood; and will fly in the face of a dog or a sow in defence of those chickens which in a few weeks she will drive before her with relentless cruelty.

This affection sublimes the passions, quickens the invention, and sharpens the sagacity of the brute creation. Thus an hen, just become a mother, is no longer that placid bird she used to be, but with feathers standing on end, wings hovering, and clucking note, she runs about like one possessed. Dams will throw themselves in the way of the greatest danger in order to avert it from their progeny. Thus a partridge will tumble along before a sportsman in order to draw away the dogs from her helpless covey. In the time of nidification the most feeble birds will assault the most rapacious. All the *hirundines* of a village are up in arms at the sight of a hawk, whom they will persecute till he leaves that district. A very exact observer has often remarked that a pair of ravens nesting in the rock of Gibraltar would suffer no vulture or eagle to rest near their station, but would drive them from the hill with an amazing fury: even the blue thrush at the season of breeding would dart out from the clefts of the rocks to chase away the kestril, or the sparrowhawk. If you stand near the nest of a bird that has young she will not be induced to betray them by an inadvertent fondness, but will wait about at a distance with meat in her mouth for an hour together.

Should I farther corroborate what I have advanced above by some anecdotes which I probably may have mentioned before in conversation, yet you will, I trust, pardon the repetition for the sake of the illustration.

The flycatcher of the Zoology (the Stoparola of Ray) builds every year in the vines that grow on the walls of my house. A pair of these little birds had one year inadvertently placed their nest on a naked bough, perhaps in a shady time, not being aware of the inconvenience that followed. But a hot sunny season coming on before the brood was half fledged, the reflection of the wall became insupportable, and must inevitably have destroyed the tender young, had not affection suggested an expedient, and prompted the parent birds to hover over the nest all the hotter hours, while with wings expanded, and mouths gaping for breath, they screened off the heat from their suffering offspring.

A farther instance I once saw of notable sagacity in a willow wren, which had built in a bank in my fields. This bird a friend and myself had observed as she sat in her nest; but were particularly careful not to disturb her, though we saw she eyed us with some degree of jealousy. Some days after, as we passed that way, we were desirous of remarking how this brood went on; but no nest could be found, till I happened to take up a bundle of long green moss as it were carelessly thrown over the nest in order to dodge the eye of any impertinent intruder.

A still more remarkable instance of sagacity and instinct occurred to me one day, as my people were pulling off the lining of a hotbed in order to add some fresh dung. From out of the side of this bed leaped an animal with great agility that made a most grotesque figure; nor was it without great difficulty that it could be taken; when it proved to be a large white bellied field mouse with three or four young clinging to her teats by their mouths and feet. It was amazing that the desultory and rapid motions of this dam should not oblige her litter to quit their hold, especially when it appeared that they were so young as to be both naked and blind! To these instances of tender attachment, many more of which might be daily discovered by those that are studious of nature: may be opposed that rage of affection, that monstrous perversion of the στοργή, which induces some females of the brute creation to devour their young because their owners have handled them too freely or removed them from place to place! Swine, and sometimes the more gentle race of dogs and cats are guilty of this horrid and preposterous murder. When I hear now and then of an abandoned mother that destroys her offspring, I am not so much amazed; since reason perverted, and the bad passions let loose are capable of any enormity; but why the parental feelings of brutes, that usually flow in one most uniform tenour should sometimes be so extravagantly perverted, I leave to abler philosophers than myself to determine.

The Natural History of Selborne.

P. 207, l. 15. Himself. *An instance of the scientific spirit worth noting. It was not common in White's days.*

TOBIAS SMOLLETT.

Tobias Smollett was born at Dalquhurn in 1721, of the house of Bonhill. He was bred to medicine, served on board a man-of-war, but finally settled down to literature. Most of his work has the faults of hack writing, but his novels, though less universal and more given to "humours" than Fielding's, show genius. He died at Leghorn in 1771.

A BUDGET OF PARADOXES.

OUR adventures, since we left Scarborough, are scarce worth reciting; and yet I must make you acquainted with my sister Tabby's progress in husband-hunting. After her disappointments in Bath and London, she actually begun to practise upon a certain adventurer, who was in fact a highwayman by profession; but he had been used to snares much more dangerous than any she could lay, and escaped accordingly. Then she opened her batteries upon an old weatherbeaten Scotch lieutenant, called Lismahago, who joined us at Durham, and is, I think, one of the most singular personages I ever encountered. His manner is as harsh as his countenance; but his peculiar turn of thinking, and his pack of knowledge, made up of the remnants of rarities, rendered his conversation desirable, in spite of his pedantry and ungracious address. I have often met with a crab-apple in a hedge, which I have been tempted to eat for its flavour, even while I was disgusted by its austerity. The spirit of contradiction is naturally strong in Lismahago, that I believe in my conscience he has rummaged, and read, and studied with indefatigable attention, in order to qualify himself to refute established maxims, and thus raise trophies for the gratification of polemical pride. Such is the asperity of his self-conceit, that he will not even acquiesce in a transient compliment made to his own individual in particular, or to his country in general.

When I observed, that he must have read a vast number of books to be able to discourse on such a variety of subjects, he declared he had read little or nothing, and asked how he should find books among the woods of America, where he had spent the greatest part of his life. My nephew remarking that the Scotch in general were famous for their learning, he denied the imputation, and defied him to prove it from their works. "The Scotch," said he, "have a slight tincture of letters, with which they make a parade among people who are more illiterate than themselves; but they may be said to float on the surface of science, and they have made very small advances in the useful arts."—"At least," cried Tabby, "all the world knows that the Scotch behaved gloriously in fighting and conquering the savages of America."—"I can assure you, madam, you have been misinformed," replied the Lieutenant; "in that continent the Scotch did nothing more than their duty, nor was there one corps in his Majesty's service that distinguished itself more than another. Those who affected to extol the Scotch for superior merit, were no friends to that nation."

Though he himself made free with his countrymen, he would not suffer any other person to glance a sarcasm at them with impunity. One of the company chancing to mention Lord B——'s inglorious peace, the Lieutenant immediately took up the cudgels in his lordship's favour, and argued very strenuously to prove that it was the most honourable and advantageous peace that England had ever made since the foundation of the monarchy. Nay, between friends, he offered such reasons on this subject, that I was really confounded, if not convinced. He would not allow that the Scotch abounded above their proportion in the army and navy of Great Britain, or that the English had any reason to say his countrymen had met with extraordinary encouragement in the service. "When a South or North Briton," said he, "are competitors for a place or commission, which is in the disposal of an English minister, or an English general, it would be absurd to suppose that the preference will not be given to the native of England, who has so many advantages over his rival.—First and foremost, he has in his favour that laudable partiality, which, Mr. Addison says, never fails to cleave to the heart of an Englishman; secondly, he has more powerful connections, and a greater share of parliamentary interest, by which these contests are generally decided; and lastly, he has a greater command of money to smooth the way to his success. For my own part," said he, "I know no Scotch officer who has risen in the army above the rank of a subaltern, without purchasing every degree of preferment either with money or recruits; but I know many gentlemen of that country, who, for want of money and interest, have grown grey in the rank of lieutenants; whereas very few instances of this ill-fortune are to be found among the natives of South Britain. Not that I would insinuate that my countrymen have the least reason to complain. Preferment in the service, like success in any other branch of traffic, will naturally favour those who have the greatest stock of cash and credit, merit and capacity being supposed equal on all sides."

But the most hardy of all this original's positions were these:—That commerce would, sooner or later, prove the ruin of every nation, where it flourishes to any extent—that the parliament was the rotten part of the British constitution—that the liberty of the press was a national evil—and that the boasted institution of juries, as managed in England, was productive of shameful perjury, and flagrant injustice. He observed, that traffic was an enemy to all the liberal passions of the soul, founded on the thirst of lucre, a sordid disposition to take advantage of the necessities of our fellow-creatures. He affirmed the nature of commerce was such, that it could not be fixed or perpetuated, but, having flowed to a certain height, would immediately begin to ebb, and so continue till the channels should be left almost dry; but there was no instance of the tide's rising a second time to any considerable influx in the same nation. Meanwhile, the sudden affluence occasioned by trade, forced open all the sluices of luxury, and overflowed the land with every species of profligacy and corruption; a total depravity of manners would ensue, and this must be attended with bankruptcy and ruin. He observed of the parliament, that the practice of buying boroughs, and canvassing for votes, was an avowed system of venality, already established on the ruins of principle, integrity, faith, and good order; in consequence of which, the elected, and the electors, and, in short, the whole body of the people, were equally and universally contaminated and corrupted. He affirmed, that, of a parliament thus constituted, the crown would always have influence enough to secure a great majority in its dependence, from the great number of posts, places, and pensions it had to bestow; that such a parliament would, as it had already done, lengthen the term of its sitting and authority, whenever the prince should think it for his interest to continue the representatives; for, without doubt, they had the same right to protract their authority *ad infinitum*, as they had to extend it from three to seven years. With a parliament, therefore, dependent upon the crown, devoted to the prince, and supported by a standing army, garbled and modelled for the purpose, any king of England may, and probably some ambitious sovereign will, totally overthrow all the bulwarks of the constitution; for it is not to be supposed, that a prince of high spirit will tamely submit to be thwarted in all his measures, abused and insulted by a populace of unbridled ferocity, when he has it in his power to crush all opposition under his feet with the concurrence of the legislature. He said, he should always consider the liberty of the press as a national evil, while it enabled the vilest reptile to soil the lustre of the most shining merit, and furnished the most infamous incendiary with the means of disturbing the peace, and destroying the good order of the community. He owned, however, that, under due restrictions, it would be a valuable privilege; but affirmed, that at present there was no law in England sufficient to restrain it within proper bounds.

With respect to juries, he expressed himself to this effect:—Juries are generally composed of illiterate plebeians, apt to be mistaken, easily misled, and open to sinister influence; for if either of the parties to be tried can gain over one of the twelve jurors, he has secured the verdict in his favour; the juryman thus brought over, will, in despite of all evidence and conviction, generally hold out till his fellows are fatigued, and harassed, and starved into concurrence, in which case the verdict is unjust, and the jurors are all perjured;—but cases will often occur, when the jurors are really divided in opinion, and each side is convinced in opposition to the other; but no verdict will be received, unless they are unanimous, and they are all bound, not only in conscience, but by oath, to judge and declare according to their conviction. What then will be the consequence? They must either starve in company, or one side must sacrifice their conscience to their convenience, and join in a verdict which they believe to be false.—This absurdity is avoided in Sweden, where a bare majority is sufficient; and in Scotland, where two-thirds of the jury are required to concur in the verdict.

You must not imagine that all these deductions were made on his part, without contradiction on mine. No—the truth is, I found myself piqued in point of honour, at his pretending to be so much wiser than his neighbours. I questioned all his assertions, started innumerable objections, argued and wrangled with uncommon perseverance, and grew very warm, and even violent in the debate. Sometimes he was puzzled, and once or twice, I think, fairly refuted; but from those falls, he rose again, like Antæus, with redoubled vigour, till at length I was tired, exhausted, and really did not know how to proceed, when luckily he dropped a hint, by which he discovered he had been bred to the law; a confession which enabled me to retire from the dispute with a good grace, as it could not be supposed that a man like me, who had been bred to nothing, should be able to cope with a veteran in his own profession. I believe, however, that I shall for some time continue to chew the cud of reflection upon many observations which this original discharged.

Humphrey Clinker.

P. 211, l. 17. Strong . . . that. *We should expect "so strong" or "so that, and it may be a mere printer's error. But the omission of "so" in similar passages was not uncommon.*

P. 212, l. 28. Lord B——. *Of course, Bute.*

P. 214, l. 19. Garbled. *The word properly means to sift, and there is no reason for its modern limitation to literary selection of an unfair kind. As often used, to signify falsification by insertion as well as omission, it is positively wrong.*

ADAM SMITH.

Adam Smith was born at Kirkaldy in 1723, and died at Edinburgh after an uneventful life in 1790. Like his friend Hume, Smith attained rare excellence in two different lines. His Wealth of Nations *is undoubtedly the Bible of political economy, and his* Theory of the Moral Sentiments, *if precariously based, is a model of ingenious system-making.*

PROFESSIONAL GAINS.

FIFTHLY, The wages of labour in different employments vary according to the probability or improbability of success in them.

The probability that any particular person should ever be qualified for the employment to which he is educated, is very different in different occupations. In the greater part of mechanic trades, success is almost certain; but very uncertain in the liberal professions. Put your son apprentice to a shoemaker, there is little doubt of his learning to make a pair of shoes: But send him to study the law, it is at least twenty to one if ever he makes such a proficiency as will enable him to live by the business. In a perfectly fair lottery, those who draw the prizes ought to gain all that is lost by those who draw the blanks. In a profession where twenty fail for one that succeeds, that one ought to gain all that should have been gained by the unsuccessful twenty. The counsellor at law, who, perhaps, at near forty years of age, begins to make something by his profession, ought to receive the retribution, not only of his own so tedious and expensive education, but of that of more than twenty others who are never likely to make anything by it. How extravagant soever the fees of counsellors at law may sometimes appear, their real retribution is never equal to this. Compute in any particular place, what is likely to be annually gained, and what is likely to be annually spent, by all the different workmen in any common trade, such as that of shoemakers or weavers, and you will find that the former sum will generally exceed the latter. But make the same computation with regard to all the counsellors and students of law, in all the different inns of court, and you will find that their annual gains bear but a very small proportion to their annual expense, even though you rate the former as high, and the latter as low, as can well be done. The lottery of the law, therefore, is very far from being a perfectly fair lottery; and that, as well as many other liberal and honourable professions, is, in point of pecuniary gain, evidently under-recompensed.

Those professions keep their level, however, with other occupations, and, notwithstanding these discouragements, all the most generous and liberal spirits are eager to crowd into them. Two different causes contribute to recommend them. First, the desire of the reputation which attends upon superior excellence in any of them; and, secondly, the natural confidence which every man has more or less, not only in his own abilities, but in his own good fortune.

To excel in any profession, in which but few arrive at mediocrity, is the most decisive mark of what is called genius or superior talents. The public admiration which attends upon such distinguished abilities, makes always a part of their reward; a greater or smaller in proportion as it is higher or lower in degree. It makes a considerable part of that reward in the profession of physic; a still greater perhaps in that of law; in poetry and philosophy it makes almost the whole.

There are some very agreeable and beautiful talents of which the possession commands a certain sort of admiration; but of which the exercise for the sake of gain is considered, whether from reason or prejudice, as a sort of public prostitution. The pecuniary recompense, therefore, of those who exercise them in this manner, must be sufficient, not only to pay for the time, labour, and expense of acquiring the talents, but for the discredit which attends the employment of them as the means of subsistence. The exorbitant rewards of players, opera-singers, opera-dancers, etc., are founded upon those two principles; the rarity and beauty of the talents, and the discredit of employing them in this manner. It seems absurd at first sight that we should despise their persons, and yet reward their talents with the most profuse liberality. While we do the one, however, we must of necessity do the other. Should the public opinion or prejudice ever alter with regard to such occupations, their pecuniary recompense would quickly diminish. More people would apply to them, and the competition would quickly reduce the price of their labour. Such talents, though far from being common, are by no means so rare as is imagined. Many people possess them in great perfection, who disdain to make this use of them; and many more are capable of acquiring them, if anything could be made honourably by them.

The Nature and Causes of the Wealth of Nations.

SIR JOSHUA REYNOLDS.

Sir Joshua Reynolds was born at Plympton in 1723, and died in London in 1792. More usually thought of as a painter only, Sir Joshua in his Discourses, Essays, and Notes on Art, exhibits to the full the good sense, the measure, and the order in thought and expression, which are the chief glories of the eighteenth century.

THE CRITERION OF BEAUTY.

I SUPPOSE it will be easily granted, that no man can judge whether any animal be beautiful in its kind, or deformed, who has seen only one of that species : this is as conclusive in regard to the human figure ; so that if a man, born blind, was to recover his sight, and the most beautiful woman was brought before him, he could not determine whether she was handsome or not ; nor, if the most beautiful and most deformed were produced, could he any better determine to which he should give the preference, having seen only those two. To distinguish beauty, then, implies the having seen many individuals of that species. If it is asked, how is more skill acquired by the observation of greater numbers ? I answer that, in consequence of having seen many, the power is acquired, even without seeking after it, of distinguishing between accidental blemishes and excrescences which are continually varying the surface of Nature's works, and the invariable general form which Nature most frequently produces, and always seems to intend in her productions.

Thus, amongst the blades of grass or leaves of the same tree, though no two can be found exactly alike, yet the general form is invariable: a naturalist, before he chose one as a sample, would examine many, since, if he took the first that occurred, it might have by accident or otherwise, such a form as that it would scarcely be known to belong to that species; he selects, as the painter does, the most beautiful, that is, the most general form of nature.

Every species of the animal, as well as the vegetable creation, may be said to have a fixed or determinate form towards which Nature is continually inclining, like various lines terminating in the centre; or it may be compared to pendulums vibrating in different directions over one central point; and as they all cross the centre, though only one passes through any other point, so it will be found that perfect beauty is oftener produced by Nature than deformity; I do not mean than deformity in general, but than any one kind of deformity. To instance in a particular part of a feature: the line that forms the ridge of the nose is beautiful when it is straight; this then is the central form, which is oftener found than either concave, convex, or any other irregular form that shall be proposed. As we are then more accustomed to beauty than deformity, we may conclude that to be the reason why we approve and admire it, as we approve and admire customs and fashions of dress for no other reason than that we are used to them; so that, though habit and custom cannot be said to be the cause of beauty, it is certainly the cause of our liking it; and I have no doubt but that, if we were more used to deformity than beauty, deformity would then lose the idea now annexed to it, and take that of beauty; as, if the whole world should agree that *yes* and *no* should change their meanings, *yes* would then deny, and *no* would affirm.

Whoever undertakes to proceed further in this argument, and endeavours to fix a general criterion of beauty respecting different species, or to show why one species is more beautiful than another, it will be required from him first to prove that one species is really more beautiful than another. That we prefer one to the other, and with very good reason, will be readily granted; but it does not follow from thence that we think it a more beautiful form; for we have no criterion of form by which to determine our judgment. He who says a swan is more beautiful than a dove, means little more than that he has more pleasure in seeing a swan than a dove, either from the stateliness of its motions, or its being a more rare bird; and he who gives the preference to the dove, does it from some association of ideas of innocence that he always annexes to the dove; but, if he pretends to defend the preference he gives to one or to the other by endeavouring to prove that this more beautiful form proceeds from a particular gradation of magnitude, undulation of a curve, or direction of a line, or whatever other conceit of his imagination he shall fix on as a criterion of form, he will be continually contradicting himself, and find at last, that the great Mother of Nature will not be subjected to such narrow rules. Among the various reasons why we prefer one part of her works to another, the most general, I believe, is habit and custom; custom makes, in a certain sense, white black, and black white; it is custom alone determines our preference of the colour of the Europeans to the Ethiopians; and they for the same reason, prefer their own colour to ours. I suppose nobody will doubt, if one of their painters were to paint the goddess of beauty, but that he would represent her black, with thick lips, flat nose, and woolly hair; and, it seems to me, he would act very unnaturally if he did not; for by what criterion will any one dispute the propriety of his idea? We, indeed, say, that the form and colour of the European is preferable to that of the Ethiopian; but I know of no reason we have for it, but that we are more accustomed to it. It is absurd to say, that beauty is possessed of attractive powers, which irresistibly seize the corresponding mind with love and admiration, since that argument is equally conclusive in favour of the white and the black philosopher.

The black and white nations must, in respect of beauty, be considered as of different kinds, at least a different species of the same kind; from one of which to the other, as I observed, no inference can be drawn.

Novelty is said to be one of the causes of beauty: that novelty is a very sufficient reason why we should admire, is not denied; but, because it is uncommon, is it, therefore, beautiful? The beauty that is produced by colour, as when we prefer one bird to another, though of the same form, on account of its colour, has nothing to do with this argument, which reaches only to form. I have here considered the word *beauty* as being properly applied to form alone. There is a necessity of fixing this confined sense; for there can be no argument, if the sense of the word is extended to everything that is approved. A rose may as well be said to be beautiful, because it has a fine smell, as a bird because of its colour. When we apply the word *beauty* we do not mean always by it a more beautiful form, but something valuable on account of its rarity, usefulness, colour, or any other property. A horse is said to be a beautiful animal; but, had a horse as few good qualities as a tortoise, I do not imagine that he would be then esteemed beautiful.

A fitness to the end proposed, is said to be another cause of beauty; but supposing we were proper judges of what form is the most proper in an animal to constitute strength or swiftness, we always determine concerning its beauty, before we exert our understanding to judge of its fitness.

From what has been said, it may be inferred, that the works of nature, if we compare one species with another, are all equally beautiful; and that preference is given from custom, or some association of ideas: and that, in creatures of the same species, beauty is the medium or centre of all various forms.

To conclude, then, by way of corollary: If it has been proved, that the painter, by attending to the invariable and general ideas of nature, produces beauty, he must, by regarding minute particularities and accidental discriminations, deviate from the universal rule, and pollute his canvas with deformity.

The Idler.

P. 220, l. 19. *Oftener found. A very dubious assertion even in regard to the Caucasian type.*

P. 222, l. 7. *A fine smell. Did Miss Ferrier, who seems to laugh at this phrase as a Scotticism in Marriage, know that it had Sir Joshua's authority as writer and Dr. Johnson's as editor?*

OLIVER GOLDSMITH.

Oliver Goldsmith, born at Pallas in Ireland in 1728, studied medicine, wandered through Europe, returned to England, emerged through usherhood into literature, and for the last ten years of his life enjoyed sufficient means. He died in 1774. The simplicity of his pathos and the gentleness of his humour have never been equalled.

THE STROLLING PLAYER.

I AM fond of amusement, in whatever company it is to be found; and wit, though dressed in rags, is ever pleasing to me. I went some days ago to take a walk in St. James's Park, about the hour in which company leave it to go to dinner. There were but few in the walks, and those who stayed seemed, by their looks, rather more willing to forget that they had an appetite than gain one. I sat down on one of the benches, at the other end of which was seated a man in very shabby clothes.

We continued to groan, to hem, and to cough, as usual upon such occasions; and at last ventured upon conversation. "I beg pardon, sir," cried I, "but I think I have seen you before; your face is familiar to me."—"Yes, sir," replied he, "I have a good familiar face, as my friends tell me. I am as well known in every town in England as the dromedary or live crocodile. You must understand, sir, that I have been these sixteen years Merry Andrew to a puppet-show; last Bartholomew Fair my master and I quarrelled, beat each other, and parted; he to sell his puppets to the pincushion-makers in Rosemary Lane, and I to starve in St. James's Park."

"I am sorry, sir, that a person of your appearance should labour under any difficulties." "Oh, sir," returned he, "my appearance is very much at your service; but though I cannot boast of eating much, yet there are few that are merrier: if I had twenty thousand a year, I should be very merry; and, thank the Fates, though not worth a groat, I am very merry still. If I have three pence in my pocket, I never refuse to be my three-halfpence; and if I have no money, I never scorn to be treated by any that are kind enough to pay my reckoning. What think you, sir, of a steak and a tankard? You shall treat me now; and I will treat you again, when I find you in the Park in love with eating, and without money to pay for a dinner."

As I never refuse a small expense for the sake of a merry companion, we instantly adjourned to a neighbouring ale-house, and in a few moments had a frothing tankard and a smoking steak spread on the table before us. It is impossible to express how much the sight of such good cheer improved my companion's vivacity. "I like this dinner, sir," says he, "for three reasons: first, because I am naturally fond of beef; secondly, because I am hungry; and, thirdly and lastly, because I get it for nothing: no meat eats so sweet as that for which we do not pay."

He therefore now fell to, and his appetite seemed to correspond with his inclination. After dinner was over, he observed that the steak was tough: "and yet, sir," returns he, "bad as it was, it seemed a rump-steak to me. Oh, the delights of poverty and a good appetite! We beggars are the very fondlings of Nature; the rich she treats like an arrant stepmother; they are pleased with nothing: cut a steak from what part you will, and it is insupportably tough; dress it up with pickles, and even pickles cannot procure them an appetite. But the whole creation is filled with good things for the beggar; Calvert's butt outtastes champagne, and Sedgeley's home-brewed excels Tokay. Joy, joy, my blood! though our estates lie nowhere, we have fortunes wherever we go. If an inundation sweeps away half the grounds of Cornwall, I am content—I have no lands there; if the stocks sink, that gives me no uneasiness—I am no Jew."

The fellow's vivacity, joined to his poverty, I own, raised my curiosity to know something of his life and circumstances; and

I entreated that he would indulge my desire. "That I will, sir," said he, "and welcome; only let us drink to prevent our sleeping: let us have another tankard while we are awake—let us have another tankard; for, ah, how charming a tankard looks when full!"

Essays.

P. 223, l. 18. Pincushion makers, *to whom their sawdust stuffing would be useful.*

P. 224, l. 8. To be my three-halfpence. *This good old phrase, signifying to club or subscribe the amount, is not quite extinct. At a recent inquiry before the magistrate into the death of an unfortunate girl in Westminster, one of the witnesses described himself as having said to another, "If you'll be sixpence, Clara, I'll be sixpence," the proposal being that they should club their money for medicine.*

P. 224, l. 25. A rump-steak. *It is sad to think that out of London and a few large towns this distinction is not universally known even yet.*

P. 224, ll. 31, 32. Calvert *is frequent in the eighteenth century writers as a brewer;* Sedgeley *less common.*

EDMUND BURKE.

Edmund Burke was born at Dublin in 1730. A private secretaryship brought him into politics, and he became one of the chief Parliamentary Whigs. His strenuous assaults on Warren Hastings and the French Revolution are the most famous events in his life. Burke spoke well but wrote better, and his political writing has, in the grand style, few equals. He died in 1797.

ON REFORM.

MANY of the changes, by a great misnomer called parliamentary reforms, went, not in the intention of all the professors and supporters of them, undoubtedly, but went in their certain, and, in my opinion, not very remote effect, home to the utter destruction of the constitution of this kingdom. Had they taken place, not France, but England, would have had the honour of leading up the death-dance of democratic revolution. Other projects, exactly coincident in time with those, struck at the very existence of the kingdom under any constitution. There are who remember the blind fury of some, and the lamentable helplessness of others; here, a torpid confusion, from a panic fear of the danger; there, the same inaction from a stupid insensibility to it; here, well-wishers to the mischief; there, indifferent lookers-on. At the same time, a sort of national convention, dubious in its nature, and perilous in its example, nosed parliament in the very seat of its authority; sat with a sort of superintendence over it; and little less than dictated to it, not only laws, but, the very form and essence of legislature itself. In Ireland things ran in a still more eccentric course. Government was unnerved, confounded, and in a manner suspended. Its equipoise was totally gone. I do not mean to speak disrespectfully of Lord North. He was a man of admirable parts; of general knowledge; of a versatile understanding fitted for every sort of business; of infinite wit and pleasantry; of a delightful temper; and with a mind most perfectly disinterested. But it would be only to degrade myself by a weak adulation, and not to honour the memory of a great man, to deny that he wanted something of the vigilance and spirit of command, that the time required. Indeed, a darkness, next to the fog of this awful day, loured over the whole region. For a little time the helm appeared abandoned—

> Ipse diem noctemque negat discernere cœlo,
> Nec meminisse viæ media Palinurus in unda.

At that time I was connected with men of high place in the community. They loved liberty as much as the Duke of Bedford can do; and they understood it at least as well. Perhaps their politics, as usual, took a tincture from their character, and they cultivated what they loved. The liberty they pursued was a liberty inseparable from order, from virtue, from morals, and from religion; and was neither hypocritically nor fanatically followed. They did not wish, that liberty, in itself one of the first of blessings, should in its perversion become the greatest curse which could fall upon mankind. To preserve the constitution entire, and practically equal to all the great ends of its reformation, not in one single part, but in all its parts, was to them the first object. Popularity and power they regarded alike. These were with them only different means of obtaining that object; and had no preference over each other in their minds, but as one or the other might afford a surer or a less certain prospect of arriving at that end. It is some consolation to me in the cheerless gloom, which darkens the evening of my life, that with them I commenced my political career, and never for a moment, in reality, nor in appearance, for any length of time, was separated from their good wishes and good opinion.

By what accident it matters not, nor upon what desert, but just then, and in the midst of that hunt of obloquy, which ever has pursued me with a full cry through life, I had obtained a very considerable degree of public confidence. I know well enough how equivocal a test this kind of popular opinion forms of the merit that obtained it. I am no stranger to the insecurity of its tenure. I do not boast of it. It is mentioned to show, not how highly I prize the thing, but my right to value the use I made of it. I endeavoured to turn that short-lived advantage to myself into a permanent benefit to my country. Far am I from detracting from the merit of some gentlemen, out of office or in it, on that occasion. No!—It is not my way to refuse a full and heaped measure of justice to the aids that I receive. I have, through life, been willing to give every thing to others; and to reserve nothing for myself, but the inward conscience, that I had omitted no pains to discover, to animate, to discipline, to direct the abilities of the country for its service, and to place them in the best light to improve their age, or to adorn it. This conscience I have. I have never suppressed any man; never checked him for a moment in his course, by any jealousy, or by any policy. I was always ready, to the height of my means, and they were always infinitely below my desires, to forward those abilities which overpowered my own. He is an ill furnished undertaker, who has no machinery but his own hands to work with. Poor in my own faculties, I ever thought myself rich in theirs. In that period of difficulty and danger, more especially, I consulted, and sincerely co-operated with, men of all parties, who seemed disposed to the same ends, or to any main part of them. Nothing to prevent disorder was omitted: when it appeared, nothing to subdue it was left uncounselled, nor unexecuted, as far as I could prevail. At the time I speak of, and having a momentary lead, so aided and so encouraged, and as a feeble instrument in a mighty hand—I do not say I saved my country; I am sure I did my country important service.

Letter to a noble Lord.

GROUNDS OF SYMPATHY WITH FRANCE.

IT is observed, that this party has never spoken of an ally of Great Britain with the smallest degree of respect or regard;

on the contrary, it has generally mentioned them under opprobrious appellations, and in such terms of contempt or execration, as never had been heard before, because no such would have formerly been permitted in our public assemblies. The moment, however, that any of those allies quitted this obnoxious connexion, the party has instantly passed an act of indemnity and oblivion in their favour. After this, no sort of censure on their conduct; no imputation on their character! From that moment their pardon was sealed in a reverential and mysterious silence. With the gentlemen of this minority, there is no ally from one end of Europe to the other, with whom we ought not to be ashamed to act. The whole college of the states of Europe is no better than a gang of tyrants. With them all our connexions were broken off at once. We ought to have cultivated France, and France alone, from the moment of her Revolution. On that happy change, all our dread of that nation as a power was to cease. She became in an instant dear to our affections, and one with our interests. All other nations we ought to have commanded not to trouble her sacred throes, whilst in labour to bring into a happy birth her abundant litter of constitutions. We ought to have acted under her auspices, in extending her salutary influence upon every side. From that moment England and France were become natural allies, and all the other states natural enemies. The whole face of the world was changed. What was it to us if she acquired Holland and the Austrian Netherlands? By her conquests she only enlarged the sphere of her beneficence; she only extended the blessings of liberty to so many more foolishly reluctant nations. What was it to England, if by adding these, among the richest and most peopled countries of the world, to her territories, she thereby left no possible link of communication between us and any other power with whom we could act against her? On this new system of optimism, it is so much the better;—so much the further are we removed from the contact with infectious despotism. No longer a thought of a barrier in the Netherlands to Holland against France. All that is obsolete policy. It is fit that France should have both Holland and the Austrian Netherlands too, as a barrier to her against the attacks of despotism. She cannot multiply her securities too much; and as to our security, it is to be found in hers. Had we cherished her from the beginning, and felt for her when attacked, she, poor good soul, would never have invaded any foreign nation; never murdered her sovereign and his family; never proscribed, never exiled, never imprisoned, never been guilty of extrajudicial massacre, or of legal murder. All would have been a golden age, full of peace, order, and liberty! and philosophy, raying out from Europe, would have warmed and enlightened the universe: but unluckily, irritable philosophy, the most irritable of all things, was put into a passion, and provoked into ambition abroad, and tyranny at home. They find all this very natural and very justifiable. They choose to forget, that other nations, struggling for freedom, have been attacked by their neighbours; or that their neighbours have otherwise interfered in their affairs. Often have neighbours interfered in favour of princes against their rebellious subjects; and often in favour of subjects against their prince. Such cases fill half the pages of history, yet never were they used as an apology, much less as a justification, for atrocious cruelty in princes, or for general massacre and confiscation on the part of revolted subjects; never as a politic cause for suffering any such powers to aggrandize themselves without limit and without measure. A thousand times have we seen it asserted in public prints and pamphlets, that if the nobility and priesthood of France had staid at home, their property never would have been confiscated. One would think that none of the clergy had been robbed previous to their deportation, or that their deportation had, on their part, been a voluntary act. One would think that the nobility and gentry, and merchants and bankers, who staid at home, had enjoyed their property in security and repose. The assertors of these positions well know, that the lot of thousands who remained at home was far more terrible; that the most cruel imprisonment was only a harbinger of a cruel and ignominious death; and that in this mother country of freedom there were no less than *Three Hundred Thousand* at one time in prison. I go no further. I instance only these representations of the party, as stating indications of partiality to that sect, to whose dominion they would have left this country nothing to oppose but her own naked force, and consequently subjected us, on every reverse of fortune, to the imminent danger of falling under those very evils in that very system, which are attributed, not to its own nature, but to the perverseness of others. There is nothing in the world so difficult as to put men in a state of judicial neutrality. A leaning there must ever be, and it is of the first importance to any nation to observe to what side that leaning inclines—whether to our own community, or to one with which it is in a state of hostility.

On a Regicide Peace.

P. 226, l. 8. Time. *Burke is speaking of the last years of Lord North's administration in 1778-1782. The Duke of Bedford referred to below was Francis, 5th Duke, a busy but not very able or high-minded politician.*

P. 226, l. 16. Nosed. *Not in the sense common earlier, of "scented" or "tracked," but "met face to face," "confronted."*

i
l
p
b
rc
th
B
du
Lt
no
wo
of
anc
thi
of
hei
of ;
hop
all
smc
wot
voic
recl
like
drav
how
parti
ascer
there
our
that
how
do ev
numl
to be

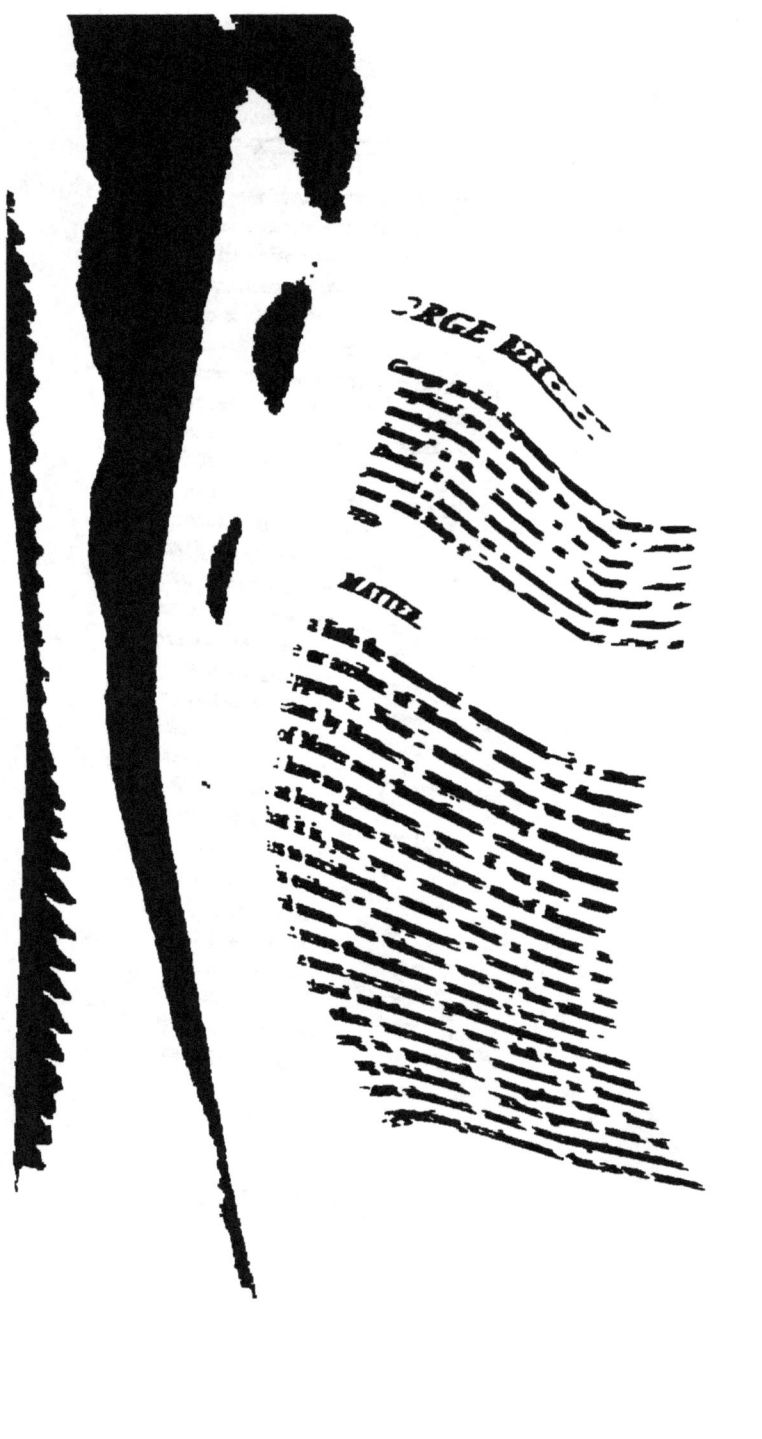

EDWARD GIBBON.

Edward Gibbon, one of the great historians of the world, was born at Putney in 1737. His early vacillations in love and religion are famous; his later occupations as a member of Parliament and a placeman have left no mark. For knowledge, judgment, range, and style combined, his History has no rival in literature. He died in 1794.

THE HERESY OF APOLLINARIS.

ALL those who believe the immateriality of the soul, a specious and noble tenet, must confess, from their present experience, the incomprehensible union of mind and matter. A similar union is not inconsistent with a much higher, or even with the highest, degree of mental faculties; and the incarnation of an æon or archangel, the most perfect of created spirits, does not involve any positive contradiction or absurdity. In the age of religious freedom, which was determined by the Council of Nice, the dignity of Christ was measured by private judgment according to the indefinite rule of Scripture, or reason, or tradition. But when his pure and proper divinity had been established on the ruins of Arianism, the faith of the Catholics trembled on the edge of a precipice where it was possible to recede, dangerous to stand, dreadful to fall; and the manifold inconveniences of their creed were aggravated by the sublime character of their theology. They hesitated to pronounce— *that* God himself, the second person of an equal and consubstantial trinity, was manifested in the flesh; *that* a being who pervades the universe had been confined in the womb of Mary;

that his eternal duration had been marked by the days, and months, and years of human existence ; *that* the Almighty had been scourged and crucified ; *that* his impassible essence had felt pain and anguish ; *that* his omniscience was not exempt from ignorance; and *that* the source of life and immortality expired on Mount Calvary. These alarming consequences were affirmed with unblushing simplicity by Apollinaris, bishop of Laodicea, and one of the luminaries of the church. The son of a learned grammarian, he was skilled in all the sciences of Greece ; eloquence, erudition, and philosophy, conspicuous in the volumes of Apollinaris, were humbly devoted to the service of religion. The worthy friend of Athanasius, the worthy antagonist of Julian, he bravely wrestled with the Arians and Polytheists, and, though he affected the rigour of geometrical demonstration, his commentaries revealed the literal and allegorical sense of the Scriptures. A mystery which had long floated in the looseness of popular belief was defined by his perverse diligence in a technical form ; and he first proclaimed the memorable words, " One incarnate nature of Christ," which are still re-echoed with hostile clamours in the churches of Asia, Egypt and Æthiopia. He taught that the Godhead was united or mingled with the body of a man ; and that the *Logos*, the eternal wisdom, supplied in the flesh the place and office of an human soul. Yet, as the profound doctor had been terrified at his own rashness, Apollinaris was heard to mutter some faint accents of excuse and explanation. He acquiesced in the old distinction of the Greek philosophers between the rational and sensitive soul of man ; that he might reserve the *Logos* for intellectual functions, and employ the subordinate human principle in the meaner actions of animal life. With the moderate Docetes he revered Mary as the spiritual, rather than as the carnal, mother of Christ, whose body either came from heaven, impassible or incorruptible, or was absorbed, and as it were transformed, into the essence of the Deity. The system of Apollinaris was strenuously encountered by the Asiatic and Syrian divines, whose schools are honoured by the names of Basil, Gregory, and Chrysostom, and tainted by those of Diodorus, Theodore, and Nestorius. But the person of the aged bishop of Laodicea, his character and dignity, remained inviolate; and his rivals, since we may not suspect them of the weakness of toleration, were astonished perhaps, by the novelty of the argument, and diffident of the final sentence of the Catholic church. Her judgment at length inclined to their favour; the heresy of Apollinaris was condemned, and the separate congregations of his disciples were proscribed by the Imperial laws. But his principles were secretly entertained in the monasteries of Egypt, and his enemies felt the hatred of Theophilus and Cyril, the successive patriarchs of Alexandria.

The grovelling Ebionite and the fantastic Docetes were rejected and forgotten: the recent zeal against the errors of Apollinaris reduced the Catholics to a seeming agreement with the double nature of Cerinthus. But instead of a temporary and occasional alliance, *they* established, and *we* still embrace, the substantial, indissoluble, and everlasting union of a perfect God with a perfect man, of the second person of the trinity with a reasonable soul and human flesh. In the beginning of the fifth century the *unity* of the *two natures* was the prevailing doctrine of the church. On all sides it was confessed that the mode of their co-existence could neither be represented by our ideas nor expressed by our language. Yet a secret and incurable discord was cherished between those who were most apprehensive of confounding, and those who were most fearful of separating the divinity and humanity of Christ. Impelled by religious frenzy, they fled with adverse haste from the error which they mutually deemed most destructive of truth and salvation. On either hand they were anxious to guard, they were jealous to defend, the union and the distinction of the two natures, and to invent such forms of speech, such symbols of doctrine, as were least susceptible of doubt or ambiguity. The poverty of ideas and language tempted them to ransack art and nature for every possible comparison, and each comparison misled their fancy in the explanation of an incomparable mystery. In the polemic microscope an atom is enlarged to a monster, and each party was skilful to exaggerate the absurd or impious conclusions that might be extorted from the principles of their adversaries. To escape from each other they wandered through many a dark and devious thicket, till they were astonished by the horrid phantoms of Cerinthus and Apollinaris, who guarded the opposite issues of the theological labyrinth. As soon as they beheld the twilight of sense and heresy, they started, measured back their steps, and were again involved in the gloom of impenetrable orthodoxy. To purge themselves from the guilt or reproach of damnable error, they disavowed their consequences, explained their principles, excused their indiscretions, and unanimously pronounced the sounds of concord and faith. Yet a latent and almost invisible spark still lurked among the embers of controversy: by the breath of prejudice and passion it was quickly kindled to a mighty flame, and the verbal disputes of the Oriental sects have shaken the pillars of the church and state.

The History of the Decline and Fall of the Roman Empire.

HIS CONVERSION TO THE ROMAN CHURCH.

It might at least be expected than an ecclesiastical school should inculcate the orthodox principles of religion. But our venerable mother had contrived to unite the opposite extremes of bigotry and indifference; an heretic, or unbeliever, was a monster in her eyes; but she was always, or often, or sometimes, remiss in the spiritual education of her own children. According to the statutes of the university, every student, before he is matriculated, must subscribe his assent to the Thirty-nine Articles of the church of England, which are signed by more than read, and read by more than believe them. My insufficient age excused me, however, from the immediate performance of this legal ceremony; and the vice-chancellor directed me to return as soon as I should have accomplished my fifteenth year; recommending me, in the mean while, to the instruction of my college. My college forgot to instruct; I forgot to return, and was myself forgotten by the first magistrate of the university. Without a single lecture, either public or private, either Christian or Protestant, without any academical subscription, without any episcopal confirmation, I was left by the dim light of my catechism to grope my way to the chapel and communion-table, where I was admitted, without a question how far, or by what means, I might be qualified to receive the sacrament. Such almost incredible neglect was productive of the worst mischiefs. From my childhood I had been fond of religious disputation. My poor aunt has been often puzzled by the mysteries which she strove to believe; nor had the elastic spring been totally broken by the weight of the atmosphere of Oxford. The blind activity of idleness urged me to advance without armour into the dangerous mazes of controversy; and, at the age of sixteen, I bewildered myself in the errors of the church of Rome.

The progress of my conversion may tend to illustrate at least the history of my own mind. It was not long since Dr. Middleton's Free Inquiry had sounded an alarm in the theological world: much ink and much gall had been spilt in the defence of the primitive miracles; and the two dullest of their champions were crowned with academic honours by the university of Oxford. The name of Middleton was unpopular; and his proscription very naturally led me to peruse his writings, and those of his antagonists. His bold criticism, which approaches the precipice of infidelity, produced on my mind a singular effect; and had I persevered in the communion of Rome, I should now apply to my own fortune the prediction of the Sibyl,

——Via prima salutis,
Quod minime reris, Graia pandetur ab urbe.

The elegance of style and freedom of argument were repelled by a shield of prejudice. I still revered the character, or rather the names, of the saints and fathers whom Dr. Middleton exposes; nor could he destroy my implicit belief that the gift of miraculous powers was continued in the church during the first four or five centuries of Christianity. But I was unable to resist the weight of historical evidence, that within the same period most of the leading doctrines of popery were already introduced in theory and practice: nor was my conclusion absurd, that miracles are the test of truth, and that the church must be orthodox and pure which was so often approved by the visible interposition of the Deity. The marvellous tales which are so boldly attested by the Basils and Chrysostoms, the Austins and

Jeromes, compelled me to embrace the superior merits of celibacy, the institution of the monastic life, the use of the sign of the cross, of holy oil, and even of images, the invocation of saints, the worship of relics, the rudiments of purgatory in prayers for the dead, and the tremendous mystery of the sacrifice of the body and blood of Christ, which insensibly swelled into the prodigy of transubstantiation. In these dispositions, and already more than half a convert, I formed an unlucky intimacy with a young gentleman of our college. With a character less resolute, Mr. Molesworth had imbibed the same religious opinions; and some popish books, I know not through what channel, were conveyed into his possession. I read, I applauded, I believed: the English translations of two famous works of Bossuet, Bishop of Meaux, the Exposition of the Catholic Doctrine, and the History of the Protestant Variations, achieved my conversion, and I surely fell by a noble hand. I have since examined the originals with a more discerning eye, and shall not hesitate to pronounce that Bossuet is indeed a master of all the weapons of controversy. In the Exposition, a specious apology, the orator assumes, with consummate art, the tone of candour and simplicity; and the ten-horned monster is transformed, at his magic touch, into the milkwhite hind, who must be loved as soon as she is seen. In the History, a bold and well-aimed attack, he displays, with a happy mixture of narrative and argument, the faults and follies, the changes and contradictions of our first reformers; whose variations, as he dexterously contends, are the mark of historical error, while the perpetual unity of the Catholic church is the sign and test of infallible truth. To my present feelings it seems incredible that I should ever believe that I believed in transubstantiation. But my conqueror oppressed me with the sacramental words, "Hoc est corpus meum," and dashed against each other the figurative half-meanings of the Protestant sects: every objection was resolved into omnipotence; and after repeating at St. Mary's the Athanasian Creed, I humbly acquiesced in the mystery of the real presence.

"To take up half on trust, and half to try,
Name it not faith, but bungling bigotry.
Both knave and fool the merchant we may call,

> To pay great sums, and to compound the small,
> For who would break with Heaven, and would not break for all?"

No sooner had I settled my new religion than I resolved to profess myself a Catholic. Youth is sincere and impetuous; and a momentary glow of enthusiasm had raised me above all temporal considerations.

Memoirs of my Life and Writings.

P. 232, l. 8. Determined. *In the proper sense, "put an end to."*

P. 234, l. 26. Mutually. *This word and its congeners have been rightly classed among the greatest cruces of the correct use of English. It does not here form an exception to Gibbon's general impeccableness of style. The opponents respectively regarded confusion and identification as capital errors.*

P. 236, l. 13. Dr. Middleton. *Conyers Middleton. The book in question, and others of his works, while nominally directed against Rome, were thought to adopt a line of argument unfriendly to Christianity generally.*

P. 237, l. 22. The milkwhite hind. *A reference, of course, to Dryden's famous poem.*

JAMES BOSWELL.

James Boswell of Auchinleck was born in 1740, travelled, drank, wrote, haunted Johnson, and practised at the bar till 1795. A paradox in himself, Boswell has been a great cause of paradoxes. The virtue of his incomparable Life *of Johnson, though apparently parasitic, has been recognised by the best judges as original. He died in 1795.*

CHARACTER OF DR. JOHNSON.

DR. SAMUEL JOHNSON'S character, religious, moral, political, and literary, nay his figure and manner, are, I believe, more generally known than those of almost any man; yet it may not be superfluous here to attempt a sketch of him. Let my readers then remember that he was a sincere and zealous Christian, of high church of England and monarchial principles, which he would not tamely suffer to be questioned; steady and inflexible in maintaining the obligations of piety and virtue, both from a regard to the order of society, and from a veneration for the Great Source of all order; correct, nay stern in his taste; hard to please, and easily offended, impetuous and irritable in his temper, but of a most humane and benevolent heart; having a mind stored with a vast and various collection of learning and knowledge, which he communicated with peculiar perspicuity and force, in rich and choice expression. He united a most logical head with a most fertile imagination, which gave him an extraordinary advantage in arguing; for he could reason close or wide, as he saw best for the moment. He could, when he chose it, be the greatest sophist that ever wielded a weapon in the schools of declamation; but he indulged this only in conversation; for he owned he sometimes talked for victory; he was too conscientious to make error permanent and pernicious, by deliberately writing it. He was conscious of his superiority. He loved praise when it was brought to him; but was too proud to seek for it. He was somewhat susceptible of flattery. His mind was so full of imagery, that he might have been perpetually a poet. It has been often remarked, that in his poetical pieces, which it is to be regretted are so few, because so excellent, his style is easier than in his prose. There is deception in this: it is not easier, but better suited to the dignity of verse; as one may dance with grace, whose motions, in ordinary walking,—in the common step, are awkward. He had a constitutional melancholy, the clouds of which darkened the brightness of his fancy, and gave a gloomy cast to his whole course of thinking: yet, though grave and awful in his deportment, when he thought it necessary or proper, he frequently indulged himself in pleasantry and sportive sallies. He was prone to superstition, but not to credulity. Though his imagination might incline him to a belief of the marvellous, and the mysterious, his vigorous reason examined the evidence with jealousy. He had a loud voice, and a slow deliberate utterance, which no doubt gave some additional weight to the sterling metal of his conversation. His person was large, robust, I may say approaching to the gigantic, and grown unwieldy from corpulency. His countenance was naturally of the cast of an ancient statue, but somewhat disfigured by the scars of that *evil*, which, it was formerly imagined the *royal touch* could cure. He was now in his sixty-fourth year, and was become a little dull of hearing. His sight had always been somewhat weak; yet, so much does mind govern, and even supply the deficiency of organs, that his perceptions were uncommonly quick and accurate. His head, and sometimes also his body, shook with a kind of motion like the effect of a palsy; he appeared to be frequently disturbed by cramps, or convulsive contractions, of the nature of that distemper called *St. Vitus's dance*. He wore a full suit of plain brown clothes, with twisted-hair-buttons of the same colour, a large bushy greyish wig, a plain shirt, black worsted stockings,

and silver buckles. Upon this tour, when journeying, he wore boots, and a very wide brown cloth great coat, with pockets which might have almost held the two volumes of his folio dictionary; and he carried in his hand a large English oak stick.
The Journal of a Tour to the Hebrides.

P. 239, l. 6. Monarchial. *We say now "monarchical," which has prevailed not merely over "monarchial," but over "monarchal."*

SIR PHILIP FRANCIS.

Sir Philip Francis, who ranks here hypothetically as Junius, was born at Dublin in 1740, and after serving in the public offices, in the diplomatic service, and on the council of Bengal, entered parliament. He died in 1818. The Letters of Junius, with which he is credited, are perhaps more famous than excellent, but still excellent.

TO THE DUKE OF GRAFTON.

WITH what force, my Lord, with what protection, are you prepared to meet the united detestation of the people of England? The city of London has given a generous example to the kingdom, in what manner a king of this country ought to be addressed; and I fancy, my Lord, it is not yet in your courage to stand between your sovereign and the addresses of his subjects. The injuries you have done this country are such as demand not only redress, but vengeance. In vain shall you look for protection to that venal vote, which you have already paid for—another must be purchased; and to save a minister, the House of Commons must declare themselves not only independent of their constituents, but the determined enemies of the constitution. Consider, my Lord, whether this be an extremity to which their fears will permit them to advance; or, if *their* protection should fail you, how far you are authorised to rely upon the sincerity of those smiles, which a pious court lavishes without reluctance upon a libertine by profession. It is not indeed the least of the thousand contradictions which attend you, that a man, marked to the world by the grossest violation of all ceremony and decorum, should be the first servant of a court, in which prayers are morality, and kneeling is religion. Trust not too far to appearances, by which your predecessors have been deceived, though they have not been injured. Even the best of princes may at last discover, that this is a contention, in which everything may be lost, but nothing can be gained; and as you became minister by accident, were adopted without choice, trusted without confidence, and continued without favour, be assured that, whenever an occasion presses, you will be discarded without even the forms of regret. You will then have reason to be thankful, if you are permitted to retire to that seat of learning, which, in contemplation of the system of your life, the comparative purity of your manners with those of their High Steward, and a thousand other recommending circumstances, has chosen you to encourage the growing virtue of their youth, and to preside over their education. Whenever the spirit of distributing prebends and bishoprics shall have departed from you, you will find that learned seminary perfectly recovered from the delirium of an installation, and, what in truth it ought to be, once more a peaceful scene of slumber and thoughtless meditation. The venerable tutors of the university will no longer distress your modesty, by proposing you for a pattern to their pupils. The learned dulness of declamation will be silent; and even the venal muse, though happiest in fiction, will forget your virtues. Yet, for the benefit of the succeeding age, I could wish that your retreat might be deferred, until your morals shall happily be ripened to that maturity of corruption, at which the worst examples cease to be contagious.

Junius's Letters.

The Duke of Grafton. *Augustus Henry, 3rd Duke, Prime Minister in 1766. He was not a model either of statesmanship or of virtue, but the invective of Junius is humorously exaggerated. The "seat of learning"* (p. 243, l. 11) *is Cambridge, and the High Steward, beside whose manners Grafton's looked pure, was the notorious Sandwich. See Gray's lampoon,* The Cambridge Courtship.

WILLIAM PALEY.

William Paley was born at Peterborough in 1743, took orders, and became Archdeacon of Carlisle. All his works, the most famous and characteristic of which is his Evidences, exhibit a peculiar hardheadedness of thought and the utmost lucidity of expression. But his writing is not engaging; nor was his character. He died in 1805.

OF THE SUCCESSION OF PLANTS AND ANIMALS.

THE generation of the animal no more accounts for the contrivance of the eye or ear, than the production of a watch by the motion and mechanism of a former watch, would account for the skill and intention evinced in the watch so produced; than it would account for the disposition of the wheels, the catching of their teeth, the relation of the several parts of the works to one another, and to their common end; for the suitableness of their forms and places to their offices; for their connection, their operation, and the useful result of that operation. I do insist most strenuously upon the correctness of this comparison; that it holds as to every mode of specific propagation; and that whatever was true of the watch, under the hypothesis above mentioned, is true of plants and animals.

I. To begin with the fructification of plants. Can it be doubted but that the seed contains a particular organization? Whether a latent plantule with the means of temporary nutrition, or whatever else it be, it encloses an organization suited to the germination of a new plant. Has the plant which produced the seed anything more to do with that organization, than the watch would have had to do with the structure of the watch which was produced in the course of its mechanical movement? I mean, Has it anything at all to do with the contrivance? The maker and contriver of one watch, when he inserted within it a mechanism suited to the production of another watch, was, in truth, the maker and contriver of that other watch. All the properties of the new watch were to be referred to his agency: the design manifested in it, to his intention: the art, to him as the artist: the collocation of each part to his placing: the action, effect, and use, to his counsel, intelligence, and workmanship. In producing it by the intervention of a former watch, he was only working by one set of tools instead of another. So it is with the plant, and the seed produced by it. Can any distinction be assigned between the two cases; between the producing watch and the producing plant; both passive, unconscious substances; both, by the organization which was given to them, producing their like, without understanding or design; both, that is, instruments?

II. From plants we may proceed to oviparous animals; from seeds to eggs. Now I say, that the bird has the same concern in the formation of the egg which she lays, as the plant has in that of the seed which it drops; and no other, nor greater. The internal constitution of the egg is as much a secret to the hen, as if the hen were inanimate. Her will cannot alter it, or change a single feather of the chick. She can neither foresee nor determine of which sex her brood shall be, or how many of either: yet the thing produced shall be, from the first, very different in its make, according to the sex which it bears. So far, therefore, from adapting the means, she is not beforehand apprised of the effect. If there be concealed within that smooth shell a provision and a preparation for the production and nourishment of a new animal, they are not of her providing or preparing: if there be contrivance, it is none of hers. Although, therefore, there be the difference of life and perceptivity between the animal and the plant, it is a difference which enters not into the account: it is a foreign circumstance: it is a difference of properties not employed. The animal function and the vegetable function are alike destitute of any design which can operate upon the form of the thing produced. The plant has no design in producing the seed, no comprehension of the nature or use of what it produces; the bird, with respect to its egg, is not above the plant with respect to its seed. Neither the one nor the other bears that sort of relation to what proceeds from them, which a joiner does to the chair which he makes. Now a cause, which bears this relation to the effect, is what we want, in order to account for the suitableness of means to an end, the fitness and fitting of one thing to another; and this cause the parent plant or animal does not supply.

It is farther observable concerning the propagation of plants and animals, that the apparatus employed exhibits no resemblance to the thing produced; in this respect holding an analogy with instruments and tools of art. The filaments, antheræ, and stigmata, of flowers, bear no more resemblance to the young plant, or even to the seed, which is formed by their intervention, than a chisel or a plane does to a table or chair. What then are the filaments, antheræ, and stigmata, of plants, but instruments strictly so called?

III. We may advance from animals which bring forth eggs, to animals which bring forth their young alive; and of this latter class, from the lowest to the highest; from irrational to rational life, from brutes to the human species; without perceiving, as we proceed, any alteration whatever in the terms of the comparison. The rational animal does not produce its offspring with more certainty or success than the irrational animal; a man than a quadruped, a quadruped than a bird: nor, for we may follow the gradation through its whole scale, a bird than a plant; nor a plant than a watch, a piece of dead mechanism, would do, upon the supposition which has already so often been repeated. Rationality, therefore, has nothing to do in the business. If an account must be given of the contrivance which we observe: if it be demanded, whence arose either the contrivance by which the young animal is produced, or the contrivance manifested in the young animal itself, it is not from the reason of the parent that any such account can be drawn. He is the cause of his offspring in the same sense as that in which a gardener is the cause of the tulip which grows upon his parterre, and in no other. We admire the flower; we examine the plant; we perceive the conduciveness of many of its parts to their end and office; we observe a provision for its nourishment, growth, protection, and fecundity; but we never think of the gardener in all this. We attribute nothing of this to his agency; yet it may still be true, that without the gardener, we should not have had the tulip: just so it is with the succession of animals even of the highest order. For the contrivance discovered in the structure of the thing produced, we want a contriver. The parent is not that contriver. His consciousness decides that question. He is in total ignorance why that which is produced took its present form rather than any other. It is for him only to be astonished by the effect. We can no more look therefore to the intelligence of the parent animal for what we are in search of, a cause of relation, and of subserviency of parts to their use, which relation and subserviency we see in the procreated body, than we can refer the internal conformation of an acorn to the intelligence of the oak from which it dropped, or the structure of the watch to the intelligence of the watch which produced it; there being no difference, as far as argument is concerned, between an intelligence which is not exerted, and an intelligence which does not exist.

Natural Theology.

THOMAS HOLCROFT.

Thomas Holcroft was born in London in 1745, and lived a Bohemian life for some years. He became a player, a playwright, a novelist, and a politician, in which last capacity his revolutionary zeal brought him into difficulties. He died in 1805. Holcroft is one of the few writers who have written of low life at once with intimate knowledge and with talent, and this is what gives him his place here.

THE LIFE OF A JOCKEY.

THERE are few trades or professions, each of which has not a uniform mode of life peculiar to it, subject only to such slight variations as are incidental and temporary. This observation is particularly applicable to the life of a stable-boy.

All the boys in the stable rise at the same hour, from half-past two in spring, to between four and five in the depth of winter. The horses hear them when they awaken each other, and neigh, to denote their eagerness to be fed. Being dressed, the boy begins with carefully clearing out the manger, and giving a feed of oats, which he is obliged no less carefully to sift. He then proceeds to dress the litter; that is, to shake the bed on which the horse has been lying, remove whatever is wet or unclean, and keep the remaining straw in the stable for another time. The whole stables are then thoroughly swept, the few places for fresh air are kept open, the great heat of the stable gradually cooled, and the horse, having ended his first feed, is roughly cleaned and dressed. In about half an hour after they begin, or a little better, the horses have been rubbed down, and reclothed, saddled, each turned in his stall, then bridled, mounted, and the whole string goes out to morning exercise ; he that leads being the first : for each boy knows his place.

Except by accident, the race-horse never trots. He must either walk or gallop; and in exercise, even when it is the hardest, the gallop begins slowly and gradually, and increases till the horse is nearly at full speed. When he has galloped half a mile, the boy begins to push him forward, without relaxation, for another half mile. This is at the period when the horses are in full exercise, to which they come by degrees. The boy that can best regulate these degrees among those of light weight, is generally chosen to lead the gallop ; that is, he goes first out of the stable, and first returns.

In the time of long exercise, this is the first *brushing gallop*. A brushing gallop signifies that the horses are nearly at full speed before it is over, and it is commonly made at last rather up hill. Having all pulled up, the horses stand some two or three minutes, and recover their wind; they then leisurely descend the hill and take a long walk; after which they are brought to water. But in this, as in every thing else, at least as soon as long exercise begins, every thing to them is measured. The boy counts the number of times the horse swallows when he drinks, and allows him to take no more gulps than the groom orders, the fewest in the hardest exercise, and one horse more or less than another, according to the judgment of the groom.— After watering, a gentle gallop is taken, and after that, another walk of considerable length ; to which succeeds the second and last brushing gallop, which is by far the most severe. When it is over, another pause thoroughly to recover their wind is allowed them, their last walk is begun, the limits of which are prescribed, and it ends in directing their ride homewards.

The morning's exercise often extends to four hours, and the evening's to much about the same time. Being once in the stable, each lad begins his labour. He leads the horse into his stall, ties him up, rubs down his legs with straw, takes off his saddle and body clothes ; curries him carefully, then with both curry-comb and brush, never leaves him till he has thoroughly cleaned his skin, so that neither spot nor wet, nor any appearance of neglect may be seen about him. The horse is then reclothed, and suffered to repose for some time, which is first employed in gratifying his hunger, and recovering from his weariness. All this is performed, and the stables are once more shut up, about nine o'clock.

Accustomed to this life, the boys are very little overcome by fatigue, except that early in the morning they may be drowsy. I have sometimes fallen slightly asleep at the beginning of the first brushing gallop. But if they are not weary, they are hungry, and they make themselves ample amends for all they have done. Nothing perhaps can exceed the enjoyment of a stable-boy's breakfast: what then may not be said of mine, who had so long been used to suffer hunger, and so seldom found the means of satisfying it? Our breakfast consisted of new milk, or milk porridge, then the cold meat of the preceding day, most exquisite Gloucester cheese, fine white bread, and concluded with plentiful draughts of table beer. All this did not overload the stomach, or in the least deprive me of my youthful activity, except that like others I might sometimes take a nap for an hour, after so small a portion of sleep.

For my own part, so total and striking was the change which had taken place in my situation, that I could not but feel it very sensibly. I was more conscious of it than most boys would have been, and therefore not a little satisfied. The former part of my life had most of it been spent in turmoil, and often in singular wretchedness. I had been exposed to every want, every weariness, and every occasion of despondency, except that such poor sufferers become reconciled to, and almost insensible of suffering, and boyhood and beggary are fortunately not prone to despond. Happy had been the meal where I had enough; rich to me was the rag that kept me warm; and heavenly the pillow, no matter what, or how hard, on which I could lay my head to sleep. Now I was warmly clothed, nay, gorgeously, for I was proud of my new livery, and never suspected that there was disgrace in it; I fed voluptuously, not a prince on earth perhaps with half the appetite, and never-failing relish; and instead of being obliged to drag through the dirt after the most sluggish, obstinate, and despised among our animals, I was mounted on the noblest that the earth contains, had him under my care, and was borne by him over hill and dale, far outstripping the wings of the wind. Was not this a change, such as might excite reflection even in the mind of a boy!

Autobiography.

P. 249, l. 22. Groom. *Holcroft apparently uses this as we should now use "trainer," or at least "stud-groom."*

P. 250, l. 26. Except that. *It is not certain whether "that" is pronoun or conjunction. In neither case is the construction quite clear, while "and" in "and boyhood" further obscures it.*

HENRY MACKENZIE.

Henry Mackenzie, the last survivor of the school of sensibility in England, was born at Edinburgh in 1745, and died there in 1831. Lucrative employments assisted him to indulge his literary tastes. In himself Mackenzie has no very great value, but he is eminently representative of a school which long dominated English and European light literature.

HARLEY'S COMPASSION.

IT was with some difficulty that Harley prevailed on the old man to leave the spot where the remains of his son were laid. At last, with the assistance of the school-mistress, he prevailed, and she accommodated Edwards and him with beds in her house, there being nothing like an inn nearer than the distance of some miles.

In the morning, Harley persuaded Edwards to come with the children to his house, which was distant but a short day's journey. The boy walked in his grandfather's hand; and the name of Edwards procured him a neighbouring farmer's horse, on which a servant mounted, with the girl on a pillow before him.

With this train Harley returned to the abode of his fathers; and we cannot but think that his enjoyment was as great as if he had arrived from the tour of Europe, with a Swiss valet for his companion, and half a dozen snuff boxes, with invisible hinges, in his pocket. But we take our ideas from sounds which folly has invented; Fashion, Bon-ton, and Vertú, are the names of certain idols, to which we sacrifice the genuine pleasures of the soul; in this world of semblance, we are contented with personating happiness; to feel it, is an art beyond us.

It was otherwise with Harley; he ran upstairs to his aunt, with the history of his fellow-travellers glowing on his lips. His aunt was an economist, but she knew the pleasure of doing charitable things, and withal, was fond of her nephew, and solicitous to oblige him. She received old Edwards, therefore, with a look of more complacency than is perhaps natural to maiden ladies of threescore, and was remarkably attentive to his grand-children. She roasted apples with her own hands for their supper, and made up a little bed beside her own for the girl. Edwards made some attempts towards an acknowledgment for these favours, but his young friend stopped them in their beginnings. "Whosoever receiveth any of these children"—said his aunt; for her acquaintance with her Bible was habitual.

Early next morning, Harley stole into the room where Edwards lay; he expected to have found him a-bed, but in this he was mistaken; the old man had risen, and was leaning over his sleeping grandson, with the tears flowing down his cheeks. At first he did not perceive Harley; when he did, he endeavoured to hide his grief, and crossing his eyes with his hands, expressed his surprise at seeing him so early astir. "I was thinking of you," said Harley, "and your children. I learned last night that a small farm of mine in the neighbourhood is now vacant; if you will occupy it, I shall gain a good neighbour, and be able, in some measure, to repay the notice you took of me when a boy; and as the furniture of the house is mine, it will be so much trouble saved." Edwards' tears gushed afresh, and Harley led him to see the place he intended for him.

The house upon this farm was indeed little better than a hut; its situation, however, was pleasant, and Edwards, assisted by the beneficence of Harley, set about improving its neatness and convenience. He staked out a piece of the green before for a garden, and Peter, who acted in Harley's family as valet, butler, and gardener, had orders to furnish him with parcels of the different seeds he chose to sow in it. I have seen his master at work in this little spot, with his coat off, and his dibble in his hand: it was a scene of tranquil virtue to have stopped an angel on his errands of mercy! Harley had contrived to lead a little bubbling brook through a green walk in the middle of the ground, upon which he had erected a mill in miniature for the diversion of Edwards' infant grandson, and made shift in its construction to introduce a pliant bit of wood, that answered with its fairy clack to the murmuring of the rill that turned it. I have seen him stand, listening to these mingled sounds, with his eye fixed on the boy, and the smile of conscious satisfaction on his cheek, while the old man, with a look half turned to Harley, and half to Heaven, breathed an ejaculation of gratitude and piety.

Father of mercies! I also would thank thee, that not only hast thou assigned eternal rewards to virtue, but that, even in this bad world, the lines of our duty, and our happiness, are so frequently woven together.

The Man of Feeling.

FRANCES BURNEY, MADAME D'ARBLAY.

Frances Burney was born at King's Lynn in 1752 and died at Bath in 1840. Miss Burney was not the first Englishwoman to write novels of merit, but she was the first to become extremely popular, and she founded a tradition which has never since ceased. The natural vivacity of her first novel, Evelina, and of her early memoir-writing, is delightful.

A MIDDLE CLASS EXQUISITE.

SUCH was the conversation till tea-time, when the appearance of Mr. Smith gave a new turn to the discourse.

Miss Branghton desired me to remark with what a *smart air* he entered the room, and asked me if he had not very much a *quality look?*

"Come," cried he, advancing to us, "you ladies must not sit together; wherever I go, I always make it a rule to part the ladies."

And then, handing Miss Branghton to the next chair, he seated himself between us.

"Well, now, ladies, I think we sit very well. What say you? For my part, I think it was a very good motion."

"If my cousin likes it," said Miss Branghton, "I'm sure I've no objection."

"O," cried he, "I always study what the ladies like,—that's my first thought. And, indeed, it is but natural that you should like best to sit by the gentlemen, for what can you find to say to one another?"

"Say!" cried young Branghton; "O, never you think of that,

they'll find enough to say, I'll be sworn. You know the women are never tired of talking."

"Come, come, Tom," said Mr. Smith, "don't be severe upon the ladies; when I'm by, you know I always take their part."

Soon after, when Miss Branghton offered me some cake, this man of gallantry said, "Well, if I was that lady, I'd never take anything from a woman."

"Why not, Sir?"

"Because I should be afraid of being poisoned for being so handsome."

"Who is severe upon the ladies *now?*" said I.

"Why, really, Ma'am, it was a slip of the tongue; I did not intend to say such a thing; but one can't always be on one's guard."

Soon after, the conversation turning upon public places, young Branghton asked if I had ever been to *George's* at Hampstead?

"Indeed, I never heard the place mentioned."

"Didn't you, Miss," cried he eagerly; "why, then you've a deal of fun to come, I'll promise you; and, I tell you what, I'll treat you there some Sunday soon. So now, Bid and Poll, be sure you don't tell Miss about the chairs, and all that, for I've a mind to surprise her; and if I pay, I think I've a right to have it my own way."

"George's at Hampstead!" repeated Mr. Smith contemptuously; "how came you to think the young lady would like to go to such a low place as that! But, pray, Ma'am, have you ever been to Don Saltero's at Chelsea?"

"No, Sir."

"No! nay, then, I must insist on having the pleasure of conducting you there before long. I assure you, Ma'am, many genteel people go, or else, I give you my word, *I* should not recommend it."

"Pray, cousin," said Mr. Branghton, "have you been at Sadler's Wells yet?"

"No, Sir."

"No! why, then you've seen nothing!"

"Pray, Miss," said the son, "how do you like the Tower of London?"

"I have never been to it, Sir."

"Goodness!" exclaimed he, "not seen the Tower!—why, maybe, you ha'n't been o' top of the Monument, neither?"

"No, indeed, I have not."

"Why, then, you might as well not have come to London for aught I see, for you've been no where."

"Pray, Miss," said Polly, "have you been all over Paul's Church yet?"

"No, Ma'am."

"Well, but, Ma'am," said Mr. Smith, "how do you like Vauxhall and Marybone?"

"I never saw either, Sir."

"No—God bless me!—you really surprise me,—why Vauxhall is the first pleasure in life!—I know nothing like it.—Well, Ma'am, you must have been with strange people, indeed, not to have taken you to Vauxhall. Why you have seen nothing of London yet. However, we must try if *we* can't make you amends."

In the course of this *catechism*, many other places were mentioned, of which I have forgotten the names; but the looks of surprise and contempt that my repeated negatives incurred were very diverting.

"Come," said Mr. Smith after tea, "as this lady has been with such a queer set of people, let's show her the difference; suppose we go somewhere to-night!—I love to do things with spirit!—Come, ladies, where shall we go? For my part I should like Foote's—but the ladies must choose; I never speak myself."

"Well, Mr. Smith is always in such spirits!" said Miss Branghton.

"Why, yes, Ma'am, yes, thank God, pretty good spirits;—I have not yet the cares of the world upon me;—I am not *married*,—ha, ha, ha!—you'll excuse me, ladies, but I can't help laughing!"—

No objection being made, to my great relief we all proceeded to the little theatre in the Haymarket, where I was extremely entertained by the performance of the Minor and the Commissary.

They all returned hither to supper.

Evelina.

P. 255, l. 1. Such. *Evelina has been dining in company with the Branghtons, vulgar relations of hers. Mr. Smith is the Miss Branghtons' beau.*

P. 256, l. 17. George's, *a tea garden.* Don Saltero's, *a museum of odds and ends.* Sadler's Wells, *not then a theatre, but a public garden, as were Vauxhall and Marybone.* Foote's Theatre, *afterwards, as appears below, the "Haymarket," and sometimes called "the Little Theatre" only. The Minor and The Commissary were among the favourite parts and pieces of Foote, who, it must be remembered, was both actor and author.*

WILLIAM GODWIN.

William Godwin was born at Wisbeach in 1756; for a time he was a dissenting minister, but soon took to miscellaneous writing of various kinds. Godwin is extremely unequal both as thinker and writer, both as politician and novelist, but his thought and his expression are frequently original and almost always more or less distinguished. He died in 1836.

OF JUSTICE.

JUSTICE is a rule of conduct originating in the connection of one percipient being with another. A comprehensive maxim which has been laid down upon the subject is, "that we should love our neighbour as ourselves." But this maxim, though possessing considerable merit as a popular principle, is not modelled with the strictness of philosophical accuracy.

In a loose and general view I and my neighbour are both of us men; and of consequence entitled to equal attention. But in reality it is probable that one of us is a being of more worth and importance than the other. A man is of more worth than a beast; because, being possessed of higher faculties, he is capable of a more refined and genuine happiness. In the same manner the illustrious archbishop of Cambray was of more worth than his valet, and there are few of us who would hesitate to pronounce, if his palace were in flames, and the life of only one of them could be preserved, which of the two ought to be preferred.

But there is another ground of preference, besides the private consideration of one of them being farther removed from the state

SI

SA.

WHEN I cons
by the gen
more than a certain
of quality have e
and the certain mi
ing letters may be
and the answer to
racter.

"My dear H
"If thou art she,
apostate! how lost
married I find is to
dismal to be shut t
my ancestors, than t
in the country, an
husband, and an aw
you may entertain y
the spouse of your p

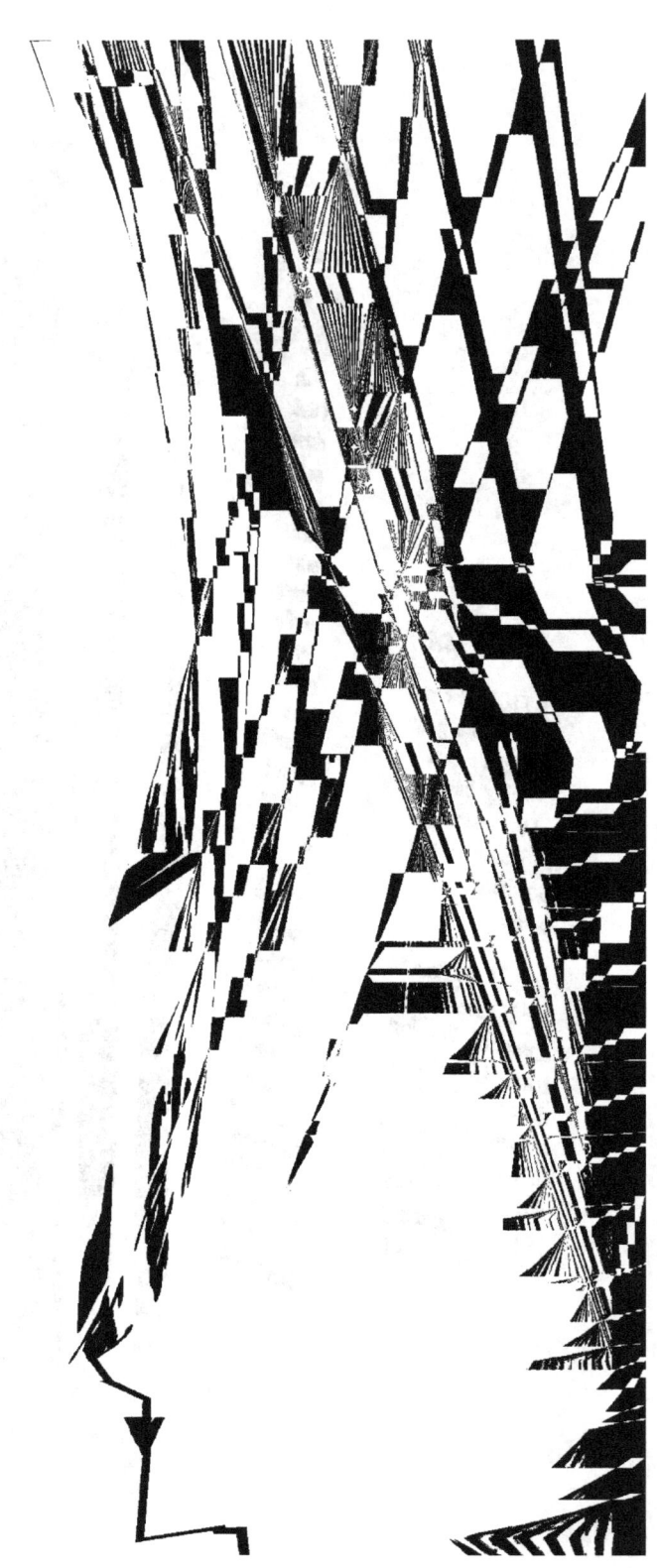

of a mere animal. We are not connected with one or two percipient beings, but with a society, a nation, and in some sense with the whole family of mankind. Of consequence that life ought to be preferred which will be most conducive to the general good. In saving the life of Fenelon, suppose at the moment he conceived the project of his immortal Telemachus, I should have been promoting the benefit of thousands, who have been cured by the perusal of that work of some error, vice and consequent unhappiness. Nay, my benefit would extend farther than this, for every individual, thus cured, has become a better member of society, and has contributed in his turn to the happiness, information and improvement of others.

Suppose I had been myself the valet; I ought to have chosen to die, rather than Fenelon should have died. The life of Fenelon was really preferable to that of the valet. But understanding is the faculty that perceives the truth of this and similar propositions; and justice is the principle that regulates my conduct accordingly. It would have been just in the valet to have preferred the archbishop to himself. To have done otherwise would have been a breach of justice.

Suppose the valet had been my brother, my father or my benefactor. This would not alter the truth of the proposition. The life of Fenelon would still be more valuable than that of the valet; and justice, pure, unadulterated justice, would still have preferred that which was most valuable. Justice would have taught me to save the life of Fenelon at the expense of the other. What magic is there in the pronoun "my" to overturn the decisions of impartial truth? My brother or my father may be a fool, or a profligate, malicious, lying or dishonest. If they be, of what consequence is it that they are mine?

"But to my father I am indebted for existence; he supported me in the helplessness of infancy." When he first subjected himself to the necessity of these cares, he was probably influenced by no particular motives of benevolence to his future offspring. Every voluntary benefit however entitles the bestower to some kindness and retribution. Why so? Because a voluntary benefit is an evidence of benevolent intention, that is, in a certain degree, of virtue. It is the disposition of the mind, not the external action separately taken, that entitles to respect. But the merit of this disposition is equal, whether the benefit were conferred upon me or upon another. I and another man cannot both be right in preferring our individual benefactor, for no man can be at the same time both better and worse than his neighbour. My benefactor ought to be esteemed, not because he bestowed a benefit upon me, but because he bestowed it upon a human being. His desert will be in exact proportion to the degree, in which that human being was worthy of the distinction conferred.

Thus every view of the subject brings us back to the consideration of my neighbour's moral worth and his importance to the general weal, as the only standard to determine the treatment to which he is entitled. Gratitude therefore, if by gratitude we understand a sentiment of preference which I entertain towards another, upon the ground of my having been the subject of his benefits, is no part either of justice or virtue.

An Enquiry concerning Political Justice.

ST. LEON'S THOUGHTS ON GAINING THE ELIXIR OF LIFE.

FROM this part of the legacy of the stranger, my mind reverted to the other. I surveyed my limbs, all the joints and articulations of my frame with curiosity and astonishment. What! exclaimed I, these limbs, this complicated but brittle frame, shall last for ever! No disease shall attack it; no pain shall seize it; death shall withhold from it for ever his abhorred grasp! Perpetual vigour, perpetual activity, perpetual youth, shall take up their abode with me! Time shall generate in me no decay, shall not add a wrinkle to my brow, or convert a hair of my head to grey! This body was formed to die; this edifice to crumble into dust; the principles of corruption and mortality are mixed up in every atom of my frame. But for me the laws of nature are suspended; the eternal wheels of the universe roll backward; I am destined to be triumphant over fate and time!

Months, years, cycles, centuries! To me all these are but as indivisible moments. I shall never become old; I shall always be, as it were, in the porch and infancy of existence; no lapse of years shall substract anything from my future duration. I was born under Louis the Twelfth; the life of Francis the First now threatens a speedy termination; he will be gathered to his fathers, and Henry his son will succeed him. But what are princes and kings and generations of men to me? I shall become familiar with the rise and fall of empires; in a little while the very name of France, my country, will perish from off the face of the earth, and men will dispute about the situation of Paris, as they dispute about the site of ancient Nineveh and Babylon and Troy. Yet I shall still be young. I shall take my most distant posterity by the hand; I shall accompany them in their career; and when they are worn out and exhausted shall shut up the tomb over them, and set forward.

There was something however in this part of my speculation that did not entirely please me. Methought the race of mankind looked too insignificant in my eyes. I felt a degree of uneasiness at the immeasurable distance that was now put between me and the rest of my species. I found myself alone in the world. Must I for ever live without a companion, a friend, anyone with whom I can associate upon equal terms, with whom I can have a community of sensations, and feelings, and hopes, and desires, and fears? I experienced something, less than a wish, yet a something very capable of damping my joy, that I also were subject to mortality. I could have been well contented to be partaker with a race of immortals, but I was not satisfied to be single in this respect. I was not pleased to recollect how trivial would appear to me those concerns of a few years, about which the passions of men are so eagerly occupied. I did not like the deadness of heart that seemed to threaten to seize me. I began to be afraid of vacancy and torpor, and that my life would become too uniformly quiet. Nor did it sufficiently console me, to recollect that, as one set of friends died off the stage, another race would arise to be substituted in their stead. I felt that human affections and passions are not made of this transferable stuff, and that we can love nothing truly, unless we devote ourselves to it heart and soul, and our life is, as it were, bound up in the object of our attachment.

It was worse when I recollected my wife and my children. When I considered for the first time that they were now in a manner nothing to me, I felt a sensation that might be said to mount to anguish. How can a man attach himself to any thing, when he comes to consider it as the mere plaything and amusement of the moment! In this statement, however, I am not accurate. Habit is more potent than any theoretical speculation. Past times had attached me deeply, irrevocably, to all the members of my family. But I felt that I should survive them all. They would die one by one, and leave me alone. I should drop into their graves the still renewing tear of anguish. In that tomb would my heart be buried. Never, never, through the countless ages of eternity, should I form another attachment. In the happy age of delusion, happy and auspicious at least to the cultivation of the passions, when I felt that I also was a mortal, I was capable of a community of sentiments and a going forth of the heart. But how could I, an immortal, hope ever hereafter to feel a serious, an elevating and expansive passion for the ephemeron of an hour!

St. Leon, a Tale of the Sixteenth Century.

P. 262, l. 3. Substract. *This form, though now regarded as a vulgarism, was once common in good writers, and has the authority of the Fr.* soustraire, *though not of the Lat.* subtrahere.

MARY WOLLSTONECRAFT.

Mary Wollstonecraft was born in 1759. She was forty years old when she married Godwin, and she died within the year. Her earlier history was romantic and unfortunate. As a novelist, as a politician, and, above all, as a defender of the rights of women and of unconventional views of marriage, she obtained a considerable reputation in the excited period of the French Revolution.

WOMAN'S TRUE POSITION.

LET woman share the rights and she will emulate the virtues of man; for she must grow more perfect when emancipated, or justify the authority that claims such a weak being to her duty.—If the latter, it will be expedient to open a fresh trade with Russia for whips; a present which a father should always make to his son-in-law on his wedding day, that a husband may keep his whole family in order by the same means; and without any violation of justice reign, wielding this sceptre, sole master of his house, because he is the only being in it who has reason:—the divine, indefeasible earthly sovereignty breathed into man by the Maker of the universe. Allowing this position, women have not any inherent rights to claim; and by the same rule, their duties vanish, for rights and duties are inseparable.

Be just then, O ye men of understanding! and mark not more severely what women do amiss than the vicious tricks of the horse or the ass for whom ye provide provender—and allow her the privileges of ignorance, to whom ye deny the rights of reason, or ye will be worse than Egyptian task-masters, expecting virtues where nature has not given understanding.

A Vindication of the Rights of Woman.

L. 3. Claim to *is not now used, "claim" having lost the simple sense of "call." But "reclaim to" would not seem strange even now.*

WILLIAM COBBETT.

William Cobbett, the raciest of all English political writers, was born in 1762. He was a soldier, a farmer, and a man of letters, a kind of Radical and a kind of Tory, a thinker of much shrewd sense and much absurd prejudice. He died in 1835. The directness and vigour of his expression are delightful.

THE WICKED BOROUGH-MONGERS.

AND, then, think of the tithes! I have talked to several farmers here about the tithes in England; and, they laugh. They sometimes almost make me angry; for they seem, at last, not to believe what I say, when I tell them, that the English farmer gives, and is compelled to give, the parson a tenth part of his whole crop, and of his fruit and milk and eggs and calves and lambs and pigs and wool and honey. They cannot believe this. They treat it as a sort of romance. I sometimes, God forgive me! almost wish them to be farmers in England. I said to a neighbour the other day, in half anger: "I wish your farm were at Botley. There is a fellow there, who would soon let you know, that your fine apple trees do not belong to you. He would have his nose in your sheep-fold, your calf-pens, your milk-pail, your sow's bed, if not in the sow herself. Your daughters would have no occasion to hunt out the hen's nests: he would do that for them." And then I gave him a proof of an English parson's vigilance by telling him the story of Baker's peeping out the name, marked on the sack, which the old woman was wearing as a petticoat. To another of my neighbours, who is very proud of the circumstance of his grandfather having been an Englishman, as, indeed, most of the Americans are, who are descended from Englishmen; to this neighbour I was telling the story about the poor woman at Holly Hill, who had nearly dipped her rushes once too often. He is a very grave and religious man. He looked very seriously at me, and said, that falsehood was falsehood, whether in jest or earnest. But, when I invited him to come to my house, and told him, that I would show him the acts which the borough-villains had made to put us in jail if we made our own soap and candles, he was quite astounded. "What!" said he, "and is old England really come to this! Is the land of our forefathers brought to this state of abject slavery! Well, Mr. Cobbett, I confess, that I was always for King George, during our Revolutionary war; but, I believe, all was for the best; for, if I had had my wishes, he might have treated us as he now treats the people of England." "He," said I, "it is not he; he, poor man, does nothing to the people, and never has done anything to the people. He has no power more than you have. None of his family have any. All put together, they have not a thousandth part so much as I have; for I am able, though here, to annoy our tyrants, to make them less easy than they would be; but, these tyrants care no more for the Royal Family than they do for so many posts or logs of wood." And then I explained to him who and what the borough-mongers were, and how they oppressed us and the king too. I told him how they disposed of the church livings, and, in short, explained to him all their arts and all their cruelties. He was exceedingly shocked; but was glad, at any rate, to know the truth.

Letter to the People of Botley.

P. 266, l. 4. The story *turns on the fact that* rushlights *could be made without interference by the Excise, but* candles *could not. An exciseman, probably in joke, had told the woman that if she had given her rushes one dip more she must have gone to jail.*

ANNE RADCLIFFE.

Anne Ward, who married a journalist named Radcliffe, was born in London in 1764, and died there in 1823. Her famous novels, once extolled to the skies, then ridiculed, now respected but little read, were all published in less than ten years, and she never wrote herself out. They show real power, marred chiefly by prolixity, and by repetition of dubious means of impressing.

EMILY'S MIDNIGHT ADVENTURE.

DURING the remainder of the day, Emily's mind was agitated with doubts and fears and contrary determinations, on the subject of meeting this Barnardine on the rampart, and submitting herself to his guidance, she scarcely knew whither. Pity for her aunt, and anxiety for herself, alternately swayed her determination, and night came, before she had decided upon her conduct. She heard the castle clock strike eleven—twelve—and yet her mind wavered. The time, however, was now come, when she could hesitate no longer : and then the interest she felt for her aunt overcame other considerations, and, bidding Annette follow her to the outer door of the vaulted gallery, and there await her return, she descended from her chamber. The castle was perfectly still, and the great hall, where so lately she had witnessed a scene of dreadful contention, now returned only the whispering footsteps of the two solitary figures gliding fearfully between the pillars, and gleamed only to the feeble lamp they carried. Emily, deceived by the long shadows of the pillars, and by the catching lights between, often stopped, imagining she saw some person moving in the distant obscurity of the perspective; and, as she passed these pillars, she feared to turn her eyes toward them, almost expecting to see a figure start out from behind their broad shaft. She reached, however, the vaulted gallery without interruption, but unclosed its outer door with a trembling hand, and, charging Annette not to quit it, and to keep it a little open, that she might be heard if she called, she delivered to her the lamp, which she did not dare to take herself, because of the men on watch, and, alone, stepped out upon the dark terrace. Everything was so still, that she feared lest her own light steps should be heard by the distant sentinels, and she walked cautiously towards the spot, where she had before met Barnardine, listening for a sound, and looking onward through the gloom in search of him. At length, she was startled by a deep voice, that spoke near her, and she paused, uncertain whether it was his, till it spoke again, and she then recognized the hollow tones of Barnardine, who had been punctual to the moment, and was at the appointed place, resting on the rampart wall. After chiding her for not coming sooner, and saying, that he had been waiting nearly half an hour, he desired Emily, who made no reply, to follow him to the door, through which he had entered the terrace.

While he unlocked it, she looked back to that she had left, and, observing the rays of the lamp stream through a small opening, was certain that Annette was still there. But her remote situation could little befriend Emily, after she had quitted the terrace; and, when Barnardine unclosed the gate, the dismal aspect of the passage beyond, shewn by a torch burning on the pavement, made her shrink from following him alone, and she refused to go, unless Annette might accompany her. This, however, Barnardine absolutely refused to permit, mingling at the same time with his refusal such artful circumstances to heighten the pity and curiosity of Emily towards her aunt, that she, at length, consented to follow him alone to the portal.

He then took up the torch, and led her along the passage, at the extremity of which he unlocked another door, whence they descended, a few steps, into a chapel, which, as Barnardine held up the torch to light her, Emily observed to be in ruins, and she immediately recollected a former conversation of Annette, concerning it, with very unpleasant emotions. She looked fearfully on the almost roofless walls, green with damps, and on the gothic points of the windows, where the ivy and the briony had long supplied the place of glass, and ran mantling among the broken capitals of some columns, that had once supported the roof. Barnardine stumbled over the broken pavement, and his voice, as he uttered a sudden oath, was returned in hollow echoes, that made it more terrific. Emily's heart sank; but she still followed him, and he turned out of what had been the principal aisle of the chapel. Down these steps, lady, said Barnardine, as he descended a flight, which appeared to lead into the vaults; but Emily paused on the top, and demanded, in a tremulous tone, whither he was conducting her.

To the portal, said Barnardine.

Cannot we go through the chapel to the portal? said Emily.

No, Signora, that leads to the inner court, which I don't choose to unlock. This way, and we shall reach the outer court presently.

Emily still hesitated: fearing not only to go on, but, since she had gone thus far, to irritate Barnardine by refusing to go farther.

Come, lady, said the man, who had nearly reached the bottom of the flight, make a little haste; I cannot wait here all night.

Whither do these steps lead? said Emily, yet pausing.

To the portal, repeated Barnardine, in an angry tone; I will wait no longer. As he said this, he moved on with the light, and Emily, fearing to provoke him by farther delay, reluctantly followed. From the steps, they proceeded through a passage, adjoining the vaults, the walls of which were dropping with unwholesome dews; and the vapours, that crept along the ground, made the torch burn so dimly that Emily expected every moment to see it extinguished, and Barnardine could scarcely find his way. As they advanced, these vapours thickened, and Barnardine, believing the torch was expiring, stopped for a moment to trim it. As he then rested against a pair of iron gates that opened from the passage, Emily saw, by uncertain flashes of light, the vaults beyond, and near her, heaps of earth, that seemed to surround an open grave. Such an object, in such a scene, would, at any time, have disturbed her; but now she was shocked by an instantaneous presentiment, that this was the grave of her unfortunate aunt, and that the treacherous Barnardine was leading herself to destruction. The obscure and terrible place, to which he had conducted her, seemed to justify the thought; it was a place suited for murder, a receptacle for the dead, where a deed of horror might be committed, and no vestige appear to proclaim it. Emily was so overwhelmed with terror, that for a moment she was unable to determine what conduct to pursue. She then considered, that it would be vain to attempt an escape from Barnardine, by flight, since the length and intricacy of the way she had passed would soon enable him to overtake her, who was unacquainted with the turnings, and whose feebleness would not suffer her to run long with swiftness. She feared equally to irritate him by a disclosure of her suspicions, which a refusal to accompany him farther certainly would do; and, since she was already as much in his power as it was possible she could be, if she proceeded, she, at length, determined to suppress, as far as she could, the appearance of apprehension, and to follow silently whither he designed to lead her. Pale with horror and anxiety, she now waited till Barnardine had trimmed the torch, and, as her sight glanced again upon the grave, she could not forbear inquiring for whom it was prepared. He took his eyes from the torch, and fixed them upon her face without speaking. She faintly repeated the question, but the man, shaking the torch, passed on; and she followed, trembling, to a second flight of steps, having ascended which, a door delivered them into the first court of the castle. As they crossed it, the light shewed the high black walls around them, fringed with long grass and dank weeds, that found a scanty soil among the mouldering stones; the heavy buttresses, with here and there between them a narrow gate, that admitted a freer circulation of air to the court, the massy iron gates, that led to the castle, whose clustering turrets appeared above, and, opposite, the huge towers and arch of the portal itself. In this scene the large, uncouth person of Barnardine, bearing the torch, formed a characteristic figure. This Barnardine was wrapt in a long dark cloak, which scarcely allowed the kind of half-boots, or sandals, that were laced upon his legs, to appear, and shewed only the point of a broadsword, which he usually wore, slung in a belt across his shoulders. On his head was a heavy flat velvet cap, somewhat resembling a turban, in which was a short feather; the visage beneath it shewed strong features, and a countenance furrowed with the lines of cunning, and darkened by habitual discontent.

The Mysteries of Udolpho.

P. 267, l. 1. *Emily the heroine is practically imprisoned in the Castle of Udolpho. She is constantly undergoing harrowing adventures, which lead to nothing in particular. Her tyrant is the husband of the aunt referred to in this passage.*

ROBERT HALL.

Robert Hall, the most renowned of modern dissenting preachers, was born in 1764. A Baptist by denomination, he ministered at Bristol and elsewhere; his sermons were of a more political tone than is usual with Anglican divines, but on the whole were distinguished by moderation and good sense, as well as by a certain eloquence and by respectable scholarship. He died in 1831.

REFLEXIONS ON WAR.

IF you had wished to figure to yourselves a country which had reached the utmost pinnacle of prosperity, you would undoubtedly have turned your eyes to France, as she appeared a few years before the revolution; illustrious in learning and genius; the favourite abode of the arts, and the mirror of fashion, whither the flower of the nobility from all countries resorted, to acquire the last polish of which the human character is susceptible. Lulled in voluptuous repose, and dreaming of a philosophical millennium, without dependence upon God, like the generation before the flood, "they ate, they drank, they married, they were given in marriage." In that exuberant soil every thing seemed to flourish, but religion and virtue. The season, however, was at length arrived, when God was resolved to punish their impiety, as well as to avenge the blood of His servants, whose souls had for a century been incessantly crying to Him from under the altar. And what method did He employ for this purpose? When He to whom vengeance belongs, when He whose ways are unsearchable, and whose wisdom is inexhaustible, proceeded to the execution of this strange work, He drew from His treasures a weapon He had never employed before. Resolving to make their punishment as signal as their crimes, He neither let loose an inundation of barbarous nations, nor the desolating powers of the universe: He neither overwhelmed them with earthquakes, nor visited them with pestilence. He summoned from among themselves a ferocity more terrible than either; a ferocity which, mingling in the struggle for liberty, and borrowing aid from that very refinement to which it seemed to be opposed, turned every man's hand against his neighbour, sparing no age, nor sex, nor rank, till, satiated with the ruin of greatness, the distresses of innocence, and the tears of beauty, it terminated its career in the most unrelenting despotism. "Thou art righteous, O Lord, which art, and which was, and which shall be, because Thou hast judged thus, for they have shed the blood of saints and prophets, and Thou hast given them blood to drink, for they are worthy."

Sermons.

SIR JAMES MACKINTOSH.

Sir James Mackintosh was born at Aldourie in 1765, and died in 1832. An orator, a lawyer, a moral philosopher, a historian, a politician, and a journalist, Mackintosh may, perhaps, be thought to have scattered his energies too much. Nor is any one part of his work very thorough or very brilliant. For facility and variety, however, combined with a certain competence, he ranks very high among miscellanists.

CHIVALRY.

THAT system of manners which arose among the Gothic nations of Europe, and of which chivalry was more properly the effusion than the source, is without doubt one of the most peculiar and interesting appearances in human affairs. The moral causes which formed its character have not, perhaps, been hitherto investigated with the happiest success: but chivalry was certainly one of the most prominent of its features and most remarkable of its effects. Candour must confess, that this singular institution was not admirable only as the corrector of the ferocious ages in which it flourished; but that in contributing to polish and soften manners it paved the way for the diffusion of knowledge and the extension of commerce, which afterwards, in some measure, supplanted it. Society is inevitably progressive. Commerce has overthrown the "feudal and chivalrous system" under whose shade it first grew; while learning has subverted the superstition whose opulent endowments had first fostered it. Peculiar circumstances connected with the manners of chivalry favoured this admission of commerce and this growth of knowledge; while the sentiments peculiar to it, already enfeebled in the progress from ferocity and turbulence, were almost obliterated by tranquillity and refinement. Commerce and diffused knowledge have, in fact, so completely assumed the ascendant in polished nations, that it will be difficult to discover any relics of Gothic manners, but in a fantastic exterior, which has survived the generous illusions through which these manners once seemed splendid and seductive. Their direct influence has long ceased in Europe; but their indirect influence, through the medium of those causes which would not perhaps have existed but for the mildness which chivalry created in the midst of a barbarous age, still operates with increasing vigour. The manners of the middle age were, in the most singular sense, compulsory: enterprising benevolence was produced by general fierceness, gallant courtesy by ferocious rudeness; and artificial gentleness resisted the torrent of natural barbarism. But a less incongruous system has succeeded, in which commerce, which unites men's interests, and knowledge, which excludes those prejudices that tend to embroil them, present a broader basis for the stability of civilized and beneficent manners.

Vindiciæ Gallicæ.

MARIA EDGEWORTH.

Maria Edgeworth (second in order of time on the roll of English lady novelists who succeed each other without break from Fanny Burney to George Eliot) was born in Berkshire in 1766, and died at Edgeworthstown in 1849. The most good-humoured and sensible of women, she wrote with more fertility than distinction, except in her Irish stories and her children's tales, both of which are unsurpassed.

THE DUBLIN SHOEBLACK.

WE proceed to establish the truth of our minor, and the first evidence we shall call is a Dublin shoeblack. He is not in circumstances peculiarly favourable for the display of figurative language; he is in a court of justice, upon his trial for life or death. A quarrel happened between two shoeblacks, who were playing at what in England is called pitch farthing, or heads and tails, and in Ireland, head or harp. One of the combatants threw a small paving stone at his opponent, who drew out the knife with which he used to scrape shoes, and plunged it up to the hilt in his companion's breast. It is necessary for our story to say, that Lamprey is a very eminent cutler in Dublin, whose name is stamped on the blade of his knives in the usual place. The shoeblack was brought to trial. With a number of significant gestures, which on his audience had all the powers that Demosthenes ascribes to action, he, in a language not purely Attic, gave the following account of the affair to his judge.

"Why, my lard, as I was going past the Royal Exchange I meets Billy—'Billy,' says I, 'will you sky a copper?'—'Done,' says he—'Done,' says I—and done and done's enough between two jantlemen.—With that I ranged them fair and even with my hook-em-snivey—up they go.—'Music!' says he—'Skull!' says I—and down they come three brown mazzards.—'By the holy you fleshed 'em,' says he—'You lie,' says I.—With that he ups with a lump of a two year old and let's drive at me—I out's with my bread-earner, and gives it him up to Lamprey in the bread basket."

To make this intelligible to the English, some comments are necessary. Let us follow the text, step by step, and it will afford our readers, as Lord Kames says of Blair's Dissertation on Ossian, a delicious morsel of criticism.

As I was going past the Royal Exchange I meets Billy.

In this apparently simple exordium, the scene and the meeting with Billy are brought before the eye, by the judicious use of the present tense.

Billy, says I, will you sky a copper?

A copper! genus pro specie! the generic name of copper for the bare individual halfpenny.

Sky a copper.

To sky is a new verb, which none but a master hand could have coined; a more splendid metonymy could not be applied upon a more trivial occasion; the lofty idea of raising a metal to the skies is substituted for the mean thought of tossing up a halfpenny. Our orator compresses his hyperbole into a single word. Thus the mind is prevented from dwelling long enough upon the figure to perceive its enormity. This is the perfection of the art. Let the genius of French exaggeration and of Eastern hyperbole hide their diminished heads—Virgil is scarcely more sublime.

"Ingrediturque solo et caput inter nubila condit."
"Her feet on earth, her head amidst the clouds."

With that I ranged them fair and even with my hook-em-snivey.

Hook-em-snivey.—An indescribable, though simple, machine, employed by boys in playing at head and harp.

Up they go, continues our orator.

Music! says he—Skull! says I.

Metaphor continually; on one side of an Irish halfpenny there is a harp; this is expressed by the general term music, which is finely contrasted with the word skull.

Down they come, three brown mazzards!

Mazzards! how the diction of our orator is enriched from the vocabulary of Shakspeare! the word head, instead of being changed for a more general term, is here brought distinctly to the eye by the term mazzard, or face, which is more appropriate to his majesty's profile than the words skull or head.

By the holy! you fleshed 'em, says he.

By the holy! is an oath in which more is meant than meets the ear; it is an ellipsis—an abridgement of an oath. The full formula runs thus—By the holy poker of Hell!—This instrument is of Irish invention or imagination. It seems a useful piece of furniture in the place for which it is intended, to stir the devouring flames, and thus to increase the torments of the damned. Great judgment is necessary to direct an orator how to suit his terms to his auditors, so as not to shock their feelings either by what is too much above, or too much below common life. In the use of oaths, where the passions are warm, this must be particularly attended to, else they lose their effect, and seem more the result of the head than the heart. But to proceed—

By the holy! you fleshed 'em.

To flesh is another verb of Irish coinage; it means, in shoeblack dialect, to touch a halfpenny, as it goes up into the air, with the fleshy part of the thumb, so as to turn it which way you please, and thus to cheat your opponent.—What an intricate explanation saved by one word!

You lie, says I.

Here no periphrasis would do the business.

With that he ups with a lump of a two year old, and lets drive at me.

With that.—These are not unmeaning words, used like expletives by some orators, merely to gain time; the phrase, *with that*, varies in signification according to circumstances; either it denotes, that one action immediately follows another as its consequence, or else it implies, that two actions happen, or two ideas occur, actually at the same time.

He ups with.—A verb is here formed of two prepositions—a novelty in grammar. Conjunctions, we all know, are corrupted Anglo-Saxon verbs; but prepositions, according to Horne Tooke, derive only from Anglo-Saxon nouns.

All this time it is possible, that the mere English reader may not be able to guess what it is, that our orator ups with or takes up. He should be apprised, that a lump of a two year old is a middle sized stone. This is a metaphor, borrowed partly from the grazier's vocabulary, and partly from the arithmetician's vade-mecum. A stone, to come under the denomination of a lump of a two year old, must be to a less stone as a two year old calf is to a yearling. It must be to a larger stone than itself, as a two year old calf is to an ox. Here the scholar sees, that there must be two statements, one in the rule of three direct, and one in the rule of three inverse, to obtain precisely the thing required; yet the untutored Irishman, without suspecting the necessity of this operose process, arrives at the solution of the problem by some short cut of his own, as he clearly evinces by the propriety of his metaphor. To be sure there seems some incongruity in his throwing this lump of a two year old calf at his adversary. No arm but that of Milo could be strong enough for such a feat. Upon recollection, however bold this figure may seem, there are precedents for its use.

"We read in a certain author," says Beattie, "of a giant, who, in his wrath, tore off the top of the promontory and flung it at the enemy; and so huge was the mass, that you might, says he, have seen goats browsing on it as it flew through the air." Compared with this, our orator's figure is cold and tame.

"*I outs with my bread-earner,*" continues he.

We forbear to comment on *outs with*, because the intelligent critic immediately perceives, that it has the same sort of merit ascribed to *ups with*. What our hero dignifies with the name of his bread-earner, is the knife with which, by scraping shoes, he earned his bread.—Pope's ingenious critic, Mr. Warton, bestows judicious praise upon the art with which this poet, in the Rape of the Lock, has used many "periphrases and uncommon expressions," to avoid mentioning the name of *scissors*, which would sound too vulgar for epick dignity;—fatal engine, forfex, meeting points, etc. Though the metonymy of *bread-earner* for shoeblack's knife may not equal these in elegance, it perhaps surpasses them in ingenuity.

I gives it him up to Lamprey in the bread-basket.[1]

Homer is happy in his description of wounds, but this surpasses him in the characteristic choice of circumstance.—*Up to Lamprey*, gives us at once a complete idea of the length, breadth and depth of the wound, without the assistance of the coroner. It reminds us of a passage in Virgil—:

"Cervice orantis *capulo tenus* abdidit ensem."
"Up to the hilt his shining fauchion sheathed."

[1] The stomach.

Essay on Irish Bulls.

P. 277, l. 3. Hook-em-snivey. *In this agreeable parody of commentatorial writing, Miss Edgeworth has left little for the commentator. But I do not know what a hook-em-snivey is, and as it is "indescribable" it is unnecessary to inquire. That before the Union Irish copper money had a harp only on the reverse is perhaps matter of common knowledge, and is, at any rate, clear from the text.*

SIR WALTER SCOTT.

Sir Walter Scott, the greatest of all novelists if quality, quantity, and originality are taken together, was born in Edinburgh in 1771. After spending many years in easy professional and literary labour, the success of his books tempted him to overwork, which, ill-fortune aiding, killed him in 1832. For attractive wholesomeness of character and varied charm of work Scott stands alone.

AN ANTIQUARY'S STUDY.

IT was indeed some time before Lovel could, through the thick atmosphere, perceive in what sort of den his friend had constructed his retreat. It was a lofty room, of middling size, obscurely lighted by high narrow latticed windows. One end was entirely occupied by book-shelves, greatly too limited in space for the number of volumes placed upon them, which were, therefore, drawn up in ranks of two or three files deep, while numberless others littered the floor and the tables, amid a chaos of maps, engravings, scraps of parchment, bundles of papers, pieces of old armour, swords, dirks, helmets, and Highland targets. Behind Mr. Oldbuck's seat (which was an ancient leathern-covered easy-chair, worn smooth by constant use), was a huge oaken cabinet decorated at each corner with Dutch cherubs, having their little duck-wings displayed, and great jolter-headed visages placed between them. The top of this cabinet was covered with busts, and Roman lamps and pateræ, intermingled with one or two bronze figures. The walls of the apartment were partly clothed with grim old tapestry, representing the memorable story of Sir Gawaine's wedding, in which full justice was done to the ugliness of the Loathly Lady; although, to judge from his own looks, the gentle knight had less reason to be disgusted with the match on account of disparity of outward favour, than the romancer has given us to understand. The rest of the room was panelled, or wainscotted, with black oak, against which hung two or three portraits in armour, being characters in Scottish history, favourites of Mr. Oldbuck, and as many in tie-wigs and laced coats, staring representatives of his own ancestors. A large old-fashioned oaken table was covered with a profusion of papers, parchments, books, nondescript trinkets and gewgaws, which seemed to have little to recommend them, besides rust and the antiquity which it indicates. In the midst of this wreck of ancient books and utensils, with a gravity equal to Marius among the ruins of Carthage, sat a large black cat, which, to a superstitious eye, might have presented the *genius loci*, the tutelar demon of the apartment. The floor, as well as the table and chairs, was overflowed by the same *mare magnum* of miscellaneous trumpery, where it would have been as impossible to find any individual article wanted, as to put it to any use when discovered.

Amid this medley, it was no easy matter to find one's way to a chair, without stumbling over a prostrate folio, or the still more awkward mischance of overturning some piece of Roman or ancient British pottery. And, when the chair was attained, it had to be disencumbered, with a careful hand, of engravings which might have received damage, and of antique spurs and buckles, which would certainly have occasioned it to any sudden occupant. Of this the Antiquary made Lovel particularly aware, adding, that his friend, the Rev. Doctor Heavysterne from the Low Countries, had sustained much injury by sitting down suddenly and incautiously on three ancient calthrops, or *craw-taes*, which had been lately dug up in the bog near Bannockburn, and which, dispersed by Robert Bruce to lacerate the feet of the English chargers, came thus in process of time to endamage the sitting part of a learned professor of Utrecht.

The Antiquary.

THE INSTALLATION OF THE ABBOT OF KENNAQUHAIR.

As she spoke, a side door, which closed a passage from the Abbot's house into the church, was thrown open, that the Fathers might enter the choir, and conduct to the high altar the Superior whom they had elected.

In former times, this was one of the most splendid of the many pageants which the hierarchy of Rome had devised to attract the veneration of the faithful. The period, during which the Abbacy remained vacant, was a state of mourning, or, as their emblematical phrase expressed it, of widowhood; a melancholy term, which was changed into rejoicing and triumph when a new Superior was chosen. When the folding doors were on such solemn occasions thrown open, and the new Abbot appeared on the threshold in full-blown dignity, with ring and mitre, and dalmatique and crosier, his hoary standard-bearers and his juvenile dispensers of incense preceding him, and the venerable train of monks behind him, with all besides which could announce the supreme authority to which he was now raised, his appearance was a signal for the magnificent *jubilate* to rise from the organ and music-loft, and to be joined by the corresponding bursts of Alleluiah from the whole assembled congregation. Now all was changed. In the midst of rubbish and desolation, seven or eight old men, bent and shaken as much by grief and fear as by age, shrouded hastily in the proscribed dress of their order, wandered like a procession of spectres, from the door which had been thrown open, up through the encumbered passage, to the high altar, there to install their elected Superior a chief of ruins. It was like a band of bewildered travellers choosing a chief in the wilderness of Arabia; or a shipwrecked crew electing a captain upon the barren island on which fate has thrown them.

They who, in peaceful times, are most ambitious of authority among others, shrink from the competition at such eventful periods, when neither ease nor parade attend the possession of it, and when it gives only a painful pre-eminence both in danger and in labour, and exposes the ill-fated chieftain to the murmurs of his discontented associates, as well as to the first assault of the common enemy. But he on whom the office of the Abbot of St. Mary's was now conferred, had a mind fitted for the situation to which he was called. Bold and enthusiastic, yet generous and forgiving—wise and skilful, yet zealous and prompt—he wanted but a better cause than the support of a decaying superstition, to have raised him to the rank of a truly great man. But as the end crowns the work, it also forms the rule by which it must be ultimately judged; and those who, with sincerity and generosity, fight and fall in an evil cause, posterity can only compassionate as victims of a generous but fatal error. Amongst these, we must rank Ambrosius, the last Abbot of Kennaquhair, whose designs must be condemned, as their success would have riveted on Scotland the chains of antiquated superstition and spiritual tyranny; but whose talents commanded respect, and whose virtues, even from the enemies of his faith, extorted esteem.

The bearing of the new Abbot served of itself to dignify a ceremonial which was deprived of all other attributes of grandeur. Conscious of the peril in which they stood, and recalling, doubtless, the better days they had seen, there hung over his brethren an appearance of mingled terror, and grief, and shame, which induced them to hurry over the office in which they were engaged, as something at once degrading and dangerous.

But not so Father Ambrose. His features, indeed, expressed a deep melancholy, as he walked up the centre aisle, amid the ruin of things which he considered as holy, but his brow was undejected, and his step firm and solemn. He seemed to think that the dominion which he was about to receive, depended in no sort upon the external circumstances under which it was conferred; and if a mind so firm was accessible to sorrow or fear, it was not on his own account, but on that of the church to which he had devoted himself.

At length he stood on the broken steps of the high altar, barefooted, as was the rule, and holding in his hand his pastoral staff, for the gemmed ring and jewelled mitre had become secular spoils. No obedient vassals came, man after man, to make their homage, and to offer the tribute which should provide their spiritual superior with palfrey and trappings. No Bishop assisted at the solemnity, to receive into the higher ranks of the Church nobility a dignitary, whose voice in the legislature was as potential as his own. With hasty and maimed rites, the few remaining brethren stepped forward alternately to give their new Abbot the kiss of peace, in token of fraternal affection and spiritual homage. Mass was then hastily performed, but in such precipitation as if it had been hurried over rather to satisfy the scruples of a few youths, who were impatient to set out on a hunting party, than as if it made the most solemn part of a solemn ordination. The officiating priest faltered as he spoke the service, and often looked around, as if he expected to be interrupted in the midst of his office, and the brethren listened as to that which, short as it was, they wished yet more abridged.

The Abbot.

P. 282, l. 30. Calthrops, *or better, caltrops, so called from the old name of the star thistle, are four-pointed iron instruments of which, however thrown, one spike sticks up. They are still occasionally used in warfare, but are more generally called now "crow's feet."*

P. 285, l. 8. Mass, *etc. A "hunting-mass" was a recognised form of the ceremonial, shortened on purpose.*

SYDNEY SMITH.

Sydney Smith, the wittiest of Englishmen, was born at Woodford in 1771, took orders, and, after some lean years, was richly beneficed. He died in London in 1845. Smith was a sincere frondeur in everything but religion, and the powers that were in his youth being Tory, he was a sincere Liberal. He brought to the service of his cause an incomparable faculty of putting things laughably and forcibly at once.

THE PRODUCTIONS OF CEYLON.

CEYLON produces the elephant, the buffalo, tiger, elk, wild hog, rabbit, hare, flying-fox, and musk-rat. Many articles are rendered entirely useless by the smell of musk, which this latter animal communicates in merely running over them. Mr. Percival asserts, and the fact has been confirmed to us by the most respectable authority, that if it even pass over a bottle of wine, however well corked and sealed up, the wine becomes so strongly tainted with musk, that it cannot be used ; and a whole cask may be rendered useless in the same manner. Among the great variety of birds, we were struck with Mr. Percival's account of the honey-bird, into whose body the soul of a common informer appears to have migrated. It makes a loud and shrill noise, to attract the notice of anybody whom it may perceive ; and thus inducing him to follow the course it points out, leads him to the tree where the bees have concealed their treasure ; after the apiary has been robbed, this feathered scoundrel gleans his reward from the hive. The list of Ceylonese snakes is hideous ; and we become reconciled to the crude and cloudy land in which we live, from reflecting, that the indiscriminate activity of the sun generates what is loathsome, as well as what is lovely; that the asp reposes under the rose; and the scorpion crawls under the fragrant flower, and the luscious fruit.

The usual stories are repeated here of the immense size and voracious appetite of a certain species of serpent. The best history of this kind we ever remember to have read, was of a serpent killed near one of our settlements, in the East Indies; in whose body they found the chaplain of the garrison, all in black, the Rev. Mr. —— somebody or other, whose name we have forgotten, and who, after having been missing for above a week, was discovered in this very inconvenient situation. The dominions of the King of Candy are partly defended by leeches, which abound in the woods, and from which our soldiers suffered in the most dreadful manner. The Ceylonese, in compensation for their animated plagues, are endowed with two vegetable blessings, the cocoa nut tree and the talipot tree. The latter affords a prodigious leaf, impenetrable to sun or rain, and large enough to shelter ten men. It is a natural umbrella, and is of as eminent service in that country as a great-coat tree would be in this. A leaf of the talipot tree is a tent to the soldier, a parasol to the traveller, and a book to the scholar. The cocoa tree affords bread, milk, oil, wine, spirits, vinegar, yeast, sugar, cloth, paper, huts, and ships.

Articles published in the Edinburgh Review.

P. 286, l. 6. Bottle of wine. *This enormous travellers' tale has been repeated to the present day, and is said to have been not inconvenient to Indian butlers.*

SAMUEL TAYLOR COLERIDGE.

Samuel Taylor Coleridge, "logician, metaphysician, bard," and, it may be added, critic and journalist of the first rank, was born at Ottery St. Mary in 1772, led a wandering life, and died at Highgate in 1834. Coleridge's prose, less unique than his verse, is more uniformly excellent, and has an almost unparalleled range of application to subjects grave and gay, easy and abstruse.

COLERIDGE AS A LITERARY CANVASSER.

SO ended my first canvass: from causes that I shall presently mention, I made but one other application in person. This took place at Manchester to a stately and opulent wholesale dealer in cottons. He took my letter of introduction, and, having perused it, measured me from head to foot, and again from foot to head, and then asked if I had any bill or invoice of the thing. I presented my prospectus to him. He rapidly skimmed and hummed over the first side, and still more rapidly the second and concluding page; crushed it within his fingers and the palm of his hand; then most deliberately and significantly rubbed and smoothed one part against the other; and lastly putting it into his pocket turned his back on me with an "*overrun* with these articles!" and so without another syllable retired into his counting-house. And, I can truly say, to my unspeakable amusement.

This, I have said, was my second and last attempt. On returning baffled from the first, in which I had vainly essayed to repeat the miracle of Orpheus with the Brummagem patriot, I dined with the tradesman who had introduced him to me. After dinner he importuned me to smoke a pipe with him, and two or three other *illuminati* of the same rank. I objected, both because I was engaged to spend the evening with a minister and his friends, and because I had never smoked except once or twice in my life-time, and then it was herb tobacco mixed with Oronooko. On the assurance, however, that the tobacco was equally mild, and seeing too that it was of a yellow colour;—not forgetting the lamentable difficulty, I have always experienced, in saying, "No," and in abstaining from what the people about me were doing,—I took half a pipe, filling the lower half of the bowl with salt. I was soon however compelled to resign it, in consequence of a giddiness and distressful feeling in my eyes, which, as I had drunk but a single glass of ale, must, I knew, have been the effect of the tobacco. Soon after, deeming myself recovered, I sallied forth to my engagement; but the walk and the fresh air brought on all the symptoms again, and, I had scarcely entered the minister's drawing-room, and opened a small pacquet of letters, which he had received from Bristol for me; ere I sank back on the sofa in a sort of swoon rather than sleep. Fortunately I had found just time enough to inform him of the confused state of my feelings, and of the occasion. For here and thus I lay, my face like a wall that is white-washing, deathy pale and with the cold drops of perspiration running down it from my forehead, while one after another there dropped in the different gentlemen, who had been invited to meet, and spend the evening with me, to the number of from fifteen to twenty. As the poison of tobacco acts but for a short time, I at length awoke from insensibility, and looked round on the party, my eyes dazzled by the candles which had been lighted in the interim. By way of relieving my embarrassment one of the gentlemen began the conversation, with "Have you seen a paper to-day, Mr. Coleridge?" "Sir!" I replied, rubbing my eyes, "I am far from convinced, that a Christian is permitted to read either newspapers or any other works of merely political and temporary interest." This remark, so ludicrously inapposite to, or rather, incongruous with, the purpose, for which I was known to have visited Birmingham, and to assist me in which they were all then met, produced an involuntary and general burst of laughter; and seldom indeed have I passed so many delightful hours, as I enjoyed in that room from the moment of that laugh till an early hour the next morning. Never, perhaps, in so mixed and numerous a party have I since heard conversation sustained with such animation, enriched with such variety of information and enlivened with such a flow of anecdote. Both then and afterwards they all joined in dissuading me from proceeding with my scheme; assured me in the most friendly and yet most flattering expressions, that neither was the employment fit for me, nor I fit for the employment. Yet, if I determined on persevering in it, they promised to exert themselves to the utmost to procure subscribers, and insisted that I should make no more applications in person, but carry on the canvass by proxy. The same hospitable reception, the same dissuasion, and, that failing, the same kind exertions in my behalf, I met with at Manchester, Derby, Nottingham, Sheffield,—indeed, at every place in which I took up my sojourn, I often recall with affectionate pleasure the many respectable men who interested themselves for me, a perfect stranger to them, not a few of whom I can still name among my friends. They will bear witness for me how opposite even then my principles were to those of Jacobinism or even of democracy, and can attest the strict accuracy of the statement which I have left on record in the 10th and 11th numbers of THE FRIEND.

Biographia Literaria.

THE BOOK OF NATURE.

IT must not, however, be overlooked that this insulation of the understanding is our own act and deed. The man of healthful and undivided intellect uses his understanding in this state of abstraction only as a tool or organ; even as the arithmetician uses numbers, that is, as the means not the end of knowledge. Our Shakspeare in agreement both with truth and the philosophy of his age names it "discourse of reason," as an instrumental faculty belonging to reason: and Milton opposes the discursive to the intuitive, as the lower to the higher,

Differing but in degree, in kind the same.

Of the discursive understanding, which forms for itself general notions and terms of classification for the purpose of comparing and arranging *phænomena*, the characteristic is clearness without depth. It contemplates the unity of things in their limits only, and is consequently a knowledge of superficies without substance. So much so, indeed, that it entangles itself in contradictions in the very effort of comprehending the idea of substance. The completing power which unites clearness with depth, the plenitude of the sense with the comprehensibility of the understanding, is the imagination, impregnated with which the understanding itself becomes intuitive, and a living power. The reason, not the abstract reason, not the reason as the mere organ of science, or as the faculty of scientific principles and schemes *à priori;* but reason as the integral spirit of the regenerated man, reason substantiated and vital, *one only,* yet *manifold, overseeing all, and going through all* understanding; *the breath of the power of God, and a pure influence from the glory of the Almighty;* which *remaining in itself* regenerateth all other powers, *and in all ages entering into holy souls maketh them friends of God and prophets;* (Wisdom of Solomon, c. vii.) this reason without being either the sense, the understanding, or the imagination, contains all three within itself, even as the mind contains its thoughts, and is present in and through them all; or as the expression pervades the different features of an intelligent countenance. Each individual must bear witness of it to his own mind, even as he describes life and light: and with the silence of light it describes itself, and dwells in us only as far as we dwell in it. It cannot, in strict language, be called a faculty, much less a personal property, of any human mind. He, with whom it is present, can as little appropriate it, whether totally or by partition, as he can claim ownership in the breathing air, or make an inclosure in the cope of heaven.

The object of the preceding discourse was to recommend the Bible, as the end and centre of our reading and meditation. I can truly affirm of myself, that my studies have been profitable and availing to me only so far as I have endeavoured to use all my other knowledge as a glass enabling me to receive more light in a wider field of vision from the word of God. If you have accompanied me thus far, thoughtful reader, let it not weary you if I digress for a few moments to another book, likewise a revelation of God—the great book of his servant Nature. That in its obvious sense and literal interpretation it declares the being and attributes of the Almighty Father, none but the fool in heart has ever dared gainsay. But it has been the music of gentle and pious minds in all ages, it is the poetry of all human nature, to read it likewise in a figurative sense, and to find therein correspondencies and symbols of the spiritual world.

I have at this moment before me, in the flowery meadow, on which my eye is now reposing, one of its most soothing chapters, in which there is no lamenting word, no one character of guilt or anguish. For never can I look and meditate on the vegetable creation without a feeling similar to that with which we gaze at a beautiful infant that has fed itself asleep at its mother's bosom, and smiles in its strange dream of obscure yet happy sensations. The same tender and genial pleasure takes possession of me, and this pleasure is checked and drawn inward by the like aching melancholy, by the same whispered remonstrance, and made restless by a similar impulse of aspiration. It seems as if the soul said to herself: From this state hast thou fallen! Such shouldst thou still become, thyself all permeable to a holier power! thyself at once hidden and glorified by its own transparency, as the accidental and dividuous in this quiet and harmonious object is subjected to the life and light of nature; to that life and light of nature, I say, which shines in every plant and flower, even as the transmitted power, love and wisdom of God over all fills, and shines through, nature! But what the plant is by an act not its own and unconsciously—that must thou make thyself to become—must by prayer and by a watchful and unresisting spirit, join at least with the preventive and assisting grace to make thyself, in that light of conscience which inflameth not, and with that knowledge which puffeth not up!

But further, and with particular reference to that undivided reason, neither merely speculative or merely practical, but both in one, which I have in this annotation endeavoured to contradistinguish from the understanding, I seem to myself to behold in the quiet objects, on which I am gazing, more than an arbitrary illustration, more than a mere *simile*, the work of my own fancy. I feel an awe, as if there were before my eyes the same power as that of the reason—the same power in a lower dignity, and therefore a symbol established in the truth of things. I feel it alike, whether I contemplate a single tree or flower, or meditate on vegetation throughout the world, as one of the great organs of the life of nature. Lo!—with the rising sun it commences its outward life and enters into open communion with all the elements, at once assimilating them to itself and to each other. At the same moment it strikes its roots and unfolds its leaves, absorbs and respires, steams forth its cooling vapour and finer fragrance, and breathes a repairing spirit, at once the food and tone of the atmosphere, into the atmosphere that feeds it. Lo!—at the touch of light how it returns an air akin to light, and yet with the same pulse effectuates its own secret growth, still contracting to fix what expanding it had refined. Lo!—how upholding the ceaseless plastic motion of the parts in the profoundest rest of the whole it becomes the visible *organismus* of the entire silent or elementary life of nature and, therefore, in incorporating the one extreme becomes the symbol of the other; the natural symbol of that higher life of reason, in which the whole series (known to us in our present state of being) is perfected, in which, therefore, all the subordinate gradations recur, and are re-ordained *in more abundant honour*. We had seen each in its own cast, and we now recognise them all as coexisting in the unity of a higher form, the crown and completion of the earthly, and the mediator of a new and heavenly series. Thus finally, the vegetable creation, in the simplicity and uniformity of its internal structure symbolising the unity of nature, while it represents the omniformity of her delegated functions in its external variety and manifoldness, becomes the record and chronicle of her ministerial acts, and inchases the vast unfolded volume of the earth with the hieroglyphics of her history.

Lay Sermons.

P. 292, l. 25. Dividuous. *This word Coleridge uses not seldom in a sense partly identical with and partly opposite to "individual." It seems to mean "that which marks off the individual."*

ROBERT SOUTHEY.

Robert Southey, the most laborious and accomplished craftsman in English letters since Dryden, was born at Bristol in 1774, and died at Keswick in 1843. His prose style is the most uniformly good of any English writer who has written on anything like the same scale and with anything like the same variety of subject and class of work.

DANIEL DOVE'S BOOKS.

HAPPILY for Daniel, he lived before the age of Magazines, Reviews, Cyclopædias, Elegant Extracts and Literary Newspapers, so that he gathered the fruit of knowledge for himself, instead of receiving it from the dirty fingers of a retail vendor. His books were few in number, but they were all weighty either in matter or in size. They consisted of the Morte d'Arthur in the fine black-letter edition of Copeland; Plutarch's Morals and Pliny's Natural History, two goodly folios, full as an egg of meat, and both translated by that old worthy Philemon, who for the service which he rendered to his contemporaries and to his countrymen deserves to be called the best of the Hollands, without disparaging either the Lord or the Doctor of that appellation. The whole works of Joshua Sylvester (whose name let me tell the reader in passing, was accented upon the first syllable by his contemporaries, not as now upon the second);—Jean Petit's History of the Netherlands, translated and continued by Edward Grimeston, another worthy of the Philemon order; Sir Kenelm Digby's Discourses; Stowe's Chronicle; Joshua Barnes' Life of Edward III.; "Ripley Revived by Eirenæus Philalethes, an Englishman styling himself Citizen of the World," with its mysterious frontispiece representing the *Domus Naturæ*, to which *Nil deest, nisi clavis;* the Pilgrim's Progress; two volumes of Ozell's translation of Rabelais; Latimer's Sermons; and the last volume of Fox's Martyrs, which latter book had been brought him by his wife. The Pilgrim's Progress was a godmother's present to his son: the odd volumes of Rabelais he had picked up at Kendal, at a sale in a lot with Ripley Revived and Plutarch's Morals: the others he had inherited.

Daniel had looked into all these books, read most of them, and believed all that he read, except Rabelais, which he could not tell what to make of. He was not, however, one of those persons who complacently suppose everything to be nonsense, which they do not perfectly comprehend, or flatter themselves that they do. His simple heart judged of books by what they ought to be, little knowing what they are. It never occurred to him that any thing would be printed which was not worth printing, any thing which did not convey either reasonable delight or useful instruction: and he was no more disposed to doubt the truth of what he read, than to question the veracity of his neighbour, or any one who had no interest in deceiving him. A book carried with it to him authority in its very aspect. The Morte d'Arthur therefore he received for authentic history, just as he did the painful chronicle of honest John Stowe, and the Barnesian labours of Joshua the self-satisfied: there was nothing in it indeed which stirred his English blood like the battles of Cressy and Poictiers and Najara; yet on the whole he preferred it to Barnes's story, believed in Sir Tor, Sir Tristram, Sir Launcelot and Sir Lamorack as entirely as in Sir John Chandos, the Captal de Buche and the Black Prince, and liked them better.

Latimer and Du Bartas he used sometimes to read aloud on Sundays; and if the departed take cognizance of what passes on earth, and poets derive any satisfaction from that posthumous applause which is generally the only reward of those who deserve it, Sylvester might have found some compensation for the undeserved neglect into which his works had sunk, by the full and devout delight which his rattling hymns and quaint collocations afforded to this reader. The silver-tongued Sylvester, however, was reserved for a Sabbath book; as a week-day author Daniel preferred Pliny, for the same reason that bread and cheese, or a rasher of hung mutton, contented his palate better than a syllabub. He frequently regretted that so knowing a writer had never seen or heard of Wethercote and Yordas caves; the ebbing and flowing spring at Giggleswick, Malham Cove, and Gordale Scar, that he might have described them among the wonders of the world. *Omne ignotum pro magnifico* is a maxim which will not in all cases hold good. There are things which we do not undervalue because we are familiar with them, but which are admired the more thoroughly they are known and understood; it is thus with the grand objects of nature and the finest works of art,—with whatsoever is truly great and excellent. Daniel was not deficient in imagination; but no description of places which he had never seen, however exaggerated (as such things always are) impressed him so strongly as these objects in his own neighbourhood, which he had known from childhood. Three or four times in his life it had happened that strangers with a curiosity as uncommon in that age as it is general in this, came from afar to visit these wonders of the West Riding, and Daniel accompanied them with a delight such as he never experienced on any other occasion.

But the author in whom he delighted most was Plutarch, of whose works he was lucky enough to possess the worthier half: if the other had perished Plutarch would not have been a popular writer, but he would have held a higher place in the estimation of the judicious. Daniel could have posed a candidate for university honours, and perhaps the examiner too, with some of the odd learning which he had stored up in his memory from these great repositories of ancient knowledge. Refusing all reward for such services, the strangers to whom he officiated as a guide, though they perceived that he was an extraordinary person, were little aware how much information he had acquired, and of how strange a kind. His talk with them did not go beyond the subjects which the scenes they came to visit naturally suggested, and they wondered more at the questions he asked, than at anything which he advanced himself. For his disposition was naturally shy, and that which had been bashfulness in youth assumed the appearance of reserve as he advanced in life; for having none to communicate with upon his favourite studies, he lived in an intellectual world of his own, a mental solitude as complete as that of Alexander Selkirk or Robinson Crusoe. Even to the Curate his conversation if he had touched upon his books, would have been heathen Greek; and to speak the truth plainly, without knowing a letter of that language, he knew more about the Greeks, than nine-tenths of the clergy at that time, including all the dissenters, and than nine-tenths of the school-masters also.

Our good Daniel had none of that confidence which so usually and so unpleasantly characterizes self-taught men. In fact, he was by no means aware of the extent of his acquirements, all that he knew in this kind having been acquired for amusement, not for use. He had never attempted to teach himself anything. These books had lain in his way in boyhood, or fallen in it afterwards, and the perusal of them, intently as it was followed, was always accounted by him to be nothing more than recreation. None of his daily business had ever been neglected for it; he cultivated his fields and his garden, repaired his walls, looked to his stable, tended his cows and salved his sheep, as diligently and as contentedly as if he had possessed neither capacity nor inclination for any higher employments. Yet Daniel was one of those men, who, if disposition and aptitude were not overruled by circumstances, would have grown pale with study, instead of being bronzed and hardened by sun and wind and rain. There were in him undeveloped talents which might have raised him to distinction as an antiquary, a virtuoso of the Royal Society, a poet, or a theologian, to whichever course the bias in his ball of fortune had inclined. But he had not a particle of envy in his composition. He thought indeed that if he had had grammar learning in his youth like the curate, he would have made more use of it; but there was nothing either of the sourness or bitterness (call it which you please) of repining in this natural reflection.

The Doctor.

P. 294, l. 7. Morte d'Arthur. *Malory's book.*
P. 294, l. 13. Doctor. *Sir Henry Holland.*
P. 294, l. 14. Sylvester. *Southey forgot or neglected a certain scandalous dialogue in verse, traditionally attributed to Sylvester and Ben Jonson.*
P. 295, l. 38. Neglect. *Sylvester has recently had justice done to him by a stately reprint in Dr. Grosart's* Chertsey Worthies.
P. 296, l. 9. Wonders. *All these natural curiosities are in the limestone district of Craven in Yorkshire; nor did Daniel overrate them. The caves and spring describe themselves, but those who do not know them may be told that Malham Cove is a vast semicircular wall of rock overhanging a valley, and Gordale Scar a small but extraordinarily wild and fantastic waterfall.*
P. 296, l. 26. Worthier half. *After allowing for the facts that the miscellanies called the* Moralia *are pretty certainly not all Plutarch's, and that they are extremely unequal in value, there is much truth in this.*
P. 297, l. 31. Bias *in the proper sense, as used in the game of bowls.*

JANE AUSTEN.

Jane Austen was born at Steventon in 1775, and died at Chawton in 1817. Furnished with matter by an exquisite and not too satirical observation, equipped by nature and reading with a style not striking to the vulgar, but infinitely flexible and instinct with humour, Miss Austen achieved perhaps the most perfect, if not the largest or noblest work, yet done in the English novel.

A STRAWBERRY PARTY.

IT was now the middle of June and the weather fine; and Mrs. Elton was growing impatient to name the day, and settle with Mr. Weston as to pigeon pies and cold lamb, when a lame carriage horse threw everything into sad uncertainty. It might be weeks, it might be only a few days before the horse were useable; but no preparations could be ventured on, and it was all melancholy stagnation. Mrs. Elton's resources were inadequate to such an attack.

"Is not this most vexatious, Knightley?" she cried; "and such weather for exploring! these delays and disappointments are quite odious. What are we to do? The year will wear away at this rate and nothing done. Before this time last year, I assure you, we had a delightful exploring party from Maple Grove to King's Weston."

"You had better explore to Donwell," replied Mr. Knightley. "That may be done without horses. Come and eat my strawberries: they are ripening fast."

If Mr. Knightley did not begin seriously he was obliged to proceed so; for his proposal was caught at with delight; and the "Oh! I should like it of all things" was not plainer in words than in manner. Donwell was famous for its strawberry beds, which seemed a plea for the invitation: but no plea was necessary; cabbage-beds would have been enough to tempt the lady, who only wanted to be going somewhere. She promised him again and again to come—much oftener than he doubted—and was extremely gratified by such a proof of intimacy, such a distinguishing compliment, as she chose to consider it.

"You may depend upon me," said she; "I certainly will come. —Name your day, and I will come.—You will allow me to bring Jane Fairfax?"

"I cannot name a day," said he, "till I have spoken to some others, whom I would wish to meet you."

"Oh, leave all that to me; only give me a carte-blanche.—I am Lady Patroness, you know. It is my party. I will bring friends with me."

"I hope you will bring Elton," said he; "but I will not trouble you to give any other invitations."

"Oh, now you are looking very sly;—but consider, you need not be afraid of delegating power to *me*. I am no young lady on her preferment. Married women, you know, may be safely authorised. It is my party, leave it all to me. I will invite your guests."

"No," he calmly replied, "there is but one married woman in the world whom I can ever allow to invite what guests she pleases to Donwell, and that one is——"

"Mrs. Weston, I suppose," interrupted Mrs. Elton, rather mortified.

"No,—Mrs. Knightley; and till she is in being, I will manage such matters myself."

"Ah, you are an odd creature!" she cried, satisfied to have no one preferred to herself. "You are a humourist, and may say what you like. Quite a humourist. Well, I shall bring Jane with me—Jane and her aunt. The rest I leave to you. I have no objections at all to meeting the Hartfield family. Don't scruple, I know you are attached to them."

"You certainly will meet them if I can prevail; and I shall call on Miss Bates on my way home."

"That is quite unnecessary; I see Jane every day;—but as you please. It is to be a morning scheme, you know, Knightley; quite a simple thing. I shall wear a large bonnet, and bring one of my little baskets hanging on my arm. Here,—probably this basket with pink riband. Nothing can be more simple, you see. And Jane will have such another. There is to be no form, or parade—a sort of gypsy party. We are to walk about your gardens, and gather the strawberries ourselves, and sit under trees; and whatever else you may like to provide, it is to be all out of doors; a table spread in the shade, you know. Everything as simple and natural as possible. Is not that your idea?"

"Not quite. My idea of the simple and the natural will be to have the table spread in the dining room. The nature and the simplicity of gentlemen and ladies, with their servants and furniture, I think is best observed by meals within doors. When you are tired of eating strawberries in the garden, there shall be cold meat in the house."

"Well, as you please; only don't have a great set-out. And, by the bye, can I or my housekeeper be of any use to you with our opinion? Pray be sincere, Knightley. If you wish me to talk to Mrs. Hodges, or to inspect anything———"

"I have not the least wish for it, I thank you."

"Well, but if any difficulties should arise, my housekeeper is extremely clever."

"I will answer for it that mine thinks herself full as clever, and would spurn anybody's assistance."

"I wish we had a donkey. The thing would be for us all to come on donkeys. Jane, Miss Bates, and me, and my caro sposo walking by. I really must talk to him about purchasing a donkey. In a country life, I conceive it to be a sort of necessary; for, let a woman have ever so many resources, it is not possible for her to be always shut up at home; and very long walks, you know—in summer there is dust, and in winter there is dirt."

"You will not find either between Donwell and Highbury. Donwell lane is never dusty, and now it is perfectly dry. Come on a donkey, however, if you prefer it. You can borrow Mrs. Cole's. I would wish everything to be as much to your taste as possible."

"That I am sure you would. Indeed I do you justice, my good friend. Under that peculiar sort of dry, blunt manner, I know you have the warmest heart. As I tell Mr. E., you are a thorough humourist. Yes, believe me, Knightley, I am fully sensible of your attention to me in the whole of this affair. You have hit upon the very thing to please me."

Emma.

CHARLES LAMB.

Charles Lamb—most exquisite and peculiar of English humourists, most appreciative within his range of English critics—was born in London in 1775, and died at Edmonton in 1834. Lamb's prose style is, undoubtedly, modelled upon the Jacobean and Caroline writers, but he has put in it so much of his own that it is practically as original as it is charming.

THE CONVALESCENT.

A PRETTY severe fit of indisposition which, under the name of a nervous fever, has made a prisoner of me for some weeks past, and is but slowly leaving me, has reduced me to an incapacity of reflecting upon any topic foreign to itself. Expect no healthy conclusions from me this month, reader; I can offer you only sick men's dreams.

And truly the whole state of sickness is such; for what else is it but a magnificent dream for a man to lie a-bed, and draw daylight curtains about him; and, shutting out the sun, to induce a total oblivion of all the works which are going on under it? To become insensible to all the operations of life, except the beatings of one feeble pulse?

If there be a regal solitude, it is a sick-bed. How the patient lords it there; what caprices he acts without control! how king-like he sways his pillow—tumbling, and tossing, and shifting, and lowering, and thumping, and flatting, and moulding it, to the ever-varying requisitions of his throbbing temples.

He changes *sides* oftener than a politician. Now he lies full length, then half length, obliquely, transversely, head and feet quite across the bed; and none accuses him of tergiversation. Within the four curtains he is absolute. They are his Mare Clausum.

How sickness enlarges the dimensions of a man's self to himself! he is his own exclusive object. Supreme selfishness is inculcated upon him as his only duty. 'Tis the Two Tables of the Law to him. He has nothing to think of but how to get well. What passes out of doors, or within them, so he hear not the jarring of them, affects him not.

A little while ago he was greatly concerned in the event of a lawsuit, which was to be the making or the marring of his dearest friend. He was to be seen trudging about upon this man's errand to fifty quarters of the town at once, jogging this witness, refreshing that solicitor. The cause was to come on yesterday. He is absolutely as indifferent to the decision as if it were a question to be tried at Pekin. Peradventure from some whispering, going on about the house, not intended for his hearing, he picks up enough to make him understand that things went cross-grained in the court yesterday, and his friend is ruined. But the word "friend," and the word "ruin," disturb him no more than so much jargon. He is not to think of anything but how to get better.

What a world of foreign cares are merged in that absorbing consideration!

He has put on the strong armour of sickness, he is wrapped in the callous hide of suffering; he keeps his sympathy, like some curious vintage, under trusty lock and key, for his own use only.

He lies pitying himself, honing and moaning to himself; he yearneth over himself; his bowels are even melted within him, to think what he suffers; he is not ashamed to weep over himself.

He is for ever plotting how to do some good to himself; studying little stratagems and artificial alleviations.

He makes the most of himself; dividing himself by an allowable fiction, into as many distinct individuals as he hath sore and sorrowing members. Sometimes he meditates—as of a thing apart from him—upon his poor aching head, and that dull pain which, dozing or waking, lay in it all the past night like a log, or palpable substance of pain, not to be removed without opening the very skull as it seemed, to take it thence. Or he pities his long, clammy, attenuated fingers. He compassionates himself all over; and his bed is a very discipline of humanity and tender heart.

He is his own sympathizer; and instinctively feels that none can so well perform that office for him. He cares for few spectators to his tragedy. Only that punctual face of the old nurse pleases him, that announces his broths and his cordials. He likes it because it is so unmoved, and because he can pour forth his feverish ejaculations before it as unreservedly as to his bedpost.

To the world's business he is dead. He understands not what the callings and occupations of mortals are; only he has a glimmering conceit of some such thing, when the doctor makes his daily call; and even in the lines on that busy face he reads no multiplicity of patients, but solely conceives of himself as *the sick man*. To what other uneasy couch the good man is hastening, when he slips out of his chamber, folding up his thin douceur so carefully, for fear of rustling—is no speculation which he can at present entertain. He thinks only of the regular return of the same phenomenon at the same hour to-morrow.

Household rumours touch him not. Some faint murmur, indicative of life going on within the house, soothes him, while he knows not distinctly what it is. He is not to know anything, not to think of anything. Servants gliding up or down the distant staircase, treading as upon velvet, gently keep his ear awake, so long as he troubles not himself further than with some feeble guess at their errands. Exacter knowledge would be a burden to him: he can just endure the pressure of conjecture. He opens his eye faintly at the dull stroke of the muffled knocker, and closes it again without asking "Who was it?" He is flattered by a general notion that inquiries are making after him, but he cares not to know the name of the inquirer. In the general stillness, and awful hush of the house, he lies in state, and feels his sovereignty.

To be sick is to enjoy monarchal prerogatives. Compare the silent tread and quiet ministry, almost by the eye only, with which he is served—with the careless demeanour, the unceremonious goings in and out, slapping of doors, or leaving them open, of the very same attendants, when he is getting a little better—and you will confess, that from the bed of sickness, throne let me rather call it, to the elbow-chair of convalescence, is a fall from dignity, amounting to a deposition.

How convalescence shrinks a man back to his pristine stature! Where is now the space, which he occupied so lately, in his own, in the family's eye?

The scene of his regalities, his sick room, which was his presence-chamber, where he lay and acted his despotic fancies —how is it reduced to a common bedroom! The trimness of the very bed has something petty and unmeaning about it. It is *made* every day. How unlike to that wavy, many-furrowed, oceanic surface, which it presented so short a time since, when to *make* it was a service not to be thought of at oftener than three or four day revolutions, when the patient was with pain and grief to be lifted for a little while out of it, to submit to the encroachments of unwelcome neatness, and decencies which his shaken frame deprecated; then to be lifted into it again, for another three or four days' respite, to flounder it out of shape again, while every fresh furrow was an historical record of some shifting posture, some uneasy turning, some seeking for a little ease; and the shrunken skin scarce told a truer story than the crumpled coverlid.

Hushed are those mysterious sighs—those groans—so much more awful, while we knew not from what caverns of vast hidden suffering they proceeded. The Lernean pangs are quenched. The riddle of sickness is solved; and Philoctetes is become an ordinary personage.

Perhaps some relic of the sick man's dream of greatness survives in the still lingering visitations of the medical attendant. But how is he, too, changed with everything else? Can this be he—this man of news—of chat—of anecdote—of everything but physic—can this be he, who so lately came between the patient and his cruel enemy, as on some solemn embassy from Nature, erecting herself into a high mediating party?—Pshaw! 'tis some old woman.

Farewell with him all that made sickness pompous—the spell that hushed the household—the desert-like stillness, felt throughout its inmost chambers—the mute attendance—the inquiry by looks—the still softer delicacies of self-attention—the sole and single eye of distemper alonely fixed upon itself—world-thoughts excluded—the man a world unto himself—his own theatre—

What a speck is he dwindled into !

In this flat swamp of convalescence, left by the ebb of sickness, yet far enough from the terra-firma of established health, your note, dear Editor, reached me, requesting—an article. In Articulo Mortis, thought I ; but it is something hard—and the quibble, wretched as it was, relieved me. The summons, unseasonable as it appeared, seemed to link me on again to the petty businesses of life, which I had lost sight of ; a gentle call to activity, however trivial ; a wholesome weaning from that preposterous dream of self-absorption—the puffy state of sickness —in which I confess to have lain so long, insensible to the magazines and monarchies of the world alike ; to its laws, and to its literature. The hypochondriac flatus is subsiding ; the acres, which in imagination I had spread over—for the sick man swells in the sole contemplation of his single sufferings, till he becomes a Tityus to himself—are wasting to a span ; and for the giant of self-importance, which I was so lately, you have me once again in my natural pretensions—the lean and meagre figure of your insignificant Essayist.

Essays of Elia.

P. 303, l. 5. This month. *July, 1825. The* Essays of Elia *originally appeared in the* London Magazine.

P. 304, l. 2. Mare Clausum. *A play on the title of Selden's treatise (in answer to Grotius) defending the rights of England over the adjacent seas.*

P. 304, l. 29. Honing. *Lamb did not invent this word, for it occurs in his favourite period, though with a somewhat different sense. But the jingle with moaning and the suggestion of the Irish "ochone" no doubt weighed with him.*

P. 307, l. 5. Alonely. *Used by Latimer.*

WALTER SAVAGE LANDOR.

Walter Savage Landor was born at Ipsley, Warwickshire, in 1775, and died at Florence in 1864. A violent temper and unbusinesslike habits brought Landor, who ought to have been a rich man, into various troubles, and much of his life was spent in almost enforced exile. In his prose and verse, but especially in the former, romantic fancy and classical precision of form meet as they meet nowhere else.

THE DREAM OF BOCCACCIO.

IN the next moment she was again at my side, with the cup quite full. I stood motionless: I feared my breath might shake the water over. I looked her in the face for her commands.. and to see it.. to see it so calm, so beneficent, so beautiful. I was forgetting what I had prayed for, when she lowered her head, tasted of the cup, and gave it me. I drank; and suddenly sprang forth before me, many groves and palaces and gardens, and their statues and their avenues, and their labyrinths of alaternus and bay, and alcoves of citron, and watchful loopholes in the retirements of impenetrable pomegranate. Farther off, just below where the fountain slipt away from its marble hall and guardian gods, arose, from their beds of moss and drosera and darkest grass, the sisterhood of oleanders, fond of tantalising with their bosomed flowers and their moist and pouting blossoms the little shy rivulet, and of covering its face with all the colours of the dawn. My dream expanded and moved forward. I trod again the dust of Posilipo, soft as the feathers in the wings of Sleep. I emerged on Baia; I crossed her innumerable arches; I loitered in the breezy sunshine of her mole; I trusted the faithful seclusion of her caverns, the keepers of so many secrets; and I reposed on the buoyancy of her tepid sea. Then Naples, and her theatres and her churches, and grottoes and dells and forts and promontories, rushed forward in confusion, now among soft whispers, now among sweetest sounds, and subsided, and sank and disappeared. Yet a memory seemed to come fresh from every one: each had time enough for its tale, for its pleasure, for its reflection, for its pang. As I mounted with silent steps the narrow staircase of the old palace, how distinctly did I feel against the palm of my hand the coldness of that smooth stonework, and the greater of the cramps of iron in it!

"Ah me! is this forgetting?" cried I anxiously to Fiametta.

"We must recall these scenes before us," she replied: "such is the punishment of them. Let us hope and believe that the apparition, and the compunction which must follow it, will be accepted as the full penalty, and that both will pass away almost together."

I feared to lose anything attendant on her presence: I feared to approach her forehead with my lips: I feared to touch the lily on its long wavy leaf in her hair, which filled my whole heart with fragrance. Venerating, adoring, I bowed my head at last to kiss her snow-white robe, and trembled at my presumption. And yet the effulgence of her countenance vivified while it chastened me. I loved her ever . . . I must not say *more* than ever . . . *better* than ever; it was Fiametta who had inhabited the skies. As my hand opened toward her,

"Beware!" said she, faintly smiling; "beware, Giovanni! Take only the crystal; take it, and drink again."

"Must all be then forgotten?" said I sorrowfully.

"Remember your prayer and mine, Giovanni! Shall both have been granted . . . O how much worse than in vain?"

I drank instantly; I drank largely. How cool my bosom grew; how could it grow so cool before her! But it was not to remain in its quiescency; its trials were not yet over. I will not, Francesco! no, I may not commemorate the incidents she related to me, nor which of us said, "I blush for having loved *first;*" nor which of us replied, "Say *least*, say *least*, and blush again."

The Pentameron.

CRITICS AS GENTLEMEN-USHERS.

Southey. We must see through many ages before we see through our own distinctly. Few among the best judges, and even among those who desired to judge dispassionately and impartially, have beheld their contemporaries in those proportions in which they appeared a century later. The ancients have greatly the advantage over us. Scarcely can any man believe that one whom he has seen in coat and cravat, can possibly be so great as one who wore a chlamys and a toga. Those alone look gigantic whom Time " *multo aëre sepsit,*" or whom childish minds, for the amusement of other minds more childish, have lifted upon stilts. Nothing is thought so rash as to mention a modern with an ancient : but when both are ancient, the last-comer often stands first. The present form one cluster, the past another. We are petulant if some of the existing have pushed by too near us : but we walk up composedly to the past, with all our prejudices behind us. We compare them leisurely one with another, and feel a pleasure in contributing to render them a plenary, however a tardy, justice. In the fervour of our zeal we often exceed it ; which we never are found doing with our contemporaries, unless in malice to one better than the rest. Some of our popular and most celebrated authors are employed by the booksellers to cry up the wares on hand or forthcoming, partly for money and partly for payment in kind. Without such management the best literary production is liable to moulder on the shelf.

Landor. A wealthy man builds an ample mansion, well proportioned in all its parts, well stored with the noblest models of antiquity ; extensive vales and downs and forests stretch away from it in every direction ; but the stranger must of necessity pass it by, unless a dependant is stationed at a convenient lodge to admit and show him in. Such, you have given me to understand, is become the state of our literature. The bustlers who rise into notice by playing at leap-frog over one another's shoulders, will disappear when the game is over ; and no game

is shorter. But was not Milton himself kept beyond the paling?
Nevertheless, how many *toupees* and *roquelaures*, and other odd
things with odd names, have fluttered among the jays in the cherry
orchard, while we tremble to touch with the finger's end his grave
close-buttoned gabardine! He was called strange and singular
long before he was acknowledged to be great: so, be sure, was
Shakespeare; so, be sure, was Bacon; and so were all the rest,
in the order of descent. You are too generous to regret that
your liberal praise of Wordsworth was seized upon with avidity
by his admirers, not only to win others to their party, but also to
depress your merits. Nor will you triumph over their folly in
confounding what is pitiful with what is admirable in him;
rather will you smile, and, without a suspicion of malice, find
the cleverest of these good people standing on his low joint-stool
with a slender piece of wavering tape in his hand, measuring him
with Milton back to back. There is as much difference between
them as there is between a celandine and an ilex. The one lies
at full length and full breadth along the ground; the other rises
up stiff, strong, lofty, beautiful in the play of its slenderer
branches, overshadowing with the infinitude of its grandeur.

Imaginary Conversations.

P. 308, l. 5. What I had prayed for. *Forgetfulness of his love for Fiametta and of his indulgence in passion.*

P. 309, l. 11. The greater. *It is curious how even Landor in classicising slips into the old forgetfulness of the limits of a non-inflected language. Greater what? Coldness of course, but the mere momentary doubt distracts the reader's attention.*

P. 311, l. 2. Toupees. *Small wigs, or even arrangements of the natural hair, with tufts in front.* Roquelaures. *Buttoned cloaks.*

HENRY HALLAM.

Henry Hallam was born at Windsor in 1777, and died in London in 1859. Industrious, sober-minded, accomplished, and as judicial in his views as was consistent with a certain want of catholicity of taste and with strong views in general politics, Hallam is an authority to be cautiously differed with. The style in him exactly corresponds to the thought.

THE SUPPRESSION OF CONVOCATION.

THE new government at first permitted the convocation to hold its sittings. But they soon excited a flame which consumed themselves by an attack on Hoadley, bishop of Bangor, who had preached a sermon abounding with those principles concerning religious liberty, of which he had long been the courageous and powerful assertor. The lower house of convocation thought fit to denounce, through the report of a committee, the dangerous tenets of this discourse, and of a work not long before published by the bishop. A long and celebrated war of pens instantly commenced, known by the name of the Bangorian controversy; managed, perhaps on both sides, with all the chicanery of polemical writers, and disgusting both from its tediousness, and from the manifest unwillingness of the disputants to speak ingenuously what they meant. But, as the principles of Hoadley and his advocates appeared, in the main, little else than those of protestantism and toleration, the sentence of the laity, in the temper that was then gaining ground as to ecclesiastical subjects, was soon pronounced in their favour; and the high church party discredited themselves by an opposition to what now pass for the incontrovertible truisms of religious liberty. In the ferment of that age, it was expedient for the state to scatter a little dust over the angry insects; the convocation was accordingly prorogued in 1717, and has never sat again for any business. Those who are imbued with high notions of sacerdotal power have sometimes deplored this extinction of the Anglican great council; and though its necessity, as I have already observed, cannot possibly be defended as an ancient part of the constitution, there are not wanting specious arguments for the expediency of such a synod. It might be urged that the church, considered only as an integral member of the commonwealth, and the greatest corporation within it, might justly claim that right of managing its own affairs which belongs to every other association; that the argument from abuse is not sufficient, and is rejected with indignation when applied, as historically it might be, to representative governments and to civil liberty; that, in the present state of things, no reformation even of secondary importance can be effected without difficulty, nor any looked for in greater matters, both from the indifference of the legislature, and the reluctance of the clergy to admit its interposition.

It is answered to these suggestions, that we must take experience when we possess it, rather than analogy, for our guide; that ecclesiastical assemblies have in all ages and countries been mischievous, where they have been powerful, which those of our wealthy and numerous clergy must always be; that if, notwithstanding, the convocation could be brought under the management of the state, which by the nature of its component parts might seem not unlikely, it must lead to the promotion of servile men, and the exclusion of merit still more than at present; that the severe remark of Clarendon, who observes that of all mankind none form so bad an estimate of human affairs as churchmen, is abundantly confirmed by experience; that the representation of the church in the House of Lords is sufficient for the protection of its interests; that the clergy have an influence which no other corporation enjoys over the bulk of the nation, and may abuse it for the purposes of undue ascendancy, unjust restraint, or factious ambition; that the hope of any real good in reformation of the church by its own assemblies, to whatever sort of reform we may look, is utterly chimerical; finally, that as the laws now stand, which few would incline to alter, the ratification of parliament must be indispensable for any material change. It seems to admit of no doubt that these reasonings ought much to outweigh those on the opposite side.

The Constitutional History of England.

P. 312, l. 4. *A sermon. In* 1717. *It is only justice to the opponents of Hoadley to say that it contained a great deal besides "principles concerning religious liberty," unless this phrase is to be interpreted in a very wide sense indeed. Hoadley was understood to maintain that no Church derived authority from Christ, a tenet as offensive to orthodox dissenters as to High Churchmen.*

WILLIAM HAZLITT.

William Hazlitt was born at Maidstone in 1778, tried various arts and professions, underwent domestic and pecuniary difficulties, drifted into literature, and died in 1830. Hazlitt, the acutest perhaps of all English critics, is too full of crotchet and partisanship to be the most trustworthy. His work, in great part hastily written, is unequal, but admirable at its best in matter and in form.

THE ELGIN MARBLES.

FARTHER, in a cast from nature there would be, as a matter of course, the same play and flexibility of limb and muscle, or, as Sir Thomas Lawrence expresses it, the same "alternate action and repose," that we find so admirably displayed in the Elgin Marbles. It seems here as if stone could move: where one muscle is strained, another is relaxed; where one part is raised, another sinks in, just as in the ocean, where the waves are lifted up in one place, they sink proportionally low in the next: and all this modulation and affection of the different parts of the form by others arise from an attentive and co-instantaneous observation of the parts of a flexible body, where the muscles and bones act upon, and communicate with, one another, like the ropes and pulleys in a machine, and where the action or position given to a particular limb or membrane naturally extends to the whole body. This harmony, this combination of motion, this unity of spirit diffused through the wondrous mass and every part of it, is the glory of the Elgin Marbles. Put a well-formed human body in the same position and it will display the same character throughout; make a cast from it while in that position and action, and we shall still see the same bold, free, and comprehensive truth of design. There is no alliteration or antithesis in the style of the Elgin Marbles, no setness, squareness, affectation, or formality of appearance. The different muscles do not present a succession of *tumuli*, each heaving with big throes to rival the other. If one is raised, the other falls quietly into its place. Neither do the different parts of the body answer to one another, like shoulder-knots on a lacquey's coat or the different ornaments of a building. The sculptor does not proceed on architectural principles. His work has the freedom, the variety, and stamp of nature. The form of corresponding parts is indeed the same, but it is subject to inflection, from different circumstances. There is no primness or *petit maître-ship*, as in some of the later antiques, where the artist seemed to think that flesh was glass or some other brittle substance; and that if it were put out of its exact shape, it would break in pieces. Here, on the contrary, if the foot of one leg is bent under the body, the leg itself undergoes an entire alteration. If one side of the body is raised above the other, the original, or abstract, or *ideal* form of the two sides is not preserved strict and inviolable, but varies, as it necessarily must do, in conformity to the law of gravitation, to which all bodies are subject. In this respect, a cast from nature would be the same. Chantrey once made a cast from Wilson the Black. He put him into an attitude at first, and made the cast, but not liking the effect when done, got him to sit again, and made use of the plaster of Paris once more. He was satisfied with the result; but Wilson, who was tired with going through the operation, as soon as it was over, went and leaned upon a block of marble with his hands covering his face. The sagacious sculptor was so struck with the superiority of this natural attitude over those into which he had been arbitrarily put, that he begged him (if possible) to continue in it for another quarter of an hour, and another impression was taken off. All three casts remain, and the last is a proof of the superiority of nature over art. The effect of lassitude is visible in every part of the frame, and the strong feeling of this affection, impressed on every limb and muscle, and venting itself naturally in an involuntary attitude which gave immediate relief, is that which strikes everyone who has seen this fine study from the life. The casts from this man's figure have been much admired—it is from no superiority of form: it is merely that, being taken from nature, they bear her "image and superscription."

Essays on the Fine Arts.

COLERIDGE.

BUT I may say of him here, that he is the only person I ever knew who answered to the idea of a man of genius. He is the only person from whom I ever learnt anything. There is only one thing he could learn from me in return, but *that* he has not. He was the first poet I ever knew. His genius at that time [1798] had angelic wings, and fed on manna. He talked on for ever; and you wished him to talk on for ever. His thoughts did not seem to come with labour and effort, but as if borne on the gusts of genius, and as if the wings of his imagination lifted him from off his feet. His voice rolled on the ear like the pealing organ, and its sound alone was the music of thought. His mind was clothed with wings; and raised on them, he lifted philosophy to heaven. In his descriptions, you then saw the progress of human happiness and liberty in bright and never-ending succession, like the steps of Jacob's Ladder, with airy shapes ascending and descending, and with the voice of God at the top of the ladder. And shall I, who heard him then, listen to him now? Not I! . . . That spell is broken; that time is gone for ever; that voice is heard no more: but still the recollection comes rushing by with thoughts of long-past years, and rings in my ears with never-dying sound.

Lectures on English Poets.

P. 316, l. 3. Alliteration or antithesis. *Hazlitt in thus using the terms of one art to describe the subject of another has set a bad example too widely followed.*

THOMAS MOORE.

Thomas Moore was born at Dublin in 1779, and died in 1852, having, like Scott and Southey, outworked, or at least outlived, his intellectual powers. His prose, less known than his poetry, is facile, elegant, and, on the whole, correct. It is interesting, like some other styles of which example is given here for the same reason, as showing a certain school and period in a good light.

A FESTIVAL ON THE NILE.

THE rising of the Moon, slow and majestic, as if conscious of the honours that awaited her upon earth, was welcomed with a loud acclaim from every eminence, where multitudes stood watching for her first light. And seldom had that light risen upon a more beautiful scene. The city of Memphis—still grand, though no longer the unrivalled Memphis, that had borne away from Thebes the crown of supremacy, and worn it undisputed through ages—now, softened by the mild moonlight that harmonised with her decline, shone forth among her lakes, her pyramids, and her shrines, like one of those dreams of human glory that must ere long pass away. Even already ruin was visible around her. The sands of the Libyan desert were gaining upon her like a sea; and there, among solitary columns and sphinxes, already half sunk from sight, Time seemed to stand waiting, till all that now flourished around him should fall beneath his desolating hand, like the rest.

On the waters all was gaiety and life. As far as eye could reach, the lights of innumerable boats were seen studding, like rubies, the surface of the stream. Vessels of every kind—from the light coracle, built for shooting down the cataracts, to the large yacht that glides slowly to the sound of flutes—all were afloat for this sacred festival, filled with crowds of the young and the gay, not only from Memphis and Babylon, but from cities still farther removed from the festal scene.

As I approached the island, I could see, glittering through the trees on the bank, the lamps of the pilgrims hastening to the ceremony. Landing in the direction which those lights pointed out, I soon joined the crowd; and, passing through a long alley of sphinxes, whose spangling marble gleamed out from the dark sycamores around them, reached in a short time the grand vestibule of the temple, where I found the ceremonies of the evening already commenced.

In this vast hall, which was surrounded by a double range of columns, and lay open over-head to the stars of heaven, I saw a group of young maidens, moving in a sort of measured step, between walk and dance, round a small shrine, upon which stood one of those sacred birds, that, on account of the variegated colour of their wings, are dedicated to the worship of the moon. The vestibule was dimly lighted—there being but one lamp of naphtha hung on each of the great pillars that encircled it. But, having taken my station beside one of those pillars, I had a clear view of the young dancers, as in succession they passed me.

The drapery of all was white as snow; and each wore loosely, beneath the bosom, a dark-blue zone, or bandelet, studded, like the skies at midnight, with small silver stars. Through their dark locks was wreathed the white lily of the Nile—that sacred flower being accounted no less welcome to the moon, than the golden blossoms of the bean-flower are known to be to the sun. As they passed under the lamp, a gleam of light flashed from their bosoms, which, I could perceive, was the reflection of a small mirror, that, in the manner of the women of the East, each of the dancers wore beneath her left shoulder.

There was no music to regulate their steps; but, as they gracefully went round the bird on the shrine, some, to the beat of the castanet, some, to the shrill ring of a sistrum—which they held uplifted in the attitude of their own divine Isis—continued harmoniously to time the cadence of their feet; while others, at every step, shook a small chain of silver, whose sound, mingling with those of the castanets and sistrums, produced a wild, but not unpleasing harmony.

They seemed all lovely; but there was one—whose face the light had not yet reached, so downcast she held it—who attracted, and, at length, riveted all my looks and thoughts. I know not why, but there was a something in those half-seen features—a charm in the very shadow, that hung over their imagined beauty —which took my fancy more than all the outshining loveliness of her companions. So enchained was I by this coy mystery, that her alone, of all the group, could I either see or think of— her alone I watched, as, with the same downcast brow, she glided gently and aërially round the altar, as if her presence, like that of a spirit, was something to be felt, not seen.

Suddenly, while I gazed, the loud crash of a thousand cymbals was heard;—the massy gates of the Temple flew open, as if by magic, and a flood of radiance from the illuminated aisle filled the whole vestibule; while, at the same instant, as if the light and the sounds were born together, a peal of rich harmony came mingling with the radiance.

The Epicurean.

P. 319, l. 4. Babylon. *Moore has not made a slip here, as some hasty readers may suppose. There was actually a Babylon opposite the Pyramids in Roman times, and "Babiloine" in the* Chansons de Gestes *and other mediæval French books always means Cairo.*

P. 319, l. 36. Sistrum. *The sacred rattle of Isis, in shape between a hand-mirror and the stand used for flat-irons, with loose cross bars of metal.*

JOHN WILSON.

John Wilson was born at Paisley in 1785. For some time he led, at Elleray on Windermere, a life of ease. Losing his fortune, he became a pillar of Blackwood's Magazine *under the name of Christopher North. Wilson's energy and versatility are amazing; his attempts at prose poetry sometimes beautiful. His humour, chiefly exercised in dialect, cannot easily be shown here. He died in 1854.*

THE FAIRY'S FUNERAL.

THERE it was, on a little river island, that once, whether sleeping or waking we know not, we saw celebrated a Fairy's Funeral. First we heard small pipes playing, as if no bigger than hollow rushes that whisper to the night winds; and more piteous than aught that trills from earthly instrument was the scarce audible dirge! It seemed to float over the stream, every foam-bell emitting a plaintive note, till the airy anthem came floating over our couch, and then alighted without footsteps among the heather. The pattering of little feet was then heard, as if living creatures were arranging themselves in order, and then there was nothing but a more ordered hymn. The harmony was like the melting of musical dewdrops, and sang, without words, of sorrow and death. We opened our eyes, or rather sight came to them when closed, and dream was vision! Hundreds of creatures, no taller than the crest of the lapwing, and all hanging down their veiled heads, stood in a circle on a green plot among the rocks; and in the midst was a bier, framed as it seemed of flowers unknown to the Highland hills; and on the bier a Fairy, lying with uncovered face, pale as the lily, and motionless as the snow. The dirge grew fainter and fainter, and then died quite away; when two of the creatures came from the circle, and took their station, one at the head and the other at the foot of the bier. They sang alternate measures, not louder than the twittering of the awakened wood-lark before it goes up the dewy air, but dolorous and full of the desolation of death. The flower-bier stirred; for the spot on which it lay sank slowly down, and in a few moments the greensward was smooth as ever —the very dews glittering above the buried Fairy. A cloud passed over the moon, and, with a choral lament, the funeral troop sailed duskily away, heard afar off, so still was the midnight solitude of the glen. Then the disenthralled Orchy began to rejoice as before through all her streams and falls; and at the sudden leaping of the waters and outbursting of the moon, we awoke.

Age is the season of Imagination, youth of Passion; and having been long young, shall we repine that we are now old? They alone are rich who are full of years—the Lords of Time's Treasury are all on the staff of Wisdom; their commissions are enclosed in furrows on their foreheads, and secured to them for life. Fearless of fate, and far above fortune, they hold their heritage by the great charter of nature for behoof of all her children, who have not, like impatient heirs, to wait for their decease; for every hour dispenses their wealth, and their bounty is not a late bequest but a perpetual benefaction. Death but sanctifies their gifts to gratitude; and their worth is more clearly seen and profoundly felt within the solemn gloom of the grave.

And said we truly that Age is the season of Imagination? that Youth is the season of Passion your own beating and bounding hearts now tell you—your own boiling blood. Intensity is its characteristic; and it burns like a flame of fire, too often but to consume. Expansion of the soul is ours, with all its feelings and all its "thoughts, that wander through eternity;" nor needeth then the spirit to have wings, for power is given her, beyond the dove's or the eagle's, and no weariness can touch her on that heavenward flight.

Yet we are all of "the earth earthy," and young and old alike, must we love and honour our home. Your eyes are bright—ours are dim ; but "it is the soul that sees," and "this diurnal sphere" is visible through the mist of tears. In that light how more than beautiful—how holy—appears even this world! All sadness, save of sin, is then most sacred ; and sin itself loses its terrors in repentance, which alas ! is seldom perfect but in the near prospect of dissolution. For temptation may intercept her within a few feet of her expected rest, nay, dash the dust from her hand that she has gathered from the burial-place to strew on her head ; but Youth sees flowery fields and shining rivers far-stretching before her path, and cannot imagine for a moment that among life's golden mountains there is many a Place of Tombs !

But let us speak only of this earth—this world—this life—and is not Age the season of Imagination ? Imagination is Memory imbued by joy or sorrow with creative power over the past, till it becomes the present, and then, on that vision "far off the coming shines" of the future, till all the spiritual realm overflows with light. Therefore was it that, in illumined Greece, Memory was called the Mother of the Muses ; and how divinely indeed they sang around her as she lay in the pensive shade !

You know the words of Milton—

"Till old experience doth attain
To something like prophetic strain ;"

and you know, while reading them, that Experience is consummate Memory, Imagination wide as the world, another name for Wisdom, all one with Genius, and in its "prophetic strain" —Inspiration.

Recreations of Christopher North.

THOMAS DE QUINCEY.

Thomas De Quincey was born near Manchester in 1785, lived chiefly at the lakes or near Edinburgh, and died in 1859. His literary activity dates from his later years. De Quincey was a man of wide knowledge, of great though capricious critical power, of peculiar imaginative faculty. His views on ornate prose were questionable, but he was equally master of the chaster and simpler style.

THE POWER AND DANGER OF THE CÆSARS.

TO this view of the imperial character and relations must be added one single circumstance, which in some measure altered the whole for the individual who happened to fill the office. The emperor *de facto* might be viewed under two aspects; there was the man, and there was the office. In his office he was immortal and sacred: but as a question might still be raised, by means of a mercenary army, as to the claims of the particular individual who at any time filled the office, the very sanctity and privilege of the character with which he was clothed might actually be turned against himself; and here it is, at this point, that the character of Roman emperor became truly and mysteriously awful. Gibbon has taken notice of the extraordinary situation of a *subject* in the Roman empire who should attempt to fly from the wrath of the Cæsar. Such was the ubiquity of the emperor that this was metaphysically hopeless. Except across pathless deserts or amongst barbarous nomads, it was impossible to find even a transient sanctuary from the imperial pursuit. If the fugitive went down to the sea, there he met the emperor: if he took the wings of the morning, and fled to the uttermost parts of the earth, there was also Cæsar in the person of his lieutenants. But, by a dreadful counter-charm, the same omnipresence of imperial anger and retribution which withered the hopes of the poor humble prisoner, met and confounded the emperor himself, when hurled from his elevation by some fortunate rival. All the kingdoms of the earth, to one in that situation, became but so many wards of the same infinite prison. Flight, if it were even successful for the moment, did but a little retard his inevitable doom. And so evident was this, that hardly in one instance did the fallen prince *attempt* to fly; passively he met the death which was inevitable, in the very spot where ruin had overtaken him. Neither was it possible even for a merciful conqueror to show mercy; for, in the presence of an army so mercenary and factious, his own safety was but too deeply involved in the extermination of rival pretenders to the crown.

Such, amidst the sacred security and inviolability of the office, was the hazardous tenure of the individual. Nor did his dangers always arise from persons in the rank of competitors and rivals. Sometimes it menaced him in quarters which his eye had never penetrated, and from enemies too obscure to have reached his ear. By way of illustration we will cite a case from the life of the Emperor Commodus, which is wild enough to have furnished the plot of a romance, though as well authenticated as any other passage in that reign. The story is narrated by Herodian, and the outline was this:—A slave of noble qualities, and of magnificent person, having liberated himself from the degradations of bondage, determined to avenge his own wrongs by inflicting continual terror upon the town and neighbourhood which had witnessed his humiliation. For this purpose he resorted to the woody recesses of the province (somewhere in the modern Transylvania), and, attracting to his wild encampment as many fugitives as he could, by degrees he succeeded in training a very formidable troop of freebooters. Partly from the energy of his own nature, and partly from the neglect and remissness of the provincial magistrates, the robber captain rose from less to more, until he had formed a little army, equal to the task of assaulting fortified cities. In this stage of his adventures, he encountered and defeated several of the imperial officers commanding large detachments of troops; and at length grew of consequence sufficient to draw upon himself the emperor's eye, and the honour of his personal displeasure. In high wrath and disdain at the insults offered to his eagles by this fugitive slave, Commodus fulminated against him such an edict as left him no hope of much longer escaping with impunity.

Public vengeance was now awakened; the imperial troops were marching from every quarter upon the same centre; and the slave became sensible that in a very short space of time he must be surrounded and destroyed. In this desperate situation he took a desperate resolution: he assembled his troops, laid before them his plan, concerted the various steps for carrying it into effect, and then dismissed them as independent wanderers. So ends the first chapter of the tale.

The next opens in the passes of the Alps, whither, by various routes, of seven or eight hundred miles in extent, these men had threaded their way in manifold disguises through the very midst of the emperor's camps. According to this man's gigantic enterprise, in which the means were as audacious as the purpose, the conspirators were to rendezvous, and first to recognise each other, at the gates of Rome. From the Danube to the Tiber did this band of robbers severally pursue their perilous routes through all the difficulties of the road and the jealousies of the military stations, sustained by the mere thirst of vengeance—vengeance against that mighty foe whom they knew only by his proclamations against themselves. Everything continued to prosper; the conspirators met under the walls of Rome; the final details were arranged; and those also would have prospered but for a trifling accident. The season was one of general carnival at Rome; and, by the help of those disguises which the license of this festival time allowed, the murderers were to have penetrated as maskers to the emperor's retirement, when a casual word or two awoke the suspicions of a sentinel. One of the conspirators was arrested; under the terror and uncertainty of the moment, he made much ampler discoveries than were expected of him; the other accomplices were secured: and Commodus was delivered from the uplifted daggers of those who had sought him by months of patient wanderings, pursued through all the depths of the Illyrian forests, and the difficulties of the Alpine passes. It is not easy to find words of admiration commensurate to the energetic hardihood of a slave—who, by way of answer and reprisal to an edict summarily consigning him to persecution and death, determines to cross Europe in quest of its author, though no less a person than the master of the world—to seek him out in the inmost recesses of his capital city, of his private palace, of his consecrated bed-chamber—and there to lodge a dagger in his heart, as the adequate reply to the imperial sentence of proscription against himself.

Such, amidst the superhuman grandeur and hallowed privileges of the Roman emperor's office, were the extraordinary perils which menaced the individual officer. The office rose by its grandeur to a region above the clouds and vapours of earth: the officer might find his personal security as unsubstantial as those wandering vapours. Nor is it possible that these circumstances of violent opposition can be better illustrated than in this tale of Herodian. Whilst the emperor's mighty arms were stretched out to arrest some potentate in the heart of Asia, a poor slave is silently and stealthily creeping round the base of the Alps, with the purpose of winning his way as a murderer to the imperial bed-chamber; Cæsar is watching some potent rebel of the Orient, at a distance of two thousand leagues, and he overlooks the dagger which is within three stealthy steps, and one tiger's leap, of his own heart. All the heights and the depths which belong to man's frailty, all the contrasts of glory and meanness, the extremities of what is highest and lowest in human casualties, meeting in the station of the Roman Cæsar Semper Augustus—have combined to call him into high marble relief, and to make him the most interesting study of all whom history has emblazoned with colours of fire and blood, or has crowned most lavishly with diadems of cypress and laurel.

The Cæsars.

OUR LADY OF DARKNESS.

But the third sister, who is also the youngest——! Hush! whisper whilst we talk of *her!* Her kingdom is not large, or else no flesh should live; but within that kingdom all power is hers. Her head, turreted like that of Cybele, rises almost beyond the reach of sight. She droops not; and her eyes rising so high *might* be hidden by distance. But, being what they are, they cannot be hidden; through the treble veil of crape which she wears, the fierce light of a blazing misery, that rests not for matins or for vespers, for noon of day or noon of night, for ebbing or for flowing tide, may be read from the very ground. She is the defier of God. She also is the mother of lunacies, and the suggestress of suicides. Deep lie the roots of her power; but narrow is the nation that she rules. For she can approach only those in whom a profound nature has been upheaved by central convulsions; in whom the heart trembles and the brain rocks under conspiracies of tempest from without and tempest from within. Madonna moves with uncertain steps, fast or slow, but still with tragic grace. Our Lady of Sighs creeps timidly and stealthily. But this youngest sister moves with incalculable motions, bounding, and with a tiger's leap. She carries no key; for, though coming rarely amongst men, she storms all doors at which she is permitted to enter at all. And *her* name is *Mater Tenebrarum,*—Our Lady of Darkness.

The Opium Eater.

SIR WILLIAM FRANCIS PATRICK NAPIER.

Sir William Napier, born at Castletown in Ireland in 1785, fought in the Peninsular War, held various military appointments, and died at Clapham in 1860. Napier is deservedly held our best military historian; his accounts of battles and military situations are admirably clear, and he can rise on occasion to a becoming and not empty pomp of style.

THE BRITISH SOLDIER.

THAT the British infantry soldier is more robust than the soldier of any other nation can scarcely be doubted by those who, in 1815, observed his powerful frame, distinguished amidst the united armies of Europe; and notwithstanding his habitual excess in drinking, he sustains fatigue and wet and the extremes of cold and heat with incredible vigour. When completely disciplined, and three years are required to accomplish this, his port is lofty and his movements free, the whole world cannot produce a nobler specimen of military bearing: nor is the mind unworthy of the outward man. He does not indeed possess that presumptuous vivacity which would lead him to dictate to his commanders, or even to censure real errors, although he may perceive them; but he is observant and quick to comprehend his orders, full of resources under difficulties, calm and resolute in danger, and more than usually obedient and careful of his officers in moments of imminent peril. It has been asserted that his undeniable firmness in battle is the result of a phlegmatic constitution uninspired by moral feeling. Never was a more stupid calumny uttered! Napoleon's troops fought in bright fields where every helmet caught some beams of glory, but the British soldier conquered under the cold shade of aristocracy. No honours awaited his daring, no despatch gave his name to the applauses of his countrymen, his life of danger and hardship was uncheered by hope, his death unnoticed. Did his heart sink therefore? Did he not endure with surpassing fortitude the sorest of ills, sustain the most terrible assaults in battle unmoved, overthrow with incredible energy every opponent, and at all times prove, that while no physical military qualification was wanting, the fount of honour was also full and fresh within him! The result of a hundred battles and the united testimony of impartial writers of different nations have given the first place amongst the European infantry to the British: but in a comparison between the troops of France and England, it would be unjust not to admit that the cavalry of the former stands higher in the estimation of the world.

History of the War in the Peninsula.

P. 329, l. 19. Stupid calumny. *Napier's generous and well-grounded enthusiasm for the British soldier has been forced into a curious paralogism here by his political prejudices. Indifference to the "cold shade" would surely prove a phlegmatic constitution, not disprove it.*

MARY RUSSELL MITFORD.

Mary Russell Mitford was born at Alresford in 1786, lived chiefly at Swallowfield in Berkshire, and died there in 1855. The charming country sketches of Our Village rank not far below White's Selborne in accuracy, and surpass them in variety and ornament.

THE COWSLIP BALL.

THESE meadows consist of a double row of small enclosures of rich grass-land, a mile or two in length, sloping down from high arable grounds on either side to a little nameless brook that winds between them, with a course which in its infinite variety, clearness, and rapidity, seems to emulate the bold rivers of the north, of whom, far more than of our lazy southern streams, our rivulet presents a miniature likeness. Never was water more exquisitely tricksy:—now darting over the bright pebbles, sparkling and flashing in the light with a bubbling music, as sweet and wild as the song of the woodlark; now stretching quietly along, giving back the rich tufts of the golden marsh-marygolds which grow on its margin; now sweeping round a fine reach of green grass, rising steeply into a high mound, a mimic promontory, whilst the other side sinks softly away, like some tiny bay, and the water flows between, so clear, so wide, so shallow, that Lizzy, longing for adventure, is sure she could cross unwetted; now dashing through two sand-banks, a torrent deep and narrow, which May clears at a bound; now sleeping half-hidden beneath the alders and hawthorns and wild roses, with which the banks are so profusely and variously fringed, whilst flags, lilies, and other aquatic plants, almost cover the surface of the stream. In good truth it is a beautiful brook, and one that Walton himself might have sitten by and loved, for trout are there; we see them as they dart up the stream, and hear and start at the sudden plunge when they spring to the surface for the summer flies. Isaac Walton would have loved our brook and our quiet meadows; they breathe the very spirit of his own peacefulness, a soothing quietude that sinks into the soul. There is no path through them, not one; we might wander about a whole spring day, and not see a trace of human habitation. They belong to a number of small proprietors, who allow each other access through their respective grounds, from pure kindness and neighbourly feeling, a privilege never abused; and the fields on the other side of the water are reached by a rough plank, or a tree thrown across, or some such homely bridge. We ourselves possess one of the most beautiful; so that the strange pleasure of property, that instinct which makes Lizzy delight in her broken doll, and May in the bare bone which she has pilfered from the kennel of her recreant admirer of Newfoundland, is added to the other charms of this enchanting scenery; a strange pleasure it is, when one so poor as I can feel it! Perhaps it is felt most by the poor, with the rich it may be less intense—too much diffused and spread out, becoming thin by expansion, like leaf-gold; the little of the poor may be not only more precious, but more pleasant to them: certainly that bit of grassy and blossomy earth, with its green knolls and tufted bushes, its old pollards wreathed with ivy, and its bright and babbling waters, is very dear to me. But I must always have loved these meadows, so fresh, and cool, and delicious to the eye and to the tread, full of cowslips, and of all vernal flowers: Shakspeare's Song of Spring bursts irrepressibly from our lips as we step on them:

> "When daisies pied, and violets blue,
> And lady-smocks all silver white,
> And cuckoo-buds of yellow hue,
> Do paint the meadows with delight,
> The cuckoo then on every tree—"

"Cuckoo! cuckoo!" cried Lizzy, breaking in with her clear childish voice; and immediately, as if at her call, the real bird, from a neighbouring tree, for these meadows are dotted with timber like a park, began to echo my lovely little girl, "cuckoo! cuckoo!" I have a prejudice very unpastoral and unpoetical, but I cannot help it, I have many such, against this "harbinger of spring." His note is so monotonous, so melancholy, and then the boys mimic him; one hears "cuckoo! cuckoo!" in dirty streets, amongst smoky houses, and the bird is hated for faults not his own. But prejudices of taste, likings and dislikings, are not always vanquishable by reason; so, to escape the serenade from the tree, which promised to be of considerable duration, (when once that eternal song begins, on it goes ticking like a clock)—to escape that noise I determined to excite another, and challenged Lizzy to a cowslip-gathering: a trial of skill and speed, to see which should soonest fill her basket. My stratagem succeeded completely. What scrambling, what shouting, what glee from Lizzy! twenty cuckoos might have sung unheard whilst she was pulling her own flowers, and stealing mine, and laughing, screaming, and talking through all.

At last the baskets were filled, and Lizzy declared victor: and down we sate, on the brink of the stream, under a spreading hawthorn, just disclosing its own pearly buds, and surrounded with the rich and enamelled flowers of the wild hyacinth, blue and white, to make our cowslip-ball. Every one knows the process; to nip off the tuft of flowerets just below the top of the stalk, and hang each cluster nicely balanced across a riband, till you have a long string like a garland; then to press them closely together, and tie them tightly up. We went on very prosperously, *considering;* as people say of a young lady's drawing, or a Frenchman's English, or a woman's tragedy, or of the poor little dwarf who works without fingers, or the ingenious sailor who writes with his toes, or generally of any performance which is accomplished by means seemingly inadequate to its production. To be sure we meet with a few accidents. First, Lizzy spoiled nearly all her cowslips by snapping them off too short; so there was a fresh gathering; in the next place May overset my full basket, and sent the blossoms floating, like so many fairy favours, down the brook; then when we were going on pretty steadily, just as we had made a superb wreath, and were thinking of tying it together, Lizzy, who held the riband, caught a glimpse of a gorgeous butterfly, all brown and red and purple, and skipping off to pursue the new object, let go her hold; so all our treasures were abroad again. At last, however, by dint of taking a branch of alder as a substitute for Lizzy, and hanging the basket in a pollard-ash, out of sight of May, the cowslip-ball was finished. What a concentration of fragrance and beauty it was! golden and sweet to satiety! rich to sight, and touch, and smell! Lizzy was enchanted, and ran off with her prize, hiding amongst the trees in the very coyness of ecstacy, as if any human eye, even mine, would be a restraint on her innocent raptures.

Our Village.

P. 331, l. 18. May. *A greyhound.*
P. 332, l. 31. Song of Spring. *Miss Mitford had apparently not made the remarkable discovery of some modern critics that this exquisite song is "very improper."*

THOMAS LOVE PEACOCK.

Thomas Love Peacock was born in 1788, passed much of his life in the service of the East India Company, and died at Halliford in 1866. His satirical novels have never been widely read, but are unapproached in their kind. He is as much the critic's novelist as Spenser is the poet's poet. His humour and the style embodying it are comparable to one thing only—very old and perfect wine.

THE DRUNKENNESS OF SEITHENYN.

ELPHIN seated himself at the right hand of Seithenyn. Teithrin remained at the end of the hall: on which Seithenyn exclaimed, "Come on, man, come on. What if you be not the son of a king, you are the guest of Seithenyn ap Seithyn Saidi. The most honourable place to the most honourable guest, and the next most honourable place to the next most honourable guest; the least honourable guest above the most honourable inmate; and, where there are but two guests, be the most honourable who he may, the least honourable of the two is next in honour to the most honourable of the two, because there are no more but two; and, where there are only two, there can be nothing between. Therefore sit, and drink. GWIN O EUR: wine from gold."

Elphin motioned Teithrin to approach, and sit next to him.

Prince Seithenyn, whose liquor was "his eating and his drinking solely," seemed to measure the gastronomy of his guests by his own; but his groom of the pantry thought the strangers might be disposed to eat, and placed before them a choice of provision, on which Teithrin ap Tathral did vigorous execution.

"I pray your excuses," said Seithenyn, "my stomach is weak, and I am subject to dizziness in the head, and my memory is not so good as it was, and my faculties of attention are somewhat impaired, and I would dilate more upon the topic, whereby you should hold me excused, but I am troubled with a feverishness and parching of the mouth, that very much injures my speech, and impedes my saying all I would say, and will say before I have done, in token of my loyalty and fealty to your highness and your highness's house. I must just moisten my lips, and I will then proceed with my observations. Cupbearer, fill."

"Prince Seithenyn," said Elphin, "I have visited you on a subject of deep moment. Reports have been brought to me, that the embankment, which has been so long entrusted to your care, is in a state of dangerous decay."

"Decay," said Seithenyn, "is one thing, and danger is another. Everything that is old must decay. That the embankment is old, I am free to confess; that it is somewhat rotten in parts, I will not altogether deny; that it is any the worse for that, I do most sturdily gainsay. It does its business well: it works well: it keeps out the water from the land, and it lets in the wine upon the High Commission of Embankment. Cupbearer, fill. Our ancestors were wiser than we: they built it in their wisdom; and, if we should be so rash as to try to mend it, we should only mar it."

"The stonework," said Teithrin, "is sapped and mined: the piles are rotten, broken, and dislocated: the floodgates and sluices are leaky and creaky."

"That is the beauty of it," said Seithenyn. "Some parts of it are rotten, and some parts of it are sound."

"It is well," said Elphin, "that some parts are sound: it were better that all were so."

"So I have heard some people say before," said Seithenyn; "perverse people, blind to venerable antiquity: that very unamiable sort of people, who are in the habit of indulging their reason. But I say, the parts that are rotten give elasticity to those that are sound: they give them elasticity, elasticity, elasticity. If it were all sound, it would break by its own obstinate stiffness: the soundness is checked by the rottenness, and the stiffness is balanced by the elasticity. There is nothing so dangerous as innovation. See the waves in the equinoctial storms, dashing and clashing, roaring and pouring, spattering and battering, rattling and battling against it. I would not be so presumptuous as to say, I could build anything that would stand against them half an hour; and here this immortal old work, which God forbid the finger of modern mason should bring into jeopardy, this immortal work has stood for centuries, and will stand for centuries more, if we let it alone. It is well: it works well: let well alone. Cupbearer, fill. It was half rotten when I was born, and that is a conclusive reason why it should be three parts rotten when I die."

The whole body of the High Commission roared approbation.

"And after all," said Seithenyn, "the worst that could happen would be the overflow of a spring-tide, for that was the worst that happened before the embankment was thought of; and, if the high water should come in, as it did before, the low water would go out again, as it did before. We should be no deeper in it than our ancestors were, and we could mend as easily as they could make."

"The level of the sea," said Teithrin, "is materially altered."

"The level of the sea!" exclaimed Seithenyn. "Who ever heard of such a thing as altering the level of the sea? Alter the level of that bowl of wine before you, in which, as I sit here, I see a very ugly reflection of your very good-looking face. Alter the level of that: drink up that reflection: let me see the face without the reflection, and leave the sea to level itself."

"Not to level the embankment," said Teithrin.

"Good, very good,". said Seithenyn. "I love a smart saying, though it hits at me. But whether yours is a smart saying or no, I do not very clearly see; and, whether it hits at me or no, I do not very sensibly feel. But all is one. Cupbearer, fill."

"I think," pursued Seithenyn, looking as intently as he could at Teithrin ap Tathral, "I have seen something very like you before. There was a fellow here the other day very like you: he stayed here some time: he would not talk: he did nothing but drink: he used to drink till he could not stand, and then he went walking about the embankment. I suppose he thought it wanted mending; but he did not say anything. If he had, I should have told him to embank his own throat, to keep the liquor out of that. That would have posed him: he could not have answered that: he would not have had a word to say for himself after that."

"He must have been a miraculous person," said Teithrin, "to walk when he could not stand."

"All is one for that," said Seithenyn. "Cupbearer, fill."

"Prince Seithenyn," said Elphin, "if I was not aware that wine speaks in the silence of reason, I should be astonished at your strange vindication of your neglect of duty, which I take shame to myself for not having sooner known and remedied. The wise bard has well observed, 'Nothing is done without the eye of the king.'"

"I am very sorry," said Seithenyn, "that you see things in a wrong light: but we will not quarrel, for three reasons: first, because you are the son of the king, and may do and say what you please without any one having a right to be displeased: second, because I never quarrel with a guest, even if he grows riotous in his cups: third, because there is nothing to quarrel about; and perhaps that is the best reason of the three; or, rather, the first is the best, because you are the son of the king; and the third is the second, that is, the second best, because there is nothing to quarrel about: and the second is nothing to the purpose, because, though guests will grow riotous in their cups, in spite of my good orderly example, God forbid I should say that is the case with you. And I completely agree in the truth of your remark, that reason speaks in the silence of wine."

The Misfortunes of Elphin.

P. 335, l. 1. *Seithenyn is the convivial and careless noble charged with the supervision of the embankment which keeps out the sea from the fated land of Gwaelod (now Cardigan Bay). Prince Elphin, son of Gwythno, the king of the country, with his attendant Teithrin, visits him to remonstrate on the condition of the dyke.*

P. 337, l. 2. *All this, as the reader will readily understand, is satire on the stock arguments against Parliamentary Reform. The book was published in 1829.*

HENRY HART MILMAN.

Henry Hart Milman was born in London in 1791, and died Dean of St. Paul's in 1868. His great work, The History of Latin Christianity, deserves the high praise that it sustains the inevitable comparison with Gibbon not wholly ill in point of erudition, and is not too far below him in point of style.

MONASTICISM.

THE calm example of the domestic virtues in a more polished, but often, as regards sexual intercourse, more corrupt state of morals, is of inestimable value, as spreading around the parsonage an atmosphere of peace and happiness, and offering a living lesson on the blessings of conjugal fidelity. But such Christianity would have made no impression, even if it could have existed, on a people who still retained something of their Teutonic severity of manners, and required therefore something more imposing—a sterner and more manifest self-denial—to keep up their religious veneration. The detachment of the clergy from all earthly ties left them at once more unremittingly devoted to their unsettled life as missionaries, more ready to encounter the perils of this wild age; while (at the same time) the rude minds of the people were more struck by their unusual habits, by the strength of character shown in their labours, their mortifications, their fastings, and perpetual religious services. All these being, in a certain sense, monks, the bishop and his clergy coenobites, or if they lived separate only less secluded and less stationary than other ascetics, wherever Christianity spread, monasteries, or religious foundations with a monastic character, arose. These foundations, as the religion aspired to soften the habits, might seem to pacify the face of the land. They were commonly placed, by some intuitive yearning after repose and security, in spots either themselves beautiful by nature, by the bank of the river, in the depth of the romantic wood, under the shelter of the protecting hill; or in such as became beautiful from the superior care and culture of the monks,—the draining of the meadows, the planting of trees, the home circle of garden or orchard, which employed or delighted the brotherhood. These establishments gradually acquired a certain sanctity: if exposed like other lands to the ravages of war, no doubt at times the fear of some tutelary saint, or the influence of some holy man, arrested the march of the spoiler. If the growth of the English monasteries was of necessity gradual, the culture around them but of slow development (agricultural labour does not seem to have become a rule of monastic discipline), it was not from the want of plentiful endowments, or of ardent votaries. Grants of land and of moveables were poured with lavish munificence on these foundations; sometimes tracts of land, far larger than they could cultivate, and which were thus condemned to sterility. The Scottish monks are honourably distinguished as repressing, rather than encouraging this prodigality. The Roman clergy, if less scrupulous, might receive these tributes not merely as offerings of religious zeal to God, but under a conviction that they were employed for the improvement as well as the spiritual welfare of the people. Nor was it only the sacred mysterious office of ministering at the altar of the new God, it was the austere seclusion of the monks, which seized on the religious affections of the Anglo-Saxon convert. When Christianity first broke upon their rude but earnest minds, it was embraced with the utmost fervour, and under its severest forms. Men were eager to escape the awful punishments, and to secure the wonderful promises of the new religion, by some strong effort, which would wrench them altogether from their former life. As the gentler spirit of the Gospel found its way into softer hearts, it made them loathe the fierce and rudely warlike occupations of their forefathers. To the one class the monastery offered its rigid course of ceremonial duty and its ruthless austerities, to the other its repose. Nobles left their halls, queens their palaces, kings their thrones, to win everlasting life by the abandonment of the pomp and the duties of their secular state, and, by becoming churchmen or monks, still to exercise rule, or to atone for years of blind and sinful heathenism.

History of Latin Christianity.

P. 339, l. 15. Habits. *Evidently in the proper sense of "dress," not "customs."*

PERCY BYSSHE SHELLEY.

Percy Bysshe Shelley was born in 1792, and was drowned in the Gulf of Spezia in 1822. To prefer or to equal Shelley's prose to his poetry is a merely uncritical freak of judgment. His prose is, however, of excellent quality, both in his letters, which are among the most charming of their kind, and in his too few essays and miscellaneous writings.

THE LAKE OF COMO.

SINCE I last wrote to you we have been to Como, looking for a house. This lake exceeds any thing I ever beheld in beauty, with the exception of the arbutus islands of Killarney. It is long and narrow, and has the appearance of a mighty river winding among the mountains and the forests. We sailed from the town of Como to a tract of country called the Tremezina, and saw the various aspects presented by that part of the lake. The mountains between Como and that village, or rather cluster of villages, are covered on high with chesnut forests (the eating chesnuts, on which the inhabitants of the country subsist in time of scarcity), which sometimes descend to the very verge of the lake, overhanging it with their hoary branches. But usually the immediate border of this shore is composed of laurel-trees, and bay, and myrtle, and wild fig-trees, and olives, which grow in the crevices of the rocks, and overhang the caverns, and shadow the deep glens, which are filled with the flashing light of the waterfalls. Other flowering shrubs, which I cannot name, grow there also. On high, the towers of village churches are seen white among the dark forests. Beyond, on the opposite shore, which faces the south, the mountains descend less precipitously to the lake, and although they are much higher, and some covered with perpetual snow, there intervenes between them and the lake a range of lower hills, which have glens and rifts opening to the other, such as I should fancy the *abysses* of Ida or Parnassus. Here are plantations of olive, and orange, and lemontrees, which are now so loaded with fruit, that there is more fruit than leaves,—and vineyards. This shore of the lake is one continued village, and the Milanese nobility have their villas here. The union of culture and the untameable profusion and loveliness of nature is here so close, that the line where they are divided can hardly be discovered. But the finest scenery is that of the Villa Pliniana; so called from a fountain which ebbs and flows every three hours, described by the younger Pliny, which is in the court-yard. This house, which was once a magnificent palace, and is now half in ruins, we are endeavouring to procure. It is built upon terraces *raised from* the bottom of the lake, together with its garden, at the foot of a semicircular precipice, overshadowed by profound forests of chesnut. The scene from the colonnade is the most extraordinary, at once, and the most lovely that eye ever beheld. On one side is the mountain, and immediately over you are clusters of cypress-trees of an astonishing height, which seem to pierce the sky. Above you, from among the clouds, as it were, descends a waterfall of immense size, broken by the woody rocks into a thousand channels to the lake. On the other side is seen the blue extent of the lake and the mountains, speckled with sails and spires. The apartments of the Pliniana are immensely large, but ill furnished and antique. The terraces, which overlook the lake, and conduct under the shade of such immense laurel-trees as deserve the epithet of Pythian, are most delightful.

Letters from Italy.

POETRY.

POETRY is indeed something divine. It is at once the centre and circumference of knowledge; it is that which comprehends all science, and that to which all science must be referred. It is at the same time the root and blossom of all other systems of thought; it is that from which all spring, and that which adorns all; and that which, if blighted, denies the fruit and the seed, and withholds from the barren world the nourishment and the succession of the scions of the tree of life. It is the perfect and consummate surface and bloom of all things; it is as the odour and the colour of the rose to the texture of the elements which compose it, as the form and splendour of unfaded beauty to the secrets of anatomy and corruption. What were virtue, love, patriotism, friendship,—what were the scenery of this beautiful universe which we inhabit; what were our consolations on this side of the grave—and what were our aspirations beyond it, if poetry did not ascend to bring light and fire from those eternal regions where the owl-winged faculty of calculation dare not ever soar? Poetry is not like reasoning, a power to be exerted according to the determination of the will. A man cannot say, " I will compose poetry." The greatest poet even cannot say it; for the mind in creation is as a fading coal, which some invisible influence, like an inconstant wind, awakens to transitory brightness; this power arises from within, like the colour of a flower which fades and changes as it is developed, and the conscious portions of our nature are unprophetic either of its approach or its departure. Could this influence be durable in its original purity and force, it is impossible to predict the greatness of the results; but when composition begins, inspiration is already on the decline, and the most glorious poetry that has ever been communicated to the world is probably a feeble shadow of the original conceptions of the poet. I appeal to the greatest poets of the present day, whether it is not an error to assert that the finest passages of poetry are produced by labour and study. The toil and the delay recommended by critics, can be justly interpreted to mean no more than a careful observation of the inspired moments, and an artificial connexion of the spaces between their suggestions, by the intertexture of conventional expressions; a necessity only imposed by the limitedness of the poetical faculty itself: for Milton conceived the Paradise Lost as a whole before he executed it in portions. We have his own authority also for the muse having "dictated" to him the "unpremeditated song." And let this be an answer to those who would allege the fifty-six various readings of the first line of the Orlando Furioso. Compositions so produced are to poetry what mosaic is to painting. The instinct and intuition of the poetical faculty is still more observable in the plastic and pictorial arts : a great statue or picture grows under the power of the artist as a child in the mother's womb ; and the very mind which directs the hands in formation, is incapable of accounting to itself for the origin, the gradations, or the media of the process.

Poetry is the record of the best and happiest moments of the happiest and best minds. We are aware of evanescent visitations of thought and feeling, sometimes associated with place or person, sometimes regarding our own mind alone, and always arising unforeseen and departing unbidden, but elevating and delightful beyond all expression: so that even in the desire and the regret they leave, there cannot but be pleasure, participating as it does in the nature of its object. It is as it were the interpenetration of a diviner nature through our own; but its footsteps are like those of a wind over the sea, which the morning calm erases, and whose traces remain only, as on the wrinkled sand which paves it. These and corresponding conditions of being are experienced principally by those of the most delicate sensibility and the most enlarged imagination; and the state of mind produced by them is at war with every base desire. The enthusiasm of virtue, love, patriotism, and friendship, is essentially linked with such emotions; and whilst they last, self appears as what it is, an atom to a universe. Poets are not only subject to these experiences as spirits of the most refined organization, but they can colour all that they combine with the evanescent hues of this ætherial world; a word, a trait in the representation of a scene or a passion, will touch the enchanted chord, and reanimate, in those who have ever experienced these emotions, the sleeping, the cold, the buried image of the past. Poetry thus makes immortal all that is best and most beautiful in the world ; it arrests the vanishing apparitions which haunt the interlunations of life, and veiling them, or in language or in form, sends them forth among mankind, bearing sweet news of kindred joy to those with whom their sisters abide—abide, because there is no portal of expression from the caverns of the spirit which they inhabit into the universe of things. Poetry redeems from decay the visitations of the divinity in man.

Poetry turns all things to loveliness; it exalts the beauty of that which is most beautiful, and it adds beauty to that which is most deformed; it marries exultation and horror, grief and pleasure, eternity and change; it subdues to union, under its light yoke, all irreconcilable things. It transmutes all that it touches, and every form moving within the radiance of its presence is changed by wondrous sympathy to an incarnation of the spirit which it breathes: its secret alchemy turns to potable gold the poisonous waters which flow from death through life; it strips the veil of familiarity from the world, and lays bare the naked and sleeping beauty, which is the spirit of its forms.

A Defence of Poetry.

P. 343, l. 10. Culture—*cultivation*.

P. 344, l. 30. An error. *There is an obvious fallacy here. The finest passages are not originally inspired by labour and study, but in their finest shape they are the result of labour and study spent on the immediate result of inspiration. Shelley speaks as if the first proposition, which is true, involved the second, which is false.*

EDWARD IRVING.

Edward Irving was born in 1792, preached chiefly in London as a Presbyterian minister, was deposed for heresy, and died at Glasgow of consumption in 1834. Irving's sermons were for a time one of the wonders of London; when read they perhaps hardly sustain their reputation, yet they are noteworthy among the comparatively few really remarkable examples of recent English homiletics.

TRUE COURAGE.

THERE be those who confound the foresight of death with a fearfulness of death, and talk of meeting death like brave men; and there be institutions in human society which seem made on purpose to hinder the thoughts of death from coming timeously before the deliberation of the mind. And they who die in war, be they ever so dissipated, abandoned, and wretched, have oft a halo of everlasting glory arrayed by poetry and music around their heads; and the forlorn hope of any enterprise goeth to their terrible post amidst the applauding shouts of all their comrades. And "to die game" is a brutal form of speech which they are now proud to apply to men. And our prize-fights, where they go plunging upon the edge of eternity, and often plunge through, are applauded by tens of thousands, just in proportion as the bull-dog quality of the human creature carries it over every other. And to run hair-breadth escapes, to graze the grass that skirts the grave, and escape the yawning pit, the impious, the daring wretches call cheating the devil; and the watchword of your dissolute, debauched people is, "a short life, and a merry one." All which tribes of reckless, godless people lift loud the laugh against the saints, as a sickly, timorous crew, who have no upright gait in life, but are always cringing under apprehensions of death and the devil. And these bravos think they play the man in spurning God and his concerns away from their places; that there would be no chivalry, nor gallantry, nor battle-brunt in the temper of man were he to stand in awe of the sequel which followeth death. And thus the devil hath built up a strong embattled tower from which he lordeth it over the spirits of many men, winning them over to himself, playing them off for his sport, in utter darkness all their life long, till in the end they take a leap in the dark, and plunge into his yawning pit, never to rise again.

And here I would try these flush and flashy spirits with their own weapons, and play a little with them at their own game. They do but prate about their exploits at fighting, drinking, and death-despising. I can tell them of those who fought with savage beasts; yea of maidens, who durst enter as coolly as a modern bully into the ring to take their chance with infuriated beasts of prey; and I can tell them of those who drank the molten lead as cheerfully as they do the juice of the grape, and handled the red fire and played with the bickering flames as gaily as they do with love's dimples or woman's amorous tresses. And what do they talk of war? Have they forgot Cromwell's iron band, who made their chivalry to skip? or the Scots Cameronians, who seven times, with their Christian chief, received the thanks of Marlborough, that first of English captains? or Gustavus of the North, whose camp sung psalms in every tent? It is not so long, that they should forget Nelson's Methodists, who were the most trusted of that hero's crew. Poor men, they know nothing, who do not know out of their country's history, who it was that set at naught the wilfulness of Henry VIII. and the sharp rage of the virgin Queen against liberty, and bore the black cruelty of her popish sister; and presented the petition of rights and the bill of rights, and the claim of rights. Was it chivalry? was it blind bravery? No, these second-rate qualities may do for a pitched field, or a fenced ring; but when it comes to death or liberty, death or virtue, death or religion, they wax dubious, generally bow their necks under hardships or turn their backs for a bait of honour, or a mess of solid and substantial meat. This chivalry and brutal bravery can fight if you feed them well and bribe them well, or set them well on edge.; but in the midst of hunger and nakedness, and want and persecution, in the day of a country's direst need, they are cowardly, treacherous and of no avail.

Of Judgment to Come.

P. 347, l. 5. They. *Here and elsewhere in the passage Irving is, after the fashion of seventeenth century writers, rather loose in his pronouns.*
P. 348, l. 6. Battle-brunt. *There is authority if not reason for this use of "brunt" (meeting with, or endurance of), though it is now quite obsolete.*

JOHN GIBSON LOCKHART.

John Gibson Lockhart was born at Cambusnethan in 1793, was educated at Oxford, married Scott's daughter, was in 1826 appointed editor of the Quarterly Review, and died in 1854. Lockhart's Life of his father-in-law is one of the most perfect examples of good taste and good workmanship in biography, while all his abundant miscellaneous work is full of thought, judgment, scholarship, and style.

CHARACTER OF HOOK.

HIS defects are great; but Theodore Hook is, we apprehend, the only male novelist of this time, except Mr. Dickens, who has drawn portraits of contemporary English society destined for permanent existence. A selection from his too numerous volumes will go down with Miss Edgeworth and Miss Austen. His best works are not to be compared with theirs, either for skilful compactness of fable or general elegance of finish. His pace was too fast for that. But he is never to be confounded for a moment either with their clumsier and weaker followers, or with the still more tedious imitators of their only modern superior. He understood London thoroughly, with all the tributary provinces within reach either of St. Peter's bell or St. Paul's. The man of that world was known to him *intus et in cute*, and its woman also, or at least not a few of the most interesting, amusing, and absurd varieties of its womankind. Strong, terrible, sinful, and fatal passions were not beyond his sphere—witness especially "Cousin William"; but his serious power is more usually revealed in brief pauses of commentary on the tragic results of trivial machinery. He is to the upper and middle life of that region, what Dickens alone is to its low life—a true authentic expositor; but in manner he is entirely original, and can be likened to no one. In the exuberance of exulting glee with which he elaborates detached scenes of pretension, affectation, the monomanias of idiosyncrasy, he has had no parallel since Smollett and Foote; and he perhaps leaves even them behind him in the magical felicity of phrase with which he brings out the ludicrous picturesque. Like all other first-rate humourists, he betrays everywhere the substratum of solid sagacity; and like them all, except Swift, he is genial. He comprehends human nature, and no one makes better sport with it; but it is never doubtful that he loved his kind, and contemplated the follies of others with a consciousness of his own frailty. That with such an education, and such an external course of life, he should have left so little to be complained of in the morality of his fictitious narratives, seemed to us one of the least intelligible things in the history of literature, until these careless diaries—for we never saw any that could be less supposed to have been written with any view to inspection—withdrew in part the veil under which the natural shyness of genius and the jealousy of conscience had concealed very much of the man from many who thought they understood him.

We have already expressed our opinion, however, that Theodore Hook's ability in conversation was above what he ever exemplified in his writings. We have seen him in company with very many of the most eminent men of his time; and we never, until he was near his end, carried home with us the impression that he had been surpassed. He was as entirely, as any parent of *bon-mots* that we have known, above the suspicion of having premeditated his point; and he excelled in a greater variety of ways than any of them. No definition either of wit or humour could have been framed that must not have included him; and he often conveyed what was at once felt to be the truest wit in forms, as we believe, entirely new. He could run riot in conundrums—but what seemed at first mere jingle, was often perceived, a moment after, to contain some allusion or insinuation that elevated the vehicle. Memory and knack may suffice to furnish out an amusing narrator; but the teller of good stories seldom amuses long if he cannot also say good things. Hook shone equally in both. In fact he could not tell any story without making it his own by the ever-varying, inexhaustible invention of the details and the aspects, and above all, by the tact that never failed to connect it with the persons, the incidents, the topics of the evening. Nothing was with him a patch—all was made to assert somehow its coherence with what had gone before, or was passing. His play of feature, the compass and music of his voice, his large and brilliant eye, capable of every expression from the gravest to the most grotesquely comical, the quiet aptness of every attitude and gesture, his power of mimicry, unrivalled but by Mathews—when to all this we add the constant effect of his innate, imperturbable good humour—the utter absence of spleen—and ever and anon some flash of strong sterling sense, bursting through such an atmosphere of fun and drollery—we still feel how inadequately we attempt to describe the indescribable. The charm was that it was all Nature, spontaneous as water from the rock. No wonder that he should have been courted as he was : but the most honourable part is, that he was far from assentation. There was sad weakness in allowing himself to be hunted out for the amusement of others, at such a heavy sacrifice of time and health and ultimate peace of mind: but once in society, of whatever class, he showed no shabby weakness of any sort. He had undoubtedly a degree of respect for mere rank and worldly splendour, which savoured of his humble origin and early associations; but his abstinence from all the arts of meanness was the more remarkable and creditable, for being shown in the midst of a superstition that otherwise brought much damage to him. Well says *The Rambler*—" It is dangerous for mean minds to venture themselves within the sphere of greatness. Few can be assiduous without servility, and none can be servile without corruption." He was never servile. Those who did not know with what pertinacity he was sought, might speak of him as a tuft-hunter—but neither ignorance nor envy ever presumed to class him with toad-eaters.

We have not endeavoured to conceal or even palliate his errors. To do so, even in the slightest biographical sketch, seems to us most culpable. We believe we have by our—however rapid—retrospect both afforded evidence of good feelings and good principles, preserved and cherished where they had been commonly supposed to be obliterated, and recalled many forgotten circumstances which must be considered as likely to operate powerfully and permanently on the development of any character, however originally amiable and upright. The example of such talents, exerted so much to the delight of others, so little to their possessor's profit—of a career so chequered by indiscretion and so darkly closed at a period so untimely—ought not, at all events, to be destitute of instructiveness. May it have its effect with those who knew Theodore Hook only afar off. We are not afraid that any of his real friends will suspect us of regarding his memory without tenderness, because we have discharged our duty by telling what we believed to be the truth.

Life of Theodore Hook.

P. 350, l. 2. Only male novelist. *When this was written Thackeray was not known as a novelist, and in a note to a reprint of it Lockhart specially recorded the fact.*

THOMAS CARLYLE.

Thomas Carlyle was born at Ecclefechan in 1795, and died in London in 1881. His life, the prey of biographers and the stumbling-block of fools, had chiefly literary eventfulness; his work is copious, characteristic, and masterful as that of few other English writers. Its peculiarities of style have been the subject of pedantic horror and of disgusting imitation, but the result of them is unique.

OLD DRAGOON DROUET.

IN this manner, however, has the Day bent downwards. Wearied mortals are creeping home from their field labour; the village artisan eats with relish his supper of herbs, or has strolled forth to the village street for a sweet mouthful of air and human news. Still summer-eventide every where! The great Sun hangs flaming on the utmost Northwest; for it is his longest day this year. The hill-tops rejoicing will ere long be at their ruddiest, and blush Good-night. The thrush in green dells, on long shadowed leafy spray, pours gushing his glad serenade, to the babble of brooks grown audibler; silence is stealing over the Earth. Your dusty Mill of Valmy, as all other mills and drudgeries, may furl its canvass, and cease swashing and circling. The swenkt grinders in this treadmill of an Earth have ground out another Day; and lounge there, as we say, in village groups; moveable, or ranked on social stone seats; their children, mischievous imps, sporting about their feet. Unnotable hum of sweet human gossip rises from this Village of Sainte-Menehould, as from all other villages. Gossip mostly sweet, unnotable; for the very Dragoons are French and gallant: nor yet has the

Paris-and-Verdun diligence, with its leathern bag, rumbled in, to terrify the minds of men.

One figure, nevertheless, we do note at the last door of the Village: that figure in loose-flowing nightgown of Jean Baptiste Drouet, Master of the Post here. An acrid, choleric man, rather dangerous-looking : still in the prime of life, though he has served in his time as a Condé Dragoon. This day, from an early hour Drouet got his choler stirred, and has been kept fretting. Hussar Goguelat in the morning saw good, by way of thrift, to bargain with his own Innkeeper, not with Drouet, regular *Maître de Poste*, about some gig-horse for the sending back of his gig ; which thing Drouet perceiving, came over in red ire, menacing the Innkeeper, and would not be appeased. Wholly an unsatisfactory day. For Drouet is an acrid Patriot too, was at the Paris Feast of Pikes : and what do these Bouillé soldiers mean? Hussars—with their gig, and a vengeance to it ! have hardly been thrust out, when Dandoins and his fresh Dragoons arrive from Clermont, and stroll. For what purpose? Choleric Drouet steps out and steps in, with long-flowing nightgown ; looking abroad with that sharpness of faculty which stirred choler gives to man.

On the other hand, mark Captain Dandoins on the street of that same village ; sauntering with a face of indifference, a heart eaten of black care ! For no Korff Berline makes its appearance. The great Sun flames broader towards setting : one's heart flutters on the verge of dread unutterabilities.

By Heaven ! here is the yellow Bodyguard Courier ; spurring fast in the ruddy evening light ! Steady, O Dandoins, stand with inscrutable indifferent face ; though the yellow blockhead spurs past the Posthouse ; inquires to find it and stirs the Village, all delighted with his fine livery.—Lumbering along with its mountain of bandboxes, and Chaise behind, the Korff Berline rolls in ; huge Acapulco Ship, with its Cockboat, having got thus far. The eyes of the Villagers look enlightened, as such eyes do, when a coach transit, which is an event, occurs for them. Strolling Dragoons respectfully, so fine are the yellow liveries, bring hand to helmet ; and a Lady in gypsy hat responds with a grace peculiar to her. Dandoins stands with folded arms, and what look of indifference and disdainful garrison-air a man can, while the heart is like leaping out of him. Curled disdainful moustachio; careless glance,—which however surveys the Village-groups, and does not like them. With his eye he bespeaks the yellow Courier, Be quick, be quick! Thickheaded Yellow cannot understand the eye; comes up mumbling to ask in words: seen of the village!

Nor is Post-master Drouet unobservant all this while: but steps out and steps in, with his long-flowing nightgown, in the level sunlight; prying into several things. When a man's faculties, at the right time, are sharpened by choler it may lead to much. That Lady in slouched gypsy hat, though sitting back in the Carriage, does she not resemble some one we have seen, some time;—at the Feast of Pikes, or elsewhere? And this *Grosse-Tête* in round hat and peruke, which, looking rear-ward, pokes itself out from time to time, methinks there are features in it ——? Quick Sieur Guillaume, Clerk of the *Directoire*, bring me a new Assignat! Drouet scans the new Assignat; compares the Paper money Picture with the Gross Head in round hat there; by Day and Night you might say the one was an attempted Engraving of the other. And this march of Troops; this sauntering and whispering,—I see it!

Drouet, Post master of this Village, hot Patriot, Old Dragoon of Condé, consider, therefore, what thou wilt do. And fast, for behold the new Berline, expeditiously yoked, cracks whipcord, and rolls away!—Drouet dare not, on the spur of the instant, clutch the bridles in his own two hands; Dandoins with broad sword might hew you off. Our poor Nationals, not one of them here, have three hundred fusils, but then no powder; besides, one is not sure, only morally-certain. Drouet, as an adroit Old Dragoon of Condé, does what is advisablest; privily bespeaks Clerk Guillaume, Old Dragoon of Condé he too; privily, while Clerk Guillaume is saddling two of the fleetest horses, slips over to the Townhall to whisper a word; then mounts with Clerk Guillaume; and the two bound eastward in pursuit to *see* what can be done.

They bound eastward in sharp trot; their moral-certainty permeating the Village, from the Townhall outwards, in busy whispers. Alas! Captain Dandoins orders his Dragoons to mount; but they, complaining of long fast, demand bread-and-cheese first;—before which brief repast can be eaten, the whole Village is permeated; not whispering now, but blustering, and shrieking! National Volunteers, in hurried muster, shriek for gunpowder; Dragoons halt between Patriotism and Rule of the Service, between bread and cheese and fixed bayonets: Dandoins hands secretly his pocket book with its secret despatches to the rigorous Quarter Master: the very Ostlers have stable forks and flails. The rigorous Quarter Master, half saddled, cuts out his way with the sword's edge amid levelled bayonets, amid Patriot vociferations, adjurations, flail strokes; and rides frantic;—few or even none following him; the rest, so sweetly constrained, consenting to stay there.

And thus the new Berline rolls; and Drouet and Guillaume gallop after it, and Dandoins' Troopers or Trooper gallops after them; and Sainte Menehould, with some leagues of the King's Highway, is in explosion; and your Military thunder-chain has gone off in a self-destructive manner; one may fear with the frightfullest issues.

The French Revolution. A History.

COLERIDGE.

THE good man, he was now getting old, towards sixty perhaps; and gave you the idea of a life that had been full of sufferings; a life heavy-laden, half-vanquished, still swimming painfully in seas of manifold physical and other bewilderment. Brow and head were round, and of massive weight, but the face was flabby and irresolute. The deep eyes, of a light hazel, were as full of sorrow as of inspiration; confused pain looked mildly from them, as in a kind of mild astonishment. The whole figure and air, good and amiable otherwise, might be called flabby and irresolute; expressive of weakness under possibility of strength. He hung loosely on his limbs, with knees bent, and stooping attitude; in walking he rather shuffled than decisively stept; and a lady once remarked, he never could fix which side of the garden-walk would suit him best, but continually shifted, in corkscrew fashion, and kept trying both. A heavy-laden, high-aspiring and surely much-suffering man. His voice, naturally soft and good, had contracted itself into a plaintive snuffle and singsong; he spoke as if preaching,—you would have said, preaching earnestly and also hopelessly the weightiest things. I still recollect his 'object' and 'subject,' terms of continual recurrence in the Kantean province; and he sung and snuffled them into "om-m-mject" and "sum-m-mject," with a kind of solemn shake or quaver, as he rolled along. No talk, in his century or in any other, could be more surprising.

Sterling, who assiduously attended him, with profound reverence, and was often with him by himself, for a good many months, gives a record of their first colloquy. Their colloquies were numerous, and he had taken note of many, but they are all gone to the fire, except this first which Mr. Hare has printed,—unluckily without date. It contains a number of ingenious, true and half-true observations, and is of course a faithful epitome of the things said; but it gives small idea of Coleridge's way of talking;—this one feature is perhaps the most recognisable, 'Our interview lasted for three hours, during which he talked two hours and three quarters.' Nothing could be more copious than his talk; and furthermore it was always, virtually or literally, of the nature of a monologue; suffering no interruption, however reverent; hastily putting aside all foreign additions, annotations, or most ingenious desires for elucidation, as well-meant superfluities which would never do. Besides, it was talk not flowing anywhither like a river, but spreading everywhither in inextricable currents and regurgitations like a lake or sea; terribly deficient in definite goal or aim, nay often in logical intelligibility; *what* you were to believe or do, on any earthly or heavenly thing, obstinately refusing to appear from it. So that, most times, you felt logically lost; swamped near to drowning in this tide of ingenious vocables, spreading out boundless as if to submerge the world.

To sit as a passive bucket and be pumped into, whether you consent or not, can in the long-run be exhilarating to no creature, how eloquent soever the flood of utterance that is descending.

But if it be withal a confused unintelligible flood of utterance, threatening to submerge all known landmarks of thought, and drown the world and you!—I have heard Coleridge talk, with eager musical energy, two stricken hours, his face radiant and moist, and communicate no meaning whatsoever to any individual of his hearers,—certain of whom, I for one, still kept eagerly listening in hope; the most had long before given up, and formed, if the room were large enough, secondary humming groups of their own. He began anywhere: you put some question to him, made some suggestive observation: instead of answering this, or decidedly setting out towards answer of it, he would accumulate formidable apparatus, logical swim-bladders, transcendental life-preservers and other precautionary and vehiculatory gear, for setting out; perhaps did at last get under way,—but was swiftly solicited, turned aside by the glance of some radiant new game on this hand or that, into new courses; and ever into new; and before long into all the Universe, where it was uncertain what game you would catch, or whether any.

His talk, alas, was distinguished, like himself, by irresolution: it disliked to be troubled with conditions, abstinences, definite fulfilments;—loved to wander at its own sweet will, and make its auditor and his claims and humble wishes a mere passive bucket for itself! He had knowledge about many things and topics, much curious reading; but generally all topics led him, after a pass or two, into the high seas of theosophic philosophy, the hazy infinitude of Kantean transcendentalism, with its 'summ-mjects' and 'om-m-mjects.' Sad enough; for with such indolent impatience of the claims and ignorances of others, he had not the least talent for explaining this or anything unknown to them; and you swam and fluttered in the mistiest wide unintelligible deluge of things, for most part in a rather profitless uncomfortable manner.

Glorious islets, too, I have seen rise out of the haze; but they were few, and soon swallowed in the general element again. Balmy sunny islets, islets of the blest and the intelligible:—on which occasions those secondary humming groups would all cease humming, and hang breathless upon the eloquent words; till once your islet got wrapt in the mist again, and they could recommence humming. Eloquent artistically expressive words you always had; piercing radiances of a most subtle insight came at intervals; tones of noble pious sympathy, recognisable as pious though strangely coloured, were never wanting long: but in general you could not call this aimless, cloudcapt, cloud-based, lawlessly meandering human discourse of reason by the name of 'excellent talk,' but only of 'surprising ;' and were reminded bitterly of Hazlitt's account of it: "Excellent talker, very,—if you let him start from no premises and come to no conclusion." Coleridge was not without what talkers call wit, and there were touches of prickly sarcasm in him, contemptuous enough of the world and its idols and popular dignitaries; he had traits even of poetic humour: but in general he seemed deficient in laughter; or indeed in sympathy for concrete human things either on the sunny or on the stormy side. One right peal of concrete laughter at some convicted flesh-and-blood absurdity, one burst of noble indignation at some injustice or depravity, rubbing elbows with us on this solid Earth, how strange would it have been in that Kantean haze-world, and how infinitely cheering amid its vacant air-castles and dim melting ghosts and shadows! None such ever came. His life had been an abstract thinking and dreaming, idealistic, passed amid the ghosts of defunct bodies and of unborn ones. The moaning singsong of that theosophico-metaphysical monotony left on you, at last, a very dreary feeling.

The Life of John Sterling.

ON STATUES.

IF the world were not properly *anarchic*, this question 'Who shall have a Statue?' would be one of the greatest and most solemn for it. Who is to have a Statue? means, Whom shall we consecrate and set apart as one of our sacred men? Sacred; that all men may see him, be reminded of him, and by new example added to old perpetual precept, be taught what is real worth in man. Whom do you wish us to resemble? Him you set on a high column, that all men, looking on it, may be continually apprised of the duty you expect from them. What man to set there, and what man to refuse forevermore the leave to be set there: this, if a country were not anarchic as we say,—ruleless, given up to the rule of Chaos, in the primordial fibres of its being,—would be a great question for a country!

And to the parties themselves, lightly as they set about it, the question is rather great. Whom shall I honour, whom shall I refuse to honour? If a man have any precious thing in him at all, certainly the most precious of all the gifts he can offer is his approbation, his reverence to another man. This is his very soul, this fealty which he swears to another: his personality itself, with whatever it has of eternal and divine, he bends here in reverence before another. Not lightly will a man give this, —if he is still a man. If he is no longer a man, but a greedy blind two-footed animal, 'without soul, except what saves him the expense of salt and keeps his body with its appetites from putrefying,'—alas, if he is nothing now but a human money-bag and meat trough, it is different! In that case his 'reverence' is worth so many pounds sterling; and these, like a gentleman, he will give willingly. Hence the British Statues, such a populace of them as we see. British Statues, and some other more important things! Alas, of how many unveracities, of what a world of *ir*reverence, of sordid debasement, and death in 'trespasses and sins,' is this light unveracious bestowal of one's approbation the fatal outcome! Fatal in its origin; in its developments and thousandfold results so fatal. It is the poison of the universal Upas-tree, under which all human interests, in these bad ages, lie writhing as if in the last struggle of death. Street-barricades rise for that reason, and counterfeit kings have to shave off their whiskers, and fly like coiners; and it is a world gone mad in misery, by bestowing its approbation wrong!

Give every man the meed of honour he has merited, you have the ideal world of poets; a hierarchy of beneficences, your noblest man at the summit of affairs, and in every place the due gradation of the fittest for that place: a maximum of wisdom works and administers, followed, as is inevitable, by a maximum of success. It is a world such as the idle poets dream of,—such as the active poets, the heroic and the true of men, are incessantly toiling to achieve, and more and more realise. Achieved, realised, it never can be; striven after, and approximated to, it must forever be,—woe to us if at any time it be not! Other aim in this Earth we have none. Renounce such aim as vain and hopeless, reject it altogether, what more have you to reject? You have renounced fealty to Nature and its Almighty Maker; you have said practically, "We can flourish very well without minding Nature and her ordinances; perhaps Nature and the Almighty—what are they? A Phantasm of the brain of Priests, and of some chimerical persons that write books?"—"Hold!" shriek others wildly: "You incendiary infidels;—you should be quiet infidels, and believe! Haven't we a Church? Don't we keep a Church, this long while; best behaved of Churches, which meddles with nobody, assiduously grinding its organs, reading its liturgies, homiletics, and excellent old moral hornbooks, so patiently as Church never did? Can't we doff our hat to it; even look in upon it occasionally, on a wet Sunday; and so, at the trifling charge of a few millions annually, serve *both* God and the Devil? Fools, you should be quiet infidels, and believe!"

To give our approval aright,—alas to do every one of us what lies in him, that the honourable man everywhere, and he only have honour, that the able man everywhere be put into the place which is fit for him, which is his by eternal right: is not this the sum of all social morality for every citizen of this world? This one duty perfectly done, what more *could* the world have done for it? The world in all departments and aspects of it were a perfect world; everywhere administered by the best wisdom discernible in it, everywhere enjoying the exact maximum of success and felicity possible for it. Imperfectly, and not perfectly done, we know this duty must always be. Not done at all; no longer remembered as a thing which God and Nature and the Eternal Voices do require to be done,—alas, we see too well what kind of a world that ultimately makes for us! A world no longer habitable for quiet persons; a world which in these sad days is bursting into street-barricades, and pretty rapidly turning out its 'Honoured Men,' as intrusive dogs are turned out, with a kettle tied to their tail. To Kings, Kaisers,

Spiritual Papas and Holy Fathers, there is universal "*Apage!* Depart thou, go thou to the—Father of thee!" in a huge world-voice of mob-musketry and sooty execration, uglier than any ever heard before.

Hudson's Statue. Latter Day Pamphlets.

P. 354, l. 13. Swenkt. *Carlyle was doubtless thinking of Milton's "swinkt hedger." The word, so more properly spelt, means "hard-worked." I do not know any authority for the e.*

THOMAS BABINGTON, LORD MACAULAY.

Thomas Babington Macaulay was born at Rothley Temple in 1800. His political services to his party secured him an Indian appointment, which in a few years gave him a competency. He died in 1859. His Essays and his History exhibit the most popular style which any English author has ever possessed. Competent critics object to its glaring defects, but have never denied its power.

THE RELIEF OF LONDONDERRY.

IT was the twenty-eighth of July. The sun had just set: the evening sermon in the cathedral was over; and the heart-broken congregation had separated; when the sentinels on the tower saw the sails of three vessels coming up the Foyle. Soon there was a stir in the Irish camp. The besiegers were on the alert for miles along both shores. The ships were in extreme peril: for the river was low; and the only navigable channel ran very near to the left bank, where the headquarters of the enemy had been fixed, and where the batteries were most numerous. Leake performed his duty with a skill and spirit worthy of his noble profession, exposed his frigate to cover the merchantmen, and used his guns with great effect. At length the little squadron came to the place of peril. Then the Mountjoy took the lead, and went right at the boom. The huge barricade cracked and gave way: but the shock was such that the Mountjoy rebounded, and stuck in the mud. A yell of triumph rose from the banks: the Irish rushed to their boats, and were preparing to board; but the Dartmouth poured on them a well-directed broadside, which threw them into disorder. Just then the Phœnix dashed at the breach which the Mountjoy had made, and was in a moment within the fence. Meantime the tide was rising fast. The Mountjoy began to move, and soon passed safe through the broken stakes and floating spars. But her brave master was no more. A shot from one of the batteries had struck him; and he died by the most enviable of all deaths, in sight of the city which was his birthplace, which was his home, and which had just been saved by his courage and self-devotion from the most frightful form of destruction. The night had closed in before the conflict at the boom began: but the flash of the guns was seen, and the noise heard, by the lean and ghastly multitude which covered the walls of the city. When the Mountjoy grounded, and when the shout of triumph rose from the Irish on both sides of the river, the hearts of the besieged died within them. One who endured the unutterable anguish of that moment has told us that they looked fearfully livid in each other's eyes. Even after the barricade had been passed, there was a terrible half hour of suspense. It was ten o'clock before the ships arrived at the quay. The whole population was there to welcome them. A screen made of casks filled with earth was hastily thrown up to protect the landing place from the batteries on the other side of the river; and then the work of unloading began. First were rolled on shore barrels containing six thousand bushels of meal. Then came great cheeses, casks of beef, flitches of bacon, kegs of butter, sacks of pease and biscuit, ankers of brandy. Not many hours before, half a pound of tallow and three quarters of a pound of salted hide had been weighed out with niggardly care to every fighting man. The ration which each now received was three pounds of flour, two pounds of beef, and a pint of pease. It is easy to imagine with what tears grace was said over the suppers of that evening. There was little sleep on either side of the wall. The bonfires shone bright along the whole circuit of the ramparts. The Irish guns continued to roar all night; and all night the bells of the rescued city made answer to the Irish guns with a peal of joyous defiance. Through the three following days the batteries of the enemy continued to play. But, on the third night, flames were seen arising from the camp; and, when the first of August dawned, a line of smoking ruins marked the site lately occupied by the huts of the besiegers ; and the citizens saw far off the long column of pikes and standards retreating up the left bank of the Foyle towards Strabane.

So ended this great siege, the most memorable in the annals of the British Isles. It had lasted a hundred and five days. The garrison had been reduced from about seven thousand effective men to about three thousand. The loss of the besiegers cannot be precisely ascertained. Walker estimated it at eight thousand men. It is certain from the despatches of Avaux that the regiments which returned from the blockade had been so much thinned that many of them were not more than two hundred strong. Of thirty-six French gunners who had superintended the cannonading, thirty-one had been killed or disabled. The means both of attack and of defence had undoubtedly been such as would have moved the great warriors of the Continent to laughter ; and this is the very circumstance which gives so peculiar an interest to the history of the contest. It was a contest, not between engineers, but between nations ; and the victory remained with the nation which, though inferior in number, was superior in civilization, in capacity for self-government, and in stubbornness of resolution.

History of England.

WARREN HASTINGS.

WITH all his faults,—and they were neither few nor small,—only one cemetery was worthy to contain his remains. In that temple of silence and reconciliation where the enmities of twenty generations lie buried, in the Great Abbey which has during many ages afforded a quiet resting-place to those whose minds and bodies have been shattered by the contentions of the Great Hall, the dust of the illustrious accused should have mingled with the dust of the illustrious accusers. This was not to be. Yet the place of interment was not ill chosen. Behind the chancel of the parish church of Daylesford, in earth which already held the bones of many chiefs of the house of Hastings, was laid the coffin of the greatest man who has ever borne that ancient and widely extended name. On that very spot probably, four-score years before, the little Warren, meanly clad and scantily fed, had played with the children of ploughmen. Even then his young mind had revolved plans which might be called romantic. Yet, however romantic, it is not likely that they had been so strange as the truth. Not only had the poor orphan retrieved the fallen fortunes of his line. Not only had he repurchased the old lands, and rebuilt the old dwelling. He had preserved and extended an empire. He had founded a polity. He had administered government and war with more than the capacity of Richelieu. He had patronised learning with the judicious liberality of Cosmo. He had been attacked by the most formidable combination of enemies that ever sought the destruction of a single victim; and over that combination, after a struggle of ten years, he had triumphed. He had at length gone down to his grave in the fulness of age, in peace, after so many troubles, in honour, after so much obloquy.

Those who look on his character without favour or malevolence will pronounce that, in the two great elements of all social virtue, in respect for the rights of others, and in sympathy for the sufferings of others, he was deficient. His principles were somewhat lax. His heart was somewhat hard. But while we cannot with truth describe him either as a righteous or as a merciful ruler, we cannot regard without admiration the amplitude and fertility of his intellect, his rare talents for command, for administration, and for controversy, his dauntless courage, his honourable poverty, his fervent zeal for the interests of the state, his noble equanimity, tried by both extremes of fortune, and never disturbed by either.

Essays.

CHISWICK PRESS:—C. WHITTINGHAM AND CO. TOOKS COURT,
CHANCERY LANE.

CPSIA information can be obtained
at www.ICGtesting.com
Printed in the USA
BVHW012140020421
604106BV00002B/17